P9-DBK-596

FUNDAMENTALS OF LITIGATION FOR PARALEGALS

FUNDAMENTALS OF LITIGATION FOR PARALEGALS

FIFTH EDITION

MARLENE A. MAEROWITZ

City Attorney
Tempe, Arizona

THOMAS A. MAUET

Milton O. Riepe Professor of Law and Director of Trial Advocacy
University of Arizona

ASPEN
PUBLISHERS

111 Eighth Avenue, New York, NY 10011
www.aspenpublishers.com

Copyright © 2006 by Marlene A. Maerowitz and Thomas A. Mauet

All rights reserved. No part of this publication may be reproduced or transmitted in any form or by any means, electronic or mechanical, including photocopy, recording, or any information storage and retrieval system, without permission in writing from the publisher. Requests for permission to make copies of any part of this publication should be mailed to:

Aspen Publishers
Attn: Permissions Department
111 Eighth Avenue, 7th Floor
New York, NY 10011–5201

Printed in the United States of America

1 2 3 4 5 6 7 8 9 0

ISBN 0-7355-5114-6

Library of Congress Cataloging-in-Publication Data

Maerowitz, Marlene A.
   Fundamentals of litigation for paralegals/Marlene A. Maerowitz, Thomas A. Mauet.—5th ed.
        p. cm.
    Includes index.
    ISBN 0-7355-5114-6
    1. Civil procedure—United States. 2. Pre-trial procedure—United States. 3. Legal assistants—United States—Handbooks, manuals, etc.
I. Mauet, Thomas A.   II. Title.

KF8841.M37 2005
347.73'5—dc22

2005024195

To our students—
Past, Present, and Future

SUMMARY OF CONTENTS

CONTENTS

PART I: INVESTIGATING AND PLANNING THE LITIGATION

CHAPTER 3: CASE EVALUATION AND STRATEGY

PART II: PRETRIAL LITIGATION

CHAPTER 6: LAW AND MOTIONS   **191**

CHAPTER 9: EVIDENCE   243

CHAPTER 10: DISCOVERY   271

PART III: SETTLEMENT, TRIAL, AND POST-TRIAL

PREFACE

APPROACH

Since the very first edition our approach to a litigation textbook for paralegals has been to include information on all areas of civil litigation, even though due to time constraints not all areas are covered in a litigation course. The purpose for including this additional information is to allow you to use this book not only as a text for learning, but as a reference book once you are in practice.

We have found that civil litigation can often be oversimplified, which hinders the learning and understanding process; on the other hand, although civil litigation is very rule-oriented and can be complex, easy-to-follow steps can be given to help you learn the rules. Thus, we attempt to strike a balance between giving sufficient detail for you to learn and understand this area of law, and, at the same time, making the steps as clear as possible. You will find that the text breaks down each civil procedure rule into easy-to-follow steps. Each step explains the process so that you are not just following the rules, but understanding them as well. We believe that as you progress through your litigation course and through your career, you will come to appreciate even more the detailed approach taken.

ORGANIZATION

This book takes you through each stage of the litigation process from the initial fact-gathering stage through post-judgment proceedings. Because there are alternative ways to resolve disputes through either arbitration or mediation, the book also covers these topics. Each chapter is designed to give you a thorough understanding of the procedural rules governing the litigation process as well as a system for transferring your knowledge of the procedural rules into the litigation skills necessary to draft litigation documents such as pleadings, discovery requests, and motions.

Always remember that behind every litigation case there are clients who are either suing or being sued and witnesses who have knowledge of the facts and events surrounding the dispute. Thus, important skills for collecting data, interviewing clients, and taking witness statements are not only discussed, but are also demonstrated throughout the text. Checklists for locating witnesses, including Internet resource sites, are also provided.

KEY FEATURES

You will note that many of the legal terms that are central to the discussion in any given chapter appear in boldface type. Each of these boldfaced terms is defined in the margin of the book where the word appears and also in the Glossary at the end of the book. The Glossary also provides definitions of the other legal terms that are used in the text; should you encounter any legal term that is unfamiliar, you can refer to the Glossary for an explanation.

At the beginning of each chapter you will find two sections. The first section is an outline of the chapter. You may use this section to obtain a quick overview of the chapter and also to help you locate a particular area. The next section identifies the chapter's objectives. Keep these objectives in mind as you go through the chapter.

At the end of each chapter you will find four important sections. The first section is a "Chapter Summary," which highlights the primary concepts in each chapter. The Summary, of course, should never be used as a substitute for reading the chapter. However, the Summary is useful when you wish to review the content of each chapter.

The "Key Terms" section acts as a checklist to ensure that you have identified and understood the legal terms that were defined and explained in the chapter. The third section at the end of each chapter is a series of questions. The "Review Questions" may be used as a study guide to further test your understanding of the main concepts discussed in each chapter.

In addition to the review questions in this book, a workbook on computer disk is included with the text. The workbook is designed to give you an opportunity to work thoroughly with the rules and concepts discussed in the text and contains additional questions and assignments. The fifth edition has been expanded and amended to complement the changes in the main text, as well as the changes in technology. Projects requiring computer usage and the Internet are included as optional assignments.

New in this edition is an *Additional Resources* section at the end of each chapter, should you choose to explore further any of the concepts discussed in that chapter. The sites and publications listed are not necessarily endorsed by the authors, but are provided to you as a convenience.

ACKNOWLEDGMENTS

No textbook can be written without the help and guidance from numerous individuals. Elizabeth Kenny has worked with us since the very first edition and we were fortunate enough to work with her again on this edition. Once more she has provided us with a tremendous amount of guidance, suggestions, substantive comments, and support. Kaesmene Harrison Banks, at Aspen Publishers, kept us all on track as she oversaw the editing and proofreading of the text. Finally, we gratefully acknowledge the permission of West Publishing Company to reprint the federal judicial circuit map (Exhibit 1.1) and the permission of Aspen Publishers to reprint Exhibits 1.2, 1.3, and 2.1.

Thomas A. Mauet
Marlene A. Maerowitz
October 2005

FUNDAMENTALS
OF LITIGATION
FOR PARALEGALS

Part

I

INVESTIGATING AND PLANNING THE LITIGATION

Chapter 1

INTRODUCTION TO LITIGATION

A	Introduction
B	The Litigation Process
C	The Paralegal's Role
D	Use of Computers in Litigation
E	Ethical Considerations

CHAPTER OBJECTIVES

In this introductory chapter to litigation you will learn

- What the differences are between civil litigation and other types of litigation
- Where to find the law applicable to litigation matters
- How the court system is structured
- How a case moves through the process
- What types of remedies an aggrieved party may seek from the court
- What the paralegal's role is in the litigation process
- What ethical standards paralegals must follow

A. INTRODUCTION

You have just been called into the office of an attorney in the firm that recently hired you. The attorney tells you that a prospective client will be coming to the office shortly who has a "problem" that might lead to litigation—a problem that appears to be just right for you to assist with and help manage. With a smile, the attorney hands you a note containing the prospective client's name and appointment time. Apprehensively, you walk out of the attorney's office, thinking: "My God—what do I do now?"

What you do, when you do it, how you do it, and why you do it is what this book on litigation is all about. This first chapter provides an overview of the litigation process and your role in that process. Each step in the process will be discussed in detail in the following chapters.

B. THE LITIGATION PROCESS

Litigation
Resolution of disputes through the court system

Civil litigation
Resolution of disputes between private parties through the court system

Litigation is the resolution of disputes through the court system. This book is about the civil litigation process, as compared to criminal or administrative litigation. **Civil litigation** is the resolution of disputes between private parties through the court system.[1] Criminal litigation is

---

1. An alternative to the use of courts, arbitration is becoming a popular method by which civil disputes are resolved. See Chapter 14.

not between private parties; rather, in criminal litigation the government prosecutes an action against individuals who have committed crimes against society. If the crime also results in damages to the victim's person or property, the victim may bring a civil action to obtain recovery for the damages. This civil action is separate from the criminal action.

Administrative litigation is the process by which administrative agencies resolve disputes that concern their administrative rules and regulations. For example, if an employee is injured on the job and a worker's compensation claim is filed, the worker's compensation agency will determine the claim and hear any appeal or dispute the employee has regarding the determination of the claim. In general, if an administrative remedy exists, the claimant must first exhaust the administrative remedies before proceeding with a court action.

Civil litigation permits parties to settle their disputes in an orderly and nonviolent manner. The entire litigation process is governed by formal rules that specify the procedures the parties must follow from commencement of the litigation until the litigation terminates. Accordingly, once a dispute is submitted to the courts for resolution, all parties to the litigation must carefully follow the court's procedural rules.

Each state has its own rules of procedure. A party filing an action in a state court must follow the procedural rules of that particular state court. Actions filed in federal court are governed by the Federal Rules of Civil Procedure. Always consult the appropriate rules of procedure before handling any litigation matter.

The rules discussed in this book are the Federal Rules of Civil Procedure. However, most states have rules modeled, at least in part, after the Federal Rules. Accordingly, once you master the Federal Rules, you can easily apply that understanding to your particular state rules.

1. Sources of law

Where do you find the law applicable to the matter you are handling? There are three sources of law that you will need to consult for every litigation matter: statutes, court cases, and constitutions.

a. Statutes

Statutes are laws enacted by state or federal legislatures that govern substantive and legal rights and principles, as well as procedural rules. In some instances, statutes are referred to as codes. All laws enacted by Congress are found in the United States Code. The United States Code is divided into various Titles, which deal with specific subject matters such as agriculture, banking, copyrights, education, and so on. State statutes are usually similarly divided. In these codes, you will also find the rules of civil procedure that exist at both the federal and state level.

In addition to the United States Code and state statutes or codes, individual municipalities, such as your town or city, may also enact their own laws, which apply only in their municipality. The municipal laws are often referred to as ordinances. These ordinances typically govern matters such as rent control, parking, and items of local interest. A municipality may not enact ordinances that conflict in any way with the law of the federal or state governments.

An individual court also may adopt procedural rules governing the cases filed in that particular court as long as the rules are not in conflict with state statutes. These rules are referred to as the local rules of court. The local rules govern everything from the type of paper on which a complaint must be filed to the dates on which motions may be heard.

All of these statutes, codes, ordinances, and rules help to determine the legal rights of parties and help to regulate the litigation process. Accordingly, they are all sources that must be referred to when handling any litigation matter.

b. Court cases

Cases are decisions of the courts interpreting the law. Once a decision has been made, the court will generally write an opinion. Certain opinions that address a unique or important legal issue are published in bound volumes and are used by other litigants to determine how the law may be interpreted with respect to their particular dispute. Throughout the course of our nation's history, thousands of opinions have been published and relied on as precedents to decide new controversies as they arise.

Even prior to the published opinions of our courts, the early American colonists brought with them a body of law from England referred to as the **common law**. Common law developed in England from usage and custom, and was affirmed by the English judges and courts. Common law, to the extent it is not inconsistent with the constitutions or laws of the United States or of the individual states, is generally still applicable in the United States.

Common law
Body of law developed in England from custom and usage

c. Constitutions

The federal Constitution is the highest law of the land. In addition to the United States Constitution, each of the 50 states has its own constitution. No rule of law enacted by a state may violate the state's constitution. Moreover, no state constitution or state or federal law may violate the federal Constitution.

2. The court system

Litigation begins when the aggrieved party files a complaint in the appropriate court. The aggrieved party is called the **plaintiff**. The party whom the complaint is filed against is called the **defendant**. In the **complaint** the plaintiff must state the basis of the claim against the defendant so that the defendant will be apprised of the action giving rise to the claim. As discussed in section 4, the plaintiff must also request specific relief from the court. The complaint is served upon the defendant along with a **summons** commanding the defendant to appear before the court.

Complaint
Document filed by an aggrieved party to commence litigation

Summons
Notice accompanying the complaint that commands the defendant to appear and defend against the action within a certain period of time

The complaint is always filed in the **trial court**. Under the federal court system, this trial court is called the **United States District Court**. There are 90 district courts in the United States. Each state has at least one district court, and several states have two or more, depending on the state's population.

In the state court system, the name of the trial court varies from state to state. In some states, the trial court is called the superior court or the court of common pleas. In all states, other, inferior courts exist to hear certain smaller and less complex matters. These inferior courts are sometimes referred to as municipal courts, justice courts, city and parish courts, and small claims courts. These inferior courts are an important part of the litigation process because they are designed to hear matters more quickly and less expensively than the general trial courts.

If a party loses in the trial court, that party has an automatic right to appeal to the next highest court. In the federal system, the party appeals to the **Court of Appeals** for the appropriate circuit in which the district court sits. The fifty states are divided into eleven circuits plus the District of Columbia, which is its own circuit. In addition, there is one Court of Appeals for the Federal Circuit that hears appeals from special courts such as the United States Claims Court and the Court of International Trade. (See Exhibit 1.1.)

On appeal, the appellate court is limited to a review of the record of the court below. The court will not hear from any witnesses or take new evidence. The party appealing the decision of the trial court must demonstrate that there was an error in the court below that affected the outcome of the case. The appellate court will determine whether the law was incorrectly applied on the facts, or if the decision reached is not supported by the facts. Even though new evidence may not be presented to the court, all parties to the appeal will have an opportunity to submit a written brief on the issues before the appellate court. After the parties

Exhibit 1.1. The Thirteen Federal Judicial Circuits

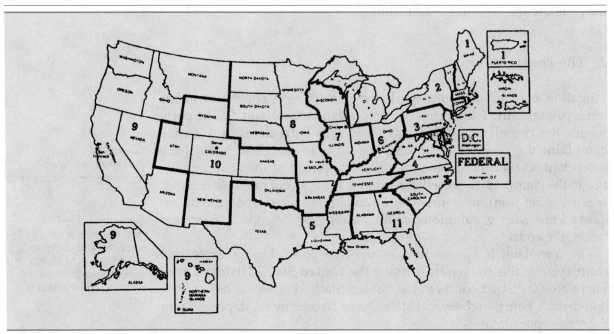

Reprinted from Federal Reporter (West's National Reporter System) with permission of West Publishing Company.

submit briefs, the court will hear oral argument. Oral argument is an opportunity for the lawyers to answer any questions the appellate judges may have and to explain their clients' positions more fully.

After oral argument, the court will render one of four decisions. The court will either **affirm, affirm with modification, reverse**, or **reverse and remand**. A decision is affirmed if the court rules the same way as the trial court. Sometimes, the court will rule the same way, but modify some element of the decision below. For example, assume that a trial court rules in an action for unlawful detainer that the plaintiff is entitled to possession of property and back rent in the amount of $1,200. If the appellate court agrees that the plaintiff should be entitled to possession of the property, but believes the back rent owed is only $998, the appellate court will affirm the trial court's decision and modify the amount of back rent.

If the court disagrees with the trial court, the appellate court will reverse the decision. Sometimes, however, the appellate court is not certain, based on the record before it, whether it disagrees with the trial court. In this situation the court gives an opinion stating how it would rule assuming that certain facts are true. The appellate court will then reverse the decision and send it back (remand) to the trial court for a decision in accordance with the opinion expressed by the appellate court.

If a party loses in the appellate court, the losing party may petition the next highest court for review. In the federal court system this is the **United States Supreme Court**. The Supreme Court is the highest court in the federal system. In addition to hearing appeals from the Courts of Appeals, the Supreme Court also has discretion to hear appeals from a state's highest court if the decision in the state court involves a constitutional issue.

Appeal to the Supreme Court is not automatic, but rather is discretionary with the Court. The losing party must petition the Supreme Court to review the matter. If review is granted, the Court will affirm, affirm with modification, reverse, or reverse and remand the decision of the appellate court. If review is denied, the decision of the appellate court will become final.

An organizational chart for the federal court system is shown in Exhibit 1.2. You will note that special courts such as bankruptcy courts and the Court of International Trade exist to hear specific cases. The typical organization for a state court system is shown in Exhibit 1.3.

3. Overview for litigation cases

Litigation consists of four basic stages: (1) information gathering, (2) pleading, (3) discovery and motions, and (4) trial and post-trial proceedings. Each of these stages is discussed in detail in subsequent chapters. However, this section gives you a brief overview of the four stages and a sample path for a typical litigation case.

Exhibit 1.2. The Federal Court System

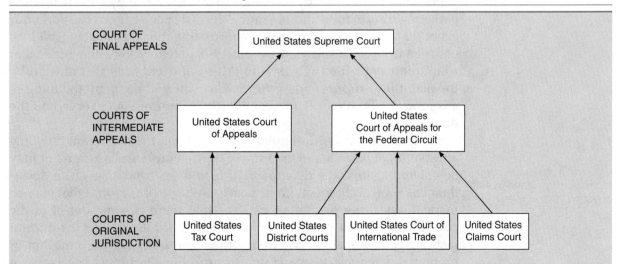

Exhibit 1.3. The State Court System

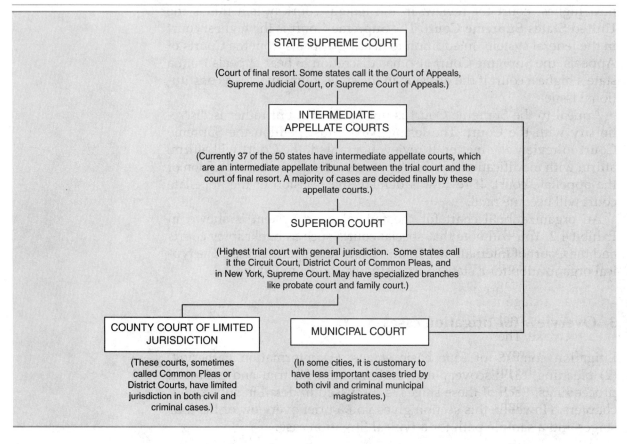

Prior to the filing of any lawsuit, you and the attorney will spend time gathering information and obtaining the facts necessary to support your client's case. This is the first stage of litigation. This stage will be engaged in by both sides since a potential defendant is often aware that a lawsuit may be filed against him. After sufficient facts are gathered by the plaintiff to support a lawsuit, the lawsuit will begin by the filing of a complaint. The complaint, along with the summons, is served on the defendant.

Upon receipt of the summons and complaint, the defendant must file a response, or else the defendant will be in **default** and a judgment may be entered against the defendant. This is the second stage. The defendant has several choices with respect to the type of response that may be made. First, if the defendant believes that there is some defect in the complaint, either a procedural rule that is not followed or insufficient facts alleged against the defendant, the defendant may file a **motion**. A motion is a request to the court for an order or ruling. The types of

Default
Failure of a party to respond to the pleading of the opposing party

motions that may be filed by the defendant are discussed in Chapter 5. If the defendant does not file a motion or if the motion is denied by the court, the defendant will answer the complaint. The **answer** is the defendant's response to the specific allegations in the complaint and states any defenses the defendant may have. Once an answer is filed, the pleading stage — that is, formal written documents by the parties to either start litigation or respond to litigation — is complete.

The third stage is the **discovery and motion stage**. At this point the parties will conduct formal factual investigation through written responses and oral testimony received from the other side. The parties may also obtain discovery formally from other individuals who are not parties but who may be witnesses or in possession of information that is helpful to the case. During this stage, there may also be a number of **pre-trial motions**. These motions may include a request to the court to enter judgment without the necessity of trial if none of the facts are in dispute, or involve requests to obtain discovery from the other side if one side does not voluntarily provide the information. The bulk of litigation time is spent at this stage, and it is usually at this stage that cases will settle.

The final stage is the **trial and post-trial proceedings**. Both during trial and after trial, there are a number of different motions that either side can make. These motions include requests for judgments if one side has failed to prove its case, or requests to the court to enter a different judgment if the jury's verdict is not consistent with the evidence produced at trial. As discussed earlier, at this stage the losing party also has an automatic right to appeal the decision. An appellate court could reverse the judgment and require a new trial, which would start this stage over again. This explains why some cases go on for several years winding their way through the trial court, appellate courts, and back to the trial court again.

The chart in Exhibit 1.4 gives an example of how a litigation case may move through the several stages.

4. Remedies

When a party brings a civil action, the party must request some relief or remedy from the court. Remedies may be divided into two categories: legal and equitable.

The most common **legal remedy** is money **damages**. For example, if a party suffers a personal injury or is the victim of a breach of contract, the party will request to be compensated by payment from the defendant. Money damages are further divided into two main categories: compensatory and punitive.

Compensatory damages are all those damages that "compensate" the injured party, including damages that directly flow from the injury or

Damages
Monetary compensation requested by plaintiff from defendant

Exhibit 1.4. Path of a Litigation Case

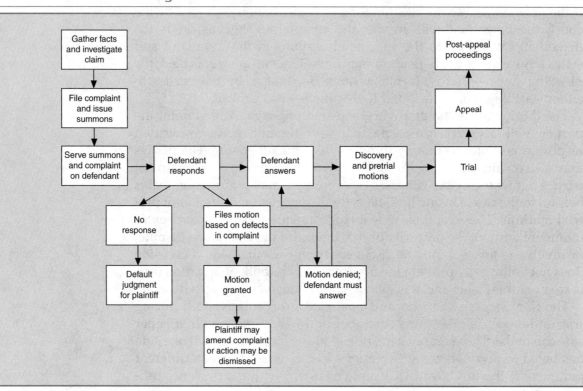

breach. Compensatory damages may be either general (i.e., compensation for pain and suffering) or specific (i.e., payment for medical expenses or loss of income from time missed at work).

In some types of action where the defendant's conduct is willful or malicious, the plaintiff may be entitled to **punitive damages**. Punitive damages, also called exemplary damages, are meant to "punish" the wrongdoer for his or her conduct. Such damages may be awarded in addition to the compensatory damages.

If the legal remedy is inadequate to compensate the plaintiff fully, the plaintiff may be able to obtain an **equitable remedy**. There are many kinds of equitable remedies. The two most commonly used in civil litigation are injunctions and declaratory relief. An **injunction** is used to stop certain conduct or actions. For example, if a plaintiff wants to stop the defendant from building a house that will impair the plaintiff's view, the plaintiff will seek an injunction from the court to stop the defendant from building the house.

Declaratory relief is used when a controversy arises over the rights and obligations of the parties and neither party has yet failed to live

Equitable remedy
Relief requested by plaintiff from defendant that is usually designed to prevent some future harm

up to these obligations. The parties request a declaration from the court to settle the controversy so they may govern their future conduct accordingly.

C. THE PARALEGAL'S ROLE

Paralegals play a vital role in the efficient handling of litigation. Law firms are finding that paralegals can, and do, handle many tasks that were previously performed by attorneys. Use of paralegals not only frees the attorney to engage in other matters, but also helps reduce litigation expenses for the client.

As a paralegal, you will find that, aside from appearing in court, representing witnesses at deposition, and giving legal advice, there is virtually nothing a lawyer can do that, as a litigation paralegal, you cannot do under the supervision of an attorney. Thus, you have the opportunity to play a significant role in analyzing, planning, and executing the lawsuit.

The following is just a sampling of the numerous tasks you may be called on to undertake in litigation:

1. Preparing for litigation
   - Interview the client
   - Gather background facts
   - Locate witnesses
   - Interview witnesses
   - Obtain medical records, tax records, educational records, etc.
   - Research claims the client may have against other parties
   - Draft demand letters
   - Obtain and analyze documents from client
2. Conducting the litigation
   - Draft pleadings
   - Prepare summons
   - Prepare pretrial motions
   - Prepare discovery to propound upon the opposing parties
   - Prepare responses to discovery propounded by the opposing parties
   - Review and organize documents produced by opposing parties
   - Arrange for the taking of depositions
   - Prepare witnesses for deposition
   - Prepare deposition summaries
   - Take notes on testimony given at depositions
   - Calendar due dates for filing briefs, motions, pretrial orders, etc.
   - Prepare discovery plan

3. Trial preparation
   - ◆ Prepare trial notebooks
   - ◆ Organize exhibits
   - ◆ Prepare witness files
   - ◆ Prepare demonstrative exhibits
   - ◆ Draft jury instructions
   - ◆ Subpoena witnesses
   - ◆ Draft trial brief
   - ◆ Coordinate scheduling of trial witnesses
   - ◆ Take notes at trial
   - ◆ Assist attorney with exhibits at trial
   - ◆ Coordinate electronic media during trial
4. Post-trial work
   - ◆ Assist with any post-trial motions
   - ◆ Prepare record for appeal
   - ◆ Enforce judgment
5. Settlement
   - ◆ Prepare settlement agreement
   - ◆ Prepare releases
   - ◆ Assist in closing file and obtaining necessary dismissals

Do not be alarmed by the breadth and complexity of these tasks. The purpose of this book and your litigation course is to familiarize and train you in each of them so that you may perform your job competently and confidently.

D. USE OF COMPUTERS IN LITIGATION

With the increase in the use of computers, has also come an increase in the use of computers during all stages of the litigation process. Not only will you use computers to research basic fact information, but also to assist you in organizing your fact investigation, organizing the information obtained, and during presentation of information to a jury during trial. In addition, many courts allow for electronic filings of motions and briefs in an effort to reduce the amount of paper filed with the court.

As discussed in Chapter 2, the use of the Internet for locating witnesses and gathering factual information about your case has become invaluable. You may be able to locate the home address or business address of possible parties and witnesses, without the necessity of hiring private detectives. In addition, the computer has allowed you to become an "expert" in virtually any field without the necessity of spending time and money in researching or retaining consultants. For example, assume you have a case involving the uniqueness of a particular name of a business for a possible claim of tradename infringement. With a click of a mouse, you can find out if other similar names of businesses exist throughout the world. This information may have taken months to locate previously, which is now available in a matter of minutes.

However, computers are not just used during the preliminary stages of litigation. Litigation software packages are now available that allow you to manage the litigation data including the documents received from other parties, documents produced by your party, and transcripts of interviews and depositions. The nice feature about using litigation software is that once the information is stored in the computer, you can search for and retrieve the information by using word or name searches, making the management of information much easier. Imaging software also exists to permit you to project on a screen during trial the text of actual documents, and to highlight important information for the jury. There are many litigation software packages available, and your firm, if involved in extensive trial work, will probably already have such software installed on the office computers. Throughout the text, the main features that are common to many of the litigation software packages will be discussed.

E. ETHICAL CONSIDERATIONS

Any discussion of litigation would be remiss in not mentioning the ethical considerations that underlie the practice of law. The conduct of lawyers is governed by the rules of professional conduct enacted in their particular states. The American Bar Association has recommended professional standards that have been adopted by many states. Although there are no rules specifically governing paralegals, certain ethical guidelines must be followed by all employees.[2]

One of the primary ethical guidelines involves confidentiality. The communication between an attorney and client is **privileged**. This means that the attorney cannot reveal any information received by the client to anyone else. The privileged nature of a client's communications extends to paralegals as well. Accordingly, any information you receive in the course of your employment from the client or in connection with the client or the client's business must be kept confidential and not be disclosed to third parties. In addition, given the private nature of attorney-client communications, you must also be careful to

Privileges
Rules providing that certain communications are inadmissible because the communications are deemed confidential

---

2. Some state bar associations have published guidelines for attorneys who use paralegals. In addition, some paralegal associations, such as the National Association of Legal Assistants, have adopted a code of ethics to be followed by their members.

Conflict of interest
When two or more parties with adverse interests are represented by the same counsel

avoid discussing a client's case in public places where eavesdroppers may be present.

Conflicts of interest should also be considered. A lawyer may never represent two or more parties who have adverse interests. Accordingly, as a paralegal charged with fact gathering, you should be cognizant of situations in which a conflict may arise. For example, your office may be representing two defendants who, at least initially, appear to have no conflict in their interests. Should a conflict develop, however, the lawyer has an ethical obligation to withdraw from representing one or both of the clients. Accordingly, immediately notify the attorney if you discover any facts in your investigation of a case indicating that a conflict may exist between two or more of your clients.

Another ethical consideration for paralegals is to avoid communicating directly with an adverse party who is represented by counsel. A party represented by counsel is entitled to be free of any direct contact with the opposing party's counsel or that counsel's employees. Even if the adverse party contacts you directly, you must refuse to speak with the client without the presence of the party's attorney. In essence, a party who is represented by counsel may not represent himself until he formally relieves that counsel from representation.

Finally, you are not authorized to practice law and therefore must never give anyone the impression that you are a lawyer. When speaking with a client, opposing counsel, or other parties, always identify yourself as a legal assistant. Similarly, when writing any letter on behalf of the law firm, place a notation of "Legal Assistant" or "Paralegal" directly below your signature to avoid any misunderstandings as to your position with the law firm.[3] In addition, remember that you may not represent a client in any legal proceeding, even though the client knows you are not a lawyer.

These ethical considerations are by no means exclusive. You, of course, must be guided by a sense of moral integrity. If something doesn't seem right to you, it probably isn't. If you are unsure if something is ethically correct, check with the lawyer in charge or contact your local paralegal association for information.

CHAPTER SUMMARY

Civil litigation involves the resolution of disputes through the court system and starts with the plaintiff filing a complaint against the defendant in the trial court. In the complaint, the plaintiff will request either

---

3. The terms "Legal Assistant" and "Paralegal" generally are used interchangeably by most legal professionals.

monetary or equitable relief (or both) from the court. The losing party in the trial court has an automatic right to appeal the decision to the next highest court.

As a paralegal, you will take on significant responsibility during all aspects of the litigation process from the initial fact gathering through trial preparation and post-trial proceedings. Throughout this entire process, it is essential that your conduct conform to the following ethical guidelines discussed in this chapter:

♦ Keep confidential all client communications
♦ Avoid all conflicts of interest
♦ Do not communicate directly with an adverse party who is represented by counsel
♦ Always identify yourself as a paralegal

KEY TERMS

Affirm	Injunction
Affirm with modification	Legal remedy
Answer	Litigation
Cases	Motion
Civil litigation	Plaintiff
Common law	Pleading
Compensatory damages	Pretrial motions
Complaint	Privileges
Conflict of interest	Punitive damages
Constitutions	Reverse
Court cases	Reverse and remand
Court of Appeals	Statutes
Damages	Summons
Declaratory relief	Trial and post-trial proceedings
Default	Trial court
Defendant	United States District Court
Discovery and motion stage	United States Supreme Court
Equitable remedy	

REVIEW QUESTIONS

1. What is civil litigation, and how does it differ from other types of litigation?

2. How is the federal court system structured? How is the court system structured in your state?

3. What are the differences between equitable and legal remedies? Identify two types of equitable remedies.

4. Where do you find the sources of law applicable to litigation matters? Explain the differences between the various sources of law.

5. Once a litigation matter is appealed, what are the four types of decision that an appellate court may make? Explain each type.

6. What are the four stages of the litigation process?

7. What is the role of a paralegal in the litigation process?

8. What ethical rules must be followed by paralegals? What are the goals of the ethical rules?

ADDITIONAL RESOURCES

www.uscourts.gov. Contains information about the federal court system.

usgovinfo.about.com. Describes the structure and purpose of the U.S. Federal Court system and provides links to other sites.

www.loc.gov/law/guide/usjudic.html. Overview of the court system and federal procedure, and links to opinions of the Supreme Court and Court of Appeals.

www.paralegals.org. Information on ethics and their application to paralegals from the National Federation of Paralegals Association.

www.washlaw.edu/doclaw/primary5m.html. Link to administrative law, case law, and statutory law resources.

Cannon, Therese A., *Ethics and Professional Responsibility*, (Aspen Publishers, 2004).

Chapter 2

INFORMAL FACT GATHERING AND INVESTIGATION

This chapter introduces you to several important aspects of the preliminary gathering and investigation of facts to support your client's position. You will learn

◆ How to structure a factual investigation

◆ Where to obtain the necessary facts to prove your client's position

◆ How to interview clients

◆ When and how to gather documents that may be used as evidence

◆ Where to locate witnesses

◆ How to use the Internet to gather facts

A. INTRODUCTION

Properly gathering and assimilating information, before a complaint is even filed, are the critical initial components of successful litigation. Litigation outcomes are usually decided not by legal interpretations but according to which party's version of disputed events the **factfinder**—that is, the judge or the jury—accepts as true. Hence, much time is spent identifying and acquiring admissible evidence that supports your party's contentions and that refutes the other side's contentions. The party who is more successful in doing this will have a better chance of convincing the factfinder that its version of the facts is what "really happened."

Your role as a paralegal will be to assist the lawyer in identifying and gathering the evidence. Many times the paralegal is charged with complete responsibility for this initial fact gathering, a responsibility that is critical to the lawyer's determination of whether to proceed with the case and how to properly advise the client. If the lawyer decides to proceed, these initial facts are also necessary to draft the complaint and make the required factual allegations.

This chapter provides a step-by-step approach for you to use when you are asked to gather and investigate the initial facts of any case. Each step will assist you in developing a complete and accurate account of the facts.

B. STRUCTURING FACT INVESTIGATIONS

Facts are the collective pieces of information explaining your client's version of what happened. For example, facts may consist of what people said, did, or heard regarding the particular incident. There are two ways of "getting the facts." You can obtain facts informally before filing suit, and you can get them through formal discovery (as discussed in Chapter 10, section B) after suit is filed. A common mistake inexperienced paralegals make is using the investigation, such as an initial client interview and the reviewing of an accident report, just to provide the lawyer with enough facts to decide whether to take the case, and using formal discovery methods as the principal fact-gathering method. This is a serious mistake. Consider the following advantages of informal discovery:

- First, information is power, and the party that has a better grasp of the favorable and unfavorable facts is in a stronger position to evaluate the case accurately.
- Second, information obtained early on, particularly from witnesses, is more likely to be accurate and complete.
- Third, information sought before the action is formalized is more likely to be obtained, since a lawsuit often makes people cautious or uncooperative.
- Fourth, information obtained before suit has been filed is less expensive to acquire. Formal discovery is the most expensive way to get information. It is usually more effective and less expensive to use informal discovery before filing suit, and to use formal discovery methods to obtain missing information, pin down witnesses, obtain specific information and records from the opposing party, and for other such focused purposes.
- Fifth, Rule 11 of the Federal Rules of Civil Procedure requires that before any suit is filed, there must be a reasonable inquiry into the facts to ensure a pleading that is well grounded.
- Finally, you can get information informally without the opposing parties participating, or even being aware that you are conducting an investigation.

For all these reasons, then, you should use informal discovery as much as possible.

If your firm represents the defendant, you may also be involved in informal fact gathering and investigation before a complaint is filed. Many times the defendant is aware of a potential lawsuit as a result of oral or written communication received from the plaintiff or because of direct involvement in an accident or other incident. In these situations, it is likely that the potential defendant will consult with an attorney prior to receiving the summons and complaint. Your fact gathering and investigation will be similar, regardless of which party your firm represents.

1. What facts do I need to get?

Your job as a litigation paralegal is to obtain enough admissible evidence to prove your client's claims and to disprove the other side's claims. If you are representing the plaintiff, enough facts must be gathered to state in the complaint a **cause of action**, sometimes called a claim for relief. A cause of action is a theory of recovery that entitles the plaintiff to recover against the defendant. If you represent the defendant, you will want to gather facts to support an affirmative defense. An **affirmative defense** is a defense pled by the defendant in the answer that, if proven, denies recovery to the plaintiff.

Cause of action
Theory of recovery that
entitles the plaintiff to recover
against the defendant

Identify in advance, with the assistance of the lawyer in charge, what you must prove or disprove. This is determined by the substantive law underlying the claims, relief, and defenses in the case. However, how do you research that law if you do not yet know what the pleadings will allege? What do you research first, the facts or the law?

There is no easy answer here. In litigation, the facts and law are intertwined. The investigation of one affects the investigation of the other. You will usually go back and forth periodically as the theory of the case develops.

EXAMPLE

You have been asked to assist with what appears to be a routine personal injury case, involving an automobile accident between your client, George Andrews, and another driver, Mildred Jones. You conduct the initial interview with George, who appears to have a simple negligence case against the other driver— Ms. Jones clearly ran a stop sign. You do preliminary research on the negligence claim to see if the damages are sufficient to recommend litigation to the lawyer. You then continue your fact investigation and discover that Ms. Jones is uninsured. Since George may not be able to collect damages from an uninsured driver, you start wondering if there may be a claim against the municipality for not maintaining intersection markings and safe road conditions. Of course, you need to research the law here. If there is a legal theory supporting such a claim, you then need to go back and see if there are facts that support that theory. Back and forth you go between getting the facts and researching the law until you have identified those legal theories that have factual support.

2. How do I structure my fact investigation?

a. Use of a litigation chart

The easiest way to give structure to your investigation is to use a system of organizing the law and facts based on what the attorney will need to prove if the case goes to trial. In short, this is a good time to start a "litigation chart."[1] A litigation chart is simply a diagram that sets out what needs to be proven or disproven in a case and how to do it. The chart is not a formal court document but an aid to you and your attorney. The chart is a graphic way of identifying four major components of the litigation plan:

1. Elements of claims
2. Sources of proof
3. Informal fact investigation
4. Formal discovery

The litigation chart has two principal benefits. First, it helps you identify what needs to be proven or disproven, so that you can focus your fact investigation on getting admissible evidence for each required element. Second, a litigation chart helps you pinpoint the strengths and weaknesses of your side's case as well as your opponent's. In most trials, the side that wins is the one that convinces the factfinder to resolve disputed issues in its favor. The litigation chart will help to identify the disputed matters for which additional admissible evidence must be developed to strengthen the client's version and to rebut the other party's version.

b. How to structure a litigation chart

Start with the "elements" of each potential claim, relief, and defense in the case. Most jurisdictions have pattern **jury instructions** for commonly tried claims, such as negligence, products liability, and contract claims. The instructions will itemize what elements must be proved for each claim, relief, or defense. If pattern jury instructions do not exist, more basic research will be necessary. If the claim is based on a statute, read the statute and look at the case annotations that deal with elements and jury instructions. If the claim is based on common law, consult treatises covering the claim, and research the recent case law in the applicable

Jury instructions
Instructions that itemize the elements for various claims, reliefs, and defenses

---

1. The litigation chart will become a "trial chart" if the case is ultimately tried.

jurisdiction. After you find the applicable law and determine the specific elements, review the litigation chart with the lawyer to ensure that you have properly covered all elements. When you have done this, you will have completed the first step on your litigation chart.

Two of the more common causes of action that you will encounter are **negligence** and **breach of contract**. Regardless of your jurisdiction, certain elements are applicable to each of these causes of action. For example, to state a cause of action for negligence, the plaintiff must allege each of the following elements:

Negligence
A cause of action in which the plaintiff must allege a duty of care by one party to another that was breached and that was the cause of plaintiff's damages

♦ A duty of care owed by one party to another
♦ A breach of that duty of care
♦ Causation (defendant's actions were the actual and proximate (probable) cause of plaintiff's injuries)
♦ Damages

Once the plaintiff has proven each of these elements, the plaintiff will be entitled to relief against the defendant, unless the defendant can prove an affirmative defense.

Breach of contract
A cause of action that alleges a contract was breached by the defendant, causing damages to the plaintiff. Also, plaintiff must allege that he performed under the contract or is excused from performing

To state a cause of action for breach of contract, the plaintiff must similarly allege a number of elements. These elements are:

♦ An executed contract
♦ Plaintiff's performance, or excuse for nonperformance
♦ Defendant's breach
♦ Plaintiff's damages

Again, only if all these elements are proven does the plaintiff have a cause of action against the defendant. The example that follows illustrates how each of these elements is placed on a litigation chart.

E X A M P L E

You are assisting in the representation of Mary Garcia in a potential contract case. Mary had a contract with Wholesale Sporting Goods (WSG) to provide baseballs for the regional baseball league. She says she obtained baseballs from WSG and paid for them, but the balls were defective, missing stitching on one side. From the initial client interview, and from reviewing the documents and records Mary provided, the lawyer decides to bring a contract claim against WSG. Your jurisdiction's pattern jury instructions for contract claims list the elements that must be proven to establish liability and damages.

You set up the following chart to help keep track of the claims:

**LITIGATION CHART
FOR MARY GARCIA'S CONTRACT CLAIM**

Elements of Claims	Sources of Proof	Informal Fact Investigation	Formal Discovery
1. Contract			
(a) Contract executed			
(b) Mary Garcia's Performance			
(c) Wholesale Sporting Goods' breach			
(d) Mary Garcia's damages			

This approach should be used for every other possible claim. For example, since the contract is for the sale of goods, a claim based on a breach of a warranty may be appropriate. If so, you should put the elements of this claim on your litigation chart. The defendant can use a similar litigation chart to place the elements that must be proven for each affirmative defense as well as the elements that the plaintiff must prove for each claim.

---

3. What are the likely sources of proof?

Facts come from five basic sources:

1. The client
2. Exhibits
3. Witnesses
4. Experts
5. The opposing party

Of these categories, most can often be reached by informal investigations. The client, of course, must be interviewed. Whenever possible, obtain exhibits in the client's possession and other evidence such as physical objects, photographs, documents, and records in the possession of third parties. Witnesses can frequently be interviewed. You also may be asked to work with consulting experts who are hired to help analyze and prepare the case.

On the other hand, formal discovery, as discussed in Chapter 10, may sometimes be the only way to get essential information. For example, important witnesses may be uncooperative and need to be deposed. Exhibits in the possession of uncooperative third parties may need to be subpoenaed. Information from the opposing party can usually be obtained only through interrogatories, depositions, and other discovery methods. However, it is always worthwhile to try the informal approach first because it is quicker, less expensive, and may be more accurate and complete. The only exception concerns other parties. Ethics rules forbid lawyers to make direct contact with an opposing party who they know is represented by counsel. As previously discussed, paralegals are bound by the same ethical obligations. Accordingly, if a party is represented by a lawyer, you must deal with the other party's lawyer.

Although informal fact investigations should always be conducted, their usefulness depends significantly on the case at hand. Some cases can be almost completely investigated through informal means, while others must rely principally on formal discovery. For example, in a routine personal injury case resulting from an automobile accident, you should be able to get all the basic information informally, since the principal sources will be the client, police officers, police reports, medical reports, and disinterested nonparty witnesses. In contrast, in a products liability case brought against the manufacturer of a consumer product, most of the information about the product's design, manufacture, distribution, and safety history will be in the possession of the defendant manufacturer and can be obtained only through formal discovery methods.

Regardless of the type of case, you must first identify the likely sources of proof, then decide how that proof can be obtained. The second step on your developing litigation chart is to list the likely sources of proof and correlate them to the required elements of the claims.

EXAMPLE

In Mary Garcia's case, determine the witnesses and exhibits that will provide the facts about the case. Mary is an obvious witness, and the contract for the sale of the baseballs is a central exhibit. Other than these obvious sources, where else can you go for proof? For example, what proof is there that Mary performed her obligations under the contract? Here again, Mary herself is a source of proof. In addition, Mary may have business records showing her performance. Wholesale Sporting Goods (WSG) may have written letters acknowledging Mary's performance. WSG may also have business records proving performance. There also may be nonparty witnesses, such as the secretary of the regional league, who have knowledge of Mary's performance. Because Mary needed to have the baseballs before opening day, she bought replacement balls from Balls R Us. Their records could help prove damages.

Put these sources on your developing litigation chart:

LITIGATION CHART
FOR MARY GARCIA'S CONTRACT CLAIM

Elements of Claims	Sources of Proof	Informal Fact Investigation	Formal Discovery
1. Contract			
(a) Contract executed	◆ Mary Garcia ◆ WSG ◆ Contract for sale of baseballs ◆ League secretary		
(b) Mary Garcia's Performance	◆ Mary Garcia ◆ Garcia's records ◆ WSG's records		
(c) Wholesale Sporting Goods' breach	◆ Mary Garcia ◆ Garcia's correspondence ◆ WSG's correspondence ◆ Garcia's records ◆ WSG's records ◆ Experts to testify that lack of stitching constitutes a defective baseball		
(d) Mary Garcia's damages	◆ Mary Garcia ◆ Garcia's records ◆ Balls R Us ◆ Balls R Us's records ◆ Experts on measure of damages for defective baseballs		

The third step is to determine whether these sources of proof can be reached by informal fact investigation and, if so, what method is best suited to getting the necessary information. Witnesses can be interviewed; exhibits in the client's possession should be obtained and reviewed; exhibits possessed by third parties can frequently be obtained from friendly or neutral third parties simply by requesting them; experts can be interviewed, and you can sometimes obtain their reports. Once again, think expansively here, since obtaining information informally is quicker, less expensive, frequently more candid and accurate, and can be obtained without the opposing party participating or perhaps even being aware that you are investigating the case. Put the methods by which you plan to obtain the information on the litigation chart (see page 29).

The last step is to decide what to use formal discovery methods for, and how and when to use them. These considerations are discussed in Chapters 3 and 10.

4. How much time should I spend?

You cannot buy a Cadillac on a Ford budget, and the same holds true for litigation. The client's financial resources are an important consideration. The "value" of the case, the amount the client can reasonably expect in a jury verdict, is another. The amount of work the case requires for adequate preparation is a third consideration. Consequently, before spending numerous hours gathering facts and engaging in investigation, consult with the lawyer responsible for the matter to determine how much time you can devote to the case and whether the case can be adequately handled within that time.

5. What sources should I investigate?

The basic sources for informal investigations are fourfold:

- The client
- Exhibits
- Witnesses
- Experts

Your litigation chart will provide the directions for your informal fact investigation. That investigation should focus on obtaining basic facts—favorable and unfavorable—about the case and identifying credible, admissible evidence for each claim you are considering.

How extensive should your fact investigation be? It needs to be thorough enough to fill out your litigation chart, to the extent that you can do so through informal fact investigation. Practically, this means several things. First, the client must be interviewed as often as necessary to learn everything she knows about the case. You will also need to interview her periodically as you gather additional information from other sources.

Second, you should try to obtain all key documents, records, and other exhibits. In a personal injury case, this includes the police accident reports, hospital and doctor's records, insurance claims records, and employment history. These can often be obtained informally, and many

LITIGATION CHART
FOR MARY GARCIA'S CONTRACT CLAIM

Elements of Claims	Sources of Proof	Informal Fact Investigation	Formal Discovery
1. Contract			
(a) Contract executed	◆ Mary Garcia ◆ WSG ◆ Contract for sale of baseballs ◆ League secretary	Interview Obtained from Garcia Interview	
(b) Mary Garcia's Performance	◆ Mary Garcia ◆ Garcia's records ◆ WSG's records	Interview Obtained from Garcia	
(c) Wholesale Sporting Goods' breach	◆ Mary Garcia ◆ Garcia's correspondence ◆ WSG's correspondence ◆ Garcia's records ◆ WSG's records ◆ Experts to testify that lack of stitching constitutes a defective baseball	Interview Obtained from Garcia Obtained from Garcia Interview	
(d) Mary Garcia's damages	◆ Mary Garcia ◆ Garcia's records ◆ Balls R Us ◆ Balls R Us' records ◆ Experts on measure of damages for defective baseballs	Interview Obtained from Garcia Interview Request letter Interview	

jurisdictions have statutes that require that they be released to the client on request. In a contract case, this includes the contract, correspondence, invoices, shipping records, and related business records. Where physical evidence is important, it should be safeguarded or photographed before such evidence is altered or possibly lost.

Third, witnesses usually need to be identified, located, and interviewed, although what you do will depend on the particular case. In most cases, what witnesses say is critical. For example, in a personal injury case, where the plaintiff and defendant are likely to have contradictory versions of how the accident happened, the testimony of neutral witnesses will frequently control the liability issue. You need to identify, locate, and interview them whenever possible. On the other hand, witness testimony is not invariably critical at trial. For example, in a contract or commercial case, the issues are frequently decided by the documents, records, or substantive law. In such a case, there may be no advantage in interviewing witnesses quickly.

Finally, in some cases it may be necessary to consult appropriate experts early in the investigation. For example, in medical malpractice and products liability cases, plaintiff's lawyers usually have the case reviewed by a physician and a technical expert before filing suit.

C. CLIENT INTERVIEWS

Client interviewing has two components: what information to get and how to get it. What to get will be determined by your litigation chart. How to get it is based on interviewing techniques that must be fully understood in order to obtain the vital information from the client.

As a paralegal your role is simply to obtain the facts. You are not licensed to give legal advice and you cannot represent yourself as a lawyer. Some clients may never have consulted with a lawyer and may not realize that, as a paralegal, you cannot give them advice about the case or answer questions regarding the merits of their claim or defense. Accordingly, when you first speak with the client, identify yourself as a paralegal. Explain that you are gathering the facts for review by the lawyer, who will ultimately make all decisions with respect to the case. By making such statements in the beginning, you avoid any undue embarrassment for you and the client.

1. Client attitudes and disclosure

The typical client is unsure of his rights and obligations, and a law office is an unfamiliar, imposing environment. The interviewer who empathizes with the client's psychological needs knows the factors that promote and inhibit client disclosure and will be more successful in getting an accurate picture of the problems that brought the client to seek legal assistance in the first place.

A client comes to the law office to determine if there are actual legal issues relative to his problems and, if so, how to deal with them. The client must be interviewed so the legal issues can be identified and all relevant available information can be obtained and analyzed. How do you go about getting that information from the client?

There are several factors that can inhibit a client from a full disclosure of information. First, a client being interviewed often feels that he is being judged. This causes the client to withhold or distort facts that may create negative impressions about himself or his case. Second, a client being interviewed often tries to satisfy what he feels are the interviewer's expectations. This causes the client to tell the interviewer what he thinks will be a pleasing story and, again, to withhold negative and contradictory facts. Third, a client may have a variety of internal reasons—such as embarrassment, modesty, and fear—that, once again, prevent him from disclosing all information.

On the other side, there are positive factors that promote full disclosure. First, a client is more likely to disclose fully if he feels that the interviewer has a personal interest in him. A friendly, sympathetic interviewer is more likely to get all the facts from a client. Second, a client is more likely to disclose fully if he senses that the lawyer is identifying with him. The interviewer who lets the client know that "she's been there too," or is familiar with and understands the client's situation, is more likely to draw out all the facts. Third, some clients enjoy being the center of attention. Supplying critical information makes the client feel important and may lead him to supply more information. Fourth, a client enjoys feeling that he is doing the right thing. The interviewer who can instill the feeling that full disclosure is the proper, decent approach is more likely to achieve it.

You will obtain the fullest possible disclosure by stressing the positive psychological influences and by understanding and minimizing negative influences that inhibit disclosure. Paralegals who create a comfortable physical environment and show an understanding and appreciation of the client will be more successful in obtaining all the facts, both good and bad. This sensitivity will establish a positive context for client relations during the course of the litigation process.

2. Interview preparation

Interview preparation has several components. What kind of physical setting should you have? How will you record what the client says?

What should the client do to prepare for the interview? What topics will you cover during the actual interview?

Many clients will be uncertain and insecure during the first interview. After all, it may be the first time they have ever been to a law office. A physical setting that is informal, friendly, and private will help make a client feel relaxed and comfortable. Your private office is a good place to conduct an interview; a small conference room is another.

Strive for informality. Sit in a place other than behind your desk, have coffee and soft drinks available, perhaps play quiet background music. Avoid interruptions. Leave the telephone alone, and close the door to keep others out. Schedule the interview so that you will have enough time to accomplish what you have planned. An initial interview with a client can easily take one or two hours, but perhaps much more. If possible, schedule client interviews as the last appointment for the day, provided you are still mentally sharp at that time. This will allow you to continue the interview without running out of time due to other appointments.

In addition to establishing rapport and gaining the client's trust, a principal function of a client interview is, again, to obtain information. This information needs to be recorded; there are two ways to do this. First, you can take notes yourself. This has the advantage of allowing for privacy, but has the disadvantage of interfering with your interview. Second, you can tape-record the interview with the client's permission. Here the advantage is completeness. However, you will still need to make a summary of the interview, and many clients are uncomfortable having their statements recorded.

The paramount consideration is creating an atmosphere in which the client feels comfortable and tells everything she knows about the problems that brought her there. Most interviewers conduct the initial part of the interview without note taking. After the client becomes comfortable with you and the interview environment, and you begin to get the details of her story, you can discuss the need to record what she says and then ask her if she will feel comfortable with the method you suggest. Once you explain why it is so important for you to have an accurate record of what she says and how the attorney-client privilege will prevent anyone else from getting it, the client will usually agree.[2]

What can you have the client do to prepare for the first interview? First, the client should be told to collect available paperwork, such as letters, documents, bills, and other records. Second, consider asking the client to write down everything she can remember about the legal problems, particularly if they involve a recent event. If the memo is

---

2. As explained in Chapter 1, the attorney-client privilege applies to client communications with a paralegal. The client should understand that, even though you are not an attorney, everything the client says to you is protected from disclosure to anyone outside the law office.

directed to the lawyer, and no one outside the lawyer's staff is permitted to see it, the memo should be protected by the attorney-client privilege, even though the attorney-client relationship may not yet formally exist. The records and memo should be brought to the initial interview.

3. Initial client interview

The initial client interview should have several objectives. First, conduct yourself in a manner that establishes a good working relationship. When the client arrives at your office, don't make her wait. Greet her personally. Have the client make herself comfortable in your office or conference room, and spend a little time making small talk—about traffic or the weather, for instance. Offer her coffee or a soft drink. Remember that you are a representative of your law firm and that the client will make a judgment about the firm and its lawyers based on her impressions of you.

E X A M P L E

Paralegal: Good afternoon, Ms. Garcia. I'm so glad you could come meet with me today. Did you have any trouble finding the office?

Ms. Garcia: No, not at all. Your directions were very clear.

Paralegal: Before we go into the conference room, is there anything I can get for you? Water? Coffee?

Ms. Garcia: No. Nothing at this time. Thank you.

Second, spend a few minutes learning about the client's background. This shows the client that you see her as a human being and not as just another case. It also helps you evaluate the client as a witness and provides important biographical and financial information.

E X A M P L E

Paralegal: I was very interested in learning that you worked with the regional baseball league. I go out and see their games on occasion. How long have you been involved with the league?

Ms. Garcia: Almost six years now. I became interested in working with the league when my oldest son started T-Ball. His T-Ball coach was playing at the time with the baseball league, and he told me that the league needed an administrative director.

Paralegal: Sounds like a great position. Do you get to see many of the games?

Ms. Garcia: Oh, every chance I get. I have two other children, so we sometimes take the whole family out to watch the games.

Third, let the client know what is going to happen during the interview, what you need to accomplish, and the reasons for it. Explain that you need to get all the important facts in order to provide the lawyer with an accurate description of the client's legal problems.

EXAMPLE

Paralegal: Ms. Garcia, I want to take a few minutes to explain to you what is going to happen today. I would like to try and get a chronological overview from you of all the events that transpired between you and Wholesale Sporting Goods. I will be taking notes of what you tell me and will be asking you questions to obtain more specific details concerning certain of the events. The facts that you tell me are important so that after we are done, I can discuss the facts of your case with the lawyer in charge of this matter, Ms. Robbins, and give to her an accurate description of your legal problem. Do you have any questions?

Ms. Garcia: No.

Fourth, have the client identify the general nature of her problems. You will usually have a general idea—a "car accident," a "contract problem"—when the client makes the appointment. However, it is always useful to have the client initially tell her story in her own way, without interruptions, which allows you to size her up as a trial witness. You may also discover facts you might never otherwise have stumbled upon, and it allows the prospective client to get the matter off her chest in her own words. These considerations are well worth "wasting time" on, even if the client talks about seemingly irrelevant things. The usual way to get the client to tell the story her way is to ask open-ended, non-leading questions. For example, simply asking "I know you were in an accident. Why don't you tell me what happened in your own words?" will usually get the client started. While the client tells her story, listen not only to what she says but also note things she omits, things that would usually be mentioned. When the client is done, you can paraphrase what she has said. This serves as a check on accuracy and shows the client that you have been listening carefully.

EXAMPLE

Paralegal: I know you have had a problem with some baseballs ordered from Wholesale Sporting Goods. Can you tell me from the beginning what happened?

Ms. Garcia: Yes. In my position as administrative director I am in charge of ordering supplies for all teams for the regional baseball league. Every year, I need to order approximately fifteen hundred baseballs. So, I placed an order for the baseballs with Wholesale Sporting Goods, which is the first time I ever ordered anything from them. I signed a contract with them for the exact type of balls that I needed, and I paid for the balls. However, when the balls arrived, they were missing stitching on one side. I tried to obtain replacement balls from Wholesale Sporting Goods, but they could not guarantee that I would have the balls by opening day. I then went out and bought the balls from Balls R Us.

Paralegal: All right. Let me make sure I have the correct facts. You signed a contract with Wholesale Sporting Goods for fifteen hundred baseballs. However, when the balls arrived, they were defective because stitching was missing on one side. You tried to obtain new balls from Wholesale Sporting Goods, but they could not guarantee that you would have the new balls before opening day. Accordingly, you then purchased new balls from Balls R Us.

Ms. Garcia: That is correct.

Fifth, after the client has told her story, you need to get a detailed chronological history of the events and other background facts. It is frequently advantageous to make an outline or checklist so that you do not overlook important topics. (See the sample checklist in section 4.) Your litigation chart, setting out the elements of the claims you are considering, should provide a start. It is sometimes useful to look at books containing form interrogatories, which are written questions to the other side, for this type of case and witness.[3] These may help you develop ideas for the topics and necessary details as you go through the history of the case. However, don't use a checklist as a questionnaire because your interview will quickly lose the personal touch. The standard method is to use the chronological story-telling approach. Most people think chronologically, and that is usually the best way to elicit details. While your checklist should be tailored to fit the particular case involved, you will usually cover the same basic topics regardless.

EXAMPLE

Paralegal: I would like to go back and get a little bit more detail on certain facts that you told me about. Can you go back to the beginning and tell me how you first came in contact with Wholesale Sporting Goods?

Ms. Garcia: I received a promotional flyer from them in the mail, and their prices seemed to be better than the company I had been using in the past.

Paralegal: What happened after that?

Ms. Garcia: I called them and spoke to a Mr. Tanner, who was one of the sales representatives.

3. A detailed discussion of formal discovery methods such as interrogatories and depositions is contained in Chapter 10.

> *Paralegal*:   What did you discuss with Mr. Tanner?
>
> *Ms. Garcia*:   I told him how many baseballs I needed, and he told me he would work up the numbers and give me a call back with a price quote.

Sixth, you need to ask follow-up questions on potential problem areas. Here, it is best to use specific, focused questions. A client naturally wants to impress the interviewer and convince him that the case is a good one, so she will often give only "her version" of what are disputed facts and omit altogether the unfavorable ones. It is always better to get the bad news early. Remind the client that your job is to get all the facts, both good and bad.[4] Remind her that the opposing lawyers will discover the bad facts soon enough, so it is better to deal with them now.

E X A M P L E

> *Paralegal*:   Part of my job here is to get all the facts, both the good and the bad. In litigation, the lawyer on the other side will discuss the bad facts, so it is best to get any facts that may be damaging to the case out in the open now, so that we can be prepared to deal with those facts. Accordingly, there are a few areas I want to cover with you. If, while we are talking, you think of any facts that could possibly be damaging, please feel free to interrupt and tell me those facts. First, have you had any problem with defective balls from companies you have used in the past?
>
> *Ms. Garcia*:   No. In the six years I have been working for the league, we have never had this problem before.
>
> *Paralegal*:   Is there some reason, other than price, that you did not go back to using the company you had used in the past?
>
> *Ms. Garcia*:   Yes. I had initially tried to place an order for the baseballs with All-Star Supplies, which is the company we had used in the past. However, I really wanted to receive the balls for the preseason training, but they could only guarantee that we would receive them before opening day. I had quite a blowup with the sales representative over their inability to accommodate my request.

Where do you probe? Look for information that might adversely affect the client's credibility. Are there problems with the client's background? Is there a spotty work history? Are there prior convictions or other such trouble with the law? Clients frequently omit negative facts in their background. Therefore, you should be asking what the client has left

---

4. This is required in any event by the "reasonable inquiry" duty of Rule 11 of the Federal Rules of Civil Procedure.

out of the story. For example, in an automobile accident case, has the client omitted the fact that he was given a traffic citation? Was driving with a suspended license? Was drinking? Had just left a bar before the accident happened? Or was using a car without permission?

A useful device in getting out these kinds of facts, without directly suggesting to the client that you don't believe his story, is to get the client to be a kind of devil's advocate. Ask him to state what he believes the other side is probably going to say to his lawyer about the event. This will frequently draw out the "other side's version" of the disputed facts. Keep in mind that under Rule 11 of the Federal Rules of Civil Procedure it is at your peril that you accept the client's version of the facts. (Under Rule 11(c) the court may also sanction parties if they are responsible for causing a violation.) The client needs to be pushed, probed, even cross-examined to test the facts he gives you. You may need to verify his version of the facts with an independent examination.

The usual topics you will need to discuss with the client during the initial interview include the following: liability, damages, client background, parties, defenses and counterclaims, statutes of limitations, witnesses, records, physical evidence, other law firms, client goals, and next steps.

a. Liability

Facts bearing on the liability of all parties must be developed fully. Details are critical. Here, a chronology of events usually works best. For example, in an automobile accident case, you will need to explore how the accident happened step by step. You need to get a detailed description of the scene of the collision. Diagrams and charts are very helpful. You need to establish the location of each car involved before the collision occurred, at the point of impact, and after the accident had run its course. You need to get details on speed, distance, time, and relationship to road markings.

b. Damages

Damages information must be obtained for both the client and all other parties. The permissible damages for each possible claim should already be on your litigation chart. For example, in an automobile collision case, damages should include out-of-pocket expenses, lost income, future expenses, and future lost income, as well as intangible damages such as permanence of injury and pain and suffering. Find out if the client suffered an injury, the extent of it, how he was treated, how he felt then and feels now, and how the injury has affected his life. Find out if he had a preexisting condition that could affect damages. You should also explore insurance coverage for all parties, as well as collateral sources such as health insurance, employer benefits, and government entitlements (e.g., Social Security and Veterans Administration benefits). In contract and commercial cases, and cases in which equitable relief is sought, you need to determine if the injuries to the client can be measured in monetary terms.

As a paralegal working for the plaintiff's side, you must determine if the defendant has the ability to pay a judgment. Find out if the defendant has insurance, the amount of the policy's coverage, and if the policy covers the event or transaction. Determine the defendant's income sources and assets, particularly those that can easily be attached to collect a judgment.

c. Client background

The client's background is significant for several reasons. The client's personal background—education, employment, family history—is important for assessing the client's credibility as a trial witness. His financial background—income and assets—is important for assessing damages. Finally, the client's financial picture bears on a mundane but consequential question: Does he have the ability to pay the legal fees? You need to get this background information from the client early on, but be sure you let the client know why this personal information is important for the lawyer's evaluation of the case.

d. Parties

It is frequently difficult to ascertain who all the parties to an event or transaction are and, if businesses are involved, their proper legal identities. Often the client does not know and has given little thought to this aspect of the case. Now is the time to begin obtaining the facts that will help you identify those parties. Once again, Rule 11 requirements must be kept in mind. For example, in an automobile accident case you will need to know not only who the other driver was, but also who owns the other vehicle and whether it is a business or rental vehicle, or was loaned or stolen. You will also need to know where the accident occurred and need to determine who owns, or is in control of, the accident location, since that entity may be responsible for designing, building, and maintaining the roadways.

From your fact investigation you will usually be able to identify the parties who should be named in the lawsuit. However, identifying parties is not the same thing as learning the proper technical identity of parties. For example, just because the truck that ran into the client had the name "Johnson Gas" on its side does not necessarily mean that the Johnson Gas Company is a properly named party. The potentially liable party may be a sole proprietorship or a corporation with a different name entirely. You need to find this out.

For individuals, learn their correct full names. For corporations, partnerships, unincorporated businesses, and other artificial entities, you must not only learn the proper names but also whether they are subsidiaries of other entities that should be brought in as parties. In each state, the secretary of state or a corporation commission usually has a list of domestic and foreign corporations licensed to do business within that state. Such lists usually show the state of incorporation and principal place of business, and list who the resident agent is for service of process. If the party is an unincorporated business operating under an assumed name, you may be able to determine the true owners and properly named parties by consulting an assumed-name index, required by many jurisdictions.[5]

e. Defenses and counterclaims

Plaintiffs and defendants alike must look closely at a frequently overlooked area: What do they have on us? And who else can be brought into the case? Cases are legion where a plaintiff has filed an action only to be hit with a much larger, previously dormant, **counterclaim**. Think expansively, particularly in the commercial area, since the parties usually will have had previous dealings that could give rise to counterclaims. During the interview, inquire about previous transactions between the parties and possible claims the other party may have against the client. Also, inquire about facts that may give rise to defenses to the claims.

Counterclaim
Claim in the form of a pleading brought by the defendant against the plaintiff as part of the same lawsuit

f. Statutes of limitation

All states have **statutes of limitation** that limit the time period in which an action may be brought against a defendant. The time period varies depending on the cause of action. For example, in California an action based on a claim of negligence must be brought within one year of the date of the incident. A claim based on a breach of a written contract must be brought within four years of the date of breach.

---

5. The capacity of individuals, corporations, and unincorporated associations to sue is governed by Rule 17 of the Federal Rules of Civil Procedure, which refers to state law. Hence, you must always check state law to determine whether a party has capacity to sue or be sued and what the technically proper party is.

Statutes of limitation have nothing to do with the substantive merits of the plaintiff's case. Rather, the concern is with the mere passage of time. Placing a limit on the time in which actions may be filed ensures that plaintiffs will not sit on their rights and allow a claim to become stale (resulting in loss of evidence or allowing memories of the witnesses to fade). Defendants are also protected since, after the time period has elapsed, they are assured that no future action will be taken against them.

When interviewing a client, always attempt to determine the exact date when the incident occurred that gives rise to the various causes of action. Sometimes a plaintiff may not consult an attorney until many months—or even years—after a claim arises. In this situation, knowing the exact date is essential in order to determine whether the applicable statute of limitations has run.

g. Witnesses

Question the client on all possible information sources, whether eyewitnesses, experts, or anyone else who possibly has useful information. Get names or any other facts that will help to identify and locate people with information. Think expansively here, and do not be concerned with the admissibility of testimony at this point. Find out who the client has already talked to about the case and what he has said.

h. Records

The client should bring to the interview all paperwork in his possession, such as accident reports, insurance claims, bills, checks, personal records, business records, and correspondence. If the client does not bring them, have him do so as soon as possible. You should keep these records; if the client needs them, make photocopies for him. A separate file labeled "client's original documents" should be set up so you do not misplace the records. Learn what other records may exist and who has them so that these can be obtained now, or later through discovery.

i. Physical evidence

Does the case involve objects such as vehicles, machinery, or consumer products? Although most common in negligence and products liability cases, such evidence can exist in other cases as well. How to locate, obtain, and preserve physical evidence is discussed in section D at page 44.

j. Other law firms

Clients often shop around for lawyers. Although a client has a perfect right to talk to more than one law firm about taking a case, there are always clients who go from door to door until they find a law firm willing to take it. It is important to find out if the client has seen other law firms about the case. On the theory that law firms turn down cases because the cases lack merit, you should be appropriately cautious.

k. Client goals

What does the client really want? In some cases, such as personal injury, the answer is often simple. The plaintiff basically wants money damages, and the defendant wants to avoid paying them. But even then it is important to probe deeper. What does the client view as a favorable outcome? Does he want the case to go to trial, or is he willing to have it settled? Is he looking for vindication, revenge, or other satisfaction not related to money damages? In other cases, such as contract and commercial disputes involving businesses, the answer may be difficult to discern. Money for damages is not always what the client wants or needs. The dispute may be with another business with which the client has an ongoing relationship, and that relationship may be more important than the money damages. Perhaps relief such as specific performance is more important than money damages. Now is the time to find out what the client thinks he wants and whether the client's expectations are realistic or need to be modified.

l. Next steps

When you are concluding the interview, advise the client that you will relate the facts to the lawyer in charge, and either the lawyer or you will be in touch with the client shortly. Do not make any commitments about the case. It is the lawyer's ultimate decision to take the case or not.

Following the client interview, write a short memo to the lawyer in charge, detailing the background facts. Also include an evaluation of the client and his story. It is easy to forget your specific impressions of a client, yet the client's credibility as a trial witness will often be critical to the success of the case. This is particularly important because the lawyer will need to evaluate the case without having met with the client.

4. Sample interview checklist

Interviewers often use a form or checklist to ensure that all the items identified in the preceding subsections are adequately covered. Your office may have a sample form or, after you have conducted several interviews, you may wish to develop your own form. (A sample interview form is provided in the computerized workbook.) If you do not have a sample form, the outline in this section may be used as a checklist when conducting the initial client interview.

Remember, however, that you should never let a checklist limit the questions you ask the client. Often, in the course of the interview, additional questions will come to mind, or other areas may be mentioned by the client. You should not hesitate to stray from your checklist to ask the additional questions or explore the other areas that may not be on the checklist.

☐ Background
  ☐ Name
  ☐ Address
  ☐ Telephone numbers: home, business
  ☐ Marital status, children
  ☐ Age
  ☐ Education (including name of institution, dates attended, degree obtained)
  ☐ Employment (starting with most recent and going backward)
  ☐ Military service
  ☐ Arrest record, if any
☐ Nature of claim
  ☐ Reasons for seeking legal advice
  ☐ Potential adverse parties
  ☐ Date of incident
  ☐ Chronology of events
  ☐ Submission of claims to insurance
  ☐ Statements made to anyone about incident (including claims adjuster, police)
☐ Damages
  ☐ Injuries sustained by client
  ☐ Injuries sustained by others
  ☐ Treatment for injuries (including dates of treatment)
  ☐ Doctors and hospitals administering treatment
  ☐ How injury has affected client's life
  ☐ Preexisting conditions
  ☐ Insurance for injuries
  ☐ Monetary loss to date

- ☐ Parties
  - ◻ Names of potential parties
  - ◻ Names of potential adverse parties
- ☐ Defenses and counterclaims
  - ◻ Potential defenses
  - ◻ Previous transactions between the parties
  - ◻ Possible claims the adverse party may have against the plaintiff
- ☐ Statutes of limitation
  - ◻ Date incident occurred
  - ◻ Date client discovered that claim existed
  - ◻ Why client has waited to consult a lawyer (if applicable)
- ☐ Witnesses
  - ◻ Names of witnesses
  - ◻ Description of witnesses whose names are unknown
  - ◻ Addresses of known witnesses
  - ◻ Any statements by witnesses to anyone
- ☐ Records
  - ◻ Identity of documents that exist
  - ◻ Was a police report made
- ☐ Physical evidence
  - ◻ List physical evidence (i.e., vehicles, machinery, consumer products)
  - ◻ Location of physical evidence
  - ◻ Condition of physical evidence
- ☐ Other law firms
  - ◻ Has client seen lawyers at other firms
  - ◻ If so, who and when
  - ◻ Why are other lawyers not representing the client
- ☐ Client goals
  - ◻ What does client want
  - ◻ What does client view as a favorable outcome

5. Follow-up client interviews

Many things should be covered during the initial interview of the client. Some cases are relatively simple, and interviewing a well-prepared client can take less than an hour. Many cases, however, will require more than one session to collect the basic information. Accordingly, you might use the first session just to build rapport with the client, get the client's story out, and compile a chronology of events. A second session could then be used to review the client's records and ask focused follow-up questions about problem areas. In more complicated cases, it may take several client interviews to acquire the necessary information.

Follow-up interviews will also be periodically necessary during the litigation process. Whenever additional information is received, whether through informal fact investigation or during formal discovery, it should be reviewed with the client. The new information may differ from what the client has previously said. Obviously, the contradictory information must be evaluated, discussed with the client, and dealt with. In some cases, the client may admit that what he previously said was not entirely true and change his story. In others, he may deny the new information and stick to his version of the facts. Whatever the client's position, the new information, if it is at odds with the client's story, must be dealt with. Is it true? Is it more accurate? What does the new information do to the client's story? This is an ongoing process, but the key point to remember is that the client must be kept informed as the fact-gathering process progresses.

D. EXHIBITS ACQUISITION

Exhibits
Tangible items of evidence presented at trial

Your interviews with the client should also identify future exhibits. **Exhibits** include the scene, physical evidence, documents, and records. In addition, interviews with witnesses and your review of documents and business records when you get them, may disclose additional exhibits.

You need to acquire these exhibits, get copies of them, or protect them from being lost or altered. The order in which you do things will depend on how important it is to obtain the particular exhibits. For example, physical evidence, such as the condition of a vehicle, machine, or consumer product, should be acquired quickly before it is repaired, altered, destroyed, or lost. Some records, such as a police accident report, are essential for you to begin your investigation.

The basic types of exhibits are the scene, physical evidence, and records.

1. Scene

If a lawsuit involves an event, such as an automobile accident, investigating the scene is vital. Whenever possible, visit the scene, even if someone else will do the technical investigation. The technical investigation should include taking photographs of all locations from a variety of perspectives and making all necessary measurements so that you can make scale diagrams. Photographs should be both in black and white and in color and be enlarged to 8 inches x 10 inches for courtroom use. Diagrams for courtroom use should be at least 24 inches x 36 inches.

However, in more complex cases, it is likely that you will use digital photographs. The photographs will then be displayed on computer monitors during the trial. This avoids the necessity of having photographs enlarged. However, you should still have copies of the photographs available for the jury to view in the jury room, and for opposing counsel.

While photographic enlargements and courtroom diagrams need not be made until shortly before trial, the necessary preparations should be made now. You should visit the scene at the same time and day of week on which the event occurred, so that your photographs will accurately show the relevant lighting, traffic, and other conditions. You might also find additional witnesses to the event—people who are there each day at that time.

If you are reasonably proficient in photography and have the equipment to take photographs that can be processed and enlarged with sufficient quality to make effective courtroom exhibits, you can take them yourself. This will not create a risk that you will become a witness at trial, since any person familiar with how the scene looked at the relevant time is competent as a witness to verify the depiction of the scene. If you are not a proficient photographer, or if you will not have any other witness who can testify to the accurate depiction of the photography, a commercial photographer should be hired to accompany you. You must tell the photographer specifically what pictures you will need.

Numerous photographs should be taken from a variety of perspectives. For example, in an intersection collision case, you will normally want pictures of how the intersection looked to both drivers as they approached it. Accordingly, pictures should be taken in the road from the appropriate lane, with the camera held the same distance above the road as the driver's head. Several pictures should be taken, starting from perhaps 300 feet away, then moving to 150 feet, and so on. The photographs will then show what each driver saw as he approached the intersection. In addition, photographs should be taken from where other eyewitnesses, such as other drivers and pedestrians, were when the crash occurred. Before you can determine what photographs you will need, you must review witness statements carefully to know where the witnesses were and what they saw and did. Finally, if there are nearby buildings, it's always useful to have overhead, bird's-eye-view pictures taken that will show lane markings, pedestrian walkways, traffic signs, and signals in the intersection.

Diagrams present a different problem. Since the person who took the measurements and made a scale diagram is often the only witness who can qualify the diagram for admission into evidence, it is better to have someone other than yourself do this so that you will not become an involuntary witness at trial. A sample diagram is shown in Exhibit 2.1 on the following page.

Exhibit 2.1.   Diagram of Accident Scene

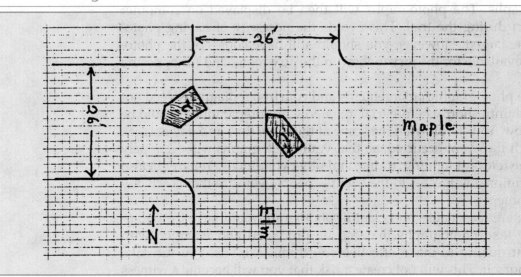

2. Physical evidence

Physical evidence
Tangible personal property
that may be used as trial
exhibits

Physical evidence, such as vehicles, machinery, and consumer products, if not already in the possession of police, other investigative agencies, or the client, must be obtained and preserved for possible use at trial. This includes not only locating the evidence, but also keeping it in the same condition and establishing the **chain of custody**—that is, who has had custody of the evidence at all times. This is particularly important if the evidence will be tested by experts before trial. When you cannot take or move evidence for safekeeping, take a thorough series of photographs and sufficient measurements so that you can make accurate diagrams and models for trial.

Preserving physical evidence often requires that you act quickly. In an automobile accident case, for example, skid marks and the condition of the vehicles involved will be lost as the skid marks wear off and the vehicles are repaired. In these situations you must take immediate steps to prevent the loss, destruction, or alteration of the evidence and to ensure a chain of custody when such a chain will be an admissibility requirement. Have someone such as an investigator do this, since he may be a necessary witness at trial.

How do you actually "preserve" physical evidence? Two concerns are involved. First, you must gain actual physical possession of the objects so that they are kept in the same condition until the trial. Second, you must either label the objects or, if they cannot readily be labeled, put them in a container that can be sealed and labeled. Both of these steps ensure admissibility at trial by establishing the two basic requirements—identity and same condition. The usual way to accomplish this is to have someone such as an investigator, who can serve as a trial witness, get the objects from wherever they are, label or put them in a container that is sealed and labeled, and have them taken to your office for safekeeping. This label should describe the object and show where it came from, who obtained it, when it was taken, and who received it at your office.

Evidence is frequently in the possession of a **third party**—that is, someone who is not a party to the lawsuit. Examples of such third parties are police departments and repair shops. If the evidence does not belong to your client, the third parties are probably under no legal obligation to preserve the evidence for you. However, most will be cooperative when they learn that what they have is important evidence. They will usually keep the evidence in an unaltered condition until you have had an opportunity to photograph and measure it. You should check if someone else, such as an investigator from the police department or insurance company, has already taken these steps. Finally, a third party will sometimes agree to preserve evidence until you can serve the third party with a **subpoena**—that is, a written court order compelling the third party to produce the evidence.

Subpoena
Court order compelling a nonparty to apear or produce documents or other tangible items

Many times, of course, a client seeks legal assistance when it is already too late to take these steps, and the evidence will be lost. If the client comes to your law firm shortly after the event, however, you should always act quickly to preserve the evidence. Many cases, particularly in the personal injury and products liability areas, are won or lost on this type of evidence.

3. Records

You should obtain all available documents and records from the client. You may as well obtain everything the client has, because once suit is filed the opposing party will be able to discover from the client anything that is relevant and not privileged. If important documents and records are in the hands of third persons, see if those persons will voluntarily turn them over or provide copies. Public records are usually available on request. A public record is one made by public officers in the course of performing their duties. Documents such as police reports, accident investigations, and personnel records of city and state employees may be obtained by simply making a proper request to the appropriate public agency.

In many jurisdictions, persons have a statutory right to obtain certain records on demand, such as their own medical reports. A written demand on behalf of the client, coupled with his written authorization, will usually suffice.

The sample letter and authorization shown in Exhibits 2.2 and 2.3, respectively, may be sent to obtain the client's medical records. The letter and authorization may be revised to send to any other type of agency that possesses records of the client.

Records are, of course, available by subpoena after suit is filed, but it is better to get them as soon as possible because the records may be essential to evaluate the case before suit is filed. For example, in a personal injury case you will need to review police accident reports, doctors' reports, hospital reports, employment records, and perhaps others.[6] In a contract action, you will need to get the contract itself as well as records that bear on the performance and nonperformance of the parties, such as orders, shipping documents, invoices, and payment records.

Exhibit 2.2.   Sample Letter

[Name of Doctor]   [Date]
[Address]

Re: John J. Smith

Dear Sir/Madam:

Our office represents John J. Smith for personal injuries sustained in an automobile accident on April 20, 2006. Mr. Smith advises that you treated him for the injuries on April 21, 2006. Accordingly, please provide us with copies of his medical records, including any notes, laboratory reports, and fee statements. Enclosed is an authorization from Mr. Smith requesting a release of records to our custody.

We will, of course, pay your copying costs. Alternatively, if you prefer, we will arrange for a copying service to come directly to your office. Please call me immediately in the event you would like us to provide the copy service.

In order for us to complete our investigation of this matter in a timely manner, please provide us with the records on or before [insert date approximately ten days after the date of the letter].

Thank you for your assistance.

Sincerely,

_____
Jane J. Jones
Paralegal [or Legal Assistant]

---

6. Since some records, such as hospital reports, will be technical, get a good dictionary or encyclopedia to help you understand them.

Exhibit 2.3.   Sample Authorization

AUTHORIZATION FOR RELEASE OF MEDICAL RECORDS

To: [Name of Doctor]   [Date]

You are hereby authorized to release a complete copy of my medical records, including all notes, laboratory reports, and fee statements, to my attorneys Mack, Meyer and Miller or their representatives. This authorization is effective immediately and remains in effect until such time as you receive written notice of my revocation of this authorization.

_____

John J. Smith

[Notary Acknowledgment]

If you can get these types of records from third parties, maintain them properly. Keep the records you receive together and in order, and do not mark them. Keep a record of how, from whom, and when you got them. Make additional copies that you can mark up and use during client and witness interviews. The sample chart that follows shows this system for maintaining the records.

RECORDS OF DOCUMENTS

Document	Date Received	How Obtained	From where
Contract	8/05/06	Client	
Shopping Order	10/23/06	Document Request	Defendant
Invoice	10/23/06	Document Request	Defendant
Letter by defendant to former employee	11/05/06	Deposition Subpoena	Jim Johnson, former employee

E. WITNESS INTERVIEWS

After you have interviewed the client and obtained the available exhibits, the next stage of your informal fact investigation is interviewing witnesses. Here, a great deal of flexibility is possible, and it is critical to plan ahead.

1. Who and when to interview

The more you know, the more accurately you can assess the strengths and weaknesses of the client's case. It makes sense, then, to interview every witness, favorable, neutral, and unfavorable, to find out what each knows. The benefits of interviewing everyone, however, are always tempered by economic realities. There are few cases in which you can interview everyone, regardless of expense. On the other hand, every case has critical witnesses whom you must try to interview regardless of the cost. In addition, once taken, the case must be handled competently, regardless of cost constraints.

In consultation with the lawyer in charge, make a list of all known witnesses who must be interviewed and a list of other witnesses who may not be known, but for whom an attempt should be made to identify and interview. For example, bystanders may not be known, but you may be able to identify them by canvassing homes or stores near the accident scene. These bystanders may be able to corroborate the client's version of the accident.

When you have the list of witnesses you need to interview, you must decide the order in which to interview them. Here again, flexibility is required. It is frequently better to interview favorable and neutral witnesses first, before you interview the unfavorable ones, since you will have better success in pinpointing the differences in their stories. Identifying and interviewing the favorable and neutral witnesses first will give you the basis for your side's version of any disputed events and will help you identify the areas of disagreement when you interview the unfavorable witnesses. These areas can then be explored in detail. Frequently, however, you won't know for sure whether a given witness will be favorable.

On the other hand, there are advantages in interviewing unfavorable witnesses early, before their attitudes and recall have solidified. For example, in an accident case you learn that a witness will be unfavorable based on quotations from that witness in a police accident report. It may be useful to interview that witness quickly. She may change her mind, or tell you that she "didn't really see it happen," or "isn't sure" about important facts. You may minimize the impact of the witness through an early interview.

2. Locating witnesses

Paralegals are capable of locating many witnesses. The client frequently knows the important ones. Records, such as business records and accident reports, will usually identify others. When their names are known, it is surprising how many witnesses can be located over the telephone or by checking basic, available sources. The telephone book, neighbors at a previous address, workers at a former job, friends, and relatives are all good sources in locating a known witness. It is often the case that a witness has merely changed a telephone number, moved to a different apartment, or changed jobs, and tracking her down is relatively simple. If these leads do not work, the following checklist of sources should be used to locate the witness. This checklist also may be used for ascertaining information about witnesses.

- ☐ Post office
- ☐ Voter registration
- ☐ Motor vehicle departments
- ☐ Utility companies
- ☐ The Veterans Administration
- ☐ Social Security office
- ☐ Unemployment agencies
- ☐ Welfare agencies
- ☐ County Assessor's office
- ☐ Board of Education
- ☐ License bureaus
- ☐ Army/Air Force register
- ☐ Credit associations
- ☐ *Who's Who in America*
- ☐ Real estate and rental agencies

The Internet is also an easy way to find people. The **Internet** links computers and databases of information from all over the world. The Internet is sometimes referred to as the World Wide Web. By searching these worldwide databases, you can locate not only information, but people and businesses. Some web sites will even give you the location of residences and businesses on a map. Yahoo's people search (http://www.yahoo.com/search/people) is a good start in locating telephone numbers and postal addresses. This database will also allow you to conduct a public records search, including court records, social security, driving records, criminal records, and background checks. If you have the city, state, and zip code, you can type in an address and pinpoint a location on the map by using Yahoo's map web site (http://maps. yahoo.com). Donnelleymarking.com has compiled information about millions of businesses. In addition, USSEARCH.com uses thousands of public records databases to find addresses and background information on individuals and businesses. To "google" a word or name has become almost standard lexicon. Go to the search engine google.com and type in a person's name. You will be surprised at how much information you find. The following additional on-line sources can be used for locating witnesses:

Internet Address Finder (http://www.iaf.net/): This site allows you to search for addresses registered on the Internet.
WhoWhere (http://www.whowhere.lycos.com/): Search for public records and background checks concerning individuals.
Big Foot (http://www.bigfoot.com/): This site will give you a choice of a directory assistance search for individuals, or a yellow page search for businesses

A word of warning: Web sites on the Internet sometimes change. If this happens, you will generally get a message advising of the new web site.

If the witness is important to the case and cannot be located through these types of leads, it may be necessary to hire an experienced investigator.

3. Purposes of the interview

There are several objectives you should try to accomplish during a witness interview. These objectives usually should be pursued in the following order:

1. Learn what the witness knows and doesn't know.
2. Get specific, admissible facts.
3. Get admissions.
4. Get information that might be used to discredit the witness.
5. Get leads to other witnesses and information.
6. Record interview, or get written statement.

Begin by learning everything the witness knows and does not know that is relevant to the case. Elicit what the witness knows by using open-ended questions. These can be followed later with specific, focused questions; however, you want details of the critical events and transactions only, not everything the witness knows that may possibly be relevant. When learning what the witness knows, make sure you pinpoint the admissible facts based on firsthand knowledge.[7] With witnesses who have unfavorable information, you should try to limit the damage by limiting the witness' testimony. Find out what the witness does not know, is not sure of, is only guessing about, or has only secondhand information about.

---

7. As discussed in later chapters, certain facts are not admissible if they are based on speculation or hearsay.

Second, pin the witness down. This means going beyond generalizations and getting to specific, admissible facts. For example, "driving fast" must be changed to an approximation of speed in miles per hour. "He looked drunk" should be pursued to get the details underlying the conclusion, such as "staggering, glassy-eyed, and smelling of alcohol." Getting only generalizations and conclusions makes it easy for a witness to change his testimony later.

Third, get admissions. With unfavorable witnesses, having the witness admit that he "isn't sure," "didn't really see it," "was only guessing," or "was told" all serve to prevent the witness from changing or expanding his testimony at trial.

Fourth, get information that might be used to discredit the witness so the witness will not be believed at trial. This is known as **impeachment**. If an unfavorable witness says something that later may be useful to impeach him, pin him down. For example, if an unfavorable witness to an accident says he was 200 feet away when it happened, make sure you commit him to that fact. Use "200 feet" in other questions to recommit him to that fact, since at trial he may claim that the distance was shorter.

Fifth, get leads to other witnesses and information. It is surprising how often a witness will name other witnesses or divulge information not previously mentioned in any report. For example, asking a witness if anyone else was present at an accident scene will sometimes get a response like: "Sure, Ellen, my supervisor, was standing right next to me and saw the whole thing."

Finally, try to record the interview or get some type of written statement. How to do this is discussed in section 6.

4. Arranging the interview

Often, the most difficult part of witness interviews is getting witnesses to agree to be interviewed in the first place. With favorable witnesses this is usually not a problem, and selecting a convenient time and place for the interview is a routine matter. Unfavorable witnesses, however, are frequently reluctant. Here, you can take either of two approaches: attempt to arrange an interview or attempt a surprise interview. A reluctant witness may agree to be interviewed at a convenient time and place, where privacy is assured, if the interview won't take too long. Let such a witness know that cooperating now may eliminate the need for a deposition, which is a formal question-and-answer period by all parties. You might also suggest that an interview at home would be both convenient and private. If the witness senses that the real question is where and when, rather than if, he is more likely to agree to an interview.

If a witness will not agree to an arranged interview, the only alternative is the unannounced interview. Frequently, a witness who doesn't want to be bothered will nevertheless agree to talk when an investigator "pops into" the witness' office or "stops by" the house. Again, it may help to reassure the witness that the questions won't take long and may eliminate the need for further involvement. However, a witness has a perfect right to refuse to be interviewed, and you cannot harass or badger the witness, hoping to change his mind. The only alternative is to depose the witness later.

5. Structuring the interview

How do you go about structuring a witness interview? First, review the case file, which should contain client interviews, exhibits such as police reports, perhaps other witness interviews, and the developing litigation chart. Second, get copies of any diagrams, photographs, and records you may use during the interview. Third, decide if and how you will record the interview. Finally, prepare an outline for the interview. A frequently followed order for witness interviews is the following:

1. Witness background
2. Story in witness' own words
3. Detailed chronological story
4. Questions focused on the theory of the case

First, witness background is important for assessing witness credibility and determining if there is any bias, interest, or other facts that affect credibility. Most witnesses don't mind talking about their work, family, and home. Asking these background questions usually puts witnesses at ease. Some witnesses, however, may resent what they consider to be intrusions into their private lives. In such cases, you may want to slip the background information into the interview or simply touch on it at the end.

EXAMPLE

Paralegal: I understand, Ms. Kramer, that you are the secretary for the regional baseball league. Can you tell me a little about your work?

Ms. Kramer: I do all the typing and act as an administrative assistant for the four staff members we have at the league.

Paralegal: How long have you been working for the league?

Ms. Kramer: Two years. Prior to that I was working as a secretary for an advertising account executive.

Paralegal: How long have you been a secretary?

Ms. Kramer: Almost fourteen years.

Second, let the witness tell her story in her own words, even at the price of hearing irrelevant facts. It gives you a good picture of the kind of witness she will be at trial, and you may discover important facts that would never have come to light.

EXAMPLE

Paralegal: As you know, we are handling the matter involving the delivery of approximately fifteen hundred baseballs ordered by Mary Garcia from Wholesale Sporting Goods. I would like for you to tell me as much as you can about what you know about the events surrounding the ordering and delivery of the baseballs.

Third, go over the story in chronological order and in detail. Get specifics on what the witness saw, heard, and did at all important times, and what she saw others do and say. Find out what exhibits the witness knows of, and other witnesses she is aware of. Find out what the witness personally knows of the facts, as opposed to the witness' opinions or speculation about the facts or what the witness was told by others. Find out to whom the witness has talked.

EXAMPLE

Paralegal: I would like to go back to the beginning where you indicated that the first time you heard of Wholesale Sporting Goods is when Mr. Tanner from Wholesale Sporting Goods called for Ms. Garcia. Did you hear any part of the conversation Mr. Tanner had with Ms. Garcia?

Ms. Kramer: I heard part of what Ms. Garcia was saying to Mr. Tanner because after I transferred the call to her, I went into her office to deliver the mail. I heard her say that if he could beat the price she was presently paying, he would have our account.

Finally, ask focused questions based on the theory of the case. For example, if the witness gives information that contradicts the client's version of the events, see how you can minimize its effect. If the witness is "not sure," "guessing," "didn't see it myself," or says other things that lessen the damage, make sure you note it. In addition, see if the witness can corroborate something useful to your client's side. Witnesses are rarely completely unfavorable; a little searching will often turn up something positive.

Paralegal: Do you know when Ms. Garcia sent payment to Wholesale Sporting
      Goods for the baseballs?

Ms. Kramer: Not exactly. I do recall filling out a check requisition for Ms. Garcia
      for payment of the baseballs soon after she received the contract.

Paralegal: Do you recall if this was before or after the baseballs had been delivered?

Ms. Kramer: Oh, it was definitely before.

---

6. Recording the interview

Regardless of the witness, you should make a record of the interview.
There are several possibilities:

- Obtain a written, signed statement
- Use a court reporter
- Make a tape recording, with the witness' consent
- Take notes during the interview
- Make notes after the interview

The approach you use depends on what will best serve your interests
and what the witness will permit. If you expect the witness to give
favorable information and be cooperative, a short, written, and signed
statement is often best. After interviewing the witness, simply type a
summary of her story and ask her to sign it. Another method is to send
the witness a confirming letter summarizing what she said, and ask the
witness to sign and return a copy acknowledging its accuracy. This will
lock a favorable witness into her basic story, and there is no damage if
the opposing side obtains the statement during discovery.[8] With unfavorable witnesses, it is often advantageous to get a detailed statement.
This improves your chances of getting contradictions, admissions, and
impeachment that may be valuable at trial. Using a court reporter or a
tape recorder is probably the most reliable method. Get the witness' permission if you plan to tape-record, since surreptitious recordings are
illegal in some jurisdictions. Avoid later criticism that the recording does
not include everything the witness said by being mindful of when conversation is off the record.

---

8. Although witness statements are usually not discoverable, under Rule 26(b)(3) of
the Federal Rules of Civil Procedure even trial preparations materials are not absolutely
protected from discovery. Upon a showing of substantial need and undue hardship,
such materials are discoverable, except that "mental impressions, conclusions, opinions,
or legal theories of an attorney or other representative of a party" are always protected
from disclosure.

What is best, and what a witness is willing to do, are two different things. Many witnesses are reluctant to talk, and they are usually under no legal obligation to talk to anyone unless compelled by legal process. Of those willing to talk, many are understandably reluctant to give a signed statement or to have their statements recorded or reduced to a writing. Hence, your priority should be to get the witness to tell what she knows so you will learn what her trial testimony is likely to be, and you will get leads on other witnesses and evidence. Only then should you try to get the most reliable type of statement the witness agrees to give. In short, it is usually better to conduct an interview without any recording than to have no interview at all. You can always dictate immediately afterward what the witness has said.

7. Interviewing techniques

Every witness is influenced by both positive and negative factors that affect the witness' willingness to be interviewed and disclose what he knows. These factors bear on both friendly and hostile witnesses. Hostile witnesses may be unwilling to talk at all; friendly witnesses, although willing to talk, are influenced by factors that inhibit or promote full disclosure. An interviewer, therefore, should understand these factors and use them to accomplish her primary purpose of finding out what the witness knows.

Negative factors inhibit witness disclosure. Some witnesses feel that they are being judged by the interviewer. Others tell the interviewer what she apparently wants to hear. Still others become inhibited by emotions such as fear or embarrassment. The interviewer must learn to recognize situations in which these factors exist and use interviewing techniques that reduce their effect.

Positive factors promote disclosure. Witnesses usually respond favorably when the interviewer shows a personal interest in them. Witnesses like to feel that they are doing the decent thing by talking to the interviewer. They tend to identify with the side that values their testimony. Witnesses enjoy feeling important and may be more likely to help if they feel that the information they can provide is important to resolve a dispute fairly. Positive reinforcement is a strong motivator.

Getting witnesses to disclose fully and accurately is best achieved by minimizing the negative factors and reinforcing the positive ones. Accordingly, pick a convenient time and place for the interview. When scheduling the interview, remind the witness that it's always better to talk when the events are fresh in mind. Remind him that it is natural to want to help others and that his disclosing information will help ensure a just and accurate result. Use open-ended, direct examination questions to get the witness talking, to obtain the basic story, and to pursue leads. For example, to find out what the witness knows about the incident you might ask, "Describe how fast you believe the defendant was traveling just prior to the accident" or "Tell me what you saw." But use narrow or closed cross-examination questions to pin the witness down and develop potential impeachment. These questions focus on specific, isolated facts and guide the witness to specific information. For example, to pin a witness down, ask him, "You're sure the car was going 40 miles per hour?" and "She couldn't have been going faster than that, could she?"

The content of questions can also effectively influence responses. Let the witness know your attitude on the matter being discussed, since he has a psychological interest in satisfying his listener's expectations. For example, telling a witness that you feel badly about your side's client having been cheated by the defendant may get a more sympathetic story from the witness. Second, word choices can influence responses. For example, it is well known that using "how fast" rather than "how slowly" will increase estimations of speed. Third, leading questions are more likely to get the kind of answer you want. For example, asking a witness, "That car was going faster than the speed limit, wasn't it?" is more likely to elicit a "yes" response. Fourth, knowing what other people have said or what other evidence has already been shown can influence witnesses, because witnesses prefer consistency and are uncomfortable with conflict. For example, telling a witness that another eyewitness has already stated that the car was speeding will often influence the witness.

8. Evaluating witnesses

Following a witness interview, write a short memo evaluating the witness and her information. It is easy to forget your impressions of the witness, yet witness credibility is frequently the critical component in case evaluation. The memo is especially important if more than one lawyer will work on the file. The memo should evaluate the witness' credibility and effectiveness as a trial witness, note the witness' attitude toward the case, and summarize where the witness' anticipated testimony will help or hurt the case.[9]

9. Under Rule 26(b)(3) of the Federal Rules of Civil Procedure, materials prepared by a lawyer, or under a lawyer's directions, are considered the lawyer's work product. Thus, a memo should also be absolutely privileged as an attorney's work product and, therefore, not discoverable by the opposing party.

F. EXPERT REVIEWS

Wrongful death, medical malpractice, product liability, major negligence, and commercial cases almost always use expert witnesses at trial. The plaintiff's case will probably require expert testimony to establish a prima facie case on liability and causation, and to make out a solid case on damages. In a **prima facie case**, the plaintiff can prove each of the elements of the claim as indicated on the litigation chart. The defense case will probably have opposing experts. Accordingly, a case investigation is often incomplete until the case file is reviewed by appropriate experts. The lawyer may need two experts: one to review the file and consult with in order to develop facts and theories for trial, the other to be a trial witness. Of course, one expert can and often does perform both roles.

Prima facie case
A case in which each element in the plaintiff's claim can be proven

If the lawyer requests that the file be reviewed by an expert, you may be asked to provide the necessary documents to the expert for review. Do not send out a file for expert review until you have collected the reports and records the expert will inevitably need. Make sure the written materials you send her give a complete and neutral picture of the case, but do not give the expert privileged materials. Keep in mind that an expert who becomes the testifying expert at trial can often be deposed and forced during cross-examination to produce all materials she received for her review. Factual materials that are given to the expert may not be protected by the work product privilege; therefore, do not give an expert any materials that contain the lawyer's mental impressions and thought processes.

In addition, rather than have the expert review the file generally, you may want to direct the expert to specific areas where there are potential problems. This is best done in conversations with the expert, after you have sent her the necessary materials. For example, in a medical malpractice case you might tell the expert that the potential case theory of liability is that the anesthetic was improperly administered, and ask the expert if the standard of reasonable care was breached. A focused review is usually more productive.

Although Rule 26 of the Federal Rules of Civil Procedure makes important discovery distinctions between consulting and testifying experts, hiring an expert as a consultant does not prevent the lawyer from using her as an expert at trial. That decision will have to be made at the discovery stage, since Rule 26 requires that the parties designate the persons who will probably be called to provide substantive evidence at trial, and Rule 37 provides that only those persons listed may be used at trial to provide substantive evidence unless the omission was with "substantial justification." Furthermore, those persons providing expert testimony must prepare a detailed written report about the testimony to be presented so the opposing parties have a reasonable opportunity to prepare for effective cross-examination or other expert testimony.

As a paralegal, you may be asked to assist the lawyer in selecting an expert. Because an expert is so important, and because a consulting expert may later be the testifying expert at trial, you must be careful in selecting one. Perhaps the best way to select an expert is simply to ask litigators you know to recommend one who is knowledgeable in the subject area of your particular kind of case, is willing to work with and educate you, and will be an effective trial witness. If this fails, or you need an expert in a specialized area, some lawyers' groups, such as the American Trial Lawyers Association, maintain expert directories, and law libraries sometimes have directories for various specialties.[10] However, the easiest way to find an expert is to do a search on the Internet. Use a search engine to put in the words "expert" and the specific topic area (i.e. medical malpractice, insurance bad faith, police brutality etc.). Popular search engines are lycos.com, altavista.com, and google.com. In addition, you can search for articles and books on the topic area for which you need to retain an expert. Often, you will find that the author of the article or book can be used as an expert, or may be able to refer you to other experts in the field.

G. COMPUTERIZED FACT GATHERING

In our fast-moving computer age, the Internet has become a significant tool to gather information in litigation matters. Accordingly, whether you want to conduct basic legal research on a specific topic or find out more information about an area, product, or even a company that is involved in the litigation, you will likely find it by surfing the Internet.

To access the World Wide Web on the Internet, you must have the necessary equipment. Most law firms have computers set up for Internet access that you may use to assist you in gathering information. If your law firm does not have Internet access, you may be able to obtain access through a computer at your local library.

There are numerous legal sites available to assist you with your research and fact gathering. The legal sites listed below are a good place to start your research. Each of the sites offers links to other legal resources.

> http://www.law.cornell.edu (provides links to court decisions, U.S. Code, and some state statutes and constitutions)
> http://www.law.emory.edu (provides links to court decisions, federal agencies, U.S. Code, as well as several legal-related databases)

---

10. TASA, the Technical Advisory Service for Attorneys, is an organization that refers experts in numerous fields. Many legal newspapers and journals also contain listings and information about experts. Local universities are also a good source.

http://www.law.indiana.edu (provides links to court decisions and legal-related databases)

http://www.law.vill.edu (provides links to court decisions, U.S. Code, and some state statutes and constitutions)

http://www.loc.gov (provides links to the Library of Congress)

http://thomas.loc.gov (information relating to congressional bills, Congressional Record, and Congressional Advisory Board Reports)

http://www.house.gov (U.S. House of Representative Internet Law Library, with links to over 2,000 other sources)

http://www.ncsconline.org (provides links to sites for state court systems)

http://cfoc.gov (provides links to state and local government sites)

http://www.kentlaw.edu (law-related discussion groups)

There are also a number of web sites for specific resources that can be helpful, depending on your topic and needs:

http://port.harbornet.com/html/search.php (state constitutions)

http://www.washlaw.edu (state laws)

http://www.access.gpo.gov (Federal Register from 1994 to the present)

http://www.law.cornell.edu (Uniform Commercial Code text)

http://www.municode.com (municipal ordinances from a number of jurisdictions)

http://www.usdoj.gov (Department of Justice)

http://www.uspto.gov (Patent and Trademark Office)

http://www.ftc.gov (Federal Trade Commission)

The state bar for your jurisdiction will probably have its own web site providing links to specific sites regarding the laws of your state. In addition, many state courts have sites that allow you to search their database for court filings. Many counties also have sites that allow you to access recorded documents such as trust deeds and property liens.

Do not overlook the value of gathering facts through the Internet. To see how valuable such a search can be, let's go back to our interview with Ms. Garcia and the shipment of defective baseballs. Using the Internet, it may be possible for us to locate background information on Wholesale Sporting Goods, such as how large a company they are, when they first started in business, and any consumer representations that they make through promotional materials placed on the Internet.

In addition, by searching the Internet you can quickly become an expert on baseballs. By searching the Internet using the query "baseball and supplies" you will find literally hundreds of sites regarding different types of baseballs and prices. This information can be valuable to you in learning something about the business, as well as in comparing the terms that were offered to the client by Wholesale Sporting Goods and what other companies could realistically offer.

The following is a partial list of sites can be used to conduct searches using key words or terms:

http://altavista.com
http://www.lycos.com
http://www.yahoo.com
http://www.google.com
http://www.askjeeves.com

CHAPTER SUMMARY

This chapter has discussed the paralegal's role in conducting an informal fact investigation, the importance of informal fact gathering, and ways in which you may structure your investigation. Facts necessary to the investigation may be obtained informally from the client, exhibits, witnesses, experts who are consulted about the client's case, and even through surfing the Internet. This informal fact gathering is usually more effective and less expensive than waiting until after a lawsuit is filed to undertake discovery.

The client and all available witnesses must be interviewed as part of the initial fact gathering. This chapter described the steps in conducting a good client interview, as well as various interviewing techniques, and provided a checklist for locating witnesses.

Equally important to the initial fact gathering is the acquisition of physical evidence, including records. Much of the evidence will be in the client's possession. However, when this is not so, you may be able to obtain evidence in the possession of third parties voluntarily and without the necessity of a subpoena. Any records you receive should be placed on a Record of Documents chart, such as the one provided in this chapter.

KEY TERMS

Affirmative defense	Counterclaim
Breach of contract	Exhibits
Cause of action	Factfinder
Chain of custody	Impeachment
Internet	Prima facie case
Jury instructions	Statute of limitations
Negligence	Subpoena
Physical evidence	Third party

REVIEW QUESTIONS

1. What is the difference between a cause of action and an affirmative defense?

2. How should you structure your fact investigation?

3. Identify at least five sources for locating the whereabouts of a witness.

4. What information should you attempt to obtain from the client during an initial interview? Why is this information important?

5. What are the purposes that should be accomplished during a witness interview? What are the question-asking techniques you can use to accomplish these purposes? Give an example of each.

6. What are the differences between a breach of contract and a negligence cause of action?

7. What is a statute of limitations? What is the statute of limitations for negligence actions in your state?

8. What documents should you attempt to obtain before a lawsuit is filed during the informal fact-gathering stage? What sources are available to you to locate these documents?

9. How can you use the Internet to help you in your informal fact gathering and investigation?

ADDITIONAL RESOURCES

www.summitconsulting.com/articles. A top ten list of effective client interviewing tips.

Find telephone numbers and residential and business addresses at the following sites:

www.peoplefinders.com
www.usa-people-search.com
www.whitepages.com
www.anywho.com

3

CASE EVALUATION AND STRATEGY

Once the preliminary factual and legal investigations are complete, attention turns to planning the litigation. In this chapter, you will discover

- How to establish the terms of the attorney-client agreement
- How a lawyer's fee is charged
- What steps to take in planning the litigation
- How to develop a litigation strategy
- What prefiling requirements should be considered

A. INTRODUCTION

Case evaluation requires that you gather enough facts and consider sufficiently the legal issues to assist the lawyer in deciding whether to take the case. If the lawyer decides to take the case, the evaluation requires a realistic, cost-effective litigation plan. This chapter gives you an overview of how the terms of the attorney-client relationship are established once the lawyer decides to take the case. This overview will familiarize you with the process the lawyer must go through, and it will enable you to assist the lawyer with that process.

In addition, once a decision has been made to take the case, you will need to assist the lawyer in developing a litigation strategy and in completing prefiling requirements. This chapter provides guidelines for preparing a litigation plan and a checklist for prefiling requirements.

B. ESTABLISHING THE TERMS OF THE ATTORNEY-CLIENT AGREEMENT

Once the lawyer decides to take the case, the terms of the attorney-client relationship should be formally established in a written agreement. There are three reasons for this. First, any contractual relationship is best established in writing. Second, the agreement will prove the existence of an attorney-client relationship for purposes of asserting the attorney-client privilege. Third, the agreement will establish the work to be done, what will not be done, and the basis for compensation, all of which must be understood to ensure a good working relationship between lawyer and client.

Unless the client is sophisticated and has experience working with lawyers, the client will have little understanding of the legal work involved in litigation and the various fee arrangements that can be made. It is in everyone's best interests that the client be educated on these matters. The lawyer will discuss with the client how fees are set and what costs can be expected.

In some jurisdictions the agreement, particularly a **contingency fee agreement** where the lawyer receives a percentage of the recovery in a lawsuit, must be in writing. It is most common to use either a written contract or a letter to the client, a copy of which the client signs and returns. Regardless of which method is used, it should cover all aspects of the relationship in detail. Unfortunately, disputes between lawyers and clients are common, but they can largely be avoided by making sure that the agreement is drafted in clear and simple English, covers all likely issues, and specifies what is not covered. The lawyer is held responsible for any ambiguities and omissions in attorney-client agreements, so it is in a lawyer's best interest to draft an agreement that leaves no room for misunderstanding. The agreement should cover the following basic subjects.

Contingency fee agreement
An agreement between the lawyer and client whereby the lawyer will receive as compensation for the lawyer's fee a certain percentage in the recovery ultimately obtained by the client

1. Work covered

The agreement should specify what work will be performed and what will not be. For example, the agreement might be to prosecute a negligence claim arising out of a car accident on a certain date and time. If the lawyer will not handle any appeal, or if there will be an additional charge for any appeal, the agreement should specify this. If the lawyer will not handle a workers' compensation claim, insurance claim, or other related matters, the agreement should say so. In general, it is important to guard against a client thinking that the lawyer will do more than the lawyer has agreed to do. Spelling out what is not covered should prevent this from happening.

2. Lawyer's fee

A lawyer's fee is the compensation the lawyer will receive for professional services rendered on behalf of the client. The amount of the lawyer's fee, the way it will be determined, and when it will be paid must be spelled out. The total fee must be reasonable in light of the work to be done, the difficulty of the work, the amount of time it will involve, and the customary range of fees for similar work in that locality.[1]

---

1. See Model Rules of Professional Conduct, Rule 1.5.

Fixed flat fee
Lawyer receives a predetermined sum as fee regardless of how much work is expended on the client's behalf

Retainer fee
Amount the client pays to the lawyer at commencement of the representation; fee is credited against fees and costs incurred by client

The agreement should specify how the fee will be determined. Three approaches are commonly employed: an **hourly rate** (common in corporate, commercial, and insurance defense cases), **a fixed flat fee** (common in criminal defense cases and in family law), and the contingency fee (common in plaintiff's personal injury cases). Obviously, the agreement can specify any number of combinations or modifications of these basic approaches, unless the fee is regulated or set by statute. For example, agreements frequently specify a minimum **retainer fee,** paid up front, that is credited against an hourly billing rate. A retainer is simply a cash payment of a sum of money to a lawyer before work begins on the client's case.

When the fee is based on an hourly rate, the client must understand that what is being paid for is the lawyer's expertise and time. Hence, any time expended on a client's case will be billed to the client, regardless of whether the time is spent on court appearances, conferences, research, drafting documents, or making telephone calls.

The agreement should define how the fee amount is determined and when it should be paid. For instance, in personal injury cases where the plaintiff's attorney's fees are usually a percentage of any recovery, it is important to specify whether the percentage is computed before or after costs are deducted and that the fee is due when any judgment is actually collected.

If a fee will be shared with another lawyer outside the principal lawyer's firm, this fact must be disclosed to the client and the client must consent to the arrangement. The division of fees must be proportionate to the work and responsibility of each lawyer.[2]

A lawyer has an ethical duty to make the fee reasonable. This may mean that the lawyer must discount the fee, even in a contingent fee situation, to make sure it is in fact reasonable before submitting it to the client.

Many statutes and rules regulate and limit attorney's fees. For example, statutory causes of action frequently either limit attorney's fees or make them subject to court approval. Any fee agreement must comply with the applicable statutes and rules.

An **attorney's lien** is a claim by the lawyer on any judgment or recovery obtained by the client and can usually be imposed to ensure payment of the lawyer's fee. This is frequently done in contingent fee situations. In some jurisdictions an attorney's lien is only enforceable if the client expressly agrees to it.

3. Retainers

In some situations, the lawyer may insist on a retainer to ensure payment of the fee and reimbursement of other costs that the lawyer advances.

---

2. See Model Rules of Professional Conduct, Rule 1.5(e).

A common arrangement is to insist on a retainer and then periodically deduct fees and costs as they are incurred. Regardless of the precise agreement, the agreement must specify the amount of the retainer, when it must be remitted, and what fees and costs will be deducted from it.

Whenever a lawyer receives advanced funds from a client, the funds must be put in a separate client trust account. Under no circumstances can any client's funds be commingled with the lawyer's funds.[3] Funds of all of a lawyer's clients can be held in one trust account; however, a separate ledger must be kept for each client showing receipts and disbursements. A number of states have adopted, through statutes or court rules, the Interest on Lawyer's Trust Accounts (IOLTA) system, which requires holding client funds in interest-bearing accounts.

4. Costs

The agreement should distinguish between fees due the lawyer for professional representation and the costs incurred during the course of that representation. **Costs** are out-of-pocket expenses incurred by the lawyer in the course of representation of the client. The lawyer is reimbursed by the client for these out-of-pocket expenses. Accordingly, the agreement should note the types of anticipated costs, such as filing fees and other court costs; expert witness fees and expenses; court reporter fees; travel expenses; photocopying, mailing, and long-distance calls. It is sometimes a good idea to estimate the usual costs for the type of case involved. The agreement should also specify when the costs will be paid; customarily the client is billed at regular intervals, such as monthly or quarterly. The agreement should make clear that costs are the client's obligation, even if no recovery is obtained.

Plaintiff's personal injury cases present a special situation. The reason for accepting a contingency fee arrangement—that the client is otherwise unable to pay for legal representation—also bears on the propriety of advancing costs. A lawyer may advance costs, such as court costs, deposition expenses, investigator fees, and expert witness fees; however, the client ultimately is still responsible for paying those costs. The most common approach is to reimburse costs to the lawyer when a judgment is actually paid. If there is no recovery, the client is still responsible for paying the costs, although a client without money will probably not be able to reimburse the lawyer. For this reason, some lawyers accept contingency fee arrangements for cases that will have substantial costs only if the client advances a sum of money sufficient to cover the expected costs.

---

3. See Model Rules of Professional Conduct, Rule 1.15.

5. Billings

The agreement should specify when fees and costs will be billed. Although monthly billing is normally best for both lawyer and client, less frequent billings are sometimes appropriate, particularly for regular business clients, or if little work is done in any given month.

6. Authorization to file suit

The agreement should contain a statement that authorizes the lawyer to file suit on behalf of the client or, if the client is a defendant, authorizes the lawyer to defend the suit. The terms of the agreement should then be put in writing, either in a letter to the client or in a written agreement. Exhibits 3.1 and 3.2 are examples of a letter and a written agreement that may be sent to the client. Although you may draft the document, the letter or agreement should always be signed by the attorney in charge and not by you.

7. Next steps

Once the lawyer has decided to take the case and has reached an agreement with the client, there are several steps that should be taken to get the relationship started on the right track and to make sure that it stays on that track.

1. If the agreement expressly includes an attorney's lien, a notice of attorney's lien must be sent to the opposing party's lawyer and any insurance carriers. Most jurisdictions have standard attorney's lien forms used in litigation. Sending out the notices will ensure that the lawyer's fee is paid when any judgment is paid.

2. The client should sign authorization forms that will allow you to obtain certain records before the lawyer files suit. Depending on your jurisdiction's laws and practice, you may need signed authorizations to get police reports and motor vehicle records; hospital, doctor, employment, and insurance records; and Social Security, Veterans Administration, and other government records. Find out what type of authorization is necessary, and become familiar with the statutes requiring that such documents be made available to the client or his lawyer on request. You can also call the particular agency to learn its requirements and procedures. Some agencies have standard authorization forms. A sample cover letter and authorization can be found in Exhibits 3.3 and 3.4.

3. The client needs to know what he should and should not do. He should be told not to talk to anyone about the matter. Either you or the lawyer should explain that persons may try to interview him or get him

Exhibit 3.1.   Hourly Fee Agreement Letter

Dear Mr. Jones:

As we discussed in my office yesterday, I have agreed to represent you in the divorce proceedings recently started by your wife Joan. I will handle all negotiations necessary to attempt a property settlement before trial. If a trial becomes necessary, I will represent you to the conclusion of the trial.   } work covered

Fees for representing you will be based on the time expended on your case, the nature of issues presented, and the services rendered. My present hourly rate is $150 per hour. You have agreed to provide a retainer of $2,000 within one week. My usual total fee in divorce cases, assuming that no unusual problems arise, is approximately $2,000 if we agree on a property settlement, and approximately $5,000 to $7,000 if the case must be tried.   } fee and retainer

In addition to my fee, there will also be certain costs expended on your case, such as court filing fees, court reporter fees, and long-distance telephone and photocopying charges. You will be responsible for paying all such costs, regardless of the outcome in the case.   } costs

I will send you an itemized statement each month showing the time I have spent on your case and the other costs that have been incurred. I will subtract each monthly statement from the $2,000 retainer until it has been used up. I will then bill you directly, and you have agreed to pay those monthly statements in full when you receive them.   } billings

Please confirm that this letter correctly reflects the terms of our agreement by signing and dating the enclosed copy of this letter on the spaces provided.

Upon receipt of the signed letter and the $2,000 retainer I will begin work on your case.   } authorization

Sincerely,

/s/ John Smith

Agreed: _____
         John Jones
Dated: _____

Exhibit 3.2. Contingency Fee Agreement

<u>AGREEMENT</u>

Date: _____

I agree to employ John Smith and his law firm, Smith & Smith, P.C., as my attorneys to prosecute all claims for damages against Frank Johnson and all other persons or entities that may be liable on account of an automobile collision that occurred on June 1, 2006, at approximately 3:00 P.M., near the intersection of Maple and Elm Streets in this city. I authorize you to file suit on my behalf. — work covered / authorization

I agree to pay my lawyers a fee that will be one-third (33⅓ percent) of any sum recovered in this case, regardless of whether received through a settlement, lawsuit, or any other way. The fee will be calculated on the sum recovered, after costs and expenses have been deducted. The fee will be paid when any moneys are actually received in this case. I agree that John Smith and his law firm have an express attorney's lien on any recovery to ensure that their fee is paid. — contingency fee

I agree to pay all necessary costs and expenses, such as court filing fees, court reporter fees, expert witness fees and expenses, travel expenses, long-distance telephone costs, and photocopying charges, but these costs and expenses will not be due until a recovery is actually received in this case. I understand that I am also responsible for paying these costs and expenses, even if no recovery is received. — costs

I agree that this agreement does not cover matters other than those described above. It does not cover an appeal from any judgment entered, any efforts necessary to collect money due because of a judgment entered, or any efforts necessary to obtain other benefits such as insurance, employment, Social Security, and Veterans Administration benefits. — work covered

Agreed: _____
         John Jones

Exhibit 3.2.   Continued

> I agree to represent John Jones in the matter described above. I will receive no fee unless a recovery is obtained. If a recovery is actually received, I will receive a fee as described above.
>
> I agree to notify John Jones of all developments in this matter promptly, and will make no settlement of this matter without his consent.
>
> Agreed: _____
> > John Smith and
> > > Smith & Smith, P.C.

Exhibit 3.3.   Letter for School Records

> Records Administrator
> University of Southern California
> University Park
> Los Angeles, California 90007
>
> Re: Stella King
>
> Dear Sir/Madam:
>
> Our office represents Stella King for personal injuries sustained in an automobile accident on March 25, 2006. We understand that Ms. King attended the University from September 1990 through June 1994. She obtained a bachelor's degree in art sciences and graduated with honors. Verification of this information may be useful to us in our preparation for trial. Accordingly, please provide us with a copy of Ms. King's transcripts indicating the course work taken, grades received, and degree awarded. Enclosed is Ms. King's signed authorization to release the records to us.
>
> Sincerely,
>
> _____
> Victoria Kelley

Exhibit 3.4.   Authorization for Release of Personnel Records

TO: The Records Administrator

You are hereby authorized to release a copy of my transcripts for all course work completed between the years 1990 through 1994 to Victoria Kelley or her representative. The authorization is effective immediately and remains in effect until such time as you receive written notice of my revocation of the authorization.

_____

Stella King

[Notary Acknowledgment]

to make or sign statements. The client should tell such persons that he is represented by a lawyer, and he should notify you or the lawyer of all such attempts. The client should also understand that he is generally not required to talk to anyone unless required through the formal discovery process; he should direct all requests for information to the lawyer. He should not sign anything without first discussing it with the lawyer. He should be told to save and collect all relevant records, documents, bills, checks, and paperwork of any kind in his possession and deliver them to you or the lawyer; he should send records and documents that subsequently come into his possession to you or the lawyer as well.

4. The client needs a blueprint for the proceedings, since he may have little idea how civil litigation is actually conducted. He should be told what needs to be done before suit is filed; what happens during the pleadings, discovery, and motion practice stages of the litigation process; and what his role in this process will be. He should have some idea of how much time each of these stages takes and how far in the future any trial is likely to be; at the same time he should be aware that most cases are settled before trial. He also needs to be reminded of the risks and costs of any lawsuit, including the risk of an adverse verdict after trial. A well-informed client will understand the process he is a part of and will be likely to assist you throughout. Some law offices use a follow-up letter or brochure that repeats this advice and contains a chronology of likely events.

5. Maintaining communication with the client is important. Litigation goes in spurts; a period of activity is often followed by weeks of inactivity. If the client has not heard from your law office recently, he may erroneously conclude that you and the lawyer do not care about

him or that your office has lost interest in his case. Accordingly, you and the lawyer should keep the client well informed. Send the client copies of all pleadings, discovery, motions, and other court papers, as well as copies of correspondence. A well-informed client will usually be a cooperative, satisfied client.

C. DECLINING REPRESENTATION

A lawyer may not always be able to take a case. The matter may not be within the lawyer's expertise. It may not have merit or be large enough to justify a suit, or the defendant may not be able to pay a judgment. The lawyer may be too busy or have a conflict of interest. Or the lawyer may be unable to agree with the client on a fee. Whatever the reason, when a lawyer declines a potential case, it should be put in writing, usually in a letter to the prospective client.

Where a lawyer represents one party but cannot represent a related party because of a potential conflict of interest, the related party should be sent a letter in which the lawyer declines the offer of employment. Also, if an attorney withdraws from representing a client, an appropriate letter should be sent.

The letter declining the case ensures that the party clearly understands that the lawyer will not be representing him, and it can help resolve any question about whether the attorney has a duty to protect the party's interests even though he has never been a client. If the lawyer asks you to draft a letter declining representation, be sure to ascertain whether a statute of limitations or other notice statute may run shortly, so that the letter can warn the party to get another lawyer in time. The lawyer should sign the letter declining representation even if you draft the letter. A sample letter is shown in Exhibit 3.5.

The letter, once signed by the lawyer, should be sent by registered mail, return receipt by addressee only requested. When the signed return receipt is returned, staple it to the copy of the letter. This will be persuasive evidence to rebut any later claim that the lawyer never actually declined the case.

D. PLANNING THE LITIGATION

Assume that the lawyer has decided to take the case and that you have gathered the facts available through informal discovery; researched the possible legal claims, remedies, defenses, and counterclaims; put them on your litigation chart; and researched other procedural questions.

Exhibit 3.5.   Letter Declining Representation

Dear Mr. Jones:

As we discussed in my office yesterday, I will not be able to represent you for any claims you may have based on an automobile collision that occurred near the intersection of Maple and Elm Streets in this city on June 1, 2006, at approximately 3:00 P.M.

Since I cannot take your case, you may wish to see another lawyer about handling this matter for you. As we discussed yesterday, if you wish to have another lawyer represent you, you should do so promptly. If you do not, there may be legal problems, such as a statute of limitations bar, that might prevent you from pursuing your claims. Since your accident happened on June 1, 2006, and the statute of limitations for tort claims in this state is two years, if you wish to file a lawsuit you must do so before June 1, 2008. To avoid such problems, I recommend that you find another lawyer promptly, so any rights you have can be protected.

Enclosed are the originals of the police reports and insurance claim forms you brought to my office.

Sincerely yours,

/s/ John Smith

Now is the time, before filing the initial pleading, to structure a litigation plan.[4]

A litigation plan consists of defining the client's objectives and developing a strategy to achieve those objectives. The basic steps in assisting the lawyer in developing a litigation plan are the following:

1. Reevaluate the client's objectives, priorities, and cost constraints
2. Define the client's litigation objectives
3. Develop a "theory of the case"
4. Plan the pleadings
5. Plan the discovery
6. Plan the dispositive motions
7. Plan the settlement approach
8. Develop a litigation timetable

4. Of course, if you have a statute of limitations problem, whereby the client's claim will be barred unless the complaint is filed immediately, you may be asked by the lawyer to prepare and file the initial pleading. In such a case, you and the lawyer will not be able to structure a litigation plan until after the complaint is filed.

1. Reevaluate the client's objectives, priorities, and cost constraints

When you first interviewed the client, she had one or more "problems" she told you about. One of your first steps was to identify her legal problems and objectives. Now is the time to reassess those problems and objectives. You will have the benefit of your partially completed litigation chart showing the fruits of your research and informal fact investigation. By this time, you should also know the client's cost constraints. Finally, time has passed. All of these factors may influence what the client's current objectives and priorities are. You or the lawyer must sit down with the client, review what has been done to date, determine if the client's thinking is the same or has changed, and analyze those objectives and priorities to see if they still make sense in light of what is now known about the case.

2. Define the client's litigation objectives

If the client's thinking is unchanged and the dispute cannot be resolved short of litigation, the next step is to decide on broad litigation objectives that serve the client's overall objectives and priorities. Always remember that the client controls the objectives of the litigation, and the lawyer decides on the means to achieve those objectives. For example, suppose that the plaintiff-client wants an early settlement of the case and to keep expenses at a minimum. The strategy may be to keep the pleadings simple, to push for focused discovery, and then to start settlement discussions. On the other hand, suppose that the plaintiff-client anticipates that a trial will be necessary. In such a case, the strategy may be to use broad pleadings with alternative theories of recovery, to engage in extensive discovery, and to prepare thoroughly for trial. The litigation objectives will then form the basis for the remainder of your litigation plan.

3. Develop a "theory of the case"

Your side's "story" is a critical part of the litigation plan. Review what you and the lawyer presently know about the uncontested and contested facts, and ask some basic questions. Is your side's story complete, or are there significant missing pieces? Are your side's witnesses reliable? Do their stories make sense? Is your side's story one that has jury appeal? Where does your side's version clash with the other side's version of the facts? How does the lawyer plan to win the credibility battle over the disputed facts?

Theory of the case
The lawyer's position on, and approach to, all the undisputed and disputed evidence that will be presented at trial

Your side's position is frequently called the **theory of the case**. Those with experience know that most trials are won on the facts, not the law. The winning side usually organizes credible witnesses and exhibits into a believable story, and wins the war over the disputed facts by presenting more persuasive evidence on its side of the dispute. Thus, before drafting the pleadings discuss with the lawyer the theory of the case.

4. Plan the pleadings

Pleadings are the vehicle by which the theory of the case is brought to court. If pleadings are based on the theory of the case, you will not make the mistake of (and violate Federal Rule of Civil Procedure 11 by) raising a number of allegations in the pleadings and then wondering how you can find facts that fit into the theories of recovery.

What claims, relief, or defenses should you assert? Inexperienced paralegals often draft pleadings by "throwing the book at them" and pleading every conceivable claim, remedy, or defense that meets Rule 11 requirements, which, as you will recall, require that before any suit is filed, there must be reasonable inquiry into the facts to ensure the pleading is well grounded. The all-inclusive approach to pleadings seldom serves any purpose and generally increases the client's costs unnecessarily. Accordingly, before drafting the pleadings, discuss with the lawyer in charge the claims, remedies, or defenses that are reasonably supported by the facts that you have obtained through informal discovery. This way, the pleadings may be drafted to reflect the theories that the lawyer will want to advance at trial.

When you and the lawyer have decided which of the possible legal theories to raise in the initial pleading, you will still need to consider the related legal issues—e.g., choice of parties, subject matter jurisdiction, venue—that will be discussed in Chapter 4. These considerations are all interconnected, and substantial legal research will be necessary when the issues are complex. The time to research is now, not after the other side files a motion to dismiss.

5. Plan the discovery

Informal discovery was discussed in Chapter 2, and the various formal discovery methods are explained in Chapter 10. As noted in earlier chapters, the formal discovery stage is usually the largest part of the litigation process, the one that consumes the most time and money. Hence, it is particularly important to plan discovery to serve the client's overall objectives and cost considerations. Without planning, discovery usually becomes unfocused and expensive—two disasters to always avoid.

Planning discovery is essentially a seven-step process:

1. What facts do we need to establish a winning case on our side's claims (or to defeat the opponent's claims)?
2. What facts have we already obtained through informal fact investigation?
3. What "missing" facts do we still need to obtain through formal discovery?

The answers to the above questions should already be established on your litigation chart. You must consider four other questions:

4. What discovery methods are the most effective for obtaining the missing facts?
5. What facts and witnesses, which we already know through informal investigation, do we need to pin down by using formal discovery methods?
6. What restrictions does our litigation budget place on the discovery plan?
7. Finally, in what order should we execute our discovery plan?

These questions obviously require some time to think through. When you have decided on what discovery methods to use for particular information, exhibits, and witnesses, put them on your litigation chart and your litigation timetable and review them with the lawyer in charge.[5]

6. Plan the dispositive motions

Dispositive motions are motions heard by the court at any stage of the litigation before trial and have the effect of terminating the lawsuit without a trial. Thus, should any dispositive motions, such as summary judgment (a motion to obtain judgment without the necessity of a trial), be planned? Will the planned discovery provide the basis for succeeding on those motions? On the other hand, if the other side will be making the motions, what discovery needs to be planned that will defeat them?

---

5. This process is discussed in detail in Chapter 10, section D.

The motions stage of the litigation process will only be successful if discovery has been coordinated with the motions plan. This means that it is important to look down the road before filing the pleadings to see what motions will be realistic, and use discovery to obtain the facts necessary to prevail when the motions are later made.

7. Plan the settlement approach

Settlement
A resolution by the parties of their dispute without the necessity of trial

When to discuss with the opposing party the possibility of resolving the dispute by **settlement**—that is, reaching a resolution without the necessity of a trial—should be part of the overall litigation plan. When the client's objective is to settle quickly and keep costs down, the lawyer might consider discussing settlement early, such as after the pleadings have been closed or after a critical witness has been deposed. Otherwise, the lawyer will probably want to consider settlement after discovery is closed, after dispositive motions have been ruled on, or when the lawyer is preparing for the final pretrial conference. At these later stages, you and the lawyer will have a better grasp of the case's strengths and weaknesses, but the client will have incurred substantial litigation expenses.

8. Develop a litigation timetable

After each of the preceding steps in the litigation plan has been developed and coordinated, a realistic timetable should be drawn up. For this, you and the lawyer need to discuss in detail the case's complexity, the likely responses of the opposing party, and the usual time between the filing of a complaint and trial date in the jurisdiction where the case is brought. You can then put the steps into a chronological sequence and include them on your master calendar to remind yourself (and the lawyer) of the due date for each step in this particular case.

The planning of litigation must be an integrated, creative, flexible, continuing process. The plan needs to be integrated because each step should be tailored to achieving the client's litigation objectives while keeping in mind that each step influences the other steps. It should be creative, because every case is different and must be planned out to account for the conditions of the particular case, rather than plugging the conditions into a standard formula. Finally, it must be flexible and continuing because developments invariably occur during the litigation process that require changes in the litigation plan.

E. EXAMPLE OF LITIGATION PLANNING: *NOVELTY PRODUCTS, INC. V. GIFT IDEAS, INC.*

The following example illustrates the thought process that is involved in each step of a coordinated litigation plan.

E X A M P L E

Novelty Products, Inc. ("Novelty") is a corporation that manufactures novelty items that are sold to gift shops throughout the United States. Its corporate headquarters and manufacturing plant are in Buffalo, New York. Gift Ideas, Inc. ("Gift") is a corporation that owns a chain of gift shops located throughout California. Its corporate headquarters is in Los Angeles.

Over the past five years, Gift has periodically ordered products from Novelty under an established procedure. Gift's purchasing department places orders over the telephone, and Novelty sends a written confirmation of the order before delivering it. Gift then pays for each shipment within thirty days of receipt.

One of the items Gift has ordered from Novelty during that time is a patented tabletop electric cigarette lighter called the "Magic Lite." Gift has ordered the lighter, in increasingly large shipments, approximately every six months. The lighter now accounts for about half of all sales from Novelty to Gift. The latest lighter order, for $30,000, was made the usual way, and was shipped last month.

A few days ago, Gift notified Novelty that the latest shipment of lighters would be returned unpaid. Gift has just decided to make and market a tabletop electric cigarette lighter itself, and from now on its shops will only carry its own lighter. The Gift lighter, called the "Magic Flame," is almost identical in appearance and design to the Novelty lighter. A few months ago, Novelty's design chief left the company, and began working for Gift.

The shipment of lighters has been returned to Novelty, but Novelty has been unable to find another buyer for the lighters. Since Novelty will soon be marketing a new version of the lighter, finding a buyer seems unlikely.

The president of Novelty now comes to your law office for help.

Assume that, at the request of the lawyer in charge of the case, you have researched potential claims against Gift, determined the elements of those claims, identified the sources of proof, and completed an informal fact investigation. You have interviewed the client and appropriate employees, and have reviewed the client's records and correspondence along with what you could obtain from other nonparty sources. At this time the litigation chart appears as follows:

Litigation Chart

Elements of Claims	Sources of Proof	Informal Fact Investigation	Formal Discovery
1. Contract			
(a) Contract executed	◆ Novelty's records ◆ Novelty's witnesses ◆ Gift's records ◆ Gift's witnesses	Obtained from client Interviews	Request to produce Depositions, interrogatories, request to admit
(b) Novelty's performance	◆ Novelty's records ◆ Novelty's witnesses ◆ Gift's records ◆ Gift's witnesses	Obtained from client Interviews	Request to produce Depositions, interrogatories, request to admit
(c) Gift's breach (nonpay-ment & return of goods)	◆ Novelty's records ◆ Novelty's witnesses ◆ Gift's records ◆ Gift's witnesses ◆ Shippers	Obtained from client Interviews	Request to produce Depositions, request to admit Subpoenas
(d) Novelty's damages	◆ Novelty's records ◆ Novelty's witnesses ◆ 3d parties who rejected lighters	Obtained from client Interviews Interviews	Subpoenas

The litigation chart would be continued for every other potential claim you have been considering. In Novelty's case, these would include:

1. Bad faith
2. Theft of trade secret

3. Trademark
4. Patent
5. Unfair competition

Now is the time to develop the litigation plan. The steps include the following:

1. Reevaluate the client's objectives, priorities, and cost constraints.
2. Define the client's litigation objectives.
3. Develop a "theory of the case."
4. Plan the pleadings.
5. Plan the discovery.
6. Plan the dispositive motions.
7. Plan the settlement approach.
8. Develop a litigation timetable.

1. Reevaluate the client's objectives, priorities, and cost constraints

From your interviews with Novelty's president, the company's objectives have become clear: Novelty wants to be paid the $30,000 due under the contract, yet it also wants to maintain its other ongoing business with Gift. It wants to accomplish these dual objectives quickly at a minimum cost. After the lawyer's demand that Gift pay the contract amount has been rejected, Novelty's president agrees that litigation will be necessary. The president still feels that litigation, if kept simple, will not adversely affect Novelty's ongoing business relationship with Gift. These client objectives remain unchanged.

2. Define the client's litigation objectives

Since Novelty's president has authorized litigation, you need to discuss with the lawyer the basic litigation objectives. The lawyer will then get the client's approval. In this case, Novelty has three possible approaches:

1. It can keep the case simple and bring only a contract claim against Gift.
2. It can bring the former design chief in as a defendant by alleging theft of a trade secret.
3. It can expand the case against Gift by alleging bad faith, copyright, trademark, and unfair competition claims.

Which one of these litigation objectives will best serve Novelty's overall objectives?

Pursuing a case against the former design chief may be difficult, since he was not under contract with Novelty, and you have not found any proof that he helped Gift design its new lighter. Pressing a theft-of-trade-secrets claim against him has Rule 11 problems and runs counter to the client's preference for handling the case simply, quickly, and cheaply.

Pursuing the complex case involving the patent, trademark, and unfair competition claims also should not be recommended to the client. Such claims would undoubtedly destroy the continuing business dealings between Novelty and Gift, which remain important to Novelty. The claims would also create lengthy, expensive, and publicity-generating litigation — all things Novelty needs to avoid. Novelty could always decide to bring a separate suit on these claims if circumstances require it.

This leaves the basic contract claim against Gift, based on either common law or statutory law. The advantages of taking this approach are that the client has an excellent chance of winning on the merits and the case can be handled relatively quickly and inexpensively. The disadvantages are that damages may be low since a party — in this case, Novelty — has a duty to mitigate damages. This means that Novelty must do everything it can to avoid damages, such as reselling the returned lighters. However, to date Novelty has been unable to resell the returned lighters, so damages near the contract price may be appropriate.

You may also suggest to the lawyer adding a bad faith claim, which, if permitted under the applicable jurisdiction's substantive tort law, might permit compensatory or punitive damages. Your thinking is that Gift is more likely to settle the case for the contract price when faced with a bad faith claim. However, your research of current bad faith law, under both New York and California law, reveals that such a claim probably cannot be brought in a contract case under your facts. Bringing such a claim would probably violate Rule 11.

3. Develop a "theory of the case"

Before dealing with the pleadings, you need to discuss with the lawyer what Novelty's theory of the case should be. You suggest portraying Novelty as a small company that had ongoing business dealings with Gift, a larger corporate chain. The specific transaction was a routine one in which Gift made an oral order and Novelty sent a confirming letter, shipped the lighters, and sent a bill. Gift refused to pay for the lighters, but had no valid reason to do so. Gift simply changed its mind after agreeing to buy because it was going to market its own lighter. When the lighters were returned, Novelty could not resell them because it was preparing to market an improved version of the original lighter. In short, according to your theory, Gift welshed on the deal, and therefore owes Novelty the full $30,000. You feel that this theory will both be simple and have jury appeal.

4. Plan the pleadings

So far, a decision has been made to bring a contract action against Gift; however, many important questions must still be answered. As we will discuss in Chapter 4, these questions include which court is the proper one to hear the case, how to serve suit on a party in another state, and in which state the case should be filed.

5. Plan the discovery

The client has two basic objectives: keep it simple and inexpensive, and try to settle it quickly. The first objective was served by keeping the pleadings simple. The second objective must be remembered when planning the discovery, as well as in the later steps of the litigation plan.

Consult your litigation chart. At this stage, the facts you have gathered come principally from Novelty's employees and business records. In a contract case, this is to be expected. The untapped sources, then, Gift's employees and records, must be reached through formal discovery.

Since a basic objective is an early settlement, your side doesn't want to get mired in lengthy discovery. In addition, the lawyer advises that she wishes to move for partial summary judgment only on the issue of liability as soon as possible. These objectives—getting the missing information, getting evidence for the summary judgment motion, and pushing for early settlement—can be served by a carefully designed discovery plan.

For example, discovery may be used to get Gift's records and witness testimony that deal with the specific transaction involved. The evidence of an established course of dealings between Novelty and Gift, which would be necessary at trial to prove the contract terms, can be established by Novelty's records and witnesses. Also, your side can again prove the contract and its breach through Novelty's records and witnesses. This will give the lawyer the information necessary for the motion for partial summary judgment on liability.

What remains to be decided is which discovery methods to use to execute the plan and what order to use them in. After consulting with the lawyer, you may send a set of interrogatories to Gift dealing with the basic chronological events involved in the transaction. You and the lawyer also may send Gift a request to produce all records dealing with the specific transaction. These should, among other things, identify the Gift employees who handled the transaction and were involved in the decision to return the lighters. Finally, depositions of those same essential Gift employees should be scheduled in succession, during one or two days, to minimize their contact with each other. When this is done, you will send a request to admit facts (discussed in more detail in Chapter 10) that covers the liability issues in the case.

The last decision is when to take these steps. In general, the lawyer will probably want to send the interrogatories and requests to produce records at the earliest permitted time, and to send out the notices for the necessary depositions a few weeks later (see Chapter 10). The request to admit facts can then follow on the heels of the depositions.

6. Plan the dispositive motions

The overall litigation objective is to seek an early settlement, preferably after pleadings are filed or discovery has begun. If this does not work, you and the lawyer plan to move for partial summary judgment on liability as soon as discovery is completed. You will then have the information necessary to support the motion and to create additional pressure for a settlement.

7. Plan the settlement approach

Early settlement has always been a priority in this case. Accordingly, the lawyer may want to make settlement overtures—if Gift does not initiate them—after the pleadings are filed, after discovery is well under way and also when completed, after the motion for partial summary judgment is heard, and at the final pretrial conference.

The lawyer's approach has been to use focused discovery, particularly the request to admit facts, and the partial summary judgment motion to eliminate liability from the settlement discussions and put pressure on Gift. Since Novelty has been unable to resell the lighters, there is no mitigation of damages problem, and damages are likely to be the full contract price. The lawyer and you decide that, with Novelty's consent, the lawyer will agree to settle for an amount close to the contract price, minus the potential litigation expenses if the matter were to go to trial. This puts the settlement "value" of the case in the range of $22,000 to $30,000, depending on how early the case is settled.

8. Develop a litigation timetable

Now that a litigation plan has been developed that will realistically serve the client's objectives and priorities, you need to put the basic components on a timetable. The basic timetable for Novelty is as follows:

LITIGATION TIMETABLE

1/1 (today)	Complete litigation plan
by 2/1	File complaint
by 3/1	Interrogatories, production requests to defendant
by 5/1	Deposition notices to defendant witnesses
by 6/1	Depose defendant witnesses (same day if possible)
by 7/1	Requests to admit facts to defendant
by 9/1	Motion for partial summary judgment on liability
by 10/1	Prepare pretrial memorandum
by 11/1	Pretrial conference
12/1	Initial trial date

Once approved by the lawyer, these dates can then be put on your general calendar to remind you when the basic steps in this case should be completed.

F. PREFILING REQUIREMENTS

We have now seen how to plan litigation in detail. Are you finally ready to begin drafting the pleadings? Not quite. There are still a few matters you need to consider before plunging ahead. The following prefiling requirements must be considered:

1. Statutory notice requirements
2. Contract requirements
3. Mediation, arbitration, and review requirements
4. Administrative procedure requirements
5. Appointment of legal guardian
6. Discovery before suit
7. Demand letters

1. Statutory notice requirements

Some actions, primarily tort claims against governmental bodies such as municipalities, often have statutory notice requirements that must be complied with or else suit will be barred. These statutes usually have time limitations substantially shorter than the applicable statute of limitations, often as short as six months or less, and usually have detailed fact requirements. These statutes are usually strictly construed, so each statutory requirement must be closely followed.

2. Contract requirements

Many contracts, particularly insurance and employment contracts and contracts with governmental bodies, have **notice and claims provisions** in them. These provisions usually require notice of intent to sue, or presentation of claims before filing suit, and require that notice be given within a short period of time, usually much shorter than the applicable statute of limitations period. Make sure your client has complied with the conditions precedent required by the contract before filing suit.

3. Mediation, arbitration, and review requirements

By statute and contract, many disputes must be submitted to binding or nonbinding mediation or arbitration before suit can be brought. For example, construction contracts frequently have arbitration clauses, and several states require by statute that medical malpractice claims must first be presented to a medical review panel.

4. Administrative procedure requirements

Claims against governmental bodies usually cannot be brought in court until administrative procedures have been followed and exhausted. For example, claims for benefits from the Social Security and Veterans Administrations must ordinarily be pursued through the administrative process before resort to the judicial system is permitted. Accordingly, determine what applicable administrative procedure statutes apply to your claim, and make sure that they have been followed before filing suit.

5. Appointment of legal guardian

Some individuals are incompetent to sue in their own name and must have a legal representative or specially appointed guardian litigate for them. Capacity to sue is governed by Rule 17 of the Federal Rules of Civil Procedure, which generally defers to local law in determining both capacity to sue and the appropriate representative party. Minors and incompetents, for example, can sue only through their legal guardians or conservators. Appropriate state court appointments of guardians or other legal representatives must be obtained before suit can properly be brought. When the statute of limitations will run shortly, this is a serious concern since obtaining such appointments may take time.

6. Discovery before suit

In certain cases, your side may depose a person before suit is filed if there is a real risk the person will die or leave the area before formal discovery can begin. A petition to depose before suit that complies with Rule 27 of the Federal Rules of Civil Procedure must be filed to enable you to take these depositions.

7. Demand letters

Although not legally required, demand letters are frequently used, especially in tort, contract, and commercial cases. For instance, if you anticipate a breach, it is advantageous to send a demand letter asserting that the other side appears to be in breach and requesting assurances of performance. Such letters, if not responded to, may constitute admissions by silence.

Demand letters also serve practical purposes. In small disputes, where a compromise is possible, a demand letter that notifies the other side of your intent to sue unless an acceptable settlement is reached can often trigger settlement discussions. A demand letter will often generate a denial letter stating the basis for rejecting your side's claim, and is sometimes a good indication of what defenses will be raised if suit is brought later. If you are requested to draft a demand letter for the attorney to send, the example in Exhibit 3.6 may be used. Remember that,

Exhibit 3.6.   *Sample Demand Letter*

Dear Mr. Jones:

We represent Sam's Landscaping Services. Our client has advised us that on January 20, 2006, you engaged our client's services to landscape your backyard at an agreed price of $15,000. You signed a contract to pay for such services by payment of one-half at the commencement of services and the balance upon completion. All work covered by the contract was completed on February 25, 2006. Although the first payment was made, no payment has been made on the balance due. As of this date, the entire balance due of $7,500, plus interest in the amount of $300, remains outstanding.

While Sam's Landscaping would like to resolve this matter amicably, in the event complete payment is not made within five business days from the date of this letter, we have been instructed to take all legal action necessary to enforce our client's claim. In addition, if any action is filed in court, our client will also seek full reimbursement of its attorney's fees as authorized by the terms of the contract.

We await prompt payment of the amounts outstanding.

Sincerely,

_____

[Name of Attorney]

while you may draft the demand letter, the letter always should be signed by the attorney.

In some cases where your ability to get the facts is limited because the important records are all in the opponent's possession, the attorney may advise you to send a draft of the complaint to the opponent and await a response. The opponent may respond by giving you information that will affect the lawyer's decision to file the lawsuit or will affect the claims that the lawyer ultimately brings. A sample letter that may be sent with the complaint is shown in Exhibit 3.7.

CHAPTER SUMMARY

This chapter has discussed the method used to establish the terms of the attorney-client agreement. The terms should be formalized in a written agreement that specifies the work that will be done, how the fee will be determined, when billings will be sent, and what the lawyer is authorized to do. Once the lawyer has decided to represent the client and the terms of the attorney-client relationship are formalized, you should structure a litigation plan.

A litigation plan consists of defining the client's objectives and a strategy for achieving the objectives. Steps for developing the litigation plan consist of developing a theory of the case and planning the pleadings, discovery, dispositive motions, and settlement approach. By developing a litigation plan, you and the lawyer are able to tailor your work to coincide with the client's objectives. However, the plan must remain flexible to respond to any changing conditions that may occur in the lawsuit.

Exhibit 3.7.   *Sample Cover Letter*

Dear Mr. Jones:

Our office represents Sam's Landscaping Services. Pursuant to [name of attorney]'s request, I am enclosing a courtesy copy of a complaint by Sam's Landscaping Services against you. The complaint has not yet been filed. [Name of attorney] intends to file the complaint on [date] if [he/she] does not hear from you prior to that time.

Sincerely,

_____

[Name]
Legal Assistant

Finally, before drafting the pleadings, consider a number of prefiling requirements. This chapter provides you with a listing and explanation of the various prefiling requirements that you need to meet before filing the lawsuit (see section F).

KEY TERMS

Attorney's lien	Hourly rate
Contingency fee	Notice and claims provisions
Costs	Retainer fee
Dispositive motions	Settlement
Fixed flat fee	Theory of the case

REVIEW QUESTIONS

1. Why do the terms of the attorney-client relationship need to be established in writing?

2. Explain the differences between a contingency fee agreement, flat fee agreement, and hourly rate agreement.

3. What is an attorney's lien?

4. What is the difference between "fees" and "costs"?

5. What is meant by the concept "litigation plan"?

6. Why might a plaintiff wish to serve a demand letter on the defendant before filing a lawsuit?

ADDITIONAL RESOURCES

For legal forms see the following sites:

> www.Findlegalforms.com
> www.xdrive.com
> www.LegalListings.net
> www.thelawencyclopedia.com

Many State Bar organizations have sample forms and information about fee agreements. For example: www.scbar.org (South Carolina), www.judiciary.statenj.us (New Jersey).

Chapter 4

PARTIES AND JURISDICTION

Prior to filing the initial complaint you must investigate various legal issues. In this chapter, you will discover

◆ Who may be a party to a lawsuit

◆ How to identify the subject matter jurisdiction of federal courts

◆ When a defendant may remove an action from state court to federal court

◆ When a party may be compelled to defend an action in a particular court

◆ What the differences are between federal and state court jurisdiction

◆ How to determine in which court to file the lawsuit

A. INTRODUCTION

As you conduct the informal fact investigation, you will also evaluate the various legal considerations that arise in every lawsuit. These considerations include determining what parties must be named in the lawsuit or "joined"; whether the court has subject matter jurisdiction over the claims; whether the court has personal or in rem jurisdiction over the parties; and where venue is proper. This chapter discusses the legal choices a plaintiff must make before filing a lawsuit, and a defendant must make before responding to one, as well as the interdependence of these legal considerations. While this discussion is based on federal district court litigation, the basic analytical sequence is also applicable to state court lawsuits.

A note of caution is in order. Issues dealing with joinder of parties, subject matter jurisdiction, personal jurisdiction, and venue can be complex, and the literature about them is extensive. A single volume can hardly deal with these issues in depth, much less one chapter in a general text on litigation. This discussion's purpose is necessarily limited to getting the new paralegal to think intelligently about these legal considerations in broad terms to avoid missing the boat on vital issues. Where a serious legal issue exists, it must always be researched thoroughly and discussed with the lawyer before the suit is filed. As always, remember that Federal Rule of Civil Procedure 11, as well as similar state rules, requires that there be a reasonable inquiry into the law and a determination that the pleading is well grounded before a lawyer may sign the pleading. The Rule, in short, requires that you do your homework.

B. PARTIES TO THE ACTION

In the previous chapters you have learned that the parties to a lawsuit may be classified as plaintiffs or defendants. Now you will learn the types of parties who may bring actions as plaintiffs or defend actions as defendants.

The **parties to an action** may be private individuals as well as partnerships, unincorporated associations, sole proprietorships, corporations, and public bodies. Although it is not difficult to understand that individuals may be parties to a lawsuit, it sometimes is difficult to comprehend how legal entities may be parties without any individuals being named. However, if you envision the legal entity as having an existence of its own, separate from the members that make up the entity, then you can see how these entities should be capable of suing and being sued in the name of the entity.

For example, a **partnership** is made up of two or more individuals who carry on a business and divide any profit or loss of the business. Assume that Matthew Miller and Kathleen James have decided to start a business selling vacuum cleaners over the telephone, and agree to call the partnership Miller & James. Dorothy Jones buys a vacuum cleaner from Miller & James, but the vacuum cleaner does not work, and Dorothy wants to return the vacuum cleaner and get her money back. Dorothy can bring a lawsuit against Miller & James without naming either Matthew Miller or Kathleen James. This is because the partnership has an existence separate from the existence of its partners.

Similarly, **an unincorporated association** is made up of individual members who operate under a common name, such as social organizations, churches, and homeowners' groups. As with partnerships, the association may sue or be sued in the name of the association.

With partnerships, **sole proprietorships** (which are entities consisting of just one person), and unincorporated associations, it is a good practice, in addition to naming the entity as a party, also to name the individual members if known. In this way, any judgment will be binding on the individual members as well as on the entity.

However, if you are bringing an action against a corporation or governmental body, the individual members that make up these entities are not proper parties to a lawsuit. For example, a **corporation** is made up of its shareholders who own the entity. However, unless the shareholders have not kept the existence of the corporation separate and distinct from their individual affairs, the shareholders are not liable for the obligations of the corporation. Thus, in general the lawsuit should be brought by and against the corporation alone. Similarly, governmental bodies such as municipal, state, or federal governments should be sued in the name of the entity alone and not in the name of the political officials who make up the entity.

C. JOINDER OF PARTIES AND CLAIMS

When you draft a complaint, a choice must be made as to which parties will be named in the action. The initial choice, of course, is to name the party who has been wronged as the plaintiff, and name the party who has done the wrong as the defendant. However, beyond this initial choice, you should ask yourself the following questions to ascertain whether you have the proper parties and whether additional parties are appropriate and necessary:

1. Who is the real party in interest?
2. Does that party have capacity to sue?
3. Is joinder of parties required?
4. Is joinder of parties permitted?
5. Do any special pleading rules apply?
6. Is joinder of claims permitted?

The following sections explain how to address these questions.

1. Real party in interest

Real party in interest
The party who, under applicable substantive law, has the right that the lawsuit seeks to enforce

Rule 17(a) of the Federal Rules of Civil Procedure requires that an action be brought "in the name of the real party in interest." The **real party in interest** is the one who, under applicable substantive law, has the right that the lawsuit seeks to enforce. The purpose of the Rule is to ensure that the parties with the real interests are the ones actually prosecuting cases. Potential issues arise when personal representatives are named parties.

Rule 17(a) also specifies exceptions to the general rule by providing that an "executor, administrator, guardian, bailee, trustee of an express trust, a party with whom or in whose name a contact has been made for the benefit of another, or a party authorized by statute" may sue in his own name. While the plaintiff has the burden of showing he is the proper real party in interest, the exceptions to Rule 17(a) have largely eliminated controversy in this area. The only areas where disputes still arise are assignments and subrogation.

In the case of **assignment**, which is a claim that has been transferred to another person or entity, the assignee is the real party in interest and has a right to sue in the assignee's own name. If the claim has been only partially assigned, then the assignee must join the assignor as a party to the lawsuit. This prevents the defendant from being harassed by multiple lawsuits.

Subrogation occurs when one party becomes obligated to pay for the loss sustained by another. In such a case, the one obligated to pay for the loss becomes subrogated to the rights of the other to collect against the person who caused the loss. For example, in an automobile accident, if the insurance company pays for the loss by its insured, the insurance company is the real party in interest and becomes subrogated to the rights of the insured to collect against the defendant. Thus, in the area of subrogation, the real party in interest will be the one paying for the loss.

2. Capacity to sue

A lawsuit must be brought by and against parties that have a legal capacity to sue or defend the action. This ensures that any judgment that ultimately is obtained will be binding on the parties.

Generally, individuals and entities have a right to sue or defend an action. This includes not only natural persons but corporations, partnerships, and unincorporated associations. However, there are a few instances when the capacity to sue or defend may be raised. For example, under Rule 17(c) an infant or incompetent can sue or be sued in the name of a representative. If no representative has been appointed, a **guardian ad litem** can bring suit or be appointed for the sued party. In addition, suspended corporations—corporations not properly qualified to do business in the state—may be unable to either sue in court or defend an action brought against it.

Guardian ad litem
A person appointed by the court to represent another, usually a minor or incompetent, in a lawsuit

If a defendant wishes to challenge plaintiff's claim of capacity to sue, the defendant must, under Rule 9 of the Federal Rules of Civil Procedure, deny the claim "with particularity." Failing to make the denial in a responsive pleading will usually result in any error being deemed waived. Similar state rules also require that the challenge to capacity be raised in the responsible pleading, or else it will be deemed waived.

3. Required joinder of parties

Joinder of parties is governed by Rules 19 and 20 of the Federal Rules of Civil Procedure. The joinder rules address a basic question: As plaintiff, what parties must, should, or may be brought into the lawsuit so

Joinder of parties
The bringing together of different parties in one lawsuit

that the claims can be properly decided? What parties must, or should be, joined is governed by Rule 19; what parties may be brought in is governed by Rule 20.

Needless to say, these esoteric distinctions have been the source of much debate and litigation over the years. The present joinder rules are an attempt to get away from rigid labels and move toward a pragmatic analysis of the competing interests involved. On the one hand, there are legal and social interests in giving every party an opportunity to litigate and at the same time avoiding multiple suits over the same issues. On the other hand, there are corresponding interests in permitting some claims to be adjudicated rather than none. The modern approach to joinder, as represented by Rules 19 and 20, is to resolve joinder issues by focusing on those competing interests.

Rule 19, dealing with required joinder, is divided into two basic rules. Rule 19(a) governs what parties are to be joined "if feasible"; Rule 19(b) governs what the court should do if all required parties cannot be joined.

Under Rule 19(a), a party should be joined if that party's presence is (1) required to grant "complete relief," or (2) the party has an interest in the action so that the party's presence is, practically speaking, necessary to protect his interest, or the party's absence may expose other parties to double or inconsistent obligations. Such a party should be joined unless he cannot be served with process, or the party's joinder would defeat federal subject matter jurisdiction (see section D). Although the Rule appears complex, in practice its application is not particularly problematical. As a practical matter, a plaintiff should join any potentially liable party who can be served, but only if the party's joinder will not defeat subject matter jurisdiction (and, of course, the Rule 11 requirements are met).

Rule 19(b) governs the situation in which a party who should be joined cannot be because the party cannot be served with process or because the party's joinder would defeat federal jurisdiction. The issue before the court then is whether to proceed without the party or dismiss the action. Rule 19(b) states four factors the court must balance in reaching an equitable decision:

1. Whether nonjoined and existing parties will be prejudiced
2. Whether an order can minimize any potential prejudice
3. Whether any judgment without the absent party can be adequate
4. Whether the plaintiff will have an adequate remedy if the action is dismissed

These practical concerns frequently compete with each other, but certain conclusions are likely. First, if the consequence of a dismissal is that the plaintiff is left without any state forum in which to pursue claims against all parties, it is highly unlikely that the court will dismiss the action. Second, if an absent party can be brought in as a third-party defendant, there is strong ground for rejecting a present defendant's claim of potential prejudice. The possibility of **intervention**—that is, where an interested party may join in a pending lawsuit—is also a strong ground for rejecting the claim of prejudice to an absent party. Third, the possibility of incomplete relief to the plaintiff will usually be rejected as a reason for dismissal, since that result alone prejudices no one. In short, the judicial tendency has been to retain federal jurisdiction rather than dismiss the case.

Intervention
The ability of a person not a party to the lawsuit to become a party to the lawsuit when such person has an interest in the outcome of the lawsuit

4. Permissive joinder of parties

Permissive joinder, governed by Rule 20, resolves the question of who may be joined as a proper party. Rule 20 provides two tests, both of which must be met before joinder will be permitted. First, there must be a question of law or fact common to all parties arising out of the action. Second, each plaintiff must have a right of relief, jointly, severally, or alternatively, against each defendant based on the same occurrences or transactions or series of transactions or occurrences.

Permissive Joinder
A joinder of parties that is allowed—but not required—by the court

The language of Rule 20 is broad and permits joinder whenever there is a legal or factual relationship between the parties, making it sensible to have all these parties present in one lawsuit. On the other hand, permissive joinder can operate to delay the litigation and make it unfairly expensive and burdensome on certain parties. For that reason, Rule 20(b) gives the court broad regulatory powers, including the power to order separate trials to prevent any unfairness.

Where there is improper joinder, Rule 21 provides simply that the case cannot be dismissed. Rather, the misjoined parties are dropped and nonjoined parties added by court order.

5. Special pleading rules

Required and permissive joinder rules, set forth in Rules 19 and 20, are not the only rules that regulate whether parties can be joined in a lawsuit. There are several pleading rules that govern a number of special types of actions. These are

Counterclaims—Rule 13
Cross-claims—Rule 13
Third-Party Practice—Rule 14
Interpleader—Rule 22
Intervention—Rule 24
Class actions—Rule 23
Shareholder derivative suits—Rule 23.1

These pleadings, and their special requirements, are discussed in Chapter 5.

6. Joinder of claims

Joinder of claims
The bringing together in one lawsuit of the different claims that a party may have against another party

Joinder of claims, whereby different claims that a party may have may be brought together in one lawsuit, is governed by Rule 18 of the Federal Rules of Civil Procedure and is always permissive. Each party can bring as many claims as the party has against every other party. These include both present and contingent claims. Deciding what claims to bring against another party is principally a practical matter.

D. SUBJECT MATTER JURISDICTION

Subject matter jurisdiction
The power of a court to hear particular matters

Subject matter jurisdiction refers to the power of a court to hear particular matters. Federal district courts are courts of limited jurisdiction and cannot hear a case unless it falls within their power (as defined in Article III of the United States Constitution) and Congress has extended jurisdiction over the particular type of case.

Because federal district courts are courts of limited jurisdiction, a party seeking to invoke the court's jurisdiction must affirmatively plead and demonstrate proper subject matter jurisdiction.[1] The basis for jurisdiction must appear on the face of a well-pleaded complaint and cannot rest on counterclaims, defenses, or anticipated defenses. On the other hand, any party or the court can raise lack of subject matter jurisdiction. Although most commonly raised by a Rule 12 motion to dismiss, it can be raised at any time, even after judgment or on appeal. If the court has no jurisdiction over the subject matter, the case must be dismissed. When there is no subject matter jurisdiction in the federal court, the complaint must be filed in the appropriate state court.

State courts also must have subject matter jurisdiction. For example, many states have different trial courts, and the question of which court to file the lawsuit in is determined by the amount in controversy or the nature of the action. For example, California has three trial courts: superior court, municipal court, and small claims court. Each court handles different matters depending on the dollar amount of the action or the nature of the action. If the amount in controversy exceeds $25,000, only the superior court has subject matter jurisdiction to hear the case, and the case must be filed in that court.

---

1. See Chapter 5, section B.

All of the following must be considered before bringing a claim in federal court:

1. Is there a case or controversy?
2. Does the case fall under federal question jurisdiction, either general or specific?
3. If the claim does not have federal question jurisdiction, can you sue based on diversity jurisdiction?
4. Does ancillary jurisdiction apply?
5. Has the case already been filed in state court, so that filing in federal court will require removal?

1. Case or controversy

The court must have an actual "case or controversy" that is ripe for adjudication. Put another way, the court will not hear moot or collusive cases, render advisory opinions, or hear controversies that are essentially political or administrative issues. This requirement limits cases to those involving real controversies in which parties have a direct stake in the outcome and will actively represent their interests.

The question of whether there is an actual case or controversy and the related issue of whether the plaintiff has **standing**—the right to raise the claim—arise frequently in public interest, constitutional, and administrative litigation. For example, a suit to enjoin enforcement of a city regulatory code provision, brought by a local resident, will raise both issues: Is the action ripe for adjudication, and does the plaintiff have a legal right to raise the claim?

Standing
The right of a person to challenge in court the conduct of another

In private litigation, there will ordinarily be an obvious controversy, with the parties having obvious standing. In public interest litigation, on the other hand, the issue of actual case or controversy and the issue of standing are common as well as complex and must be researched thoroughly.

2. Federal question jurisdiction

28 U.S.C. §1331 provides that "district courts shall have original jurisdiction of all civil actions arising under the Constitution, laws, or treaties of the United States." Section 1331 is generally referred to as conferring "general" federal question jurisdiction. This distinguishes §1331 from other "specific" grants of jurisdiction found in §§1333 et seq. and from other non-Title 28 grants.

The general-versus-specific distinction is important because of the requirement that, in federal court, a party invoking the court's jurisdiction must affirmatively show the basis for jurisdiction. Issues over jurisdiction seldom arise when the basis is a specific grant in a statutory provision. Problems frequently arise, however, when the basis for jurisdiction is the general grant under §1331.

a. "Arising under"

Jurisdictional issues occur under §1331 because its arising "under" language is so general. Section 1331 provides that jurisdiction can arise "under the Constitution, laws, or treaties of the United States." The constitutional provisions are contained in Article III, §§1 and 2. However, §1331, which contains the same language as Article III, §2, has been interpreted much more narrowly than the parallel constitutional language.

The basic requirements for jurisdiction under §1331 are that the claim be based on federal law, which must be demonstrated in the complaint, and that the federal claim be substantial rather than frivolous.[2] For example, assume the plaintiff brings an action for patent infringement. This raises federal question jurisdiction because it is brought under the Patent Act, which is federal law. Another plaintiff brings an action for an unlawful search of her house. This raises federal question jurisdiction because it is brought under the Fourth Amendment of the U.S. Constitution.

b. Specific grants of jurisdiction

There are several other sections of Title 28 that grant federal courts jurisdiction to hear particular matters. These include

§ 1333 — admiralty
§ 1334 — bankruptcy
§ 1336 — Interstate Commerce Commission/commerce
§ 1337 — commerce/antitrust
§ 1338 — patent, copyright, trademark, unfair competition
§ 1339 — postal
§ 1340 — Internal Revenue Service/customs
§§ 1341-1364 — miscellaneous provisions

---

2. Since the complaint must affirmatively show that federal jurisdiction exists, it follows that a defendant raising in the answer a defense based on federal law cannot create federal jurisdiction.

Finally, there are numerous statutory provisions outside of Title 28 that also confer jurisdiction on federal district courts. The more important ones are

Jones Act, 46 U.S.C. §688
Federal Employer's Liability Act, 45 U.S.C. §56
Securities Act, 15 U.S.C. §77
Civil Rights Act, 42 U.S.C. §1983

Where jurisdiction is based on these specific grants provided by federal law, the same pleading requirements apply: A plaintiff wishing to invoke the court's jurisdiction must always affirmatively plead a proper jurisdictional basis. This should be done in the beginning of the complaint. See Chapter 5, Pleadings.

Keep in mind that these federal grants of jurisdiction can be exclusive or concurrent with state courts. In several areas, notably admiralty, bankruptcy, and patent and copyright cases, the district courts have exclusive jurisdiction. In other areas, the plaintiff may have a choice to file in either federal or state court.

c. Pendent jurisdiction

A claim can properly be brought in federal court if the basis for jurisdiction is a federal question. What happens, however, if the plaintiff has other claims not based on federal question jurisdiction? Can these be brought with the federal claim? If the other claims each have a separate proper basis for federal jurisdiction, no problems arise. However, if there is no such basis for the claims, the question arises of whether the other claims can be "joined" to the federal claim.

The concept of **pendent jurisdiction** addresses this question and strikes a compromise between the usual requirement that federal jurisdiction must be strictly construed and the obvious advantage of hearing at one time all claims that can be brought by one party against another. A simple answer is to deny federal jurisdiction on the nonfederal claims, the result being that a plaintiff who wants to pursue all claims in one action must do so in a state forum. However, this option is not available when the federal claim is one over which federal courts have exclusive jurisdiction. In this situation, the options are to try all claims in federal court or to split the claims between federal and state courts.

The Supreme Court in United Mine Workers of America v. Gibbs, 383 U.S. 715 (1966), set forth the standards in deciding whether to permit joining federal and nonfederal claims. "Pendent jurisdiction," that is, jurisdiction over the nonfederal claims, will be permitted if both the federal and nonfederal claims "derive from a common nucleus of

Pendent jurisdiction
Jurisdiction by the federal court over nonfederal claims when both the federal and nonfederal claims derive from a common set of facts

operative fact." Id. at 725. In short, if the nonfederal claims are based on the same set of facts as the federal claims, joinder of the claims is proper, although the court retains discretion to reject the pendent claim.

d. The United States as a party

Sovereign immunity
The insulation of government from being sued when acting in its official capacity

When the United States is a plaintiff, no special jurisdictional problems arise. However, the United States cannot be sued unless it has waived its **sovereign immunity** and consented to the action. Sovereign immunity is the insulation of the government from being sued when functioning in an official government capacity. A plaintiff suing the United States, therefore, must expressly demonstrate the statutory basis under which the government has consented to be sued. The most frequently used grounds are the Court of Claims Act, Tucker Act, and Federal Tort Claims Act.

Frequently, however, a plaintiff may wish or need to sue a federal official or federal administrative agency rather than the United States directly. In this situation, there must be a specific statute that permits suit against the agency or a named federal official. Such statutes frequently permit suits brought to challenge administrative agency decisions. For example, suit is frequently brought against the Secretary of Housing and Urban Development for denial of claimed Social Security benefits. Where there is no statute permitting suit against a federal official or agency, it is still sometimes possible to sue an official individually for an alleged improper act. In determining whether a governmental entity or federal official can be sued in federal courts, always be sure to research the appropriate federal statutes and possibly even case law.

3. Diversity jurisdiction

Diversity jurisdiction
The power of the federal court to hear controversies between citizens of different states

If the claim does not have federal question jurisdiction, the plaintiff may still be able to sue in federal court based on **diversity jurisdiction**. 28 U.S.C. §1332 provides for the jurisdiction of federal courts in civil actions involving diversity of citizenship, and parallels the constitutional grant of power found in Article III, §2 of the Constitution. This provision of Title 28 sets out four categories of actions for which diversity jurisdiction is proper:

1. Between citizens of different states
2. Between citizens of a state and citizens or subjects of a foreign state

3. Between citizens of different states and in which citizens or sub-jects of a foreign state are additional parties
4. Between a foreign state as plaintiff and citizens of a state or of different states

Of these four categories, the first is the predominantly used section. The other three are usually referred to as the alienage sections. Diversity jurisdiction does not apply to domestic relations and probate matters, which are considered local matters properly raised only in state courts.

If the claim does not have federal question jurisdiction, and you and the lawyer wish to file an action in federal court, consider whether you can meet the following three requirements for diversity jurisdiction, which are discussed in detail below:

1. Citizenship
2. Complete diversity
3. Jurisdictional amount

If each of these three requirements are met, the complaint may be filed in federal court.

a. "Citizenship" requirement

Section 1332 is based on "citizenship," an imprecise term. The citizenship of natural persons is the state of permanent residence (called **domicile**), and no person can have more than one domicile at a time. For a corporation, §1332(a) provides that its citizenship is both the state where it is incorporated and the state where it has its **principal place of business,** which is usually defined as where a majority of its business is conducted or, if that is unclear, where the corporate headquarters is located. In direct actions against liability insurers, the insurer is considered a citizen of the state where the insured is domiciled.[3]

Unincorporated associations present particular difficulties. If the association is not an entity entitled by state law to sue or be sued in its own name, its citizenship is that of each of its members. If the association is an entity entitled to sue or be sued, the prevailing rule is that here also the association is considered to be a citizen of each state of which any member is a citizen.

---

3. Some states have so-called direct action statutes that permit suits that are brought directly against an insurance company. The typical situation is an automobile accident involving the insured.

Needless to say, what constitutes citizenship for diversity purposes when artificial entities are involved can be a complex issue involving law that is frequently unsettled; thorough research is essential.

b. *Complete diversity requirement*

Complete diversity
The plaintiff must have a different state citizenship from each defendant in order for the federal courts to have jurisdiction

Complete diversity means that each plaintiff must have a different state citizenship from each defendant in order for the federal district courts to have jurisdiction. Stated another way, if any plaintiff and any defendant are citizens of the same state, diversity will not be complete. For example, if citizens of Illinois and California sue citizens of Maine and Vermont, complete diversity exists. If citizens of Illinois and California sue citizens of Maine, Vermont, Connecticut, and California, complete diversity does not exist.

The complete diversity requirement applies to every party that is actually joined, regardless of whether that party is required or permissive. To retain the required complete diversity, a plaintiff can dismiss all but indispensable parties from the action. In addition, a plaintiff may manipulate the parties to create complete diversity. Because of this, a party's characterization as a plaintiff or defendant in the complaint is not controlling. Rather, the court can realign parties as plaintiffs or defendants, and ignore nominal or formal parties, to determine if complete diversity actually exists.

In the case of legal representatives, such as a trustee or guardian, the citizenship of the representative is controlling. However, where the legal representative is nominal, such as with a guardian ad litem, the citizenship of the represented party is determinative for diversity purposes. Collusive assignments, made solely to create diversity, are also ignored.

Complete diversity is determined according to the citizenship of parties at the time the initial complaint was filed. Later changes in citizenship by a party will not defeat jurisdiction.

c. *Jurisdictional amount requirement*

Section 1332(a) requires that the "matter in controversy exceeds the sum or value of $75,000, exclusive of interest and costs." The plaintiff's complaint is the sole basis for determining if the requirement has been met. The allegations are controlling unless there is a "legal certainty" that the jurisdictional amount cannot be obtained. This will occur only when plaintiff requests damages, such as punitive damages, to which he is not entitled under the applicable substantive law, and those damages are necessary to reach the jurisdictional amount.

The principal issue in this area involves the problem of valuation, particularly where equitable relief is requested. With injunctions, where this problem most frequently occurs, the measure of damages is the value of the right sought to be enforced or the value of the avoided injury. The value may be different depending on whether it is measured from the plaintiff's or the defendant's perspective. The courts are divided on which view of the measure of damages is appropriate, although more appear to use the plaintiff's loss approach. For example, suppose the plaintiff brings suit to enjoin the enforcement of certain statutes, such as zoning ordinances or health regulations, and to have them declared unconstitutional. The court must look to see what the amount of the loss to the plaintiff would be if the statutes continue to be enforced.

Another issue involves aggregation of claims to meet the jurisdictional amount. Here there are four basic situations. In the first, there is one plaintiff and one defendant to meet the jurisdictional amount requirement. For example, a plaintiff has two claims, each involving $40,000, against one defendant; the claims involve two separate, unrelated contracts. The plaintiff can properly aggregate the claims.

Second, where there is one plaintiff and multiple defendants, plaintiff can aggregate claims only if the claims are joint rather than several and distinct. For example, a plaintiff has two claims, each involving $40,000 against two defendants; the claims involve two separate, unrelated contracts. The plaintiff cannot aggregate these claims. However, if the liability is joint, as would be the case if the defendants are partners jointly liable on a partnership obligation, aggregation is proper.[4]

Third, where there are multiple plaintiffs and one defendant, the plaintiffs cannot aggregate separate and distinct claims. The plaintiffs can aggregate only if the claims are undivided and a single title or right is involved. For example, two plaintiffs each have a $40,000 claim against one defendant; the claims involve two separate, unrelated contracts. The plaintiffs cannot aggregate these claims; however, if the two plaintiffs are partners suing to recover a debt owed to the partnership, aggregation is proper.

Finally, where there are multiple plaintiffs and multiple defendants, the above analysis applies to the individual claims.

Interest and costs raise fewer questions. Costs include attorney's fees only if a contract or statute permits them. Interest, which is ordinarily incidental to the action, is included for purposes of determining if the jurisdictional amount is met only if the interest itself is the basis of the action.

---

4. A simple way of determining whether the plaintiff meets the jurisdictional amount is to ask yourself "what is the maximum liability that may be charged to any one defendant"? If the answer is at least $75,000, then the jurisdictional amount requirement has been met.

4. Ancillary jurisdiction

Because federal courts are courts of limited jurisdiction, the question must arise of whether a federal court can have jurisdiction over claims for which no federal jurisdictional basis exists. The competing interests are closely related to pendent jurisdiction issues. On one hand, federal jurisdiction is ordinarily interpreted narrowly. On the other hand, it makes sense, for the sake of judicial economy and consistency, to try all related claims at one time. The issue of **ancillary jurisdiction** arises whenever a plaintiff has a proper claim and another party wishes to file a counterclaim, cross-claim, or third-party complaint, but the latter claim does not have an independent jurisdictional basis.

Ancillary jurisdiction
The authority of a federal court to hear certain types of pleadings involving claims that do not have an independent basis for federal jurisdiction

The Supreme Court in Owen Equipment Co. v. Kroeger, 437 U.S. 365 (1978), held that ancillary jurisdiction should be conferred where there is a "logical dependence" between the claim having an independent jurisdictional basis and the nonindependent claims. Although this is an imprecise standard, the decision recognizes that the test can only be applied on a case-by-case basis. If the subsequent claim arises out of the same transaction or occurrence as the plaintiff's original claim, it makes sense to try the claims together.

The concept of ancillary jurisdiction is important because it permits certain types of pleadings involving claims that do not have an independent basis for federal jurisdiction. These include compulsory counterclaims, cross-claims, interpleader, intervention of right, and impleader, all of which are discussed in more detail in Chapter 5. Such pleadings commonly involve indemnity. An indemnity claim exists when one party is liable for another party's damages. For example, consider a plaintiff who properly brings a claim in federal court that has proper subject matter jurisdiction. The defendant wishes to bring in a third-party defendant on an indemnification theory. Indemnification raises no federal questions, however, and since the defendant and third-party defendant are citizens of the same state, diversity is lacking. Yet, in this situation the court will have ancillary jurisdiction over the third-party claim.

5. Removal jurisdiction

The removal jurisdiction of federal district courts is governed by 28 U.S.C. §§1441-1452. Since it is a jurisdictional statute, it is strictly construed and its requirements must be followed closely to ensure that removal is properly made.

Removal is the procedure in which the defendant may transfer a case, already filed in a state court, to the federal district court for the same district in which the state action is pending. The first requirement, then, is that the case already has been filed in state court. The second requirement is that the state court in which the action is pending must have both subject matter jurisdiction over the action and personal jurisdiction (see section E) over the defendant.

Third, the notice of removal must, under §1446(b), be filed within 30 days of the time the defendant receives a copy of plaintiff's initial pleading in state court, or within 30 days of receiving summons if the initial pleading under state practice is not required to be served on the defendant, whichever is shorter. The short time period, like all the removal requirements, is strictly enforced.

Fourth, removal is generally proper if the federal district court could have had original jurisdiction over the action had it been filed in federal court. For this reason, in your research you must determine if the federal district could have had proper subject matter jurisdiction over the plaintiff's original complaint.

There are three basic grounds for removal: diversity, federal question, and special removal statutes. Under §1441, removal jurisdiction can be based on diversity; this is usually proper when each plaintiff has a different citizenship from each defendant. The complete diversity rule for removal has one important exception: §1441(b) prevents removal if any proper defendant is a citizen of the state where the action was brought. This exception is based on the notion that a principal reason for permitting removal in diversity of citizenship cases is the possibility of local prejudice against noncitizen parties, which fails if a party is a citizen of the forum state. Accordingly, the diversity jurisdiction for removal is narrower than diversity for original diversity jurisdiction purposes. In addition, complete diversity must exist both when plaintiff's original action was filed in state court and when the removal petition is filed.

Removal can also be based on federal question jurisdiction. If an action could have been brought in district court on federal question grounds, it can ordinarily be removed. As noted above, removal generally cannot be allowed unless the claim could be brought as an original action in federal court.

The removal sections also provide for removal in certain special circumstances. These include

§1441(d)—civil actions against foreign states
§1442—federal officers
§1442a—members of armed forces
§1443—civil rights actions
§1444—foreclosure against the United States

Section 1445 makes certain actions nonremovable. These include actions under state worker's compensation acts; actions against railroads, their receivers, or trustees; and actions against a common carrier, its receivers, or trustees arising under specific federal statutes.

Where it later develops that the district court lacked subject matter jurisdiction for removal, §1447(c) provides for remand to the state court at any time before final judgment.

A plaintiff who wishes to file and keep a lawsuit in state court can use certain strategies to defeat removal. First, where diversity would otherwise permit removal, the plaintiff can add a defendant who either is not diverse from the plaintiff or is a citizen of the forum state. So long as such a joinder is not fraudulent in the sense that plaintiff does not really wish to prosecute a claim against that party, it will defeat removal. Second, where diversity does not exist, plaintiff can draft the complaint to avoid pleading a claim that would permit removal based on federal question jurisdiction. Where plaintiff has decided that a state forum is preferable, it is often possible to structure the claims and select the defendants to prevent removal.

E. PERSONAL JURISDICTION

Personal jurisdiction
The power of a court to bring a party before it and to make a decision binding on such a person

In addition to subject matter jurisdiction, the court also must have personal jurisdiction over the defendant. **Personal jurisdiction** refers to the power of a court to bring a party before it. A judgment is not enforceable against a party unless that party can lawfully be brought into court and has received notice of the lawsuit. Thus, constitutional concepts of due process (discussed below) underlie this requirement. Since personal jurisdiction is permissible only to the extent allowed by the federal Constitution, there is a great deal of overlap between federal and state law in this area.

Jurisdiction to adjudicate can be in personam, in rem, or quasi in rem. **In personam jurisdiction** refers to the court's power to personally bind the parties to the court's judgment. This jurisdiction can be either general or specific. If a court has general jurisdiction over a defendant, the defendant can be sued on any matter. It is not necessary that the claim be specifically based on the contacts that the defendant has with the forum state. For example, if a defendant in a breach of contract action resides within the state in which the action is brought, the court has jurisdiction over the defendant to personally bind the defendant to any judgment that is rendered against him.

If the jurisdiction is specific, it means that the defendant's contacts are not sufficient and pervasive enough to be sued on all matters in the forum state. Rather, the claim must arise out of specific contacts that the defendant has in the forum state. For example, a situation in which a defendant lives in another state but comes to the forum state to sell his goods and enters into a contract with the plaintiff in the forum state allows the court to exercise specific jurisdiction over the defendant for any claim concerning the contract or the sale of the goods. However, since the court does not have general jurisdiction, other claims against the defendant cannot be brought in the forum state.

An **in rem** action is one that involves property (the res) located within the state in which the court sits and in which the parties have their dispute. Jurisdiction over the party exists by virtue of the party's ownership of the property. With in rem jurisdiction, the court decides rights in the property, and that determination is then binding on any party claiming an interest in the property. Finally, **quasi in rem** is a type of jurisdiction that allows a plaintiff to use property of the defendant to satisfy a claim so long as the property is in the state. Thus, even if the defendant is not in the state and there is no in personam jurisdiction over the defendant, jurisdiction can still be obtained over the property. Only the property, however, may be used to satisfy the claim. If the property is not sufficient to satisfy the claim, the plaintiff may not try to enforce the balance of the claim or subsequent judgment against the defendant since the court does not have in personam jurisdiction against the defendant.

These distinctions have less significance today at the federal court level, where the critical concerns involve the constitutional limits of personal jurisdiction and the issue of whether service was properly made. Hence, issues surrounding personal jurisdiction involve two separate questions:

1. Can the defendant constitutionally be subject to the court's jurisdiction?
2. Was service of process on the defendant proper?

The first question involves the due process limitations on personal jurisdiction, and the second involves the service-of-process requirements of Rule 4 of the Federal Rules of Civil Procedure.

1. Due process requirements

Due process is a constitutional doctrine requiring fairness in judicial proceedings. Due process issues do not arise for plaintiffs, since by initiating suit a plaintiff is considered to have voluntarily submitted to the court's jurisdiction for all purposes, including being required to respond to counterclaims and other claims brought in that action. When a defendant is a resident of the **forum state**—that is, the state in which the action is brought—due process problems do not arise. Since the defendant is a resident of the state, it is fair to require the defendant to defend against an action brought in the state.

When a nonresident defendant, however, is sued in the forum state and does not consent to the jurisdiction of the court, due process problems may prevent that defendant from being required to defend there. Determining what the due process limitations are is a difficult

Due process
A constitutional doctrine requiring fairness in judicial proceedings

question that the Supreme Court has considered several times. The question is raised with increasing frequency as more businesses engage in national and international commerce.[5]

The leading constitutional cases include International Shoe Co. v. State of Washington, 326 U.S. 310 (1945), and World-Wide Volkswagen Corp. v. Woodson, 444 U.S. 286 (1980). Other significant Supreme Court cases are Burger King Corp. v. Rudzewicz, 471 U.S. 462 (1985), and Asahi Metal Industry Co. v. Superior Court, 480 U.S. 102 (1987).

In *International Shoe* the Court addressed the question of what activities by a corporation within a particular state will subject it to suit within that state consistent with due process concepts. It held that where a corporation's "minimum contacts" in the forum state were such that being forced to defend a suit in that state would not offend "traditional notions of fair play and substantial justice," jurisdiction was proper. 326 U.S. at 316, quoting Milliken v. Meyer, 311 U.S. 457, 463 (1940). The **minimum contacts** standard requires that there be sufficient activities of the defendant in the forum state to subject the defendant to the jurisdiction of the court. Many subsequent decisions, of course, expounded on what are sufficient minimum contacts to satisfy due process.

One of these, *World-Wide Volkswagen*, appeared to narrow the scope of such contacts. There, the Court rejected the argument that an out-of-state seller should be subjected to suit in another state simply because it was foreseeable that the vehicle sold might be involved in a collision in another state. Instead, the Court stressed that minimum contacts protect a defendant from being sued in a remote or inconvenient forum, and that foreseeability does not by itself create such contacts as would satisfy due process requirements. Requiring a defendant to defend in the forum state, the Court held, must be fair and not impose unreasonable burdens on the defendant.[6]

In order to understand the minimum contacts required for personal jurisdiction, consider the following examples:

♦ Simply posting information on a web site, even though the defendant knew that it would harm the movie industry in California, is not sufficient contact to invoke personal jurisdiction against a nonresident of California. Cornelius v. Chaney, 16 Cal. 3d 1434 (1976).

5. The issue rarely arises in tort litigation because a tort is usually seen as an event caused by a defendant that subjects him to the court's jurisdiction, and because state automobile statutes usually impose a "consent to be sued" fiction on out-of-state motorists.

6. In *Asahi Metal*, 480 U.S. 102 (1987), a closely divided Court held that merely placing a product into the stream of commerce is not an act that will subject a party to the forum state's jurisdiction, even if the party was aware that the stream of commerce would sweep the product into the forum state. Minimum contacts requires some action purposely directed toward the forum state.

However, if the defendant also came to California and handed out flyers with the information, the court probably would have specific jurisdiction over the defendant.

♦ A publisher who distributed magazines in another state can be brought to defend action for damages arising from an allegedly defamatory story. Keeton v. Hustler Magazine, 465 U.S. 770 (1984).

♦ A forum state does not have jurisdiction over a divorced father simply because the father allowed his daughter to live with her mother in the forum state. Kulko v. Superior Court, 438 U.S. 908 (1978).

The minimum-contacts analysis applies with equal force to in rem and quasi in rem actions.[7] Because of this, distinctions such as in rem or quasi in rem have no direct bearing on the due process question of a defendant's amenability to suit in a particular forum. However, the distinctions are still important for determining the enforceability of judgments.

2. Service-of-process requirements

Service of process refers to the actual delivery of the legal document (usually the initial summons and complaint) to the defendant. It is important to keep in mind that jurisdiction over the party is different from, and independent of, the adequacy of service of process. If a party is not constitutionally amenable to process, any service on that party will have no effect unless the party waives objections to the service. If a party is amenable to process, service of process on that party must still be properly made.

Service must be properly made because due process considerations require that service be made in a manner that will reasonably put defendants on notice that they have been sued. Rule 4(e) of the Federal Rules of Civil Procedure permits service by any method allowed by the state law in which the district court is sitting. This means, in practical terms, that out-of-state defendants can be served under the forum state's long-arm statutes. **Long-arm statutes** refer to state laws that allow a court to reach beyond the state's geographical boundaries and make nonresident defendants subject to suit within the state. Service of process is also permitted by any method authorized by the law of the state where the defendant is served.

Long-arm statutes
State laws that enable a court to exercise jurisdiction over a defendant who is outside the geographical boundaries of the court

---

7. The Supreme Court so held in Schaffer v. Heitner, 433 U.S. 186 (1977), deciding that a defendant's ownership of personal property by itself did not establish such contacts as would create proper personal jurisdiction over the defendant where the claims were not related to the property.

Service of process under Rule 4 is discussed in Chapter 5, section C. In general, however, courts recognize four ways service may be made upon a defendant.

- First, service may be made by personally delivering the document to the defendant. This is obviously the best method of service for due process purposes because such service ensures that the defendant has received notice and thus has an opportunity to be heard.
- Second, service may be made by leaving the legal document with an adult at either the residence or place of business of the individual or entity, and thereafter mailing a copy of the document to the address where the document was left. This method, although not as reliable as the personal delivery to the defendant, seeks to provide a reasonable substitute for personal delivery in the event the defendant cannot be located for personal service.
- A third method is by notice and acknowledgment of receipt. This method, recognized in some states, allows the plaintiff to send the defendant the summons and complaint in the mail along with a form notice and acknowledgment of receipt. Service is deemed complete when the defendant signs and returns the acknowledgment of receipt. While this method ensures that the defendant has received the document, there is very little compelling the defendant to voluntarily acknowledge receipt of the documents. Hence, you cannot count on the defendant returning the acknowledgment of receipt, and you may have to complete service of process by another method.
- A final method that is commonly recognized is service of process by publication. This method is usually a last alternative, reserved for when notice cannot be given to the defendant by any other method. Each state has certain requirements that must be met before publication is possible, and generally a court order is required to ensure that the requirements have been met. If publication is allowed, then notice of the summons and complaint will be published in a newspaper of general circulation.

F. FEDERAL VERSUS STATE COURT

If your side has the choice of filing a complaint in either federal or state court, a decision must be made before the complaint is filed as to which court you would like to commence the litigation in. Although the lawyer will be responsible for making the ultimate decision, the paralegal should be aware of certain considerations that go into the decision process.

One of the main differences between federal and state courts is the time it takes to get to trial. As a general rule, the length of time between the filing of a complaint in federal court and trial is much shorter than if the same case were filed in state court. Some state courts may take up to five years from the filing of a complaint to the time of trial; in federal court, the time to trial may be as short as six months. Obviously, from the plaintiff's point of view, this is a significant advantage.

Another potential advantage of filing in federal court is that one judge and usually a magistrate are assigned to hear all aspects of the case. In contrast, in many state courts, a different judge will hear law and motion matters, discovery disputes, and the trial. Thus, a federal judge is able to quickly become familiar with the facts of each case and may be able to move the case along to a more rapid conclusion.

Since the jury pool for federal court is usually much larger than that for state courts, consideration must also be given to the potential jurors who may ultimately hear the case at trial. The lawyer will also give substantial consideration to which law the federal court may apply. Although a federal court sitting in a diversity case must apply the substantive law of the state in which it sits, there may be differences in the way the federal court judges interpret the laws of the particular state.

In addition, consideration should be given to the differences in the federal and state rules of procedure and evidence. Many times, the procedural and evidentiary rules in federal court are more stringent than in state court. Moreover, federal courts are generally considered to be more formal and technical than state courts. All of these various considerations must be examined carefully before making a choice between federal and state court.

G. VENUE

A lawsuit must be filed in a proper place. Where a lawsuit can be filed is governed by **venue** statutes. Such statutes determine the geographic districts where the case can properly be heard.

Since venue provisions are designed in part to protect a defendant from being forced to litigate in an "unfair" forum, it follows that a defendant can waive the benefits of the venue rules. Hence, a defendant must raise improper venue in a timely manner, either by a Rule 12 motion or in the answer; otherwise, any of the defendant's objections will be deemed waived.

Venue
The geographic district where a lawsuit may properly be heard

1. Determining venue

The general venue statute for federal district courts is 28 U.S.C. §1391, which has two basic provisions. Under §1391(a), if jurisdiction is based solely on diversity, venue is proper in the district (1) where "any defendant resides, if all defendants reside in the same state," or (2) where a substantial part of the events or omissions giving rise to the claim occurred or a substantial part of the property involved in the action is located, or (3) where "any defendant is subject to personal jurisdiction" at the time the action is commenced. Under §1391(b), if jurisdiction is based other than solely on diversity, venue is proper on the same terms as parts (1) and (2) of §1391(a). However, if there is no other district, venue is also proper in the district "in which any defendant may be found."

There are numerous special venue statutes, both in the Title 28 venue section and elsewhere. The special provisions begin with §1394. Other venue provisions are scattered throughout the United States Code, usually as part of the substantive statute that creates a cause of action. Consequently, you must always check whether a special venue statute exists that overrides the general provisions of §1391.

In addition, §1392 governs venue in "local" actions that involve property. Whether the action is in rem, so that §1392 applies, is controlled by the nature of the remedy sought. Ordinarily, if the remedy is specific to the property, the action will be local, and §1392 makes the venue that of the res involved.

Once the applicable statutes are determined, the question of a party's residence arises, since §1391 is based on residence. For venue purposes "residence" is viewed in much the same way as citizenship. An individual's citizenship is where the individual has permanent residence. A corporation under §1391(c) is considered a resident of any district "in which it is incorporated or licensed to do business or is doing business." Unincorporated associations, if they have no capacity to sue under state law, are residents of each district in which any member of the association resides. If the association is an entity entitled to sue under state law, the association is a citizen of the district where it conducts its business. Aliens under §1391(d) can be sued in any district.

Finally, where a defendant is the United States or its agencies, officers, or employees, §1391(e) controls and provides that venue is generally proper — unless law provides otherwise — where the defendant resides, where a substantial part of the events or omissions giving rise to the claim occurred or a substantial part of the property involved in the action is located, or where the plaintiff resides if no property is involved.

The venue provisions control where a plaintiff files the initial complaint against the original defendants. They do not apply to counterclaims, cross-claims, or third-party claims, since these are seen as ancillary to the initial suit and hence raise no additional venue issues.

2. Change of venue

A change of venue can be based on two grounds: **improper venue**, governed by §1406, and **inconvenient venue**, governed by §1404. Under §1406, the court has discretion either to dismiss or to transfer to a proper venue any case that has been filed in an improper venue. Since the statute encourages transfer "if it be in the interest of justice," this is the usual approach. Keep in mind that proper venue is a personal right. A plaintiff, by filing an action in an improper venue, waives the right to object to it. A defendant must raise any venue objection either by a Rule 12 motion or in the defendant's answer; otherwise, objections will usually be considered waived.

Under §1404(a), the court may transfer a case from a proper venue to another venue "where it might have been brought," "for the convenience of parties and witnesses, in the interest of justice." This section recognizes that a plaintiff frequently has venue choices and that the plaintiff's choice, while proper, may not be the most convenient forum for the case seen as a whole. If this situation exists, the court can transfer the case to the more convenient forum, the only restriction being that the new forum must be in a district in which the plaintiff could have filed the action and where the court could have obtained personal jurisdiction over the defendants.

H. CHOICE OF COURT BASED ON CHOICE OF LAW

After completing your jurisdictional analysis, you may find that there are courts in several different states that may have jurisdiction over the defendant. If you determine that more than one court has jurisdiction over the defendant, how do you decide in which court the complaint should be filed? This question involves both practical and legal considerations. On the practical side, convenience and cost to the plaintiff, the plaintiff's lawyer, and witnesses will frequently dominate the decision. The plaintiff's own resident state will often be the choice if it is available. If the plaintiff's principal witnesses are in another state, that should be considered. On the legal side, **choice-of-law decisions** may be critical because applicable substantive law may differ for such matters as statutes of limitation, elements of claims, and allowable damages, and the lawyer will want to choose the jurisdiction with the laws most favorable to your client.

Choice-of-law decisions
Determining in which court a complaint should be filed

For example, suppose an Arizona driver is injured by a California driver in an automobile accident in Nevada. Certainly, it would appear that the plaintiff has, at a minimum, a choice between filing in

California (the defendant's domicile) or Nevada (where the claim arose). In deciding in which state to file the action, the plaintiff should consider the law of the forum state. If California and Nevada tort law differ, the plaintiff will obviously want to pick the more advantageous forum.

Furthermore, the subpoena power of a district is generally limited to its geographical boundaries; thus, if uncooperative witnesses are out of state, you and the lawyer may need to choose another available forum to reach these witnesses. Finally, factors such as the choice of judges, the desirability of prospective jury pools, and length of time until trial should all be considered.

The choice of deciding where to file the action applies whether the action is filed in state or federal court. In federal court actions based on diversity jurisdiction, the federal court will apply the state's substantive law. Of course, if a plaintiff brings a case in federal court based on the court's federal question jurisdiction, federal substantive law will apply.

CHAPTER SUMMARY

This chapter has considered a number of important legal issues that you must investigate before a lawsuit is filed. The first is to decide who may, or must, be a party to the litigation and what claims may, or must, be brought in the litigation. You must also consider whether the court has jurisdiction over the subject matter of the controversy. Because a court has power to hear only those cases that are properly before it, a determination of the type of case and the amount of relief sought must be made prior to the filing of a complaint. In some instances, even if a case is properly filed in state court, the defendant may have a right to remove the case to federal court.

In addition to subject matter jurisdiction, the court must also have personal jurisdiction. Personal jurisdiction is the power of the court to bring a party before it. Personal jurisdiction must meet due process and service-of-process requirements.

Many times, your side will have the choice of filing in either federal or state court. Certain matters must be considered in choosing the court. These considerations include the time it takes to get to trial, the benefit of the case being assigned to one judge, the jury pool, and the differences in the procedural and substantive law that may apply in the case.

Finally, once a determination is made as to which court to file the lawsuit in, consideration must be given to choosing the proper venue. Venue can be changed by the defendant only if the venue chosen by the plaintiff is improper or inconvenient.

KEY TERMS

Ancillary jurisdiction
Assignment
Choice-of-law decisions
Complete diversity
Corporation
Diversity jurisdiction
Domicile
Due process
Forum state
Guardian ad litem
Improper venue
Inconvenient venue
In personam jurisdiction
In rem jurisdiction
Intervention
Joinder of claims
Joinder of parties
Long-arm statutes
Minimum contacts

Parties to an action
Partnership
Pendent jurisdiction
Permissive joinder
Personal jurisdiction
Principal place of business
Quasi in rem jurisdiction
Real party in interest
Removal
Res
Service of process
Sole proprietorship
Sovereign immunity
Standing
Subject matter jurisdiction
Subrogation
Unincorporated association
Venue

REVIEW QUESTIONS

1. What is the difference between pendent and ancillary jurisdiction?

2. What are the requirements for a federal court to exercise its diversity jurisdiction?

3. What are the two places of citizenship for a corporation? Why is it important to know the citizenship of corporations?

4. Why would a defendant want to remove an action from state court to federal court? What is the procedure the defendant must follow in order to remove an action filed in state court?

5. Explain the difference between in personam, in rem, and quasi in rem jurisdiction, and give an example of each.

6. Identify the trial courts in your state and the subject matter jurisdiction of each.

7. What are the different ways in which a defendant may be served with process? Are all of these methods authorized by the courts in your state? Are additional methods authorized by your state?

ADDITIONAL RESOURCES

http://www.west.net/~smith/smjuris.htm. Overview of subject matter jurisdiction in federal court.

www.law.cornell.edu/rules/frcp/overview.htm. Access to federal rules of procedure.

Glannon, Joseph W., *Civil Procedure: Examples and Explanations* (Aspen Publishing, 2001).

Shreve, Gene R., Melvin, Richard S., Raven-Hansen, Peter, Weston, Glen Earl, *Understanding Civil Procedure,* (Matthew Bender 2002).

Part II

PRETRIAL LITIGATION

Chapter 5

PLEADINGS

Pleadings refer to all documents filed by the plaintiff to initiate a lawsuit and all documents filed by the defendant in response to the lawsuit. In this chapter, you will learn

♦ What the general requirements are for all pleadings

♦ How to draft a complaint

♦ What pleadings the defendant may file in response to the complaint

♦ How to draft an answer to a complaint

♦ How a nonparty may intervene in the lawsuit

♦ When you should amend or supplement a pleading

A. INTRODUCTION

Pleadings
Formal written documents by the parties to the litigation to either start or respond to the litigation

Modern pleading rules essentially limit the purpose of **pleadings** to notice of claims and defenses. Former purposes that included discovering facts, sharpening issues, and disposing of frivolous claims are now controlled by discovery and motion practice. Under modern rules, claims and factual issues will rarely be resolved at the pleadings stage. Hence, don't expect the pleadings to accomplish more than what they are designed to do.

Federal pleadings rules are principally contained in the Federal Rules of Civil Procedure, although other sources exist and must always be kept in mind. Under Rule 83, district courts can create local rules governing litigation in that district. Most have done so. Local rules generally do not affect the substance of pleadings, but ordinarily control mechanics such as the number of copies filed, size of paper, format, and bindings. Particular federal statutory actions, such as bankruptcy and copyright, may also have special procedure rules. Finally, specialized federal courts, such as magistrates, bankruptcy, and claims courts, may have special statutory and local procedural rules. Hence, you should always check procedural statutes and local rules, in addition to the Federal Rules of Civil Procedure, to determine what rules apply to the particular case you are working on.

Good pleadings practice is a combination of two things: a solid litigation plan and technically precise drafting. The litigation plan, which you have already developed, will control the claims and remedies (if a plaintiff) or the defenses and counterclaims, cross-claims, or third-party claims (if a defendant). The drafting of pleadings then becomes the primary concern, since pleadings that are technically precise will avoid attacks by motions and eliminate the need to file amended pleadings to cure defects that should have been avoided in the first place.

B. GENERAL PLEADING REQUIREMENTS

The Federal Rules of Civil Procedure have made simplicity and limited purpose the touchstones of the pleadings stage of the litigation process. Under Rule 7(a), the only basic pleadings allowed in civil actions are complaints, answers, and replies.

1. General "notice" requirements for claims

Rule 8(a) permits four forms of claims:

- ◆ complaint
- ◆ counterclaim
- ◆ cross-claim
- ◆ third-party complaint

All forms are actually complaints, since each asks for relief of some kind, but the various labels designate which party is bringing the claim.[1] Since they are all complaints, however, their requirements are the same. Rule 8 requires only a "short and plain statement of the claim showing the pleader is entitled to relief." This commonly is referred to as notice pleading.

Under **notice pleading**, the only requirement is that the pleading contain enough information to fairly notify the opposing party of the basis of the claim. It does not require an elaborate narration of facts, nor does it require that a legal theory of recovery of relief be set forth. Previous distinctions about whether a pleading was of fact, law, or conclusion of law now have no significance.[2] Hence, for most allegations the only requirement is a "short and plain statement" that gives fair notice of your claims to the opposing side. Forms 2 through 23 in the Appendix of Forms to the Federal Rules of Civil Procedure contain a

Notice pleading
Short and plain statement in the complaint of the claim that the plaintiff seeks to enforce and the relief that the plaintiff is requesting

---

1. In some state courts, there may not be any separate labels. For example, in California, counterclaims, cross-claims, and third-party complaints are all referred to simply as cross-complaints. (Counterclaims, cross-claims, and third-party complaints are discussed later in this chapter.)

2. If you are filing the complaint in state court, carefully review your state's rules, because some states still require a fact pleading. Under fact pleading, you must state enough facts to satisfy each element of the claim you are bringing.

variety of legally sufficient pleadings. The safest pleadings approach is to use the forms and modify them to meet the specific requirements of your case. The standard drafting technique is to state just enough facts to identify the events or transactions that the claim is based on and the legal theory of recovery. These techniques are detailed in section C2.

The only exception to the simple notice pleading requirement is Rule 9, which requires that certain matters—including capacity and authority to sue, fraud, mistake, and special damages—be alleged specifically and particularly. This type of pleading is also discussed in section C2c.

2. Alternative and inconsistent pleadings

Rule 8(e)(2) allows a party to plead multiple claims or defenses, either in one or in separate counts or defenses. In practice, each claim is usually put in a separate count, and each defense is designated separately. Keep in mind, however, that since pleadings can be read to the jury during trial, alternative or inconsistent pleadings may cast the party in a poor light. Hence, drafting must also be done with an eye toward the impression the pleading will have on the jurors.

3. Format requirements

Format requirements are set forth in Rules 10 and 11. There are several that must be followed for every pleading. Local rules may also specify additional requirements.

a. Caption

Every pleading must have a caption containing three elements:

- The file number (also called the case number)
- Names of the parties and identification of the side of the action for each
- Court in which the case is being filed

i. File number

The file number is the case number that is stamped on the complaint when it is first filed with the clerk of the court. It must appear on all successive pleadings. Although not required, the designation "Civil Action" is usually placed below the file number.

ii. Parties to the action

The complaint must list all the parties to the action. Subsequent pleadings need only list the first plaintiff and first defendant, with an appropriate reference to additional parties, such as "et al."

Make sure that your caption correctly states the proper name and legal description of each party. Under Rule 17, every action must be brought in the name of the real party in interest, and, according to this rule, the capacity to sue or be sued is controlled by the law of domicile, incorporation, or forum.[3] You must always check Rule 17(b) and (c) to see if a party has capacity to sue or be sued and that the correct person or entity is designated as a party. Examples of common designations include the following:

◆ John Smith
◆ Sharon Jones, as guardian of the Estate of Robert Jones, a minor
◆ Robert Smith, as conservator of the Estate of Ellen Smith, an incompetent
◆ Frank Watson, as executor of the Estate of James Morley, deceased
◆ Barbara Myers, as trustee in bankruptcy of the Estate of Robert Jackson, bankrupt
◆ R. J. Smith Company, a corporation
◆ Johnson Hospital, a not-for-profit corporation
◆ Robert Smith, d/b/a Smith Cleaners
◆ Barnett and Lynch, a partnership
◆ Western Ranches Association, an unincorporated association

Where a party is being sued both individually and in a representative capacity, it should be spelled out.

◆ John Smith, individually and as administrator of the Estate of Franklin Smith, deceased

A sample caption is shown in Exhibit 5.1.

Sometimes it is impossible to identify a proper party by name before filing. In these circumstances, you can designate a party as "John Doe, the true name being presently unknown," and the identity of the party can be pursued through formal discovery. This sometimes happens when a plaintiff has been able to identify some but not all liable parties.

---

3. See Chapter 4, section B.

Exhibit 5.1.   *Sample Caption*

UNITED STATES DISTRICT COURT FOR THE NORTHERN DISTRICT OF NEW YORK	
JOHN SMITH, and J. W. SMITH Company, a corporation, Plaintiffs v. RANDOLPH CONSTRUCTION, a corporation, and WILLIAM JOHNSON, d/b/a Solar Consultants, Defendants	No. _____ Civil Action

b. Designation

Each pleading should be labeled to show what type it is, such as a complaint, counterclaim, cross-claim, third-party complaint, answer, or reply. Where multiple parties are involved, it is useful to show against whom the pleading is directed. Sample designations are shown in Exhibit 5.2.

c. Signing pleadings

Every pleading or other court paper must be signed by one of the party's lawyers. The signing must be by an individual, not a law firm, although in practice the lawyer's firm is frequently shown as "of counsel." The pleading must also contain the lawyer's address and, in practice, a telephone number.

Exhibit 5.2.   *Sample Designation*

<u>COMPLAINT</u>

<u>ANSWER TO CROSS-CLAIM OF DEFENDANT FRANKLIN CORPORATION</u>

<u>THIRD-PARTY COMPLAINT AGAINST JONES CONSTRUCTION COMPANY</u>

Under the Federal Rules of Civil Procedure, pleadings are not "verified." A verified pleading is one signed by the party and notarized. In some state courts, a verified pleading requires the party to state that the facts in the pleading are true and correct to the best of the party's information and belief. Since verified pleadings remain proper procedure in many state jurisdictions and may be permitted or required by specific local rules, always check the specific rules for the court in which the pleading is filed.

4. Rule 11

As a paralegal, you will often be charged with conducting the initial fact investigation and drafting the initial pleading. Accordingly, you must be mindful of Rule 11 of the Federal Rules of Civil Procedure. Under Rule 11, a lawyer's signature on a pleading, motion, or other court paper automatically constitutes a certification that the lawyer has read the pleading and that to the best of the lawyer's knowledge, information, and belief the pleading is well grounded in fact and law — or is a good faith argument for a change in law — and is not being filed for any improper purpose.[4]

The lawyer's obligations under Rule 11 are significant. A good faith belief that the pleading is well founded is not sufficient: A lawyer must have made a **"reasonable inquiry"** into the law and facts, and concluded that there is a sound basis in law and fact for the pleading. What constitutes a "reasonable inquiry" must be considered on a case-by-case basis, and the case law concerning this standard is hardly uniform at this time.

Among the factors to be considered are the amount of time available to investigate the law and facts, the reliability of the client as a source of facts, and the extent to which an investigation could corroborate or alter those facts. If a lawyer simply relies on the client's representation of facts where a reasonable inquiry would show that the facts are otherwise, the lawyer's Rule 11 obligations have not been met. The reasonable inquiry requirement applies not only to theories of recovery and damages against the defendant but also to every party brought into the case. The lawyer must have a reasonable belief, based on a reasonable investigation, that there is a case for every claim against every defendant. Rule 11 applies with equal force to any pleading or other court paper filed by any party. Thus, if you are charged with the responsibility of drafting the

---

4. Rule 11 parallels the applicable ethics considerations. See Model Rules of Professional Conduct, Rule 3.1 (1984). For a useful discussion of Rule 11, see Golden Eagle Distributing Corp. v. Burroughs Corp., 801 F.2d 1531 (9th Cir. 1986). In addition, many jurisdictions have similar state rules requiring that a pleading must not be filed that is frivolous or brought in bad faith or for an improper purpose.

initial pleading, you must also make the necessary "reasonable inquiry" and advise the lawyer of all facts that should be considered.

Under Rule 11, the court can impose sanctions for violations of this requirement. The Rule expressly states that the court may "impose . . . an appropriate sanction" when a violation of the reasonable inquiry requirement occurs. Sanctions can include all reasonable expenses, including attorney's fees, that were incurred as a result of the improperly brought pleading. The court can impose sanctions in response to the motion of a party or on its own motion and is not required in all cases to hold a hearing before imposing sanctions. Furthermore, sanctions can be substantial in appropriate circumstances.

The message of Rule 11 should be abundantly clear: Gone are the days when a lawyer could, with relatively little preparation, file an action containing a variety of claims against a multitude of defendants and later simply dismiss those claims and defendants that never should have been raised or brought into the case in the first place. Today, the reasonable inquiry requirement has teeth, and judges are increasingly willing to impose significant sanctions for violations.

5. Service and filing

Pleadings and other court papers must be served on all parties in one of the permitted ways. Service of any complaint or summons must be made on the party in accordance with the provisions of Rule 4. When a party is represented by a lawyer, service of pleadings other than a complaint should be made on the party's lawyer. This is customarily done either by personal delivery or mail, although under Rule 5(b) delivery includes leaving the pleading or other court paper at the lawyer's office with the person in charge, as well as other infrequently used methods. If a party is not represented by a lawyer, the party himself must be served, and the permitted methods essentially parallel those for lawyers.

Unless otherwise ordered, all pleadings and other court papers that are actually served on parties must be filed with the court clerk either before service or within a reasonable time after service. The usual practice is to have the original and appropriate number of copies of the pleading or other court paper taken to the clerk of the court for filing and have another copy stamped "filed" and dated for your law firm's files. This is usually done the same day papers are being served on the lawyers for the other parties. Local rules often specify how proof of service should be made. The usual practice is to have a **certificate** or **affidavit of service** attached to the end of the pleading that shows when and how service was made and includes the signature of the attorney or the notarized signature of a member of the attorney's staff. Examples of a certificate and affidavit of service are shown in Exhibit 5.3. See also the Litigation File at the end of the book for a sample affidavit of service.

Certificate/Affidavit of Service
A notice at the end of a pleading indicating that service of the pleading has been made upon a particular party

Exhibit 5.3.   Certificate of Service and Affidavit of Service

---

CERTIFICATE OF SERVICE

I, _____[attorney]_____ , state that I served the above by mailing a copy to the attorneys for ____[plaintiff/defendant]____ at ____[state address]____ on ___[date]____ .

Dated: _____

> _____
> Name of attorney
> Address
> Tel. No.

AFFIDAVIT OF SERVICE

I, _____[name]_____ , having been first duly sworn, state that I served the above by mailing a copy to the attorneys for the other parties at their addresses of record in this case.

> _____
> Name

Signed and subscribed to before me on ___[date]___ .

_____
Notary Public

My commission expires on ____[date]____ .

C. COMPLAINTS

The **complaint** is the plaintiff's initial pleading, which, when filed, starts the litigation. There are three essential components of every complaint required by Rule 8(a):

> **Complaint**
> The document filed by the aggrieved party to commence litigation

1. Statement showing subject matter jurisdiction
2. Statement of claims showing the plaintiff is entitled to relief
3. Statement of relief requested

In addition, the complaint must show a jury demand, if a jury will be demanded, and it must be filed and served on each opposing party. A sample complaint appears in the Litigation File at the end of this book.

1. Subject matter jurisdiction

Since federal courts are courts of limited jurisdiction, jurisdiction must be alleged in the complaint, and since jurisdiction cannot be assumed, it must be demonstrated. You should be careful to state the jurisdiction grounds specifically. The jurisdictional allegation is usually the first part of a complaint and is customarily labeled as such. There are two principal ways by which subject matter jurisdiction can be acquired in federal court.

a. Federal question jurisdiction[5]

Federal jurisdiction can be based on a federal statute, constitutional provision, or treaty. To establish jurisdiction in this way, the complaint should cite the particular statute, constitutional provision, or treaty, and perhaps quote the operative wording or paraphrase it. (A sample is shown in Exhibit 5.4.) Failure to do so is not fatal, since jurisdictional allegations can be amended; however, citing a federal statute, constitutional provision, or treaty will not conclusively confer jurisdiction because facts alleged in the complaint can contradict and disprove the jurisdictional allegation. As always, the safest pleading approach is to

Exhibit 5.4.   *Jurisdictional Allegation Based on Federal Question Jurisdiction*

[Caption]

COMPLAINT

Plaintiff Ralph Johnson complains against Defendant Wilbur Jackson as follows:

Jurisdictional Allegation

1. Jurisdiction in this case is based on the existence of a federal question. This action arises under [the Constitution of the United States, Amendment _____ , § _____] [or the Act of _____ , _____ Stat. _____ , _____ U.S.C. § _____] [or the Treaty of the United States _____], as is shown more fully in this complaint.

---

5. See Chapter 4, section D2. The general federal question statute is 18 U.S.C. §1331.

track the language of the Appendix of Forms to the Federal Rules of Civil Procedure.

b. Diversity jurisdiction[6]

Federal jurisdiction can also be based on diversity of citizenship. (See Chapter 4, section D3.) The jurisdictional allegation must affirmatively show complete diversity of each plaintiff and each defendant. The essential requirement is citizenship, not residence. An individual has only one state of citizenship. A corporation, for jurisdictional purposes, is deemed a citizen of both the state where incorporated and the state where it has its principal place of business. An alien, for jurisdictional purposes, is treated as if the country of foreign citizenship were a 51st state.

Where the party is a legally recognized unincorporated association, such as a labor union or service organization, it is a citizen of every state of which any of its members is a citizen. Partnerships are considered citizens of each state where a general partner is a citizen. For legal representatives—such as a guardian of a minor, executor or administrator of an estate, and trustee of a trust—the representative's citizenship is usually controlling for diversity purposes although there may be exceptions in special circumstances.

Where a statute makes notice of a claim a prerequisite to suit, some courts have held that the fact that notice was given is a jurisdictional requirement that must be alleged in the complaint. Diversity jurisdiction under 28 U.S.C. §1332 also requires that the "matter in controversy exceeds the sum or value of $75,000, exclusive of interest and costs." Where the jurisdictional amount must be alleged in the pleadings, it is customary to simply paraphrase the statute at the end of the jurisdictional allegation. Examples of jurisdictional allegations based on diversity are shown in Exhibits 5.5, 5.6, and 5.7.

Exhibit 5.5.   *Jurisdictional Allegation Based on Diversity (Individuals)*

<u>Jurisdictional Allegation</u>

Jurisdiction in this case is based on diversity of citizenship of the parties and the amount in controversy. Plaintiff is a citizen of the State of California. Defendant is a citizen of the State of Oregon.

---

6. See Chapter 4, section D3. The diversity jurisdiction statute is 18 U.S.C. §1332.

Exhibit 5.6.   *Jurisdictional Allegation Based on Diversity (Corporations)*

<u>Jurisdictional Allegation</u>

Jurisdiction in this case is based on diversity of citizenship of the parties and the amount in controversy. Plaintiff is a corporation incorporated under the laws of the State of Delaware having its principal place of business in the State of New York. Defendant is a corporation incorporated under the laws of the State of Georgia having its principal place of business in the State of Florida.

Exhibit 5.7.   *Jurisdictional Allegation Based on Diversity (Claim over $75,000)*

<u>Jurisdictional Allegation</u>

. . . The amount in controversy exceeds the sum of seventy-five thousand dollars ($75,000), exclusive of interest and costs.

---

2. Statement of claims

Rule 8(a) merely requires that a pleading contain a "short and plain statement of the claim showing that the pleader is entitled to relief." Rule 8(e) states that each allegation in the pleading shall be "simple, concise, and direct"; only a few claims, principally fraud and mistake, must be pleaded with particularity. In short, technical requirements have been discarded, the sole requirement now being that enough be pleaded that the other party has fair notice of the claims presented sufficient to defend itself.

Since the requirements for the statement of claims are minimal, great latitude in drafting exists. Hence, the more significant drafting questions are: What is the most effective way to make a statement of the claim in a complaint? Are there any general drafting "rules" that apply?

a. Use plain English

In recent years, the trend in legal drafting has been away from legalese in favor of plain English. The same approach should be applied when drafting pleadings. Commonly used words, short sentences of simple construction, active verbs, and a preference for nouns and verbs over adjectives and adverbs create clear, forceful language. This benefits everyone in litigation—parties, lawyers, judge, and jury.

b. Keep it simple

Pleadings are not the place to disclose the detailed facts of the client's claims, nor the place to elaborate on theories of recovery. The Rules require only a "short and plain statement." One need only allege enough to put the opposing party on fair notice of what the claims against him are. Although this must be read in the light of the complexity of the case, with complex cases requiring more detailed allegations, the preference should still be for simplicity.

On the other hand, there are times when making specific factual allegations can be effective, because they are harder for the defendant to deny. In addition, specific allegations—each set out in a separate paragraph—can support subsequent specific discovery requests. If the defendant denies an allegation, then objection can hardly be taken to discovery methods that are directed at uncovering the denied facts.

The official Appendix of Forms gives excellent examples of complaints in common situations that, by virtue of Rule 84, are legally adequate yet simply written. The safest approach in drafting pleadings is to modify these forms to the claims of the case whenever practical. Examples of claims are shown in Exhibits 5.8 and 5.9.

The preference for using simple English also should apply to naming parties. Use names rather than the pleading's designations (e.g., plaintiff, defendant, cross-claimant, or third-party defendant) or other legal designations (e.g., trustee, drawer, or obligor) unless a local pleading rule requires the designation of the party. Using names keeps things clear, particularly where multiple parties are involved.

Exhibit 5.8. Statement of Claims (Negligence)

1. On August 1, 2006, at approximately 3:00 P.M., plaintiff Jones and defendant Smith were driving automobiles on Elm Street, near Maple Avenue, in Chicago, Illinois.

2. Smith negligently crossed the center lane of Elm Street with his automobile, striking Jones' automobile.

3. As a result Jones received facial injuries, a broken arm, and other injuries, experienced pain and suffering, incurred medical expenses, lost substantial income, and will incur more medical expenses and lost income in the future.

Exhibit 5.9. Statement of Claims (Contract)

> 1. On August 1, 2006, plaintiff Jones and defendant Smith entered into a contract. A true and correct copy of the contract is attached to this complaint as Exhibit A and incorporated herein by reference.
>
> 2. Jones paid Smith $1,000 and has performed all of her obligations under the contract.
>
> 3. Smith failed to paint Jones' house as he was required to do under the contract.

A common practice is to set out the full name of each party the first time it is used, then show in parentheses how you will refer to that party from then on:

* Defendant William B. Smith (hereafter "Smith") . . .
* The International Business Machines Corporation ("IBM") . . .

c. Plead "special matters" with particularity

Rule 9 is an exception to the liberal "notice pleading" approach of the Federal Rules. Under Rule 9, certain allegations must be pled "specifically" and "with particularity." This means that the allegation must be specific as to what the claim is, and the allegation must give particulars of the incident. These allegations include fraud, mistake, and special damages.[7] While capacity and authority to sue, and conditions precedent can be pled generally, denials must be made specifically and with particularity.

What constitutes appropriate specificity and particularity in pleading these special matters is unclear. While the particularity requirement should be viewed in light of Rule 8's liberal pleading standards, it is safer as well as proper to set forth the specific elements of the special matter being pled. This will ensure that the requisite particularity has been established. An example of a fraud statement of claims, which must be pled with particularity, is shown in Exhibit 5.10.

d. Use separate paragraphs

The Rules require a separate paragraph for a "single set of circumstances" whenever practicable—admittedly an imprecise standard.

---

7. Subject matter jurisdiction must also be pled specifically. See Chapter 4, section D.

Exhibit 5.10. Statement of Claims (with Particularity)

1. On August 1, 2006, plaintiff Jones and defendant Smith entered into a contract (the "Contract"). A true and correct copy of the Contract is attached to this complaint as Exhibit A and incorporated herein by reference.

2. Under the Contract, Jones agreed to pay Smith $20,000, and Smith agreed to sell Jones a parcel of land in Atlanta, Georgia. The precise location and description of the parcel are set out in the Contract.

3. Before executing the Contract, Smith represented that he had legal title to the parcel, that the parcel had no encumbrances of any kind, such as mortgages, tax liens, or judgment liens, and that Smith would be able to have the property rezoned to a B-2 zoning.

4. Those representations were false and fraudulent, Smith knew they were false and fraudulent when made, and Smith made them to induce Jones to enter into the Contract.

5. Jones relied on Smith's representations and was damaged.

When in doubt, it is probably better to use paragraphs liberally because this usually makes the pleadings simpler to follow. More important, it makes the complaint easier to answer and will minimize the likelihood that an answer will admit part and deny part of a single paragraph. As a result, the positions of the parties will be clearer, benefiting everyone. The following example shows concise, separate paragraphs:

EXAMPLE

1. On June 1, 2006, plaintiff Jones and defendant Smith entered into a contract, a copy of which is attached as Exhibit A.
2. On June 15, 2006, Jones paid Smith $10,000 as required by the contract.
3. Jones has performed each of his obligations under the contract.
4. Smith failed to deliver 1,000 folding chairs to Jones by June 30, 2006, and has failed to perform her obligations under the contract.

e. Use separate counts

Although not required by the Federal Rules of Civil Procedure, it is customary to state each claim involving a separate theory of recovery

Count
Each separate cause of action alleged in a complaint

in a separate **count**, even if all are based on the same general occurrence or transaction. This has the advantage of setting out clearly each legal theory that forms a basis for recovery.

Since setting out different theories of recovery in different counts usually requires restating some allegations, it is efficient and proper under Rule 10(c) to incorporate into the later count by reference those allegations made in earlier counts, as shown in the following example.

EXAMPLE

Count II

1-15. Plaintiff adopts Par. 1-15 of Count I as Par. 1-15 of this Count.
  16. ...
  17. ...

It is also useful to label the legal theory for each count and, where different counts are against different parties, show which parties are involved in each count:

EXAMPLE

Count I—Contract

(against defendants Jones and Roberts)
1. ...
2. ...
3. ...

Count II—Implied Warranties

(against defendant Roberts only)

---

f. Use exhibits

Rule 10(c) permits attaching exhibits to pleadings. This is most commonly done in contract cases, where the contract that forms the basis for the claim is attached to the complaint. When attached to the pleading, the exhibit becomes an integral part of it. This is usually a more efficient way of stating a claim than setting out the exhibit's contents in the body of the complaint. The following example shows how to incorporate attached exhibits into the complaint.

1. Plaintiff Jones and defendant Smith entered into a contract on June 1, 2006. A true and correct copy of this contract is attached as Exhibit A and incorporated herein by reference.

Even if the exhibit is attached to the pleading, language from the exhibit can still be quoted in the complaint.

3. Prayer for relief

Rule 8(a) requires a pleading to make a "demand for judgment for the relief to which [the pleader] deems himself entitled. Relief in the alternative or of several different types may be demanded." This is called the **prayer for relief**. The Rule makes no distinction between legal and equitable relief.

Prayer for relief
A section at the end of a complaint specifying the relief requested by the plaintiff

Care in pleading relief is important for two reasons. First, since under federal law the nature of the remedy sought is often controlling on the question of the right to a jury trial,[8] the demand for relief should be drafted to ensure the right to a jury trial, or to avoid it, as the case may be. Second, where a defendant fails to respond to the complaint and a **default judgment** is requested, the method under which default can be obtained is affected by the type of relief sought, and the relief granted is limited to that requested in the pleadings. Since default is always a possibility, you should always draft the prayer carefully.

Default judgment
Judgment entered against a defendant who fails to appear and defend against the lawsuit after having been given proper notice of the lawsuit

The prayer for relief appears at the end of the body of the complaint. It specifies the types of relief sought, including legal and equitable remedies, interest, costs, attorney's fees, and any special damages, with sufficient detail. Where several specific types of relief are sought, the better practice is to itemize and number them. An example of a prayer for relief is shown in Exhibit 5.11.

4. Jury demand

Under Rule 38, a party may demand in writing a jury trial on any claim triable as of right by a jury at any time after the complaint is filed and "not later than 10 days after the service of the last pleading directed to such issue." The party may specify in the demand which claims he

---

8. Jury trials are permitted in actions of law as opposed to equitable actions.

Exhibit 5.11.   Prayer for Relief

WHEREFORE, plaintiff demands judgment against defendant for the sum of $25,000, with interest and costs.

WHEREFORE, plaintiff demands a preliminary and permanent injunction, an accounting for all damages, and interest and costs.

WHEREFORE, plaintiff demands:
1. That defendant pay damages in the sum of $25,000;
2. That defendant be specifically ordered to perform his obligations under the contract;
3. That defendant pay interest, costs, and reasonable attorney's fees incurred by plaintiff.

wishes tried to a jury. The Rule permits the jury demand to be placed on the pleading itself, and this is the customary method of making the demand. Local rules, however, may have additional requirements for jury demands. A common practice is to place the label "Jury Trial Demanded" below the case number, and the phrase "Plaintiff Demands Trial by Jury" at the end of the complaint. Local rules sometimes have additional requirements, such as the use of jury demand forms and the payment of fees.

If one party makes a jury demand, the other parties are entitled to rely on it. However, if a party makes a jury demand on only some counts, the other parties must make a timely jury demand on other counts. Failure to make a timely demand for a jury trial constitutes a waiver of the right under Rule 38(d); courts have taken a strict view on waiver and only rarely exercise their discretion to permit a belated demand.

5. Filing and service of summons

Under Rule 3, a federal action is commenced when the complaint is filed with the clerk of the court. This is significant for statute of limitations purposes. In federal question cases, the filing of the complaint "tolls"—that is, stops—the statute of limitations. In diversity cases, however, state law controls, and if state law requires something more than the mere filing of the complaint—usually service of summons on the defendant—state law must be complied with fully before the statute of limitations is tolled.

After the action is commenced, the complaint must be served on each defendant. Under Rule 4, detailed service-of-summons rules control how the complaint and summons are to be served on defendants. There are several steps involved, and you should check local rules for any additional filing and service-of-summons requirements. For example, most districts require designation or cover sheets and appearance forms to be filed with the complaint and summons.

a. Issuing the summons

When the complaint is filed, the clerk is directed under Rule 4(b) to issue the summons. A **summons** is the notice to the defendant that commands that the defendant appear and defend against the action within a certain period of time or else judgment may be entered against the defendant. In practice, the summons form, which is available from the clerk's office, is usually filled out in advance and taken to the clerk's office when the complaint is filed. To assist in service, it is useful to list on the back of the form where and when service on each defendant can most likely be made. For example, if the service is to be made at the defendant's work address, it is useful to put down the working hours and where on the premises the defendant actually works. The clerk then "issues" the summons by signing and stamping it with the court seal, the date, and the case file number. Make sure that you have enough copies of the complaint and summons for the clerk's administrative needs, for service on each defendant, and for your law firm's files.

Summons
Notice accompanying the complaint that commands that the defendant appear and defend against the action within a certain period of time

b. Summons content

Rule 4(a) controls the summons content. Exhibit 5.12 contains the standard elements of a summons. Most summons include:

- Defendant's name and address
- Plaintiff's attorney and attorney's address
- Request for answer
- Time limit on answer
- Statement of consequences of nonreply

Another example of a summons appears in the Litigation File at the end of this book.

All courts have summons forms. To ensure that you have included everything, it is a safer practice to simply pick up a copy of a blank summons form from the clerk of the court than write your own. A sample summons form is shown in Exhibit 5.13.

Exhibit 5.12. Sample Summons

<u>SUMMONS</u>

To: _____ *[defendant and address]* _____

You are hereby summoned and required to serve upon _____, plaintiff's attorney, whose address is _____, an answer to the complaint that is hereby served upon you, within 20 days after service upon you, exclusive of the day of service.

If you fail to do so, judgment by default will be taken against you for the relief demanded in the complaint.

_____
Clerk of Court

---

c. Persons who may serve the summons

As a general rule, the complaint and summons can be served by any person who is not a party and is at least 18 years old. Service by the U.S. marshal is now required only in limited circumstances specified in Rule 4(c)(2)—on behalf of paupers or on a seaman, and by court order.

d. Methods of service

How service of summons may be made depends on the entity being served and is governed by Rule 4(e)–(k).

i. Individuals

An individual can be served a summons in several ways. First, service can be made by personally giving the individual a copy of the complaint and summons. Second, it can be made by leaving a copy of the complaint and summons "at his dwelling house or usual place of abode" with a person of suitable age and discretion residing there. Third, service can be made on an agent authorized by appointment or law to receive process. Fourth, where the individual is out of state, service may be made on any defendant using either the law of the forum state or the law in that state where the defendant is served, subject to constitutional and statutory constraints. These are the state long-arm statutes, which

Exhibit 5.13. Sample Summons

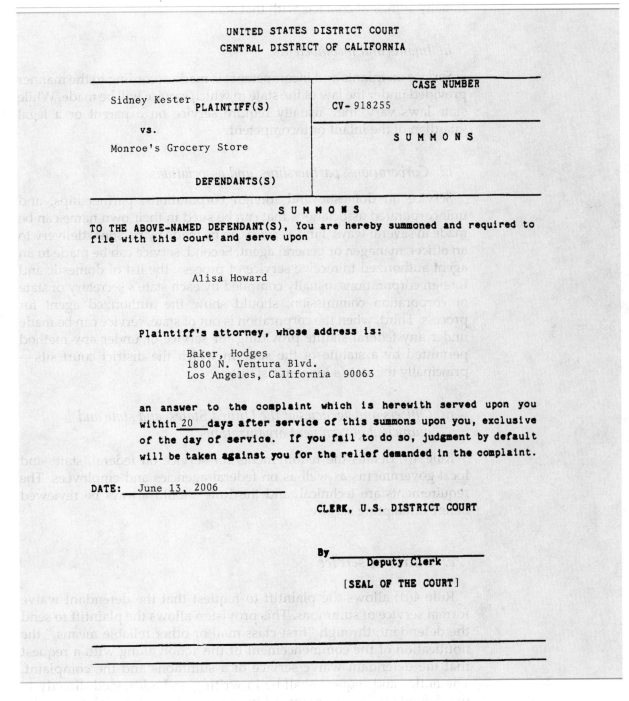

UNITED STATES DISTRICT COURT
CENTRAL DISTRICT OF CALIFORNIA

	CASE NUMBER
Sidney Kester **PLAINTIFF(S)**	CV- 918255
vs.	
Monroe's Grocery Store	**S U M M O N S**
DEFENDANTS(S)	

S U M M O N S

TO THE ABOVE-NAMED DEFENDANT(S), You are hereby summoned and required to file with this court and serve upon

Alisa Howard

Plaintiff's attorney, whose address is:

Baker, Hodges
1800 N. Ventura Blvd.
Los Angeles, California 90063

an answer to the complaint which is herewith served upon you within 20 days after service of this summons upon you, exclusive of the day of service. If you fail to do so, judgment by default will be taken against you for the relief demanded in the complaint.

DATE: June 13, 2006

CLERK, U.S. DISTRICT COURT

By_____
Deputy Clerk

[SEAL OF THE COURT]

provide for extraterritorial service on any defendant who has constitutionally sufficient contacts with that state.[9]

ii. Infants and incompetents

Service on infants and incompetents is made according to the manner provided under the law of the state in which service will be made. While state laws vary, they usually require service on a parent or a legal guardian of the infant or incompetent.

iii. Corporations, partnerships, and associations

Service on domestic and foreign corporations, partnerships, and unincorporated associations that can be sued in their own name can be made in several ways. First, service can be made by personal delivery to an officer, manager, or general agent. Second, service can be made to an agent authorized to receive service of process; the list of domestic and foreign corporations, usually compiled by each state's secretary of state or corporation commission, should show the authorized agent for process. Third, when the corporation is out of state, service can be made under any federal statute providing for service or under any method permitted by a statute of the state in which the district court sits— principally the state's long-arm statute.

iv. Officers and agencies of the United States, and state and municipal government organizations

Rule 4(i) details the requirements for service on federal, state, and local governments as well as on federal agencies and employees. The requirements are technical, and the Rule should always be reviewed before attempting service.

e. Waiver of service

Rule 4(d) allows the plaintiff to request that the defendant waive formal service of summons. This provision allows the plaintiff to send the defendant, through "first-class mail or other reliable means," the notification of the commencement of the action along with a request that the defendant waive service of a summons and the complaint. The notice and request shall be in writing and addressed directly to the defendant, be accompanied by a copy of the complaint, identify

---

9. See Chapter 4, section E.

the court in which the action is filed, inform the defendant of the consequences of compliance and the failure to comply with the request, specify the date the request was sent, and allow the defendant a reasonable time to return the waiver.

The purposes of the waiver of service are to eliminate the costs of service of a summons on many parties and to foster cooperation among the parties to the suit. In order to encourage defendants to cooperate, a defendant may be liable for those costs that could have been avoided if the defendant had reasonably cooperated under the provisions of Rule 4(d). Once the plaintiff files a waiver of service with the court, the action proceeds as if a summons and complaint had been served, and no proofs of service are required.

f. Territorial limits of service

The geographical scope of service is governed by Rule 4. There are four basic precepts.

i. The 100-mile "bulge" rule

The 100-mile "bulge" provision provides for some service within 100 miles of the place where the original action commenced, even if state lines are crossed. However, this rule applies only to parties brought in as third-party defendants under Rule 14 or as additional necessary parties to a counterclaim or cross-claim under Rules 13 and 19.

The purpose of the rule is to permit service of process on additional parties that are brought into the action after the original suit is filed and are necessary for a fair and complete disposition of the action. This is an important rule for multiparty litigation in large metropolitan areas such as New York, Chicago, and Washington, which cover several jurisdictions, since otherwise it would often be difficult to serve every party in the suit.

ii. State long-arm statutes

As discussed previously, state long-arm statutes permit service on a party outside the state in which the district court sits by service on a party in a state where the party has sufficient minimum contacts. This makes federal and state process, as far as territorial limits, essentially the same.[10]

---

10. For example, in some states service is permissible on out-of-state parties by certified mail, return receipt requested. In those states, service of a federal court complaint on an out-of-state party may be made in the same manner.

iii. Federal statute or court order

Whenever a federal statute or court order authorizes service on a party outside the state in which the district court sits, service may be made in accordance with the statute or order.

iv. The Hague Convention

If you are serving someone living in another country, you must be aware of the Hague Convention. The Convention is an international treaty that governs service of process in countries that are parties to the treaty. A list of countries that have signed the Convention, along with a copy of the Convention, is in the last volume of the Martindale-Hubbell Law Directory. The appropriate methods of service vary from country to country, so you must always check the service requirements for the particular country. If you fail to comply with the service requirements of the Hague Convention, any service on the party residing abroad will be void.

g. Timeliness of service

Under Rule 4(m) of the Federal Rules of Civil Procedure, service of the complaint and summons must be carried out within 120 days after filing of the complaint. Unless good cause can be shown for not having carried out service in time, the action will be dismissed without prejudice as to the unserved defendant. Many state jurisdictions also have timeliness requirements.

The complaint, of course, may be refiled against that same party. Refiling after the statute of limitations has run should not create a problem, so long as the original action was properly filed within the limitations period. However, when a state cause of action is asserted and state law requires more than the mere filing of the complaint to satisfy the state statute of limitations, such as actual service of summons, these additional requirements must be met within the limitations period.

h. Proof of service

Rule 4(l) requires that if service is not waived the person serving process must establish proof of service. If process is served by anyone other than the U.S. marshal, proof must be in affidavit form. In practice, the proof of service affidavit is usually found on the summons form. The person serving the summons and complaint should fill in the proof of service affidavit and return it to you for filing with the court. An example is shown in Exhibit 5.14.

i. Informal service

Sometimes you will know the lawyer who will represent the defendant in the lawsuit. You or the lawyer in charge may have already had contact with the defendant's lawyer before filing suit, or you may know the lawyer who regularly handles the defendant's legal matters. In such instances, a good practice is for you or the lawyer to call the defendant's lawyer and let her know that your client is about to file suit. Ask her if she will accept service of process and acknowledge receipt on behalf of the defendant. If so, simply deliver or mail the complaint to her.

If you think the defendant will try to avoid service of process or contest the validity of service, serve the defendant formally under Rule 4. Otherwise, informal service can be a convenient approach; it is frequently used in commercial litigation with corporate parties.

D. RULE 12 RESPONSES

When a complaint and summons have been served on a defendant, he can respond in two basic ways. First, he can answer the complaint.

Exhibit 5.14.   Proof of Service Affidavit

AFFIDAVIT OF SERVICE

I, _____, having been first duly sworn, state that I served a copy of the summons and complaint on _____ by _____ at
_____[defendent]_____   _____[method of service]_____

_____ on _____ .
_____[address]_____   _____[date]_____

_____
[signature]

Signed and sworn to before me on:

_____

_____

Notary Public

My commission expires on _____ .

Ordinarily, the defendant must answer within 20 days of service. However, under Rule 12(a)(1)(B), if a defendant has waived service consistent with Rule 4(d)(3), then he has 60 days from the date the request was mailed to respond to the complaint, or 90 days if the request to respond was sent outside the United States. Always check the code of civil procedure in your state to determine the time to respond in state court. For example, in California, the time to respond is 30 days from the date of service.[11]

Second, before filing an answer the defendant can make any of three motions attacking claimed defects in the complaint.[12] These are

- ◆ Motion to strike
- ◆ Motion for a more definite statement
- ◆ Motion to dismiss

All of these are governed by Rule 12. When a defendant decides to attack the complaint with a Rule 12 motion, he must do so within the time permitted for his answer, ordinarily within 20 days of service of the complaint.[13] The following sections provide an overview of these Rule 12 motions and the grounds for making such motions. The motions usually, but not always, must be accompanied by a notice indicating the date, time, and place of the hearing on the motion. The motions should also include a **memorandum of law**, sometimes referred to as a memorandum of points and authorities. The memorandum of law sets forth the background facts and legal authorities to support your side's position.

Memorandum of law
Legal document submitted with a motion setting forth background facts and legal authorities to support a position

1. Motion to strike

Motion to strike
A motion to eliminate certain allegations from a complaint

Under Rule 12(f), if the complaint contains "any redundant, immaterial, impertinent or scandalous matter," it can be stricken upon motion. Such a motion is referred to as a **motion to strike**. (See Exhibit 5.15.) While a motion to strike is not frequently made, it should be considered when there is a possibility that the complaint will be read to the jury during trial.

---

11. In California, the time to answer a complaint is extended if service of process was not made personally upon the defendant but by some other method. This extension of time is typical in virtually every state.

12. See section C for the requirements of a complaint.

13. If a Rule 12 motion is denied, a defendant generally has ten days to answer the complaint.

Exhibit 5.15.   Motion to Strike

[Caption]

<u>MOTION TO STRIKE</u>

Defendant Johnson Corporation moves under Rule 12(f) for an order striking certain immaterial and scandalous matters from the complaint. In support of its motion defendant states:

    1. Par. 2 of the complaint alleges that the "Johnson Corporation had gross receipts of \$102,436,000 for fiscal year 2006." This allegation is immaterial to a contract action and should be stricken.

    2. Par. 7 of the complaint alleges that the "Johnson Corporation is an international cartel that dominates the furniture polish industry." This allegation is impertinent and scandalous and should be stricken.

    WHEREFORE, defendant Johnson Corporation requests that the court enter an order striking these parts of plaintiff's complaint and requiring plaintiff to file an amended complaint that deletes the stricken matter within 10 days.

---

2. Motion for a more definite statement

Under Rule 12(e), if the complaint is "so vague or ambiguous" that the defendant cannot respond to it, the defendant may make a **motion for a more definite statement**.[14] (See Exhibit 5.16.) The motion must point out the defects and specify the details that are needed. However, since the complaint need only be a "short and plain statement," and pleadings generally should be "simple, concise and direct," and because discovery is the preferred method for flushing out details, such motions are disfavored and infrequently granted. A more commonly used approach is to move to dismiss under Rule 12(b)(6) for failure to state a claim on which relief can be granted.

3. Motion to dismiss under Rule 12(b)

Under Rule 12(b), the defendant may raise certain defenses either in the answer or by a **motion to dismiss.** This is the predominant motion for attacking the complaint, and it has several important characteristics.

Motion to dismiss
A motion by the defendant that the complaint filed by the plaintiff be dismissed because of some specified defect

---

14. In some state courts, such a motion is called a "special demurrer." A demurrer challenges defects that appear on the face of the pleading.

Exhibit 5.16. Motion for a More Definite Statement

[Caption]

<u>MOTION FOR A MORE DEFINITE STATEMENT</u>

Defendant Johnson Corporation moves under Rule 12(e) for an order requiring plaintiff to provide a more definite statement. In support of its motion defendant states:

1. Par. 3 of the complaint alleges that "plaintiff and defendant and others entered into an agreement in 2006 under which defendant was obligated to deliver such amounts of furniture polish as plaintiff may from time to time request."

2. Nowhere else in the complaint is greater detail provided, and no copy of any contract is attached to the complaint. Without additional details, defendant cannot respond to this allegation.

WHEREFORE, defendant Johnson Corporation requests that the court enter an order requiring defendant to serve and file a more definite statement within 10 days showing what date this alleged contract was entered into, where it was entered into, every part to it, the requirements under the contract, and, if in writing, a copy of the alleged contract.

---

a. The one motion requirement

If the lawyer asks you to respond to the complaint with a motion to dismiss on Rule 12(b) grounds, the Rule requires that you present all defenses that can be raised in one motion to dismiss. In other words, you must consolidate all available Rule 12(b) defenses into one motion. This requirement prevents attacking the complaint on a piecemeal basis.

b. Rule 12(b) defenses

The following defenses may be raised in a motion to dismiss:

1. Lack of subject matter jurisdiction
2. Lack of personal jurisdiction
3. Improper venue
4. Insufficiency of process
5. Insufficiency of service of process
6. Failure to state a claim upon which relief can be granted
7. Failure to join a party under Rule 19

In addition, there is some case law holding that affirmative defenses in Rule 8(c) may be asserted in a Rule 12(b) motion to dismiss.

Federal practice has eliminated the need for special appearances to contest personal jurisdiction, since under Rule 12(g) the joinder of defenses does not create a waiver of any of them. Hence, a defendant can raise any of the Rule 12(b) defenses by motion and is not held to have waived the right to assert lack of personal jurisdiction. This rule may be different in state court. In some states, such as California, failure to raise personal jurisdiction first and alone will constitute a waiver of the right to contest personal jurisdiction. Accordingly, the defect must be raised by a motion to quash service of the summons.

c. Waiver

Under Rule 12(g) and (h), defenses not consolidated into one motion to dismiss may be waived, but the waiver rules depend on the defense involved. Lack of jurisdiction over the person, improper venue, insufficiency of process, and insufficiency of service of process are all waived if not included in a motion to dismiss or, if no motion is made, in the answer. Hence, if any of these grounds are raised in a motion to dismiss, the others must be raised then as well, or they will be waived. Failure to state a claim and failure to join an indispensable party, however, may be raised in the answer, in a motion for judgment on the pleadings, or at trial. Finally, lack of subject matter jurisdiction is never waived and can be raised at any time.

The waiver rules create two categories of defenses to a claim. The procedural irregularity defenses are waived unless timely presented, while substantive defenses to a valid judgment cannot be so waived.

d. Practice approach

The underlying theory of Rule 12 must be kept in mind when you and the lawyer are deciding whether to present Rule 12(b) defenses in a motion to dismiss or in the answer. The Rule allows certain defenses to be raised in a motion so that meritless or defective complaints can be disposed of early in the litigation. If you decide to assert a defense in a motion to dismiss, you should raise the other Rule 12(b) defenses available and assert them in one consolidated motion because most of those defenses are waived if not raised then.

After you and the lawyer consider the possibilities under Rule 12, consider the types of defenses that can be raised. Three of the grounds—lack of personal jurisdiction, insufficiency of process, and insufficiency of service of process—are essentially procedural defects that usually can be cured. Since the plaintiff can ordinarily file an amended complaint or serve process on the defendant again, there may be little point in raising these defenses if the plaintiff can easily cure them. For example, when there is no proper personal jurisdiction over the defendant because of a defect in the process, but it is obvious that the defendant can be properly served later, there may be little point in raising these defenses even though they are technically available. On the other hand, when personal jurisdiction over the defendant does not properly exist, and probably cannot be obtained, the motion should be made.

If the defense is improper venue, the defense is waived if not included in a motion to dismiss that raises other 12(b) defenses.[15] Hence, if venue is in fact improper under venue rules, and the present venue is a logistically inconvenient location for the defendant, the motion should be made. If granted, the probable result will not be dismissal but transfer to a proper venue.

Finally, when the defenses are lack of subject matter jurisdiction, failure to state a claim upon which relief can be granted, and failure to join an indispensable party, the defendant has more flexibility because these may be made either in the answer, by a motion for judgment on the pleadings, or at trial, even if a motion to dismiss based on other Rule 12(b) grounds has been made. Hence, the defendant has the option of including these grounds in a motion to dismiss or raising them later. Raising them by motion to dismiss, of course, will get the issue resolved sooner than by including them in the answer. Regardless of which approach is taken, however, the plaintiff is on notice of a possible defect in his pleading and can usually file an amended complaint correcting the defect.

The history of Rule 12(b) shows that motions to dismiss rarely result in the final disposition of a lawsuit. Indeed, federal pleadings are designed to frame issues, not resolve disputes. Hence, the trend in litigation practice has been to make fewer motions under Rule 12 and to raise those defenses instead in the answer; that is, to raise those defenses in a motion to dismiss only when there is a clear strategic reason to do so, not simply because the Rules permit it.

A motion to dismiss based on Rule 12(b) should clearly set out the defenses being asserted in separate paragraphs. An example of a motion to dismiss is shown in Exhibit 5.17.

The basic allegations of Rule 12(b) grounds should be developed both factually and legally. Where facts are necessary, statements in affidavit form and exhibits should be attached to the motion, although the court under the Rule can then treat the motion as one for summary judgment.

---

15. See Chapter 4, section G; 28 U.S.C. §§ 1391 et seq.

Exhibit 5.17.   Motion to Dismiss

[Caption]

<u>MOTION TO DISMISS</u>

Defendant Jones moves under Rule 12(b) for an order dismissing the complaint. In support of his motion defendant states:

1. The court lacks jurisdiction over the subject matter of this action because it appears from the complaint that the alleged claim does not arise under the Constitution of the United States, any Act of Congress, or treaties of the United States.

2. The court lacks jurisdiction over the subject matter of this action because the controversy is not between citizens of different states, and because the amount in controversy between the plaintiff and this defendant is less than $75,000, exclusive of interest and costs.

3. The court lacks jurisdiction over the defendant because the defendant is a corporation incorporated under the laws of the State of Delaware, has its principal place of business in Delaware, and is not subject to service in the State of Maryland where service was attempted.

4. This action has been brought in an improper district, since the complaint alleges that jurisdiction is based on diversity of citizenship; plaintiff is a citizen of the State of California, defendant is a citizen of the State of Nevada, and the claims arose in the State of Nevada. Venue in the district of Arizona is therefore improper.

5. Service of process on the defendant was insufficient because service was made on the defendant's business partner at his place of business, as shown by the proof of service for the summons.

6. The complaint fails to state a claim against this defendant on which relief can be granted.

7. The complaint fails to join all indispensable parties as required by Rule 19 because the Phillips Corporation is an indispensable party, has not been joined as a party, and if so joined would destroy this court's jurisdiction since complete diversity would be lacking.

If case law is pertinent, it should be contained in a memorandum of law accompanying the motion.

The most commonly raised ground for dismissal, of course, is Rule 12(b)(6), failure to state a claim upon which relief can be granted. The motion should be granted if, based on facts alleged and applicable law, there is no possible set of facts that could support the claim under any available legal theory.[16] The motion is conceptually limited to matters alleged in the complaint. If facts outside the pleadings are presented at a hearing on the motion, the court should treat the motion as one for summary judgment and proceed in accordance with Rule 56. If the motion is granted, plaintiff will routinely be given leave to file an amended complaint. However, if the plaintiff is acting in bad faith, has repeatedly failed to amend properly, or obviously cannot amend properly, leave to amend should be denied.

E. ANSWERS

Answer
A response by the defendant to the plaintiff's complaint

When the plaintiff's complaint has been served, every defendant must respond, either by filing a Rule 12 motion (discussed in the preceding section) or by filing an **answer** to the complaint. The answer admits or denies the various allegations in the complaint and usually asserts a number of defenses. An example appears in the Litigation File at the end of the book.

1. Timing

As a general rule, under Rule 12(a) the defendant must serve an answer within 20 days of service of the complaint and summons. Different deadlines may apply if service is made out of state, if the United States government is a defendant, or if a specific federal or state statute applies.[17] When the defendant first responds with a Rule 12 motion, the answer is due within ten days after the defendant receives notice of the court's action on the motion or within ten days after service of a more definite statement.

2. General requirements

There are several rules that regulate the form and content of the answer. Rule 8(b) requires that an answer shall "state in short and plain terms" the defenses asserted. It must either admit or deny the allegations, or state that the defendant is without knowledge or information sufficient to form a belief as to their truth. Under Rule 8(c), affirmative defenses

---

16. See Conley v. Gibson, 355 U.S. 41 (1957). As with a motion for a more definite statement, in some state courts, such as California's, motion to dismiss for failure to state a claim is called a "demurrer." Other than the difference in the name of the motion, the substance of the motion is the same.

17. Remember, under Rule 12(a)(1)(B), if a defendant has waived service consistent with Rule 4(d)(3), then he has 60 days from the date the request was mailed to respond to the complaint or 90 days if the request to respond was sent outside the United States.

(see section E.5) must be set out in the answer, and under Rule 12(b), the specified defenses may be set out as well. (For Rule 12(b) defenses, see section E.4.) The defenses may be set out alternatively, inconsistently, or hypothetically. A hypothetical defense can be raised to an allegation in a complaint if it is found to be true, thus permitting a response that both denies the allegation and raises a hypothetical defense to it.

Since a complaint must be answered, failing to answer will constitute an admission of all facts alleged in the complaint; this does not apply, however, to the prayer for relief. Answering with a simple "admit," "deny," or "no knowledge or belief" is usually sufficient. Under Rule 9(a), however, where the answer raises an issue as to the "legal existence of any party or the capacity of any party to sue or be sued or the authority of a party to sue or be sued in a representative capacity," the denials must be made with particularity.

To parallel the complaint, the answer must be organized in paragraphs and by counts, setting out separate defenses in separate counts. When there is only one defendant, the answer is simply titled "Answer." If there are multiple defendants, however, the title should specify the party answering, for example, "Answer of Defendant Acme Tool Corporation." If a defendant demands a jury trial, the "Jury Trial Demanded" notice should appear in the caption of the answer, and the words "Defendant Demands Trial by Jury" at the end of the answer. Finally, the answer, like every pleading, must be signed by the lawyer; this signature constitutes a certification that the pleading is made in good faith under Rule 11.

The answer, therefore, may have three parts:

- Responses of the complaint's allegations
- Affirmative defenses
- Rule 12(b) defenses

A well-drafted answer will set out each part clearly.

3. Responses

Rule 8(b) permits three types of responses to the complaint's allegations. The answer may either admit or deny the allegations, or state that the party is without knowledge or information sufficient to form a belief as to their truth. The format, whether informally brief or more formal, is largely a matter of local custom, although the trend is toward brief responses.

If the response is "no knowledge or belief," this must be based on good faith. Such a response should not be available on matters that are common knowledge or that can easily be learned by the defendant. For example, if the complaint alleges that the defendant corporation had "gross receipts during 2007 in the amount of $6,450,000," the defendant's lawyer cannot answer "no knowledge or belief" since the lawyer can easily find out if the allegation is true or not.

The answer may admit only part of an allegation and deny the remainder or may admit having no knowledge or information as to the remainder, whichever the case may be. Each paragraph of the complaint must be responded to individually unless the defendant can in good faith collectively deny every allegation of the complaint. Sample responses are shown in Exhibits 5.18 and 5.19.

Exhibit 5.18.   Answer (Sample Response Format)

[Caption]

<u>ANSWER</u>

Defendant Jones answers the complaint as follows:
   1. Defendant admits the allegations in paragraph 1 of the complaint.
   2. Defendant admits the allegations in paragraph 2.
   3. Defendant denies each and every allegation in paragraph 3 of the complaint.
   4. Defendant denies each and every allegation in paragraph 4 of the complaint.
   5. Defendant is without knowledge or information sufficient to form a belief as to the truth of the allegations in paragraph 5 of the complaint, and therefore denies each and every allegation contained therein.

Exhibit 5.19.   Answer (Sample Response with Specific Admissions and Denials)

---

   1. Defendant admits he is a citizen of the State of California, but denies the remaining allegations in paragraph 1 of the complaint.
   2. With respect to paragraph 2 of the complaint, defendant admits he entered into a written contract with plaintiff on June 1, 2006, but denies that the contract was modified under an agreement on August 1, 2006, or on any other date.
   3. Defendant denies he owned and operated a business known as Jones Excavating in 2006 or any other year. Defendant does not have sufficient knowledge or information to form a belief as to the truth of the other allegations in paragraph 3, and therefore denies each and every remaining allegation contained therein.

Within these guidelines the Rules permit considerable drafting flexibility. The modern trend is toward brevity and conciseness. The standard approach is to simply have counts and numbered paragraphs corresponding to the counts and paragraphs of the complaint. However, it is just as effective to set out admissions, denials, and no-knowledge-or-information responses collectively when the situation is appropriate. If the complaint incorporates several paragraphs in the first count, the answer can do the same. A response following this format is shown in Exhibit 5.20.

Denying all allegations not specifically admitted is a safe practice, since this prevents a typographical error in the answer from prejudicing the client. Claims under Rule 9(a) of no capacity or authority and claims under Rule 9(c) that conditions precedent have not been performed are raised by denials, but must be particularly specified. A sample response answering these claims is shown in Exhibit 5.21.

Not every allegation in the complaint must be responded to, since not every count, or every paragraph in a count, will contain an allegation directed at the defendant your law office is representing. Where the lawyer represents one defendant in a case that has multiple defendants, and some counts or paragraphs do not apply to that defendant, the usual practice is to point this out in the answer. This avoids the possibility of "silence" in the answer being interpreted as an admission. Paragraphs

Exhibit 5.20.   *Answer (Sample Response Incorporating Several Paragraphs)*

<u>Count I</u>

1. Defendant admits the allegations of paragraphs 1, 2, 3, 4, 5, and 6 of the complaint.

2. Defendant denies the allegations of paragraphs 8, 9, and 10 of the complaint.

3. Defendant is without knowledge or information sufficient to form a belief as to the truth of the allegations in paragraph 7 of the complaint and therefore denies each and every allegation contained therein.

<u>Count II</u>

1. Defendant incorporates her answers to paragraphs 1-3 of Count I as if fully set forth.

2. Defendant denies all other allegations of the complaint not specifically admitted.

Exhibit 5.21. Answer (Sample Response to Claims Under Rules 9(a) and 9(c))

> 1. Defendant denies that plaintiff is a legal entity that has capacity to sue in its own name, and specifically denies that plaintiff has any legal existence that permits it to pursue this action in the name of "John Smith Corporation."
>
> 2. Defendant denies that plaintiff has performed all conditions precedent as required under the contract, and specifically denies that plaintiff delivered a copy of the contract to defendant within 30 days of execution, although plaintiff was required to do so before the contract would be in force.

like those in the following two examples can be incorporated into your answer to point out claims that do not apply to your client.

EXAMPLE

Count II

The allegations in this count are not directed to this defendant and accordingly no response by this defendant is made to the count. In the event it is ever determined that this count is directed to this defendant, this defendant reserves his right to respond to this count.

EXAMPLE

12. The allegations in paragraph 12 of plaintiff's complaint are not directed toward this defendant, so this defendant makes no answer to the allegations.

4. Rule 12(b) defenses

As discussed previously,[18] the defendant can raise Rule 12(b) defenses in a pre-answer motion to dismiss or can include them in the answer. If the defenses are raised in the answer, each should be labeled separately to refer to the specific defense being asserted, preferably by tracking the language of Rule 12(b) and elaborating where necessary, as is shown in the following example.

18. See pages 149-154.

<u>**FIRST DEFENSE**</u>

The complaint fails to state a claim against the defendant on which relief can be granted.

<u>**SECOND DEFENSE**</u>

This court lacks jurisdiction over the subject matter of this action, since the complaint alleges that jurisdiction is based on diversity of citizenship and there is no allegation that the amount in controversy exceeds $75,000, exclusive of interest and costs.

5. Affirmative defenses

An **affirmative defense** raises new matters not otherwise in issue by defendant's denial of an allegation in the complaint. Even if plaintiff proves the allegations of her complaint, an affirmative defense entitles the defendant to have judgment in his favor.

Rule 8(c) sets forth what it characterizes as affirmative defenses:

Affirmative defense
Defense pled by the defendant in the answer that, if proven, denies recovery to the plaintiff

> accord and satisfaction, arbitration and award, assumption of risk, contributory negligence, discharge in bankruptcy, duress, estoppel, failure of consideration, fraud, illegality, injury by fellow servant, laches, license, payment, release, res judicata, statute of frauds, statute of limitations, waiver, and any other matter constituting an avoidance or affirmative defense.

Other defenses also have been characterized as affirmative defenses, so you will need to discuss this strategy with the lawyer. When answering the complaint, the usual practice is to label each affirmative defense separately and clearly describe the affirmative defense being asserted, preferably by using the language of Rule 8(c) and elaborating when necessary, as shown below.

<u>**FIRST AFFIRMATIVE DEFENSE**</u>

Plaintiff's cause of action set out in the complaint did not occur within two years before commencement of this action and is thus barred by the applicable statute of limitations.

<u>**SECOND AFFIRMATIVE DEFENSE**</u>

Plaintiff's cause of action is barred by defendant's discharge in bankruptcy.

6. Practice approach

Drafting answers to complaints involves two basic considerations. First, you and the lawyer should respond to every allegation in every paragraph of every count of the complaint, since any allegation not responded to is deemed admitted. A safe practice is to deny, at the end of every count, all allegations not specifically admitted or otherwise answered. Where the allegations are admitted in part and denied in part, make sure that the answer clearly states the facts being admitted and clearly denies all remaining allegations. Clear, simple language is critical here.

There may be times, however, when your side may wish to admit an allegation, even though you are not required to admit it. Remember that pleadings are always interrelated with discovery. If a fact alleged is denied, a plaintiff will invariably focus some of his discovery efforts on the denied fact. On the other hand, admitting a fact may have the effect of preventing further discovery of information that would prove the fact. When that information contains harmful or embarrassing facts, it may make sense to simply admit the allegation in your answer, although you could have—consistent with Rule 11—denied it.

Second, set out all Rule 12(b) defenses and affirmative defenses that you and the lawyer can raise in good faith; it is best to list and label them separately. There is no penalty for raising inconsistent, hypothetical, or alternative defenses. If you are in doubt whether a defense is considered an affirmative defense, the safer course is to raise it in the answer. The real danger is that you will fail to raise a defense with the result that it will be waived. If you and the lawyer need additional time to study potential defenses, it is better to move for additional time to respond than to serve a hastily considered answer.

If the plaintiff has not made a jury demand with the complaint and your side wants a jury trial, you must make an appropriate jury demand on the answer. If the plaintiff has made a jury demand on the complaint, you need not make one, although the safer approach is to make the demand on the answer as well. The jury demand is usually made by putting the words "Jury Trial Demanded" below the case number and the words "Defendant Demands Trial by Jury" at the end of the answer. Local rules usually have additional requirements, such as jury demand forms and fees.

Counterclaim
Claim in the form of a pleading brought by the defendant against the plaintiff as part of the same lawsuit

F. COUNTERCLAIMS

In addition to Rule 12 motions and the answer, both of which are responses to the complaint, a defendant can also **counterclaim**. This is a pleading brought against a plaintiff within the time the defendant has to answer. The counterclaim is functionally identical to a complaint and is made part of the answer. As such, the analytical approach and the pleading strategy for the counterclaim are the same as for a complaint. The plaintiff must respond to the counterclaim, either with Rule 12 motions or a reply, within the usual time limits. Counterclaims are either compulsory or permissive, and substantially different rules apply to each.

1. Compulsory counterclaims

Compulsory counterclaims, governed by Rule 13(a), are claims that a defendant is required to bring against the plaintiff. The purpose of the compulsory counterclaim rule is clear: If the court already has jurisdiction over the plaintiff, the defendant, and the subject matter of the lawsuit, it makes sense to hear and adjudicate at one time all claims related to the occurrence or transaction involved.

A claim is compulsory if four requirements are met:

1. The claim must already exist when the defendant is required to answer the complaint.
2. The claim must arise out of the same transaction or occurrence on which the complaint is based.
3. The court must be able to obtain jurisdiction over any necessary additional parties.
4. The counterclaim must not be the subject of a pending action.

No jurisdictional dollar amount is necessary. The court has ancillary jurisdiction over the counterclaim even if the plaintiff voluntarily dismisses the complaint. However, if the complaint is dismissed for jurisdictional defects, the counterclaim will be dismissed unless it has an independent jurisdictional basis.

The principal difficulty with compulsory counterclaims is in determining if the defendant's claim involves the same transaction or occurrence that gave rise to the plaintiff's claim. While this is often easy to determine in tort claims, such as an automobile accident, it is a more difficult question in the corporate and commercial areas where numerous lengthy transactions are often involved. Courts have devised several approaches for determining whether the "same transaction or occurrence" is involved. These include deciding whether the legal or factual issues are the same, whether the trial would involve the same proof, and whether the complaint and counterclaim are logically related. The purpose of Rule 13(a) is to promote fairness and efficiency by having related claims heard in one trial with consistent results. Accordingly, the phrase in general has been broadly interpreted. The "logical relation" test, the most flexible approach, has the support of most treatises on the topic.

When there is proper jurisdiction over the plaintiff's complaint, the court will also have ancillary jurisdiction over the counterclaims. In addition, since the plaintiff by filing suit chose the venue, the plaintiff cannot complain about the same venue for the defendant's counterclaim. Hence, there are no basic jurisdiction or venue problems associated with bringing compulsory counterclaims.

2. Permissive counterclaims

Permissive counterclaims, governed by Rule 13(b), are claims that a defendant may bring, but is not required to bring, against a plaintiff in the pending lawsuit. A counterclaim is permissive if it does not arise out of the transaction or occurrence on which the plaintiff's complaint is based.

A permissive counterclaim, because it is a claim asserting different grounds from the complaint, must have a separate jurisdictional basis. The reasoning behind the requirement is that a defendant cannot use a counterclaim to bring another claim into federal court that could not have been filed there as an original claim. A permissive counterclaim, in other words, cannot enlarge federal jurisdiction. If the permissive counterclaim has an independent jurisdictional basis, but no proper venue exists in the district where the plaintiff's complaint was filed, it also cannot be brought. Both independent jurisdiction and proper venue must exist before the defendant can bring a permissive counterclaim.

The concept behind the permissive counterclaim rule is fairness. Since a plaintiff has total freedom to bring unrelated claims against the defendant, the defendant should have the same freedom, restricted only by the independent jurisdiction and venue requirements. If the counterclaims make the case too complex, the court can order separate trials on the counterclaims.

3. The United States as plaintiff

When the United States is a plaintiff, Rule 13(d) applies special rules. As a sovereign power, the United States has immunity from suit unless it has waived that immunity and has consented to be sued. No procedural rule can enlarge the types of suits that can be brought against the United States. Accordingly, no counterclaim can be asserted against the United States unless the government has expressly consented to be sued on that type of claim. The only exception is **recoupment,** which is a right of the defendant to have the amount of damages decreased because of defendant's entitlement to damages from the plaintiff. Recoupment can be asserted as a counterclaim to reduce or defeat a claim. This rule does not work the other way around: When the United States is a defendant, there is no equivalent restriction on its right to bring any proper counterclaim against the plaintiff.

4. Statutes of limitation

Statutes of limitation are usually considered substantive law. Federal statutes of limitation apply to federal claims, and state statutes apply to state claims brought under diversity jurisdiction. A counterclaim, like a complaint, must be filed within the applicable statutory period, or it will usually be barred.

5. Waiver and amended pleadings

Failure to plead a compulsory counterclaim bars the defendant from asserting the claim later in another action. Rule 13(a) operates like a statutory bar in both federal and state courts.

If a counterclaim was omitted through "oversight, inadvertence or excusable neglect, or when justice requires," the court may permit an amended answer to include the omitted counterclaim. However, the court cannot allow such a counterclaim if the statute of limitations has run because the concept of "relation back" (discussed in section M at page 183) applies only to amended pleadings, and a new counterclaim in an amended answer is viewed as a new pleading.

Under Rule 13(e), a counterclaim that matures or accrues after the defendant serves his answer may, at the court's discretion, be raised through a supplemental answer. If the court denies it, no prejudice should occur because such a counterclaim is not compulsory, and the defendant can always assert it later as an independent claim. Of course, where the defendant requests leave to file a supplemental pleading early in the litigation process and the counterclaim is based on the same transaction or occurrence as the plaintiff's complaint, leave will usually be granted.

6. Practice approach

A counterclaim is simply a complaint brought by a defendant against a plaintiff in a pending suit. In format, content, and signing, the counterclaim should be drafted like a complaint.[19] The only difference is that the counterclaim is made part of the defendant's answer and is served on the plaintiff's attorney like any post-complaint pleading, motion, or discovery document. It is usually titled "Answer and Counterclaim," with separate headings and sections for each. If there are several plaintiffs against whom counterclaims are brought, the titles should be specific.

If the counterclaim is not included in the answer, it may be waived. To set it off from the answer, it should be clearly labeled a counterclaim; if you are unsure whether the claim is in fact a counterclaim, the safe course is to label it as such because there are no penalties for an incorrect designation. If you and the lawyer are unsure whether your counterclaim is compulsory or permissive, the safe course again is to assert the counterclaim to avoid a possible waiver. Finally, since a counterclaim is analogous to a complaint, you should make a jury demand on those counterclaims that the lawyer wants tried to a jury; failure to do so may constitute a waiver. The plaintiff's demand for a jury trial will not extend to the defendant's counterclaims. An example of a counterclaim format is shown in Exhibit 5.22.

G. REPLIES

The plaintiff must consider how best to respond to the counterclaim and answer. If the answer merely admits or denies the complaint's allegations, the plaintiff ordinarily need do nothing. However, if the answer contains redundant, immaterial, impertinent, or scandalous matters, the plaintiff can move to strike. If the answer contains Rule 12(b) defenses or affirmative defenses, the plaintiff may move to strike "any insufficient defense." In short, all of the Rule 12 motions are available when responding to a complaint.

Exhibit 5.22. Format for Counterclaim in an Answer

COUNTERCLAIM

Defendant Acme Manufacturing complains of plaintiff Wilbur Johnson as follows:
    1. [If the counterclaim is permissive, you must allege the jurisdictional basis for bringing the claim in federal court.]
    2. [Draft the pleading in the same manner as any complaint.]

---

19. See section C.

The plaintiff under Rule 7(a) must reply to a "counterclaim denominated as such." A **reply** is essentially the plaintiff's answer to the counterclaim. There must be a counterclaim in fact, and it must be labeled a counterclaim on the defendant's answer. Only if both requirements are met must plaintiff reply. These requirements relieve the plaintiff of the burden of correctly guessing if the defendant's pleading is a counterclaim or an affirmative defense, since the distinction as a matter of substantive law is not always clear. However, a careful plaintiff will reply to any responsive pleading that may be a counterclaim, even to those not so labeled, since pleadings may be read to the jury during trial.

Reply
The plaintiff's answer to the defendant's counterclaim

Since a counterclaim is the functional equivalent of a complaint, the plaintiff in responding is in the same position a defendant is in when responding to the original complaint. Hence, the plaintiff can respond to the counterclaim with any Rule 12 motions or may respond with a reply. The reply itself can answer the counterclaim, assert Rule 12 defenses, and raise Rule 8(c) affirmative defenses.

Because a reply is simply an answer to a counterclaim, the reply should be drafted in the same manner as an answer[20] and should be titled "Reply." When a plaintiff must respond to more than one counterclaim, the reply should show in the title which counterclaim is being responded to. Exhibit 5.23 shows a sample reply.

H. CROSS-CLAIMS

A **cross-claim** is essentially a complaint brought by one codefendant against another codefendant. Rule 13(g) permits a cross-claim if the

Cross-claim
A complaint brought by one codefendant against another codefendant

Exhibit 5.23. Reply

[Caption]

REPLY

Plaintiff Wilbur Johnson replies to Defendant Acme Manufacturing's counterclaim as follows:
    1. Plaintiff admits the allegations in Par. 1 of the counterclaim.
    2. . . .
    3. . . .
    WHEREFORE . . .

20. See section E.

claim arises out of the same transaction or occurrence that is the subject matter of the original complaint, or relates to any property that is the subject matter of the original action. If a counterclaim has been brought against two or more plaintiffs, those plaintiffs may cross-claim against each other. Also, if a defendant has brought third-party complaints against additional parties, those third-party defendants may cross-claim against each other.

There are several cross-claim rules that must be understood.

1. Discretionary pleading

Cross-claims are always discretionary. A cross-claimant may, but is not required to, bring his claim in the pending action. The cross-claimant can always bring the claim as a separate action. Hence, there are no waiver dangers involved in this decision.

2. Subject matter

A cross-claim must be based on the subject matter of the original complaint, a counterclaim, or property involved in the original complaint. This restriction is designed to protect the original plaintiff from being unfairly forced into litigation that involves a matter totally different from the matters raised in the original complaint, and one in which he may not have any interest. Requiring the cross-claim to arise out of the same transaction or occurrence as the complaint, or counterclaim, or the property involved in the complaint involves the same test and analysis used for compulsory counterclaims.

The Rule allows both matured and contingent cross-claims. Accordingly, claims that the coparty "is or may be liable" for all or part of plaintiff's claim against him are properly raised in the cross-claim. In fact, most cross-claims raise just such issues, usually based on active-passive negligence, indemnity, or contribution.

3. Timing

Rule 13(g) requires that the cross-claim be made in a party's responsive pleading, usually the answer. Accordingly, just as a counterclaim must be made when answering a complaint, a cross-claim also must be made at that time. This promotes efficient and orderly pleadings.

4. Jurisdiction, venue, and joinder

Since cross-claims must involve the same subject matter as the original complaint or a counterclaim, jurisdiction over the cross-claim is considered ancillary, and venue is considered already established by the original pleading. Hence, there are no jurisdiction or venue problems relative to cross-claims. If the original complaint is dismissed, however, the cross-claim also will be dismissed unless it has an independent jurisdictional basis.

Difficulties may arise in a related area, however. Rule 13(h) applies the joinder requirements of Rules 19 and 20 to cross-claims as well as to counterclaims. While Rule 13(g) requires that a cross-claim be brought against a coparty, usually a codefendant, additional parties that are indispensable to the cross-claim must be joined. Where an indispensable party cannot be brought in because jurisdiction over the person cannot be obtained, the cross-claim must be dismissed, although the dismissal will necessarily be without prejudice. The cross-claim can always be brought as an independent action later. Further, if the addition of cross-claims makes the trial too complex, the court can order separate trials under Rule 13(i).

5. Cross-claims against the United States

Cross-claims against the United States cannot enlarge the scope of claims on which the United States as a sovereign power has consented to be sued. The cross-claim, like counterclaims, must be based on a claim that could have been independently brought against the United States. This result appears required by the concept of sovereign immunity, although Rule 13 explicitly requires this only for counterclaims, not cross-claims.

6. Practice approach

The cross-claim, like a counterclaim, must be part of the defendant's answer. It must be served with the answer on existing parties in the same way any pleadings, motions, or discovery documents are served. If the cross-claim brings in new parties that are indispensable under joinder rules, the cross-claim must be served on each new party under Rule 4's summons and service requirements in the same way a complaint is initially served on a defendant.

The cross-claim, like a complaint,[21] counterclaim, or third-party complaint, is a pleading that asks for relief. Hence, it should be drafted like

---

21. See section C.

a complaint. The prayer for relief will ordinarily reflect the contingent liability position of the cross-claiming party. A sample cross-claim is shown in Exhibit 5.24.

7. Responses to cross-claims

When a cross-claim has been served on a coparty, that party can respond with any of the responses permitted to a complaint. The party can make any of the Rule 12 motions or can answer the complaint and raise Rule 12(b) defenses and affirmative defenses. The party responding to the cross-claim must do so by motion or answer within the required time for answering, normally 20 days.

I. THIRD-PARTY PRACTICE (Impleader)

Third-party practice
The method for bringing into an action new parties who may be liable to a defendant for some or all of the judgment

Third-party complaint
A complaint by a defendant in the action against a new party, which brings this new party into the action

Third-party practice, also called **impleader**, is governed by Rule 14. It is a method for bringing into the action new parties who may be liable to a defendant for some or all of the judgment that the plaintiff may obtain against the defendant. The original defendant becomes a "third-party plaintiff" filing a complaint, called a **third-party complaint**, against a new party, the "third-party defendant."

Third-party practice must be distinguished from the filing of counter-claims and cross-claims, both of which involve new claims between original parties to the action. Third-party practice, by contrast, is a procedure by which new parties, the third-party defendants, are added to the action. The process helps carry out one of the principal purposes of federal pleadings: Whenever possible, consistent with jurisdictional limitations, a court should hear all related claims in one action because

Exhibit 5.24.   Cross-Claim

CROSS-CLAIM AGAINST DEFENDANT JONES

Defendant John Smith cross-claims Defendant James Jones as follows:
    1. . . .
    2. . . .
    WHEREFORE, in the event that Defendant Smith is liable to Plaintiff, Defendant Smith demands judgment against codefendant Jones in the same amount, plus interest and costs.

this is an efficient way to resolve multiparty disputes and obtain consistent results.

There are several rules for third-party practice actions that must be understood. The terms usually employed to identify the parties in third-party practice situations are the original plaintiff; the original defendant, who is now also a third-party plaintiff; and the third-party defendant.

1. Discretionary pleading

Under Rule 14(a), an original defendant can serve a third-party complaint on a third-party defendant without leave of court so long as it is done within ten days of serving the original answer to plaintiff's complaint. After that time, the defendant must obtain the court's permission to do so. The original plaintiff, if served with a counterclaim, may under Rule 14(b) also bring in a third-party defendant.

The court retains discretion to allow or deny third-party practice, and any party may move to strike a third-party claim. In deciding whether to allow third-party practice, the court must balance the preference for complete resolution of all related issues with any possible prejudice to the plaintiff. Ordinarily, the court should permit third-party practice; if the case then becomes too complex, it can simply order separate trials on the third-party claims. If the court denies third-party practice, the third-party claim can usually be brought as an independent action.

2. Subject matter

An original defendant, as a third-party plaintiff, may include in his third-party complaint any claim that asserts that the third-party defendant "is or may be liable to him for all or part of the plaintiff's claim against him." However, the original defendant's right to bring third-party claims is broader than would first appear from Rule 14. There are four types of claims that can be brought under the third-party practice rule.

First, and most commonly, an original defendant can bring a third-party practice action based on indemnity, contribution, active-passive negligence, subrogation, or any other theory that passes part or all of the defendant's liability to one or more new parties. Second, the defendant can bring a contingent claim against the third-party defendant. The "is or may be liable" language in the Rule permits accelerated contingent liability claims. Third, the original defendant may be able to bring an independent claim against a third-party defendant, since under Rule 18(a) any party can join claims against another. So long as the defendant has one claim against a third-party defendant that is proper under Rule 14(a), any other independent claims proper under the joinder rules can be added. Finally, the defendant can bring a claim against the third-party defendant that the original plaintiff could not bring directly against the third-party defendant.

3. Jurisdiction and venue

Third-party practice necessarily involves two related questions: whether the new action is proper under the rules, and whether there is proper jurisdiction and venue over the new action. Although a third-party practice action may be proper under Rule 14, this does not necessarily mean that jurisdiction and venue properly exist.

When third-party practice is based on an indemnity type of claim, for instance, ancillary jurisdiction exists, and there will be no jurisdiction or venue problems. This situation is similar to that which exists with the filing of compulsory counterclaims. When third-party practice is based on a claim that is independent of the original plaintiff's claim against the original defendant, however, there must be an independent basis for jurisdiction. This situation is similar to that involving permissive counterclaims.

4. Statutes of limitation

As with any complaint, a third-party complaint is subject to all applicable statutes of limitation. In addition, if the original plaintiff files an amended complaint directly against a third-party defendant, it is considered a new cause of action to which the relevant statute applies. The concept of relation back, applicable to amended pleadings, does not apply here.[22]

5. Practice approach

A third-party complaint under Rule 14 is the fourth type of complaint permitted by the Federal Rules of Civil Procedure, in addition to complaints, counterclaims, and cross-claims. As such, it should have the three basic parts of any complaint: a jurisdictional allegation, a statement of claims, and a prayer for relief. In short, the approach to drafting a third-party complaint is essentially identical to that of the original complaint, although it should recite the circumstances of the already pending original complaint. The document itself is entitled "Third-Party

---

22. See page 184.

Complaint." The caption should clearly show the status of the various parties.

Where leave of court is required, the defendant must move for permission to bring the third-party complaint against the new party. The usual procedure is to attach the proposed pleading and summons to the motion. A request is shown in Exhibit 5.25.

Since a third-party complaint brings new parties into the suit, each new third-party defendant must be served with the third-party complaint and summons as required by Rule 4. A third-party complaint is shown in Exhibit 5.26.

6. Third-party defendant responses

A third-party defendant who has been served with a third-party complaint can choose any of the responses of any party served with a complaint. He may make Rule 12 motions, or he may answer the third-party complaint. He can also assert any defenses that the original defendant may have against the original plaintiff. This protects the third-party defendant who might otherwise be prejudiced by the original defendant's failure to assert all available defenses against the original plaintiff.

Furthermore, a third-party defendant can counterclaim against the original plaintiff directly, so long as that counterclaim involves the same

Exhibit 5.25.   Request to Bring In Third Party

DEFENDANT JOHNSON'S MOTION TO BRING IN THIRD-PARTY DEFENDANT

Defendant Thomas Johnson requests permission to proceed as a third-party plaintiff against Frank Jones. A copy of the proposed third-party complaint is attached to this motion as Exhibit A. In support of his motion Defendant Johnson states:

      1. . . .

      2. . . .

WHEREFORE, Defendant Johnson requests that an order be entered permitting him to proceed as third-party plaintiff against Frank Jones, file the third-party complaint (Exhibit A), and to have that complaint and summons served upon Frank Jones as third-party defendant.

_____

Attorney for Defendant Johnson

Exhibit 5.26.   Third-Party Complaint

UNITED STATES DISTRICT COURT FOR THE DISTRICT OF VERMONT

Rebecca Smith 　　　Plaintiff 　　v. Thomas Johnson, 　　　Defendant and 　　　Third-Party 　　　Plaintiff 　　v. Frank Jones, 　　　Third-Party 　　　Defendant	No. ＿＿＿＿＿＿＿＿＿ Civil Action

THIRD-PARTY COMPLAINT

Defendant and Third-Party Plaintiff Johnson complains of Third-Party Defendant Frank Jones as follows:

1. Plaintiff Smith has previously filed a complaint against defendant Johnson. A copy of that complaint is attached as Exhibit A.

2. . . .

3. . . .

WHEREFORE, Defendant and Third-Party Plaintiff Johnson demands judgment against Third-Party Defendant Jones for all sums that Plaintiff may receive in judgment against Defendant Johnson.

---

transaction or occurrence that is the basis for plaintiff's claim against the original defendant. The court will have ancillary jurisdiction over such a counterclaim. The defendant can also assert cross-claims against other third-party defendants under Rule 13.

Finally, a third-party defendant can also bring a third-party complaint against a new party, who in turn may be liable to him for all or part of the original third-party complaint filed by the original defendant.

The approach for drafting each of these responses is essentially identical to the approach for responses discussed earlier in this chapter. One must be sure that the particular response chosen bears a title that makes clear what type of response it is and identifies the pleading to which it is responding. Where ancillary jurisdiction does not attach to a third-party claim, an independent jurisdictional basis must exist, and there must be personal jurisdiction over the new parties.

Although the pleading possibilities under Rule 14 appear complex, its underlying philosophy is simple: The Federal Rules broadly permit adding parties and claims so that all parties and all aspects of a dispute can be regulated and disposed of in one consolidated proceeding that produces consistent results. If the pleadings make the case too complex, the court can always order separate trials. This in fact is frequently done. The court will try the claims between the original plaintiff and original defendant first. The third-party claims can then be tried later if necessary. Ordering separate trials for the original claims and the subsequent third-party claims will also protect the original plaintiff from any unfairness that might be caused by the addition of the third-party claims.

7. Original plaintiff responses

Under Rule 14(a), after a third-party complaint has been filed, the original plaintiff can file an amended complaint directly against a third-party defendant. This in effect allows the plaintiff to do what could have, and perhaps should have, been done in the first place. However, there must be an independent jurisdictional basis for the amended complaint. If a third-party defendant has counterclaimed directly against the original plaintiff, that plaintiff must reply to the counterclaim within the usual time limits.

J. INTERPLEADER

Interpleader is the procedure under which a party, called a "stakeholder," who is or may be subjected to double liability because two or more claimants are making competing claims on a fund or property, can resolve these claims. For example, a standard situation involves multiple claims on the proceeds of an insurance policy. If the insurance company does not know who should get the proceeds, it may pay the wrong person and later be forced to pay a second time. Interpleader asks the court to decide who is entitled to the fund or property and in what amounts. In an interpleader action, the stakeholder is the plaintiff, and the competing claimants become the defendants.

> **Interpleader**
> Procedure under which a party subjected to double liability may deposit into court a fund or property

There are two types of federal interpleader: Rule 22 interpleader and so-called statutory interpleader under 28 U.S.C. 1335. Each must be considered separately, because substantial differences exist.

1. Rule 22 interpleader

Rule 22 interpleader is in some respects broad, in others restrictive. It is broad because it allows interpleading claims that "do not have a common origin, or are not identical but are adverse to and independent of one another." It also allows the defense that the plaintiff-stakeholder is "not liable in whole or in part to any or all of the claimants." Accordingly, the plaintiff need not deposit the fund in issue with the clerk of the court or post an equivalent bond. The rule allows a defendant in a pending suit to plead interpleader in a counterclaim or cross-claim.

On the other hand, Rule 22 interpleader is restrictive because the usual jurisdiction and venue rules apply. This means that when federal jurisdiction is based on diversity of citizenship under 28 U.S.C. §1332, there must be complete diversity between a plaintiff-stakeholder and each defendant-claimant, a situation that in interpleader cases will rarely exist. The amount in controversy must also exceed $75,000, a determination based on the amount of the fund or value of the property involved. Proper venue is determined under the general venue statute, 18 U.S.C. §1391.

2. 28 U.S.C. §1335 interpleader

Statutory interpleader under §1335, while conceptually identical to Rule 22 interpleader, has significant procedural advantages. First, §1335 relaxes the diversity requirement by requiring that only two of the defendant-claimants have diverse citizenship. Plaintiff's citizenship is not considered. This relaxed diversity requirement allows most interpleader actions to be filed in federal court. Venue under §1397 is proper in any district where one or more of the defendant-claimants resides. Second, the amount in controversy need only exceed $500. Third, under §2361 the court may issue an injunction against any defendant-claimant pursuing another action involving the same fund or property in state or federal courts. Finally, statutory interpleader under §2361 permits nationwide service of process.

Section 1335 requires that the claims be "adverse to and independent of one another," but the claims need not have a common origin or be identical in type. However, the plaintiff must deposit the fund or property with the clerk of the court or post a bond in the amount of the fund or property.

Furthermore, while §1335 itself is silent on whether to allow a statutory interpleader to be asserted in a counterclaim or cross-claim, most courts permit it.

3. Practice approach

An interpleader complaint based on either Rule 22 or §1335 should have all the components of an ordinary complaint: a jurisdictional statement, a statement of claims, and a prayer for relief. Under §1335, the jurisdictional statement should state whether the fund has been deposited with the court or a bond has been posted in the appropriate amount payable to the clerk. The prayer for relief should ask for all relief that is appropriate, including a determination of the amount of liability, if any; a determination of which claimants are entitled to the fund or property and in what amounts; an injunction against any claimants pursuing other actions in state or federal courts based on this claim; and fees and costs, including attorney's fees where permitted. An example of an interpleader complaint is shown in Exhibit 5.27.

K. INTERVENTION

Intervention, governed by Rule 24, is the procedure by which a nonparty having an interest in a pending action can protect its rights by becoming an additional party and presenting a claim or defense. The Rule closely parallels the joinder rules by allowing two types of intervention, intervention of right and permissive intervention.

1. Intervention of right

Rule 24(a) permits two bases for **intervention of right**. The seldom-used basis is if "a statute of the United States confers an unconditional right to intervene." The frequently used basis is Rule 24(a)(2), which sets forth three requirements for intervention of right:

Intervention of right
The ability of a person to become a party to the lawsuit when such a person has an interest in the outcome of the lawsuit

1. The intervenor must claim "an interest relating to the property or transaction which is the subject of the action" pending.

What is a sufficient "interest" remains unsettled because Rule 24 in its present form was enacted in 1966 and the case law is hardly uniform. Various courts have held that the intervenor's interest must be "direct," "substantial," or "significantly protectable." An analysis of the intervenor's claimed interest, of the relief sought, and of the nature of the claims and defenses asserted in the pending action is required.

2. The intervenor must be "so situated that the disposition of the action may as a practical matter impair or impede his ability to protect that interest."

Exhibit 5.27. Interpleader Complaint

Whole Life Insurance Co., a
corporation
Plaintiff

v.

Thomas Smith
and
James Smith,
Defendants

No. _____

Civil Action

COMPLAINT FOR INTERPLEADER

Plaintiff Whole Life Insurance Co. complains of defendants Thomas Smith and James Smith as follows:

Jurisdictional Allegation

1. Jurisdiction in this action is based on 28 U.S.C. §1335. Defendant Thomas Smith is a citizen of the State of Maine. Defendant James Smith is a citizen of the State of Vermont. The amount in controversy exceeds the sum of $500, exclusive of interest and costs.

or

1. Jurisdiction is based on Rule 22 of the Federal Rules of Civil Procedure and 18 U.S.C. §1332. Plaintiff is a citizen of the State of New York. Defendant Thomas Smith is a citizen of the State of Maine. Defendant James Smith is a citizen of the State of Vermont. The amount in controversy exceeds the sum of $75,000, exclusive of interest and costs.

2. On June 1, 2000, plaintiff issued a life insurance policy on the life of Franklin Smith. A copy of that policy is attached as Exhibit A.

3. . . .

4. . . .

5. By reason of the defendants' conflicting claims, plaintiff cannot determine with certainty which defendant[, if either,] is entitled to any proceeds of the policy [or, if either is entitled, in what amount].

6. Plaintiff has deposited the face amount of the policy, $80,000, with the clerk of the court. [Required only under §1335 interpleader.]

Exhibit 5.27. Continued

> WHEREFORE, plaintiff requests that the court enter a judgment finding that:
>
>   (1) Neither defendant is entitled to recover any money from the policy [permitted only under Rule 22 interpleader];
>
>   (2) Each defendant is permanently enjoined from pursuing any other actions or claims on this policy [permitted only under § 1335 interpleader];
>
>   (3) If this court finds the policy in force at the time of Franklin Smith's death, that the defendants be required to interplead and settle their claims on the policy between themselves, and that plaintiff be discharged from any liability except to any person in such amount as the court adjudges plaintiff is liable;
>
>   (4) Plaintiff is entitled to costs [and reasonable attorney's fees if a passive litigant].

The critical term "as a practical matter" was included to make clear that this determination should include any substantial functional difficulties that might adversely affect the intervenor's interests.

  3. The intervenor must not be "adequately represented by existing parties."

This requires a comparison of the interests of the existing parties with the claimed interests of the intervenor to determine how closely they are related. If the intervenor's interests are essentially identical to those of an existing party, so that the existing party will necessarily assert the same positions as the intervenor would, intervention should be denied.

2. Permissive intervention

Rule 24(b) permits two bases for **permissive intervention**. The seldom-used basis is if "a statute of the United States confers a conditional right to intervene." The usual situation for such a basis is where the federal or a state government can intervene in a case involving the constitutionality or interpretation of a statute.

The frequently used basis for permissive intervention is Rule 24(b)(2), which permits intervention "when the applicant's claim or defense and the main action have a question of law or fact in common." This involves an analysis similar to that made for the permissive joinder of parties under Rule 20(a). This request to intervene is addressed to the court's discretion, and the court may deny it where the intervenor's request would "delay or prejudice" the rights of the pending parties or inject unimportant issues into the case.

If a court denies intervention, there are no adverse legal consequences because **res judicata**—a legal doctrine that provides that a judgment, once final, is binding on the parties—will not apply to the unsuccessful intervenor. The common situation in which intervention is permitted is when the intervenor has a claim against the defendant that is factually and legally similar to the plaintiff's pending claim against the defendant.

3. Timing

A prospective intervenor must move to intervene in a timely fashion, regardless of whether the intervention sought is of right or is permissive. Both Rule 24(a) and (b) require a "timely application," but where intervention of right is requested, it will ordinarily be permitted regardless of when the application is made because the intervenor's right might otherwise be adversely affected. Despite this, it is possible to seek intervention of right so late in the pending action that it is considered untimely and is therefore denied.

When permissive intervention is sought, the court must consider "whether the intervention will unduly delay or prejudice the adjudication of the rights of the original parties." This requires analyzing the relief the intervenor wants, whether the intervenor will be an active or passive party, and particularly the stage that the pending action is in. Intervention obviously will be more favorably viewed when sought early in the pleading stage than if substantial discovery already has been taken.

4. Jurisdiction

The intervenor's addition to the pending action must meet jurisdiction and venue requirements. Where intervention of right is requested, the intervenor's claim is necessarily closely related to the original action and ancillary jurisdiction will attach. On the other hand, if intervention is not based on Rule 24(b)(1), independent jurisdictional grounds must exist.

Venue should not be an issue, since it is viewed as a personal right and the intervenor is generally held to accept the venue that has already been established.

5. Practice approach

Rule 24(c) requires that the intervenor make a timely motion to intervene in the district in which the original action is pending. The intervenor must attach an appropriate pleading in the event the motion is allowed. The motion, which must be served on all existing parties, should state the reason why intervention is appropriate under the circumstances. A motion to intervene is shown in Exhibit 5.28.

If the motion to intervene is granted, the intervenor becomes a party and has the rights of any party. The intervenor usually cannot contest past orders, but can counterclaim and cross-claim, present any appropriate motions, and fully participate in discovery. Note, however, that the court has power to limit intervention to certain matters if permissive intervention has been granted.

Exhibit 5.28.   Motion to Intervene

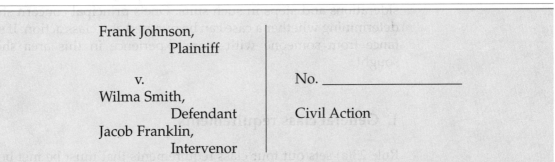

Frank Johnson,
        Plaintiff

    v.   No. _____

Wilma Smith,
        Defendant   Civil Action
Jacob Franklin,
        Intervenor

MOTION TO INTERVENE AS A DEFENDANT

Jacob Franklin moves for leave to intervene as a defendant in this action. A copy of his proposed answer is attached as Exhibit A. In support of his motion Franklin states:

    1. Intervention is appropriate because . . . .
    2. . . .

WHEREFORE, Jacob Franklin requests that he be permitted to intervene as a defendant, file his answer to the complaint, and participate in this action as a party defendant.

ANSWER OF DEFENDANT-INTERVENOR FRANKLIN

Defendant Franklin answers the complaint as follows:
    1. . . . .
    2. . . .

The denial of a motion to intervene raises the difficult issue of whether the ruling is final and appealable. While there is a split in authority on this question, it appears that a motion for intervention of right is appealable if denied, but the denial of a motion to intervene permissively is appealable only when an abuse of discretion is shown. If the motion to intervene is granted, it is not an appealable order.

L. CLASS ACTIONS

The topic of **class actions**—a lawsuit brought by individuals representing a large group of identifiable members—by itself can fill volumes, and literature on the subject in treatises, cases, and journals is extensive. It is a complicated area, one in which inexperienced litigators and paralegals should tread cautiously, if at all. Hence, this section is limited to a brief overview of the class-action requirements and the initial considerations and steps in such suits. One's principal concern should be determining whether a case can be pursued as a class action. If so, assistance from someone with more experience in this area should be sought.

1. General class requirements

Rule 23(a) sets out four class requirements that must be met before the action can proceed as a class action. These apply regardless of whether the class involves the plaintiff or the defendant.

1. The class must be so "numerous that joinder of all members is impracticable."

The Rule itself does not define what a class is or how its members should be determined. Impracticability depends on the type of claims asserted and the persons asserting those claims. Because of this, the numbers necessary for a class action are quite flexible, and the ultimate decision whether a class action is the preferred method of dealing with a claim is left to the discretion of the trial court. While it is usually clear that hundreds of potential plaintiffs or defendants make the action suitable for class-action treatment and that fewer than 30 ordinarily is not enough, the case law on class numbers in the middle range—perhaps 30 to 50 members—shows no obvious pattern. Some of such classes have been held to be of an appropriate number, others not. The outcome is as dependent on other considerations as it is on the number of class members.

2. There must be "questions of law or fact common to the class."

This requires the same type of analysis required for joinder and intervention requests.[23]

3. The "claims or defenses of the representative parties" must be "typical of the claims or defenses of the class."

Also, the representatives must be actual members of the class. In addition, the claims or defenses of the class must be reviewed, and there must be enough representative parties to ensure that each claim or defense is represented fairly. This obviously requires that lawyers and paralegals closely analyze the facts before selecting actual parties and initiating suit.

4. The representative parties must "fairly and adequately protect the interests of the class."

This requirement is directed to both the representative parties and their lawyers. The interests of the representatives must be scrutinized to determine if conflicting interests exist. If they do, a possible solution is to certify separate classes. In addition, the lawyers must have sufficient ability and experience to represent the class competently.

2. General facts requirements

Rule 23(b) sets out three fact situations in which a class action is appropriate.

1. It is appropriate when separate actions would "create a risk of inconsistent or varying adjudications" that would "establish incompatible standards of conduct" for the party opposing the class, or when separate adjudications as a practical matter would determine the interests of the others in the class who are not parties to that adjudication.

The former is commonly relied on in actions against municipal entities to declare actions invalid, such as expenditures and bond issues. The latter is frequently relied on in shareholder actions against corporations, such as to compel declaration of a dividend.

---

23. See Chapter 4, section C.

2. A class action is appropriate when the party opposing the class has "acted or refused to act on grounds generally applicable to the class."

Many of the cases brought on this basis are civil rights actions in which a party is asking for injunctive or other equitable relief under Title VII of the 1964 Civil Rights Act. Some are employment discrimination cases.

3. A class action is appropriate when "questions of law or fact common to the members of the class predominate over any questions affecting only individual members" and a class action is the best method for handling the entire controversy.

This has become the most common basis for class actions, and one that is frequently relied on in antitrust and securities fraud cases. However, a class action under this Rule—Rule 24(b)(3)—is rarely permitted in mass tort cases, such as airline crashes, because the plaintiffs' claims are usually seen as too diverse to justify class action treatment.

3. Jurisdiction

In a class action where jurisdiction is based on diversity of citizenship, the usual requirement of complete diversity between any plaintiff and any defendant is relaxed. Only the citizenship of the named representatives of the class is considered. Hence, through the simple device of selecting as named class representatives persons who are diverse in citizenship to the nonclass party, diversity for class action purposes can ordinarily be established.

The jurisdictional amount requirement is more problematical and often arises in a Rule 24(b)(3) class action. For a long time, the courts have barred aggregating claims to meet the required jurisdictional amount. In a diversity action, each plaintiff must have a claim that exceeds $75,000; in a class action, therefore, the claims of the plaintiff class members cannot be aggregated, nor can the claims of the named representatives be aggregated. This means that each named representative of the class must have a claim that exceeds the jurisdictional amount. In many potential class actions, of course, there are numerous members of the class with individual small claims. In these situations, the jurisdictional amount requirement in diversity cases cannot be met, and the claim cannot be presented in federal court. However, this problem does not exist when the claim is based on federal question jurisdiction because there is no jurisdictional amount requirement. Therefore, the common approach is to raise a federal question as the basis for jurisdiction whenever possible.

4. Procedure

Rule 23(c) governs the initial procedures in a class action. The first two steps are critical. First, the court must determine "as soon as practicable" if the action can be brought as a class action. This necessarily requires an evaluation of the Rule 23(a) and (b) requirements, a determination of what issues can be tried as a class action, and a determination of what the class or classes will be.

Second, in an action under Rule 23(b)(3), the predominantly used section, the court must direct the "best notice practicable under the circumstances," which includes "individual notice to all members who can be identified through reasonable effort." Aside from related concerns such as the actual technical requirements for notice, the ability to opt out of being a class member, and res judicata issues, the immediate concern is a practical one. Notice can be an expensive undertaking, sometimes prohibitively so. For class members whose identity can be ascertained with reasonable effort, notice by first-class mail is usually required; for unknown class members, some form of notice by publication is required. Since each side must bear its costs of litigation, the expense of actually notifying the individual class members can effectively prevent a claim from being pursued as a class action.[24]

M. AMENDMENTS OF PLEADINGS AND SUPPLEMENTAL PLEADINGS

The principal concepts behind the Federal Rules' pleading requirements are that pleadings should accurately notify the parties of the claims involved and that enough flexibility should be permitted so that substantial justice is achieved in every case. Rule 15, the amendments rule, reflects these concerns. Amended pleadings should be freely allowed when fairness requires it—that is, whenever an amendment would create a more accurate or complete pleading and the opposing parties will not be substantially prejudiced. The Rule applies to all pleadings—complaints, answers, and replies.

1. Amendments by right

Any party has a right to amend a pleading once, at any time before a responsive pleading is made. If no responsive pleading is permitted, an

---

24. The Supreme Court has held that in class-action suits brought under Rule 23(C)(2), the party seeking the class action must bear the costs of actual notice to the reasonably identifiable class members. Eisen v. Carlisle & Jacquelin et al., 417 U.S. 156 (1974).

amendment by right can be made within 20 days after service unless the case is already on the trial calendar. A motion that attacks a pleading is not considered a responsive pleading. If an amendment is by right, it is simply served on the other parties; no court action is needed.

When the amended pleading seeks to add new parties, Rule 15(a), permitting timely amendments of right, seems to conflict with Rule 21, which permits additions of parties only by leave of court. Courts have gone both ways on this issue, some holding that leave is always required, others not.

There is also some conflict between Rule 15(c) and state statutes of limitations, which apply in diversity cases. Under Rule 15(c)(1), generally the applicable statute of limitations law is state law. However, in some circumstances, the governing statute of limitations law may be federal. If the federal law would permit a claim that would otherwise be barred, it should be used to save the claim.

2. Amendments by leave of court

Rule 15(a) permits amendments by leave of court. The Rule expressly provides that "leave shall be freely given when justice so requires." The amended pleading can change the jurisdictional allegations, factual claims, legal theories of recovery, events and transactions involved, and even parties to the action. Yet the courts have been indulgent in permitting amendments, and grounds such as oversight, error, or delay by themselves are generally held insufficient to deny leave to amend.

Courts may exercise their discretion and deny leave to amend when, in addition to delay or neglect, there is some actual prejudice to the opposing party. In other situations, the court may grant leave to amend while restricting it to particular matters so that prejudice to an opposing party is minimized. Obviously, the amending party should seek leave to amend as early in the litigation process as possible to minimize prejudice. A motion during the pleading stage will in all likelihood be granted. One made after discovery is underway, however, may well encounter difficulties.

After granting a motion to dismiss for failure to state a claim on which relief can be granted, some courts will not grant a motion for leave to amend if it appears certain that the plaintiff cannot, under the existing facts, state a proper claim. Courts often look to see if the proposed amended complaint properly states a claim before granting leave to amend. If it does not, leave can properly be denied.

3. Statutes of limitation and "relation back"

An important concern in amending pleadings is whether the statute of limitations applies to amended pleadings. This question exists only if the amended pleading is filed after the applicable statute of limitations has run on a particular claim. If the statute of limitations has not run, there is, of course, no concern since the pleading can be timely filed. When the statute has run, the issue of whether the statute will bar the amended pleading depends on whether the concept of relation back, set out in Rule 15(c) of the Federal Rules of Civil Procedure, will apply. **Relation back** is a legal doctrine that permits an amended pleading to be deemed filed at the time the original pleading was filed. In other words, the amended pleading "relates back" to the initial pleading.

Relation back
Legal doctrine that permits an amended pleading to be deemed filed at the time the original pleading was filed

There are two principal types of amendments — changing facts and legal theories and changing parties — that must be considered separately in determining if the relation-back doctrine applies.

a. Changing facts and theories

Rule 15(c)(2) states that if the amended pleading's claims or defenses "arose out of the conduct, transaction or occurrence set forth or attempted to be set forth" in the original pleading, the amendment will relate back to the date the original pleading was filed so that the statute of limitations will not operate as a bar. When the amended pleading alleges an entirely new claim, the concept of relation back will not apply. Whether the claims or defenses in the amended pleading "arose out of the conduct, transaction or occurrence set forth or attempted to be set forth" in the original pleading is an imprecise standard, but courts have been reasonably lenient in permitting amendments, particularly when only a change in legal theory is involved.

b. Changing parties

The more difficult situation concerns changing parties with an amended pleading. Rule 15(c)(3) permits relation back to avoid a limitations bar when the amendment satisfies the same transaction requirement of Rule 15(c)(2) and when the new party added by amendment either actually knew of the suit and would not be prejudiced, or knew or should have known that, but for a mistake in identifying the proper party, he would have been sued.

The first situation involves actual knowledge of the action by the new party. The second involves a misnomer of a proper party, where the proper party knew or should be held to know that it was the target party all along. This is a common problem when commercial parties or the United States government is involved, where determining the technically proper defendants is difficult and sometimes impossible prior to discovery. Cases that have dealt with the question of when a party "should have known" it was the intended party are hardly uniform and should be thoroughly researched.

4. Supplemental pleadings

Under Rule 15(d), a party may move to file a supplemental pleading alleging transactions, occurrences, and events that have occurred since the time the original pleading was served. Permitting the motion is discretionary with the court, which can impose any reasonable terms to protect the other parties.

Since a supplemental pleading by definition raises new matters that have arisen since the original pleading, statute of limitations and relation-back issues will rarely be involved.

5. Practice approach

A motion of leave to amend, like any other motion, must meet the Rule 7(b) requirements. The motion must state with particularity the grounds for the motion and the relief sought. Timely notice must be sent to other parties. The better practice is to attach the amended pleading as an exhibit to the motion. In addition, it is both more convenient and a safer practice to have a complete amended pleading, rather than incorporate by reference parts of the original pleading. It is simply easier to deal with a complete pleading, and responses will likely be more accurate. A motion of leave to amend is shown in Exhibit 5.29.

If the motion is allowed, or the amended pleading is of right, a party that is required to respond to the amended pleading must do so either within the time remaining to respond to the original pleading or within ten days of service of the amended pleading, whichever is greater.

Many motions to permit an amended pleading are made after an opposing party has been granted a motion to dismiss under Rule 12. Here, the dismissed party should move for leave to file an amended pleading within ten days of dismissal. The better and more common practice, however, is that the lawyer move for leave to file an amended pleading and have the motion granted at the hearing on the motion to dismiss, if that motion is granted. In this way, the order granting the motion to dismiss will also contain an order permitting the amended pleading.

CHAPTER SUMMARY

Good pleadings require a solid litigation plan and technically precise drafting. Precise drafting includes knowing the notice requirements for

Exhibit 5.29.   Motion for Leave to Amend

[Caption]

MOTION FOR LEAVE TO FILE AMENDED COMPLAINT

Plaintiff moves for an order permitting plaintiff to file an amended complaint. A copy of the amended complaint is attached to this motion as Exhibit A. In support of this motion plaintiff states:

1. Plaintiff's original complaint was against one defendant, William Smith, and alleged one theory of liability based on negligence.

2. New information, based on both informal fact investigation and discovery, has revealed that another party, Acme Motors, may be liable to plaintiff and that a valid claim against Acme may exist, based on products liability and implied warranty.

WHEREFORE, plaintiff requests that an order be entered permitting plaintiff to file the amended complaint attached as Exhibit A, which adds Acme Motors as a defendant and alleges two additional counts, based on products liability and implied warranty, against Acme Motors.

_____
Attorney for Plaintiff

claims and the format requirements. Even in notice pleading jurisdictions, the complaint must contain a statement showing subject matter jurisdiction, a statement of the claims, and a statement of the relief requested.

The defendant has a number of options when responding to a complaint. The defendant may answer the complaint and allege a number of affirmative defenses. In addition, the defendant may file a responsive motion such as a motion to dismiss, a motion for a more definite statement, or a motion to strike. If a defendant does not file an answer or an appropriate motion, the plaintiff may take a default judgment against the defendant.

The defendant also may assert claims against the plaintiff, called a counterclaim, or against a codefendant, called a cross-complaint, or against a new party, called a third-party complaint. Each of these claims appears in the same format as a complaint. If an individual is not a party to the lawsuit, that individual may have a right to intervene in the action by filing a motion to intervene.

In the event that a party wishes to change or correct a pleading, the pleading may, under most circumstances, be amended or supplemented.

However, if a responsive pleading already has been filed, the party wishing to amend may have to seek leave of court.

KEY TERMS

Affidavit of service	Motion to dismiss
Affirmative defense	Motion to strike
Answer	Notice pleading
Certificate of service	Permissive counterclaim
Class action	Permissive intervention
Complaint	Pleadings
Compulsory counterclaim	Prayer for relief
Count	Reasonable inquiry
Counterclaim	Recoupment
Cross-claim	Relation back
Default judgment	Reply
Impleader	Res judicata
Interpleader	Summons
Intervention of right	Third-party complaint
Memorandum of law	Third-party practice
Motion for a more definite statement	

REVIEW QUESTIONS

1. What pleading is used to commence a lawsuit?

2. What are the four forms of claims that are permitted under the Federal Rules of Civil Procedure? Explain the differences and purposes of each.

3. What is meant by the term "notice pleading"?

4. What is the doctrine of "relation back"? Why is this doctrine important?

5. How may a third party intervene into a lawsuit?

6. Explain the different ways that a summons may be served on individuals.

7. What is an affirmative defense? Why is it important for the defendant to include affirmative defenses in the answer?

8. Explain the differences between a motion to strike, a motion for a more definite statement, and a motion to dismiss. What is the purpose of each?

9. In what situations would an interpleader procedure be used?

10. When does a party have an automatic right to amend a pleading?

ADDITIONAL RESOURCES

www.uscourts.gov. The U.S. Federal Courts home page.

lalaw.lib.ca.us. The Los Angeles County Law Library home page with links to legal resources.

Mauet, Thomas A., *Pretrial* (Aspen Publishers, 2002).

See also the sample form web sites listed at the ends of Chapters 7 and 8.

Chapter

6

LAW AND MOTIONS

This chapter covers the law relating to motions that may be made by the parties after a complaint is filed and before trial begins. The chapter includes

- What the general requirements are for all motions
- How to obtain an extension of time and continuances
- When to serve motions
- When there must be a substitution of parties
- Why a case may be removed to federal court

A. INTRODUCTION

Motions are a significant part of the litigation process. They are used to regulate the routine "housekeeping" matters in litigation, such as the rescheduling of discovery, hearings, and other deadlines. Motions are also used to reach dispositive results, such as motions to dismiss or motions for summary judgment. Every litigated matter will involve motions, so knowing how to present appropriate, well-drafted motions is an essential skill for every litigation paralegal.

A **motion** is simply an application to a court for an order. Presenting an effective motion, however, involves both technical requirements, such as format and service rules, and substantive requirements, which control how the body of a motion should be organized and constructed so that the motion will be persuasive to the judge.

This chapter discusses the technical requirements as well as the law relating to the filing of motions. In addition, there are a number of motions that routinely come up in cases, such as requests for extensions of time and substitution of parties. The rules relating to these motions are also discussed in this chapter. Specific motions are discussed in subsequent chapters.

B. GENERAL REQUIREMENTS FOR MOTIONS

Rules 5 through 11 of the Federal Rules of Civil Procedure govern how motions are made. However, local rules must always be checked, because they often detail matters such as page size, page limitations, format, organization, supporting memoranda and exhibits, and special service times. Although motions may present numerous matters and seek a wide variety of relief, their basic requirements are generally the same.

1. Form

Under Rule 7(b), a motion must meet three basic requirements. It must

1. Be in writing
2. "State with particularity the grounds therefor"
3. State the relief or order requested

Within these broad requirements a great deal of flexibility is allowed, and tactical considerations primarily control how a particular motion is structured.

The format requirements for motions are identical to those for pleadings. A motion must have a caption showing the name of the court, the names of the parties to the action, and a designation of the motion involved. Where there are multiple parties, the name of the first party on each side, with an "et al." designation, is sufficient.

Every motion must be signed by a lawyer representing the moving party. The motion must show the lawyer's name and address, and will customarily include a telephone number. Although some lawyers put the original of all court papers on a blue-backed sheet, Rule 7 does not require it. However, some local rules still require this formality. Again, always check your local rules for any specific format requirements. The format of a motion is shown in Exhibit 6.1.

In some jurisdictions the practice required by local rule is to state only the motion itself and put all supporting points, authority, and agreement on an attached memorandum. Where they exist, these formalities obviously must be followed.

2. Notice, service, and filing

Rule 6(d) requires that a written motion, any supporting affidavits, and notice of the motion and hearing be served on every party at least five days before the hearing date, unless the Federal Rules or a court order alters the time requirement.[1] A notice of motion is shown in Exhibit 6.2. Most local rules require a longer period of time and must be followed. As a practical matter, all documentation that accompanies a motion

---

1. For instance, a motion for summary judgment must be served at least ten days before the hearing date. See Chapter 7.

Exhibit 6.1.   Sample Motion Format

UNITED STATES DISTRICT COURT FOR THE DISTRICT OF IOWA

John Smith,	
Plaintiff	
v.	No. 90 C 182
Johnson Corporation, et al.,	
Defendants	

MOTION TO RESET HEARING DATE

Plaintiff John Smith moves this Court for an order continuing the hearing on defendant's motion for discovery sanctions, presently set for July 1, 2006, for ten days.

In support of his motion, plaintiff states:

1. . . .
2. . . .
3. . . .

WHEREFORE, plaintiff John Smith requests the Court to enter an order continuing the hearing, presently set for July 1, 2006, to July 11, 2006.

Attorney for Plaintiff
Address
Telephone

---

should be attached to and served with the motion. Under the Federal Rules, service by mail adds three days to the notice requirement. Local and state rules may add more days to the notice requirement if the motion is served by mail.

For the convenience of the court and other parties, it is good practice to give more notice than the minimum required by Rule 6 when possible under the circumstances.[2] It is also good practice to call the lawyers for the other parties to select a mutually agreeable hearing date, if possible, before sending out the written notices. This gives the court time to read the motion, avoids disputes over whether notice was adequate,

---

2. Lawyers sometimes give only the required minimum notice, without prior contact, when the motion involved is routine or when the lawyer on the other side is using delaying tactics or other improper conduct.

Exhibit 6.2.   Notice of Motion

[Caption]

<u>NOTICE OF MOTION</u>

To: Alfred Jackson
      Attorney for Johnson Corporation
      100 Madison St., Suite 1400
      Chicago, Illinois 60602

   PLEASE TAKE NOTICE that on June 14, 2006, at 9:30 A.M., or as soon as the case will be called, plaintiff will appear before the Hon. Prentice Marshall in Courtroom No. 22, United States Court House, 219 S. Dearborn St., Chicago, Illinois, and present a motion to reset a hearing date. The motion, with supporting memorandum and exhibits, is attached to this notice.

                                    _____
                                    Attorney for Plaintiff
                                    Address
                                    Telephone

minimizes continuances, and fosters a good working relationship with the lawyers for the other parties in the case.

   A motion can be served in any of the ways set out in Rule 5(b). The standard methods are to mail the motion and notice of motion to a lawyer for each party or have the motion and notice delivered to them or someone at their offices. Following service, the originals of the notice and motion should be filed with the clerk of the court along with a proof of service. Filing must occur "within a reasonable time" after service, but obviously must be done before the date set for the hearing. The usual procedure is to file the originals immediately after service. Be sure you get a copy of the motion, notice, and proof of service stamped "filed" and dated by the clerk to keep in the client's files maintained by your firm.

   Proof of service is merely a certificate, issued by a lawyer or a non-lawyer, that states that service on the other parties has been made in a proper way. The Federal Rules do not have proof of service rules, but local districts usually do. These should be checked, because some rules provide for a certificate from an attorney, while a nonattorney may be required to make a declaration under penalties of perjury or a notarized

Proof of service
A notice that usually appears at the end of a pleading or motion stating particulars about the service of the pleading or motion

affidavit of service. The certificate of service is usually attached to the end of the motion. A sample certificate is shown in Exhibit 6.3.

How do you select the day for the hearing on the motion? Check with the clerk of the court to determine on what days the court hears motions, since practices vary widely. Some judges hold daily court calls; others hear motions only on designated days. Find out what the judge's practice is so that the date you select will be one on which the motion can be heard. Next, check with the lawyer in your office who will argue the motion so that the date is cleared on her calendar. Finally, check with the clerk the day before the hearing to make sure the case will actually appear on the next day's motion calendar and to find out what time the lawyer should be in the courtroom. Many judges arrange their court calendars to hear uncontested and routine cases first and contested matters afterward.

3. Content of the motion

Under Rule 7(b) a motion must be in writing, must "state with particularity the ground therefor," and must state the relief or order requested. Since the Rule permits a great deal of flexibility, the content of a motion is principally governed by tactical considerations: What will be an effective way to present this motion?

The usual procedure is to draft a concise motion summarily setting out the matter and the relief requested and to supplement it with a memorandum of law if appropriate. A memorandum of law is a document setting forth the background facts and legal authorities to support the motion. A declaration or affidavit with any necessary exhibits and supporting documents should also be attached. In this way, a judge can scan the motion quickly, then review the more detailed supporting materials. This format is required by many local rules.

Exhibit 6.3.   Certificate of Service

<u>CERTIFICATE OF SERVICE</u>

I, Karen Brown, state that I served the above motion for a continuance by mailing a copy to the attorney for defendant Johnson Corporation at 100 Madison St. on June 6, 2006.

_____
Attorney for Plaintiff

The usual practice must be informed and modified, however, by such factors as the relative seriousness and complexity of the motion and local practice. For example, a motion to reset a hearing date because the lawyer will be on trial in another case should be brief. The motion need only point out when the hearing is presently scheduled, state where and when the conflicting trial is scheduled, and how long the case will take to try, and then suggest a new date for the hearing. In this situation, the judge will want brevity, and the factual representations by counsel in the motion and supporting declaration should be enough.

At the other extreme, a motion for summary judgment usually must be a thorough presentation of both law and facts. The motion should set out the background of the case, the relief requested, and incorporate by reference a memorandum that thoroughly discusses the applicable law and existing facts. The memorandum should also contain excerpts from the pleadings and discovery, exhibits such as documents and records, and witness statements in declaration or affidavit form. The motion and accompanying materials should be a self-contained package having everything the judge will need to decide the motion.

In short, drafting a motion requires a flexible approach. The relative complexity of the motion, local custom in presenting motions, and even the preferences of the judge all come into play. Motions that are specifically tailored to these considerations—that is, motions that do not mechanically follow a set blueprint—have a much better chance of succeeding.[3]

4. Responses to motions

Once served with a motion, the respondent has two choices: The respondent can either oppose or not oppose the motion. If the respondent is not going to oppose the motion, a common practice is to notify the opposing lawyer of this position; the opposing lawyer will tell the judge at the hearing on the motion that the responding party has no objection to the motion. This will eliminate the need of the attorney representing the respondent to come to court. However, a statement that says the respondent has no opposition to the motion should be filed, since it is good practice to have a written record of your side's position and should eliminate the danger that your position is misrepresented. A sample statement of nonopposition is shown in Exhibit 6.4.

---

3. The motion should be drafted with precision the first time, since no rule expressly allows amendments of motions; Rule 15 applies only to pleadings. In practice, however, amendments of motions are sometimes permitted.

Exhibit 6.4. Statement of Nonopposition

[Caption]

STATEMENT OF NONOPPOSITION TO DEFENDANT'S MOTION FOR ADDITIONAL TIME TO ANSWER

Plaintiff John Smith does not intend to oppose defendant's motion for additional time to answer, nor does he intend to appear at the hearing on this motion presently set before the Hon. Prentice Marshall on June 14, 2006, at 9:30 A.M.

_____
Attorney for Plaintiff

Another approach is to agree to a **consent order**, in which both parties draft an agreed-upon order that disposes of the motion. Although this does not guarantee that the judge will sign it, in practice the judge usually will. This approach is more common in state courts than in federal court.

On the other hand, if you are asked to oppose the motion, serve and file the response in advance of the hearing. The response should set out the reasons for the opposition and include case law and other authority that the judge should consider. Draft the opposition early to allow the responsible attorney sufficient time to review it before the filing deadline. A sample statement of opposition is shown in Exhibit 6.5.

5. Hearing and argument

Although a paralegal is not permitted to argue motions in court, you nonetheless should be familiar with the hearing process. This familarity will give you a better understanding of motion practice.

At the hearing, the judge will usually dispense with all routine and uncontested matters first. These matters can be handled quickly and dispensing with them ensures that attorneys need not wait while more lengthy matters are heard. If the matter is contested, the clerk will call the case. The usual practice is for the lawyers to approach the bench when their case is called and state who they are and which party they represent. Sometimes the judge will make a **tentative ruling**, in which case the party the tentative ruling is against will have the opportunity to speak first in an effort to persuade the judge to change the ruling. If no tentative ruling is given and the motion is a routine one, the judge will

Tentative ruling
A ruling by the judge based on the written briefs submitted by the parties and before oral argument is heard

Exhibit 6.5.   Statement of Opposition

[Caption]

<u>DEFENDANT'S OPPOSITION TO PLAINTIFF'S MOTION FOR LEAVE
TO FILE A SECOND AMENDED ANSWER.</u>

Defendant Wilbur Johnson opposes plaintiff's motion for leave to file a Second Amended Answer, presently set before the Hon. Prentice Marshall on June 14, 2006, at 9:30 A.M., for the following reasons:
    1. . . .
    2. . . .
    3. . . .
WHEREFORE, defendant Wilbur Johnson requests the Court to enter an order denying plaintiff's motion for leave to file a second amended answer.

_____
Attorney for Defendant

---

usually let the lawyers make brief comments, and then the judge will make a decision from the bench and immediately enter an appropriate order. If a significant motion is involved, the judge will probably permit lengthier arguments and take the case **under submission**, meaning that the judge will research and consider the issues further before deciding the motion.

Under submission
Refers to the judge's delaying decision on a motion until the judge has an opportunity for further consideration

With respect to oral argument, each judge's practice is different. Some judges disfavor oral argument and dispense with it altogether for routine motions or, for other motions, give the lawyers very little time to argue. Other judges use oral argument principally as an opportunity to ask the lawyers questions about the law or facts. In this situation, all points must be made in the written motion. At the other extreme are judges who at best scan written motions and rely heavily if not exclusively on oral argument in deciding whether to grant a motion. Most lawyers' preparation for oral argument depends a great deal on knowing what the judge wants to hear.

If the judge's practice is to allow substantial oral argument, the lawyer needs to decide what will persuade the judge to rule favorably. Sometimes, the weight of prevailing law will be persuasive; at other times, the facts of the case. Whatever it is, judges do not want the lawyers to repeat the contents of the motion unless the judge specifically requests that the judge's memory needs to be refreshed.

6. Order

Regardless of when the motion is decided, the court will enter an order. In federal court, routine motions are usually decided by a **minute order**, which is merely a form on which the clerk makes an entry reflecting the ruling. The minute order is then signed by the judge or stamped with the judge's signature, and a copy is mailed to the lawyers. If the motion is important, the judge may prepare a written opinion and order explaining the reasons for the ruling.[4]

Magistrate
An officer of the court authorized to hear routine civil pretrial matters

The court may refer certain motions to a U.S. **magistrate**, since magistrates are empowered to hear routine civil pretrial matters.[5] In recent years, it has become common for magistrates to supervise the discovery process in civil cases. The motion procedure before a magistrate is identical to that before the judge.

C. EXTENSIONS OF TIME AND CONTINUANCES

The kinds of motions that can be presented to the court are limited only by the movant's imagination. Practically, however, the routine housekeeping motions invariably deal with time and date modifications. These are the motions for extensions of time, continuances, and new hearing and trial dates.

Rule 6(b) of the Federal Rules of Civil Procedure governs extensions of time. If a motion to extend time is made before the expiration of the applicable time period, the court may grant the motion for "good cause." However, if the motion is made after the applicable time period has expired, the court may grant the motion only where "excusable neglect exists."

What constitutes "good cause" or "excusable neglect" is in the court's discretion and must be evaluated in the context of the pending case. Courts have generally been realistic and accommodating in permitting extensions of time when the applicable period has not yet run. Usually, any reason other than one involving bad faith and actual prejudice to an opponent will result in the court's granting a reasonable extension of time.

Excusable neglect, on the other hand, is judged on a substantially higher standard. Courts have usually denied extensions of time when the failure to act within the required time limitation was caused by the lawyer's inadvertence or ignorance of the applicable rule or by a lawyer's

---

4. This practice may differ from state practice, where the prevailing lawyer sometimes prepares a draft order reflecting the court's ruling, which the judge then signs.
5. See Magistrate's Act, 28 U.S.C. §§631 et seq.

busy caseload and other work demands. Before a court will find excusable neglect and permit an extension of time, usually an extraordinary situation involving good faith must be present, such as the death or serious illness of a lawyer, a delay by a client in forwarding a complaint and summons, or difficulties in substituting proper parties or different lawyers.

Some time periods for post-trial matters usually cannot be enlarged. These include a motion for judgment as a matter of law (Rule 50(b)), motion for new trial after a judgment as a matter of law has been granted (Rule 50(c)(2)), motion to amend findings and judgment (Rules 52(b) and 59(e)), motion for a new trial (Rule 59(b)), motion to set aside a judgment for reasons such as mistake, fraud, or newly discovered evidence (Rule 60(b)), and appeals from magistrates' decisions (Rule 74(a)).

Any motions for change of time or continuance should be made and decided within the applicable time period. In the motion, give the court solid reasons why an extension is necessary, and ask only for such additional time as is reasonably needed. Above all, avoid missing a deadline. Some time periods cannot be enlarged; others can only be enlarged after expiration upon a showing of excusable neglect. The best way to avoid having these disasters arise in the first place is by creating, maintaining, and following a reliable docket control system, which will remind you and the lawyer of all significant dates for each case you are handling. These vary from simple calendars to sophisticated computer systems, but are critical for every litigation paralegal.

Routine motions for extensions of time or continuances should be structured simply. The pertinent information that forms the basis for the motion can ordinarily be put in the body of the motion. A sample motion for an extension is shown in Exhibit 6.6.

Note that the motion asserts facts in the body of the motion that are based on the lawyer's own knowledge or on information already contained in the court file. In some courts, facts based on the lawyer's knowledge or information do not need to be stated in affidavit form. In other courts, an affidavit or declaration signed under penalty of perjury must be filed in support of the facts. In all courts, the facts must be in affidavit or declaration form and attached to the motion when the facts that are the basis of the motion are within someone's knowledge other than the attorney.

D. SUBSTITUTION OF PARTIES

While an action is pending, occurrences may take place that will require that a named party be replaced by another. Such a substitution of parties can be required when a party dies, becomes incompetent, or loses all legal interest in the action. A public official named as a party can die, resign, or be voted out of office. In these situations, Rule 25 of the Federal

Exhibit 6.6. Motion for Extension

[Caption]

MOTION FOR ADDITIONAL TIME TO ANSWER OR RESPOND

Defendant Robert Johnson moves this court for an order granting defendant an additional ten days to answer or respond to plaintiff's complaint. In support of his motion defendant states:

1. Defendant was served with the summons and complaint on June 3, 2006. Under the rules defendant's answer is due on or before June 23, 2006.

2. Defendant's attorney received the complaint on June 13, 2006.

3. Plaintiff's complaint has five counts and is based on an alleged series of contracts with the defendant.

4. To answer the complaint, defendant's attorney will have to evaluate numerous business records, which the defendant is presently locating, and review them with defendant.

5. Defendant's attorney believes he can prepare and serve an answer or otherwise respond if an additional ten days to answer or respond is granted.

WHEREFORE, defendant requests that this court enter an order extending defendant's time to answer or respond to July 7, 2006.

_____
Attorney for Defendant

Rules of Civil Procedure provides for substitution with a successor party. Unless death abates the action, the court, upon notification and demonstration of the change, will order a substitution. In the case of public officials, the substitution is automatic.

The usual procedure is to make a motion for substitution of parties, state the reason for the substitution in the body of the motion, and attach any necessary documents as exhibits. For example, if a party dies and will be substituted by the administrator of the estate, attach a copy of the death certificate and the probate court order appointing the administrator of the estate.

E. REMOVAL

Removal, as discussed in Chapter 4, is the procedure in which the defendant may transfer a case already filed in state court to the federal court for the same district in which the state action is pending. The right of a defendant to remove a case from state to federal court is a statutory right governed by 28 U.S.C. §§1441-1452 and the applicable law is discussed in Chapter 4, section D5. The following sections discuss the practical steps for filing a notice for removal.

1. Should you remove?

Removal is nothing more than a change from a state to a federal forum. Consequently, there is no point in removing unless the defendant will benefit from the change. The potential advantages include a quicker trial date, since federal courts frequently have less of a backlog than state courts. Many federal districts, however, make diversity cases the lowest priority on the trial calendar. Another potential advantage is the procedural differences that may exist between the state and federal courts. For example, the pleading possibilities may be greater and the discovery rights broader in federal court. Also, the Federal Rules of Evidence may be more relaxed on admissibility issues than the state evidence rules. Removing to federal court is also a way of getting the case away from an unfavorable judge. Also, federal jury panels are usually from a larger geographical pool and may have different characteristics from those of a state jury panel. Finally, changing to federal court may result in different substantive law being applied in diversity cases. These types of strategic possibilities must be carefully evaluated before proceeding further.

2. What are the procedural requirements for removal?

If the lawyer decides that removal is the proper course, make sure that you follow the procedures set out in 28 U.S.C. §§1446-1450, since case law requires that the procedures be closely followed. There are several basic steps that are requirements of the removal process.

a. Timing

Under § 1446(b), the notice for removal must be filed in the federal district court in the division in which the state action is pending within 30 days after the defendant receives notice of the plaintiff's initial pleading. Accordingly, defendants must act quickly in removing a case.

b. Notice of removal

A verified petition for removal is no longer required under the Federal Rules. Instead a party must simply give notice of the removal. A sample notice is shown in Exhibit 6.7.

Exhibit 6.7.   Notice of Removal

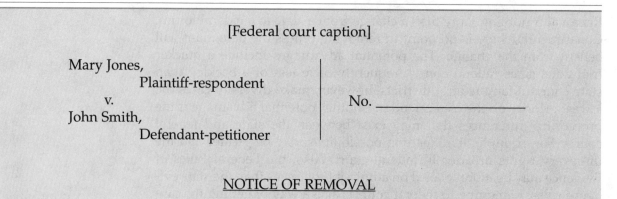

[Federal court caption]

Mary Jones,
          Plaintiff-respondent
     v.   No. _____
John Smith,
          Defendant-petitioner

NOTICE OF REMOVAL

To: The United States District Court for the District of Arizona:

Defendant John Smith hereby removes the above captioned case from the Superior Court of Pima County, Arizona, to the United States District Court for the District of Arizona, Southern Division. In support of this removal defendant states:

1. Plaintiff Mary Jones commenced this action against defendant John Smith in the Superior Court of Pima County under the caption of "Mary Jones, Plaintiff v. John Smith, Defendant," Docket No. 90 C 10478, by serving a copy of the complaint and summons on defendant on June 3, 2006.

2. A copy of the complaint and summons is attached to this petition. No other pleadings or other proceedings have been filed or taken to date.

3. This action is a civil action and is one over which this court has original jurisdiction under 28 U.S.C. §1331 [and/or §1332, etc.] and is an action that can be removed on the petition of defendant to this District Court pursuant to 28 U.S.C. §1441.

4. [If federal question:] This court has original jurisdiction over this action because it appears from plaintiff's complaint that this is a civil action that arises under the _____

Act, _____ U.S.C. § _____, [or Constitution or treaty] because plaintiff claims that . . . .

Exhibit 6.7.   *Continued*

5. [If diversity:] This court has original jurisdiction over this action because it appears from plaintiff's complaint that this is a civil action, and:

(a) Plaintiff, both when this action was commenced and now, was and is a citizen of the State of California.

(b) Defendant, both when this action was commenced and now, was and is a citizen of the State of Nevada. Defendant was not, when this action was commenced, nor is he now, a citizen of the State of Arizona.

(c) The amount in controversy, exclusive of interest and costs, exceeds $75,000.

_____
Attorney for Defendant

[Verification]

c. Filing a notice in state court

A notice of removal should be filed with the clerk of the state court. This act terminates the jurisdiction of the state court. Notice must also be given to all the adverse parties.

d. Further proceedings

Once the notice is filed, removal is complete. There is no order required to effect removal. The district court retains jurisdiction unless and until the case is remanded, and can proceed as with any other case.

The usual status of affairs after a case has been removed is that the defendant who has been served has not yet responded to the complaint, and other defendants have not been served. The served defendant must, under Rule 81(c), answer or otherwise plead within 20 days of receipt of the initial pleading or summons, or within 5 days of filing the removal petition, whichever is longer. The answer or other response must comply with the federal pleading rules. If plaintiff has not served all defendants before the removal petition is filed, service must be made in compliance with Rule 4. In short, all action taken after removal must be taken under the Federal Rules.

CHAPTER SUMMARY

This chapter has provided an overview of the general law and procedures relating to motions. All motions must be in writing and contain a caption, a statement of the grounds for the motion, the relief or order requested, and the signature of the lawyer representing the moving party. Beyond these general requirements, specific requirements must also be met depending on the type of motion. For example, the usual procedure is to draft a concise statement setting forth the matter and relief requested, and to supplement the statement with a memorandum of law. Of course, local rules must be consulted, since some courts require notices to accompany the motion and may also require affidavits or declarations.

After the motion and any opposition papers are filed, the court may hear oral argument. Sometimes, the judge issues a tentative ruling in advance of the oral argument. After the oral argument, the judge may issue a ruling from the bench or else take the matter under submission. Once a ruling is made, the clerk will enter the ruling in a minute order. A formal order also may be prepared by either the judge or the lawyer for the party in whose favor the judge ruled.

KEY TERMS

Consent order	Proof of service
Magistrate	Removal
Memorandum of law	Tentative ruling
Minute order	Under submission
Motion	

REVIEW QUESTIONS

1. What are the three basic requirements that all motions must meet?

2. What must the respondent do to oppose a motion?

3. What is a "minute order"?

4. Under what circumstances might a court deny a motion to extend time?

5. If a motion contains facts that are within someone's knowledge other than the attorney, what document must also be filed with the motion?

6. What is the procedure for substituting parties during the course of a pending lawsuit?

7. What document must the defendant file if the defendant wants to remove an action to federal court?

8. How many days does the defendant have to remove an action to federal court after the defendant receives notice of the plaintiff's state court complaint?

ADDITIONAL RESOURCES

www.washlaw.edu. Information on state, federal, and international laws.

www.lawsource.com/also. American Law Sources On-line: compilation of links to legal sites.

Chapter 7

MOTION PRACTICE

This chapter discusses the particular types of motions that a party can make after the pleadings are complete. In this chapter, you will learn

◆ How to draft a motion for judgment on the pleadings

◆ When a motion for summary judgment is appropriate

◆ What must be included in a motion for summary judgment

◆ What response the opponent should make to a summary judgment motion

◆ How to obtain a dismissal of a lawsuit

◆ How to cure a default judgment

◆ When consolidation and separation of trials may occur

A. INTRODUCTION

In Chapter 6, you learned the general requirements for all motions. However, there are certain motions that have special requirements. Two of the major motions that may be brought after the pleadings are complete, but before trial, are judgment on the pleadings and summary judgment. This chapter discusses how to make these motions and appropriate responses to the motions.

Other motions that may arise during this stage are dismissals and defaults. Voluntary dismissals can be done either by simply giving notice or by stipulation. However, involuntary dismissals require a motion as discussed in this chapter.

Motions for default judgment can be taken against a defendant that does not respond to a complaint. If a default judgment is entered, under certain circumstances a defendant may make a motion to vacate the default.

Although this chapter discusses some of the motions that may arise during the course of a lawsuit, there are many other motions that you may need to address at different stages of the lawsuit. Pleading motions are discussed in Chapter 5, section D, discovery motions are discussed in Chapter 10, section J, and motions for injunctions are discussed in Chapter 8.

B. JUDGMENT ON THE PLEADINGS

Motions for **judgment on the pleadings** are governed by Rule 12(c). After the pleadings are closed, but sufficiently before trial so that trial will not be delayed, any party can move for judgment on the pleadings. The motion determines if, based on the allegations in the pleadings, the moving party is entitled to judgment. For purposes of the motion, the movant's well-pleaded allegations that have been denied are deemed false, while the opponent's allegations are deemed true. In short, the pleadings are viewed in the light most favorable to the opponent. It is only when the undisputed facts as pled show that the movant is entitled to judgment that the motion should be granted. If a party presents matters outside the pleadings and the court decides to receive them, the motion is treated as one for summary judgment. An example of a motion for judgment on the pleadings is shown in Exhibit 7.1.

> **Judgment on the pleadings**
> A judgment entered after the pleadings have been filed, but before trial

The motion for judgment on the pleadings is usually made only in cases where "legal" defenses, such as the statute of limitations, are clearly shown to exist. Since under the Federal Rules of Civil Procedure answers need not be responded to, allegations in the answer cannot be the basis for judgment on the pleadings.

Rule 15 provides that motions to amend pleadings should be "freely given when justice so requires." Therefore, if it appears likely that a motion for judgment on the pleadings will be granted, the plaintiff should move

Exhibit 7.1.   Motion for Judgment on the Pleadings

[Caption]

MOTION FOR JUDGMENT ON THE PLEADINGS

Defendant Johnson Corporation moves this Court to enter judgment on the pleadings in favor of the defendant. On the undisputed facts in the pleadings, defendant is entitled to judgment, under Rule 12(c), as a matter of law.

In support of its motion defendant states:

      1. . . .
      2. . . .
      3. . . .

WHEREFORE, defendant Johnson Corporation requests the Court to enter judgment on the pleadings in favor of the defendant.

_____
Attorney for Defendant

---

for leave to amend if the defect can be cured. Under these circumstances, the motion for leave to amend should be attached to the proposed amended pleading. When the motion to amend is made before substantial discovery has been conducted, it should ordinarily be granted, despite the fact that a motion for judgment on the pleadings is pending.

The motion for judgment on the pleadings is closely related to the motion to dismiss under Rule 12(b).[1] Of the seven grounds for a Rule 12(b) motion, the most commonly asserted one is Rule 12(b)(6): failure to state a claim upon which relief can be granted. A Rule 12(b)(6) motion should be made after the defendant has received the plaintiff's complaint and before answering. If the motion is granted, the plaintiff will usually be given leave to file an amended complaint; usually the plaintiff can cure the defect. The litigation then continues.

By contrast, a motion for judgment on the pleadings is made after the pleadings are closed and it has become evident that there is a legal bar, such as an applicable statute of limitations, that will prevent plaintiff from recovering anything. For this reason, a motion for judgment on the pleadings should not be made unless it is clear from the facts in the pleadings, in light of applicable substantive law, that plaintiff cannot recover on his claim. Such motions are infrequently made.

C. SUMMARY JUDGMENT

Summary judgment
A judgment rendered by the court before trial

Summary judgment, a judgment rendered by the court before trial, is governed by Rule 56 of the Federal Rules of Civil Procedure. It is designed to be an efficient method of deciding a case and may be made when there are no genuine disputes over any material facts. A motion for summary judgment can be made on any claim—complaint, counterclaim, cross-claim, or third-party claim—or on a separate complaint for declaratory judgment. **Partial summary judgment** can be granted on fewer than all counts, or on one of several issues within a count, such as liability.[2]

1. When made

A complaining party may move for summary judgment on its claim 20 days after the action has been commenced or after an adverse party has moved for summary judgment. A defending party on whom any such claim has been asserted may move for summary judgment at any time.

---

1. See Chapter 5, section D.
2. In some state courts, partial summary judgment is referred to as summary adjudication of issues. In addition, some courts require that a motion for partial summary judgment must dispose of an entire count or affirmative defense, and not simply separate the issues.

A motion for summary judgment must be served on all other parties at least ten days before the hearing date.

Since Rule 56(a) allows motions for summary judgment early in the litigation process, when to bring such a motion is principally a matter of litigation strategy. While the Rule permits early motions, as a practical matter they have little chance of success before the pleadings have been closed. The motion is usually made after substantial discovery has been conducted, the important facts have become known, and it becomes increasingly apparent that there are no serious disputes over the essential facts.

2. Standards and matters considered

A moving party is entitled to summary judgment only if "there is no genuine issue as to any material fact" and "the moving party is entitled to a judgment as a matter of law." The motion merely asks the court to decide if there are any material facts in issue and whether the substantive law entitles the moving party to judgment. It is not the court's function here to determine what facts are true. In deciding if material facts are in dispute, however, the court can consider the pleadings, discovery, and witness affidavits.

What facts are material is determined by the claim involved and the allegations in the pleadings. The court will review the movant's motion and supporting matters, and determine if any material facts remain disputed. The court will resolve any doubts against the moving party. Keep in mind, however, that the formal pleadings do not dictate the court's decision. If the pleadings show a dispute, but the discovery and affidavits show that no dispute over any material fact exists, the motion should be granted.

If the motion fails to demonstrate that summary judgment should be granted, the opponent theoretically need do nothing. As a matter of practice, of course, the opposing party always responds to the motion with a memorandum and, if possible, affidavits showing why the motion should not be granted. However, if the motion with accompanying materials shows that the motion should be granted, the opponent ordinarily must, if able to, present a response and opposing affidavit to show that disputes over material issues still remain.[3] If the court then finds that disputed issues remain, the motion will be denied.

3. See Celetex Corp. v. Catratt, 477 U.S. 317 (1986), where the Court rejected the notion that the moving party must always support the motion with affidavits showing the absence of a genuine dispute over a material fact. Where a party has the burden of proof on an essential element and fails to make a sufficient showing to establish that element after an adequate time for discovery, there is no genuine dispute over a material fact, and the other party may be entitled to summary judgment without a further factual showing.

3. Hearing, order, and appealability

At the hearing on the motion for summary judgment, the judge will usually allow oral argument, and then ordinarily will take the case under advisement and enter a written order at a later time. The order will set out whether the motion is granted or, if partial summary judgment is requested, on what issues the motion is granted or denied. It will also set out the findings and reasoning that are the basis of the order.

Appealability of the order depends on whether the order disposes of all or only part of the case. When an order granting the motion disposes of the entire case, the order is final and appealable. Where the order grants only partial summary judgment, either for some but not all parties or for some but not all claims, the order may be appealable, depending on whether the court makes it an appealable one under Rule 54(b). That rule permits the judge to make the order appealable "only upon an express determination that there is no just reason for delay" and the judgment is expressly entered.

When the motion is denied, the usual reason is that material facts are still in dispute. An order denying summary judgment on that basis is not final and cannot be appealed.

4. Practice approach

A motion for summary judgment is most frequently successful in simple cases where the "facts" cannot be disputed, such as actions on contracts and notes where the signatures are conceded to be either genuine or fraudulent. The motion is unlikely to be granted in cases where a mental state or a witness' credibility is critical.

Motions for partial summary judgment should be considered in more complex cases when at least one count, or one issue in a count, can possibly be disposed of. This may at least streamline the case and make the remaining counts or issues easier to try. For example, parties in personal injury cases frequently move for summary judgment on the issue of liability, so that the trial will focus only on the amount of damages.

If you are asked to draft a motion for summary judgment, keep several points in mind. First, draft the motion sufficiently in advance of the hearing date to allow time to serve and file the motion. Although the Rule permits service to be made only 10 days before the hearing, or 13 days before if service is by mail, the court will need more time to evaluate a serious motion. In addition, since the opposing party has a right to respond, setting a hearing date well in advance will allow the other party to prepare and present a response. This approach will minimize continuances.

Second, prepare the motion in an organized, progressive way. The better practice is to have the motion itself simply state on what issues summary judgment is being sought. A supporting memorandum should then detail the material facts involved in those issues and refer to the pleadings, discovery, and affidavits to demonstrate that there is no genuine issue over those facts. Finally, an exhibits section should contain those documents and witness affidavits that are referred to in the memorandum. An example of a motion for summary judgment is shown in Exhibit 7.2.

Witness affidavits must be carefully prepared for the motion, and particular care must be taken that they conform to the requirements set out in Rule 56(e). **Affidavits** are sworn statements by witnesses, and their contents should be drafted so that the facts asserted will be admissible at trial. Accordingly, the witness must be shown to be competent and to have firsthand knowledge of the facts. The facts asserted must comply with all other evidence rules. The testimony of each witness is usually set out in statement form, although in some situations a question-and-answer

Exhibit 7.2. Motion for Summary Judgment

[Caption]

<u>MOTION FOR SUMMARY JUDGMENT</u>

Plaintiff Albert Smith moves, pursuant to Rule 56, for an order entering summary judgment in plaintiff's favor on:
   1. Count I of the complaint for the relief requested;
   2. Count II on the issue of liability only;
on the ground that there is no genuine issue as to any material fact in Count I, and no genuine issue as to any material fact regarding the issue of liability in Count II, and that plaintiff is entitled to summary judgment to the extent requested as a matter of law.

In support of his motion, attached are the following:

   1. memorandum of law and fact
   2. excerpts from the pleadings
   3. excerpts from the interrogatories and answers
   4. excerpts from depositions
   5. excerpts from requests to admit and responses
   6. three witness affidavits, marked Exhibits A, B, and C

WHEREFORE, plaintiff Albert Smith requests the Court to enter an order for summary judgment in favor of plaintiff on Count I, and on Count II on the issue of liability.

_____
Attorney for Plaintiff

format may be appropriate. The statement is then sworn to before a notary public showing that the witness has personal knowledge of the facts and that they are true. The notary's attestation and seal should be on the affidavit. A sample affidavit is shown in Exhibit 7.3.

Declarations contain the same content and are in the same format as affidavits. Under the Federal Rules, and the rules of many state courts, declarations may be used instead of affidavits. The only difference between affidavits and declarations is that, rather than containing a notary's attestation, the witness signs a declaration under penalty of perjury.

Exhibit 7.3.   Affidavit

AFFIDAVIT IN SUPPORT OF MOTION FOR SUMMARY JUDGMENT

I, Gloria Patterson, having first been sworn, state under oath:

1. I am a resident of Tucson, Arizona, and have resided there for eight years.

2. Since January 1, 1998, I have been the President of Cross-Country Transportation, an Arizona corporation having its principal place of business in Tucson, Arizona. As president of Cross-Country, I have overall responsibility for its operation, including entering in and approving contracts on behalf of Cross-Country.

3. On June 2, 2006, at approximately 10:00 A.M., I was at the office of Smith Corporation at 100 Main Street, Tucson, Arizona, for a meeting with John Smith, president of Smith Corporation, the defendant in this case. Also present was Adam York, the plaintiff in this case.

4. At the meeting, I saw John Smith sign his name to a contract, a copy of which is attached to this affidavit as Exhibit A. The signature at the bottom of page 5 of Exhibit A is that of John Smith, the defendant.

5. I have seen John Smith sign his name to various documents about 25 times over the past five years. Based on this previous experience, I recognize the signature on page 5 of Exhibit A as that of John Smith, the defendant.

_____

Gloria Patterson

State of Arizona | SS.
County of Pima

Signed and sworn to before me on _____ .

_____
Notary Public

My commission expires on _____ .

5. Opponent's responses

What should the opponent of a motion for summary judgment do? Rule 56(e) expressly states that an opposing party cannot rely on denials in the pleadings to resist the motion. Of course, if the motion on its face fails to show that the movant is entitled to relief, the adverse party theoretically need not do anything. As a practical matter, however, the adverse party should present an opposing memorandum with supporting affidavits to demonstrate that issues of material fact remain. The supporting affidavits will usually present testimony that contradicts the movant's affidavits on some material facts, thus creating an issue of witness credibility. Credibility issues that exist concerning material facts can only be decided by a trial, so the motion should be denied. If the movant's witness affidavits contain information that the witness would not be able to testify to because of evidentiary objections or because the affidavit is improperly sworn to or notarized, these defects should be raised in the opposing memorandum.

D. DISMISSALS AND DEFAULTS

Dismissals are governed by Rule 41 of the Federal Rules of Civil Procedure. There are two types of dismissals: voluntary and involuntary. While the Rule speaks only of plaintiffs, it is clear that the Rule applies to any claimant and therefore to any claim, counterclaim, cross-claim, or third-party claim. It permits dismissals of fewer than all claims against fewer than all parties.[4]

1. Voluntary dismissals

There are two ways to obtain a **voluntary dismissal**. First, if an answer or summary judgment motion has not yet been filed, a plaintiff can simply file a notice of dismissal with the clerk of the court. (See Exhibit 7.4.) No court order is required. The rationale is that the Rule permits a plaintiff to withdraw a lawsuit that is ill-considered or prematurely brought without incurring penalties.

Second, if all parties who have appeared in the action agree on a dismissal, the plaintiff need only file with the clerk of the court a stipulation of dismissal signed by all parties. (See Exhibit 7.5 and, for another example, the Litigation File in the Appendix.) Again, no court order is

Voluntary dismissal
A withdrawal of a claim by the party originally asserting the claim

---

4. Rule 15, governing amendments of pleadings, and Rule 21, governing joinder, overlap Rule 41 and should always be checked.

Exhibit 7.4.   Notice of Dismissal

[Caption]

<u>NOTICE OF DISMISSAL</u>

Please take notice that on June 14, 2006, plaintiff Wilbur Jackson filed this Notice of Dismissal to dismiss plaintiff's complaint without prejudice, pursuant to Rule 41, with the clerk of the Court.

———————————————
Attorney for Plaintiff

Exhibit 7.5.   Stipulation of Dismissal

[Caption]

<u>STIPULATION OF DISMISSAL</u>

The parties, plaintiff Wilbur Jackson and defendant Frank Johnson, agreed on June 14, 2006, to dismiss the above-captioned action, without prejudice, and for each party to bear its costs of suit.

———————————————
Attorney for Plaintiff

———————————————
Attorney for Defendant

required. This is the usual method for terminating a lawsuit following a settlement. A stipulation of dismissal can be filed at any point during a lawsuit.

In all other circumstances, plaintiff may obtain a voluntary dismissal only by court order. The court has power to impose terms and conditions that are appropriate under the circumstances, which may include the payment of costs, expenses, and attorney's fees to the defendant. Under ordinary circumstances, the motion should be granted, unless the defendant can show that some actual legal prejudice would result from a second lawsuit.

As a tactical matter, plaintiff should simply file and serve a motion for a voluntary dismissal of the action, stating reasons for granting the relief. If the court will only grant the motion upon terms that seem unduly harsh or expensive, plaintiff should consider withdrawing the motion and continuing with the action.

Regardless of whether the voluntary dismissal was obtained through a notice of dismissal or court order, the dismissal is **without prejudice**— meaning the claim can be refiled later—unless otherwise stated. However, under Rule 41(d), if a plaintiff later files the same claim against the same defendant, the court can order the plaintiff to pay the costs of the previously dismissed action to the defendant and can order a stay of the new action until plaintiff complies with the order for payment of costs.

Without prejudice
Once dismissed, the claim may be filed again

When the dismissal is made by notice of dismissal, the first one is without prejudice. However, to avoid abuse of the Rule by repeated filings and dismissals of actions, Rule 41(a)(1) has a "two dismissal rule." A second notice of dismissal is **with prejudice**, meaning that the plaintiff is barred from ever refiling the same claim again. (See the example in the Litigation File.)

With prejudice
Once dismissed, the claim may not be refiled

The court ordinarily will not look into the plaintiff's motivation in seeking a voluntary dismissal. The only issues are whether a dismissal would create a legal prejudice to the defendant and what terms the order should include so that defendant's costs and expenses will be reasonably reimbursed. For instance, a plaintiff may dismiss an action that has been removed to federal court even if the only purpose of the dismissal is to defeat the removal and resulting federal jurisdiction, since a defendant has no absolute right to have a case tried in federal court.

Under Rule 41(a)(2), a voluntary dismissal of a claim will not be allowed if a counterclaim has been pled before the plaintiff has served a motion for voluntary dismissal, if the counterclaim has no independent jurisdictional basis, or if the defendant objects to the dismissal. The reasoning behind this rule is that the plaintiff, having previously decided to sue, cannot now use a voluntary dismissal to avoid the counterclaim. When the defendant's counterclaim does have an independent basis for federal jurisdiction, the plaintiff may dismiss his complaint.

2. Involuntary dismissals

Involuntary dismissal provides a method for terminating a claim when the plaintiff or other claimant has been guilty of misconduct. While the Rule mentions only a defendant's motion to dismiss, it is clear that the court on its own motion may dismiss. There are several grounds for an involuntary dismissal.

Involuntary dismissal
Method of terminating a claim when the plaintiff or other claimant has been guilty of misconduct or inaction

First, a plaintiff's failure to prosecute a claim can result in dismissal. This depends on the nature of the case, but includes a plaintiff's lack of diligence in litigating, such as failing to respond to motions or to appear at hearings, and other repeated dilatory behavior. Involuntary dismissal is a drastic remedy and will normally not be imposed unless other remedies are inadequate. Difficult cases often involve situations in which the plaintiff's inaction is a result of his attorney's misconduct, but the plaintiff may have a valid claim. In these situations, the court will usually do something short of involuntary dismissal.

Second, the court can involuntarily dismiss when the plaintiff fails to comply with rules of procedure or with court orders. Rule 41 will govern only situations involving failures other than discovery. (Failures to comply involving discovery will be discussed in Chapter 10.)

Third, under Rule 52(c), a judgment on partial findings, a type of involuntary dismissal, may be entered at trial when the evidence presented by the plaintiff fails to demonstrate that the plaintiff is entitled to any relief. This is permissible only during a bench trial after plaintiff has rested his case-in-chief. This motion performs the same function as a motion for a directed verdict in a jury trial. However, since the judge during a bench trial is also the trier of fact, the judge may evaluate the facts that the plaintiff has presented; in a motion for judgment as a matter of law under Rule 50, the judge must consider the evidence in the light most favorable to the plaintiff.

An involuntary dismissal is with prejudice unless otherwise ordered. Hence, it is a final and appealable order.

3. Defaults

Default
A failure of a party to respond to the pleading of the opposing party

Closely related to dismissals are **defaults**, governed by Rule 55. The Rule allows any claimant to obtain a default judgment against a party that fails to plead or take any steps to defend against the pending action. The usual situation involves a defaulting defendant.

Defaults are allowed only when the claim seeks affirmative relief. If the claim is for a specific sum or a sum that can be computed to a specific amount, a default judgment can be entered by the clerk of the court, provided the defendant is not an infant or incompetent. The plaintiff must present an affidavit to the clerk of the court setting out the facts showing default and the sum due. The affidavit should be in the same form as any notarized witness affidavit.

In all other cases, the plaintiff must make a motion for default at least three days before the hearing. (An example of a motion for default is shown in Exhibit 7.6.) If the defaulting party has appeared in the case, the plaintiff must serve a notice of motion on that party at least three days before the hearing. Even if the defaulting party has never appeared in the case, it is good practice to serve a notice of motion anyway. At the hearing, the court will determine if the allegations of the claim are true and, if plaintiff is entitled to judgment, the proper amount of damages.

Defaults are most commonly obtained in simple cases where a defendant who has been properly served fails to respond in any way to the lawsuit, and enough time has passed so that it becomes obvious the defendant does not intend to defend against the claim.

Exhibit 7.6.   Motion for Default

[Caption]

<u>MOTION FOR DEFAULT</u>

Plaintiff Joan Franklin moves for an order finding defendant Thomas Johnson in default, finding that the defendant owes plaintiff the sum of $24,246.80 plus costs, and for judgment against defendant in that amount. In support of her motion plaintiff states:

    1. On March 1, 2007, defendant Thomas Johnson was personally served with the summons and the complaint, as shown by the affidavit of service on the summons.

    2. Defendant has failed to answer the complaint, has failed to make an appearance, or in any way respond or defend, although over 90 days have passed since service upon him.

    3. Defendant has not responded to three letters sent to him by plaintiff's attorneys. Copies of these letters are attached as Exhibits A, B, and C.

    4. Plaintiff is prepared to testify to her reasonable damages, which total $24,246.80.

WHEREFORE, plaintiff requests that the court find defendant Thomas Johnson in default, hold a hearing to determine the exact amount due plaintiff, and enter judgment for plaintiff and against defendant in that amount.

_____

Attorney for Plaintiff

If the sum due is clear, such as in a contract action for past due rent or in an action for an unpaid bill for purchased merchandise, an affidavit to the clerk of the court is appropriate. In many cases, however, the full damages can only be determined at a hearing, requiring that a motion for default judgment be made.

At the hearing on the motion, commonly called a **"prove up,"** the plaintiff must be prepared to show that service on the defaulting party was proper, that the allegations of the complaint are true, and what the proper damages are. Although judges vary on the formality of the prove-up hearing, all supporting documentation should be available at the hearing and any witnesses that may be necessary to prove the case should be on hand. For example, in an action on a contract, proper service can be shown with the proof of service in the court file. If necessary, the person who served the complaint and summons may testify. The existence and execution of the contract may be proven by calling a witness who was present at its execution. Another witness along with exhibits can prove performance by the plaintiff, typically payment of the contract price. Other witnesses and records can show nonperformance by the defendant and the extent of the plaintiff's damages. Although the court may not require them, or permit witnesses to summarize what they know in a narrative fashion, it is always safer to have all the witnesses available and prepared to testify as if the proceeding were a trial.

A defaulting party can only have the default judgment set aside if any of the reasons under Rule 60(b), principally excusable neglect, are shown. For that reason, take the following steps to minimize the chances that a default will be vacated. First, serve the defendant by the most direct of the permitted service methods. Second, wait an appropriate period of time, at least 60 to 90 days, before seeking a default. Third, during this time send the defendant periodic letters asking for a response and spelling out the consequences of a default. Finally, send the defendant a notice of motion for the default motion, even though this is required only if the defendant has previously appeared in the case.

Taking these steps now will support the motion itself and will make it less likely that the defaulted defendant will succeed in having the default judgment set aside later. The defendant will usually try to vacate the judgment only after steps have been taken to execute the judgment against the defendant's property, such as garnishing a savings account, and the matter suddenly has become "serious."

E. CONSOLIDATION AND SEPARATE TRIALS

Under Rule 42 of the Federal Rules of Civil Procedure, upon motion of the parties or the court's own motion, the court may consolidate separate cases for trial or have parts of a single case tried separately.

1. Consolidations

Consolidation is governed by Rule 42(a) and has several elements. First, actions can be consolidated only when all actions are "pending before the court." This means that the cases have all been filed and are presently pending in the same district court. Second, the actions must have "common questions of law or fact." Typical are personal injury actions by several plaintiffs arising out of a single accident. Third, the court may decide to consolidate only certain issues for hearing or trial, such as the liability issues. This is a discretionary matter for the court and is usually decided after discovery has been completed and the cases are scheduled on the trial calendar.

2. Separate trials

Under Rule 42(b), the court may also order separate trials. This is permitted where separation will create convenience, avoid prejudice, or permit a case to be tried more efficiently and economically. The court has broad authority to separate claims, counterclaims, cross-claims, and third-party claims and to separate issues in any claims or to separate parties. The typical situation involves unrelated permissive counterclaims or third-party claims in which it makes sense to try unrelated claims later or spin off third-party actions to keep the trials simpler. This decision is also usually made only when discovery is complete and the case is on the trial calendar. Frequently, a decision to sever is made at the pretrial conference.

Although the court has authority to separate issues, a problem often arises because the Rule expressly reserves a party's rights to a jury trial. The case law is still unclear as to when a court may order separate trials of issues before different juries. Separate trials on liability and damages issues before the same jury cause no problems, but there is some dispute over different juries deciding the separate issues.

CHAPTER SUMMARY

This chapter has described the common motions you may be asked to draft after the pleading stage is complete. If, based solely on the allegations of the pleadings, one party is entitled to judgment, then the appropriate motion to make is a motion for judgment on the pleadings. However, if the motion must discuss facts beyond the mere allegations in the pleadings, the appropriate motion is one for summary judgment. The motion for summary judgment is the more common occurrence.

A motion for summary judgment is an efficient way to dispose of a lawsuit prior to trial when there are no material issues in dispute. Either side can bring a motion for summary judgment. If the motion is brought on fewer than all counts, a motion may be made for partial summary judgment.

A lawsuit also may be terminated by either a voluntary or involuntary dismissal. If the dismissal is voluntary, notice of the dismissal must be sent to all parties, although no court order is required. If all parties agree on the dismissal, the parties may simply file a stipulation with the court.

A lawsuit also may terminate because a defendant has failed to timely respond to the complaint. If the claim is for a specific sum, the plaintiff may be able to have the default judgment entered by the clerk of the court. In all other instances, the plaintiff should make a motion for a default judgment to be entered.

KEY TERMS

Affidavit

Consolidation

Default

Involuntary dismissal

Judgment on the pleadings

Partial summary judgment

Prove up

Summary judgment

Voluntary dismissal

With prejudice

Without prejudice

REVIEW QUESTIONS

1. What is a motion for judgment on the pleadings?

2. Under what circumstances is a moving party entitled to summary judgment?

3. What are the differences between summary judgment and partial summary judgment?

4. What are the two ways a party may obtain a voluntary dismissal of an action?

5. Identify at least three grounds for an involuntary dismissal of an action.

ADDITIONAL RESOURCES

www.ilrg.com/forms/index.html. Collection of free legal forms.

www.findlaw.com. Link to forms, laws, legal news.

www.chesslaw.com. Free legal research sites; information on state and federal courts.

www.lawguru.com. Links to legal resources and forms.

www.cornell.edu. Legal services and analysis.

8

PROVISIONAL REMEDIES

CHAPTER OBJECTIVES

This chapter introduces you to the various remedies that may be obtained by a plaintiff prior to trial. In this chapter, you will learn

- Why a temporary restraining order or preliminary injunction may be necessary
- How to obtain a temporary restraining order
- When a plaintiff can make a motion for a preliminary injunction
- When a writ of attachment may be obtained
- What a writ of possession is
- How to obtain a lis pendens

A. INTRODUCTION

Provisional remedies
Under proper circumstances, these remedies allow a plaintiff to essentially obtain the relief requested from the defendant before going to trial

Provisional remedies are those remedies that may be obtained by a plaintiff prior to trial. Under the proper circumstances, they allow a plaintiff to essentially obtain the relief the plaintiff is requesting from the defendant without the necessity of trial. Of course, the plaintiff must still go to trial, and if the plaintiff should lose at trial, the plaintiff may be responsible to the defendant for any damages that the defendant may have suffered as a result of the plaintiff receiving a provisional remedy from the court.

There are a number of provisional remedies that you and the lawyer will want to consider at the commencement of a lawsuit. The type of remedy you choose to seek depends on the nature of the action against the defendant and the type of remedy the plaintiff ultimately wishes to recover from the defendant. For example, if the plaintiff brings a lawsuit against a defendant to stop the defendant from taking some action, such as building a house that destroys the plaintiff's view, the plaintiff will probably want to obtain an injunction against the defendant from building the house. However, if the plaintiff were to wait two or three years for the lawsuit to be tried before the plaintiff could receive an injunction, the defendant would probably have sufficient time to build the house before any injunction could stop the defendant. In this situation, the plaintiff will want to receive an injunction prohibiting the building of the house until such time as the lawsuit can be tried and the case decided by the judge or jury. This chapter explains how to obtain an injunction in such a situation. In addition, there are a number of other situations that might be right for some provisional relief. In addition to injunctions, the most common remedies available to the plaintiff before trial are attachments, writs of possession, and lis pendens. Each of these remedies are explained in this chapter.

B. TEMPORARY RESTRAINING ORDERS AND PRELIMINARY INJUNCTIONS

Injunctions are of three types: temporary restraining orders, preliminary injunctions, and permanent injunctions. A **permanent injunction** is a remedy that can be ordered only after a trial on the merits of the case. Temporary **restraining orders** and **preliminary injunctions**, governed by Rule 65 of the Federal Rules of Civil Procedure, are provisional remedies whose purpose is to maintain the **status quo** (i.e., the positions of the parties as they presently exist) and to avoid irreparable injury to the plaintiff until the rights of the parties can be adjudicated. A temporary restraining order can be granted **ex parte** (i.e., without notice to the other side) and can be granted only until a hearing for a preliminary injunction can be held. Its purpose is to avoid an immediate irreparable injury to the petitioning party. A preliminary injunction, by contrast, can be issued only after an adversarial hearing; it maintains the status quo until the case is tried.

> **Injunction**
> Equitable remedy used by the plaintiff to stop certain conduct or actions of the defendant

Both preliminary injunctions and temporary restraining orders are forms of injunctions. Since an injunction is an equitable remedy—a remedy designed to prevent some future harm—it can only be granted if the legal remedies are inadequate. Accordingly, make sure that the underlying complaint asks for injunctive relief and that such relief would be proper if the complaint's allegations are ultimately proved. While Rule 65 governs temporary restraining orders and preliminary injunctions, local rules often have additional requirements that must be met.

1. Temporary restraining orders

a. Law

A **temporary restraining order (TRO)** is governed by Rule 65(b). Its purpose is to maintain the status quo until a hearing upon notice can be held. Since this is an extraordinary procedure, the Rule's requirements must be followed precisely.

> **Temporary restraining order**
> An order from the court temporarily prohibiting a party from doing some act until such time as a hearing for an injunction can be heard

First, a TRO can be granted without notice to the opposing party, but only if three requirements are met. The motion must be supported by affidavit or a verified complaint alleging specific facts that show that "immediate and irreparable injury, loss or damage will result" unless the order is issued before the opposing side can be heard. In addition, the attorney representing the applicant must file an affidavit stating the "efforts, if any, which have been made to give notice" and the "reasons supporting his claim that notice should not be required." Finally, the applicant for a TRO must post security in an amount the court deems sufficient to cover the costs and damages that may be incurred if the party restrained is found to have been wrongfully restrained. All three of these requirements must be met.

Although Rule 65(b) expressly requires only that an applicant for a TRO show an "immediate and irreparable injury," case law generally holds that the applicant must make the same showing, at least on a preliminary basis, as that required for a preliminary injunction. That is, the applicant must show, in addition to an irreparable injury, that there is a likelihood of success on the merits of the case, that the threatened injury to the applicant exceeds any foreseeable injury to the adverse party if the order is granted, and that any order will not be against the public interest. As a practical matter, a court will not enter a TRO unless these considerations, taken as a whole, appear to weigh heavily in the applicant's favor.

Second, if a TRO is granted, the order must specify the injury, why it is irreparable, why it was granted without notice, and describe in reasonable detail the acts that are enjoined. It is limited to the duration set by the court, which cannot exceed ten days, although it can be extended for another ten days for good cause.

Third, the court must set a date for a hearing on a preliminary injunction at the earliest possible time whenever a TRO is granted without notice. The party against whom the TRO was issued can, with two days' notice, move to have the TRO dissolved.

b. Practice approach

Apply for a TRO only under appropriate circumstances. There is a great deal of work involved, and the court cannot properly issue a TRO unless an immediate and irreparable injury will occur without it. Since a TRO is a powerful and extraordinary judicial remedy, courts are necessarily reluctant to grant it except in the most compelling of circumstances. When drafting an application for a TRO, consider the following steps.

First, you must demonstrate in the moving papers an immediate and irreparable injury and an inadequate remedy at law. Common situations involve threatened damage to unique property and proprietary interests. For example, if someone is about to cut down mature elm trees on another's property, if a magazine is about to release personal photographs of a private person without authorization, or if a former employee is about to sell trade secrets to a business competitor, a TRO may be appropriate because in these situations the wronged party cannot be made whole through money damages.

Second, make sure that the court has both subject matter jurisdiction over the claim and personal jurisdiction over the defendant. Lack of subject matter jurisdiction will result in dismissal of the complaint. Lack of personal jurisdiction will make any injunctive relief ordered unenforceable.

Third, moving for a TRO requires that you prepare, file, and ultimately serve several things at nearly the same time. These include

- ♦ Complaint and summons
- ♦ Application for TRO and preliminary injunction
- ♦ Attorney's certificate of attempted notice
- ♦ Witness affidavits
- ♦ Security for costs and damages
- ♦ Court order

i. Complaint and summons

Where a TRO is being sought, the allegations in the complaint will form the factual basis for the motion and must be coordinated with it. The relief requested should include a TRO, preliminary injunction, and permanent injunction. The factual allegations should, like any complaint, show that the pleader is entitled to the relief requested if the allegations are proved. Finally, although not required, the allegations should be verified by the party, since this has the same evidentiary effect as an affidavit. A complaint is verified when it contains a statement that the party has read the complaint, personally knows the facts, and states that the facts are true. Also, the statement must be sworn to before a notary public or, in some courts, at least signed under penalty of perjury.

The complaint is usually filed at the same time as the application for the TRO. This means that the summons will not yet have been served. However, since the Federal Rules require that the attorney state how notification on the adverse party has been attempted, try to have service of the complaint and summons expedited, especially since Rule 4 permits service by private individuals.

The complaint, application, and supporting documents are usually filed with the emergency judge, an assignment that is usually rotated among the active judges. Find out who the present emergency judge is and notify the judge's clerk of the situation.

ii. Application for TRO and preliminary injunction

The application for a TRO should be combined with a request for a preliminary injunction, since under Rule 65(b) a hearing on a preliminary injunction must be scheduled as soon as possible after a TRO without notice is granted.

The application must allege that an immediate and irreparable injury will occur unless the TRO is granted. Since the application must be supported by facts, it usually refers to the verified complaint and accompanying witness affidavits for factual support. As with motions generally, the application itself is usually drafted briefly and refers to the supporting material for the substance. A sample application is shown in Exhibit 8.1.

Exhibit 8.1. Application for a Temporary Restraining Order and Preliminary Injunction

---

[Caption]

APPLICATION FOR TEMPORARY RESTRAINING ORDER AND PRELIMINARY INJUNCTION

Plaintiff applies, pursuant to Rule 65, for a temporary restraining order and requests that a hearing for a preliminary injunction be set. In support of his application plaintiff states:

1. Plaintiff will suffer an immediate and irreparable injury unless his application for a temporary restraining order is granted.

2. In support of his application for a preliminary injunction and a hearing date, plaintiff states:

   (a) defendant will perform the threatened acts, as more fully set out in the complaint, unless enjoined;

   (b) defendant's threatened action, if carried out, will result in irreparable injury to plaintiff;

   (c) a preliminary injunction will not injure or inconvenience the defendant.

3. In support of his application, plaintiff incorporates by reference the allegations of his verified complaint and the facts as set forth in the witness affidavits attached as Exhibits A through C.

4. Plaintiff's attorney's certificate showing her efforts to give notice to the adverse party, and why notice to the defendant should not be required, is attached as Exhibit D.

5. Plaintiff is ready to provide security in such amount as the court determines is necessary to cover the costs and expenses incurred by the defendant in the event the defendant is found to have been erroneously restrained and enjoined.

WHEREFORE, plaintiff requests that the court enter a temporary restraining order against defendant and set a hearing for a temporary injunction at the earliest practical time.

_____
Attorney for Plaintiff

iii. Attorney's certificate regarding notice

Rule 65(b) requires that the attorney for the moving party certify in writing "the efforts, if any, which have been made to give the notice and the reasons supporting his claim that notice should not be required." Notice here includes informal as well as formal notice. The court will clearly prefer any notice over none at all, such as a telephone call to the adverse party, his lawyer if known, or an agent. Accordingly, the lawyer's certificate should show all the reasonable steps she took to give some advance notice to the adverse party. Exhibit 8.2 shows a sample certificate.

iv. Witness affidavits

Rule 65 requires that the applicant for a TRO show specific facts, through a verified complaint or witness affidavits, that demonstrate the required "immediate and irreparable injury." Accordingly, you should

Exhibit 8.2.   Attorney's Certificate Regarding Notice

[Caption]

CERTIFICATE OF ATTORNEY IN SUPPORT OF APPLICATION FOR TEMPORARY RESTRAINING ORDER WITHOUT NOTICE

I, Terry Anton, attorney for plaintiff, make this certificate, in accordance with Rule 65(b), in support of plaintiff's application for a temporary restraining order without notice to the defendant.

1. On June 2, 2006, at approximately 1:00 P.M. I was first informed of defendant's imminent conduct as set forth in the complaint. I immediately began drafting the complaint, this application, and the supporting documents.

2. At the same time I telephoned defendant at his place of business to advise him of this application, but could not personally contact him. I left a message with his answering service, but have received no call from him.

3. I have attempted to locate the defendant's residence and present whereabouts without success.

4. I have no knowledge of any attorney who may presently represent the defendant, and have attempted to learn this without success.

_____
Attorney for Plaintiff

review the verified complaint and determine what additional facts must be shown, and put them in affidavit form. The affidavit should show who the witness is and demonstrate that the witness has first-hand knowledge of all the facts in the affidavit. An affidavit for this purpose is shown in Exhibit 8.3. In some courts, use of a declaration, signed under penalty of perjury, is sufficient. The format for both is similar.

v. Security for costs

Rule 65(c) requires that a TRO cannot be issued unless the applicant provides adequate security to cover any costs and damages that may be incurred by the adverse party if the TRO is wrongfully issued. Accordingly, thought must be given to the likely security requirement. Ordinarily, this means posting a cash bond with the clerk of the court, although the court can set any other security requirement. Since the court will not issue the TRO until the security has been set and met, you should always have the plaintiff prepared to deposit the likely cash bond immediately if the TRO is granted. Check with the clerk's

Exhibit 8.3.   Witness Affidavit Supporting Temporary Restraining Order

---

<u>AFFIDAVIT</u>

I, William Jones, having been first duly sworn, state:
    1. I am the plaintiff in this action, I live at 123 Maple Lane, Denver, and am the owner of that property.
    2. On June 2, 2006, at approximately 8:30 A.M. I saw . . .
    3. . . .
    4. . . .

_____

Name of Affiant

Signed and sworn to
   before me on June 3, 2006.

_____

Notary Public

My commission expires on _____ .

office to determine its requirements for receiving bonds and other security.

vi. Order and service

It is the usual procedure in federal court for the judge or his clerk to issue orders, either minute or full written orders. However, since with a TRO time is critical, it is useful to prepare a draft order for the judge in advance so that it can be immediately signed if the judge grants the TRO. Rule 65(b) requires that the order specify the date and time issued, define the injury, state why the injury is irreparable, state why the TRO was granted without notice, specify the terms and duration of the order, and set a hearing date for the temporary injunction at the earliest possible time. A sample order is shown in Exhibit 8.4.

Since the court's order is not enforceable until the defendant receives actual notice of it, you should attempt to notify the defendant by telephone of the court's order and arrange for immediate proper service of the order under Rule 4.

2. Preliminary injunctions

a. Law

Preliminary injunctions are governed by Rule 65(a). The purpose of the Rule is to maintain the status quo until a trial on the merits can be held, and it has several requirements. These requirements are quite similar to those for issuing a TRO.

Preliminary injunction
An injunction granted after a hearing; maintains the status quo until trial

First, the Rule requires notice to the adverse party. Although it does not specify the necessary time period, the five-day notice period for motions under Rule 6(d) usually applies. Also, notice of the motion must include service of the complaint and summons.

Second, the **movant**—that is, the party making the motion—must post security in an amount the court deems proper for the payment of costs and damages that may be incurred if the party is found to have been wrongly enjoined.

Third, the movant has the burden of showing, through verified pleadings or testimony and other evidence at the hearing, that (1) if the injunction is not ordered, the movant will suffer an irreparable injury; (2) the movant will likely succeed on the merits of his claims at trial; (3) the threatened injury to movant exceeds any threatened injury to the adverse party; and (4) a preliminary injunction would not be against the public interest.

Fourth, if the court orders a preliminary injunction, the order must be specific and state in reasonable detail what acts are enjoined.

Exhibit 8.4.   Order Granting Temporary Restraining Order

[Caption]

ORDER

This cause being heard on the application of plaintiff for a temporary restraining order and preliminary injunction, the plaintiff appearing ex parte without notice to the defendant, the court having considered the verified complaint, witness affidavits, and the attorney's certificate attached as exhibits to plaintiff's motion,

THE COURT FINDS:

1. Plaintiff's threatened injury as described in the verified complaint is irreparable because . . . .
2. This order is being granted without notice to defendant because . . . .

THE COURT ORDERS:

1. The defendant is hereby restrained from . . . .
2. This order shall remain in effect until June 5, 2006, at 5:00 P.M.
3. A hearing on plaintiff's motion for a preliminary injunction is set for June 5, 2006, at 2:00 P.M. and the defendant is hereby ordered to appear in this courtroom at that time.
4. A copy of this order, along with copies of the complaint, summons, motion, and supporting documentation, shall be served forthwith on the defendant.

SO ORDERED:

_____
Judge

Date: _____

Time: _____

The court can consolidate the hearing on the motion for a preliminary injunction with a trial on the merits. If consolidation is not ordered, evidence presented at the hearing on the motion for a preliminary injunction need not be repeated at the trial on the merits. Consolidation is frequently ordered where injunctive relief is the principal remedy sought and the evidence at the hearing for the preliminary injunction would be largely the same as at the trial.

An order granting or denying a preliminary injunction and a permanent injunction is appealable. An order granting or denying a TRO is not appealable. Since the issuance of injunctive orders is addressed to the court's discretion, the order will be reversed on appeal only if it was erroneous as a matter of law or the order was improvidently granted.

b. Practice approach

A preliminary injunction can come before the court in two ways. First, it can be set by the judge as part of an order granting an application for a TRO. Second, the plaintiff can move for a preliminary injunction without requesting a TRO first.

Regardless of how a motion for a preliminary injunction comes before the court, several considerations must be remembered. First, the adverse party must have notice of the motion, which must be given in accordance with the usual notice requirements. Second, the hearing is an adversarial one, with each party entitled to call and cross-examine witnesses. Third, the plaintiff has the burden of proving that an irreparable injury will occur unless the status quo is maintained during the pendency of the action, that there is a likelihood of ultimate success on the merits, that the threatened injury to the plaintiff exceeds any threatened injury to the defendant, and, where appropriate, that the relief requested will not adversely affect the public interest. Fourth, the plaintiff must provide security for costs and damages before a preliminary injunction can be issued. Fifth, if a preliminary injunction is granted, it is in effect until a final trial on the merits, although the court can modify or vacate the order if warranted.

The critical point to remember is that the hearing on the preliminary injunction is, as a practical matter, often the determinative proceeding in an injunction case. Proof presented at the hearing need not be duplicated at a later trial. Furthermore, the court can advance the trial on the merits and consolidate the trial with the hearing. When injunctive relief is the sole or principal remedy sought, the court will often accelerate and consolidate the trial and hearing. The court will frequently order that discovery be expedited. Thus, the plaintiff's lawyer must be prepared to go to trial quickly and present her entire case on short notice.

If the lawyer asks you to draft a motion for a preliminary injunction, it should be drafted both to allege the legal requirements for such relief and to specify precisely what acts are sought to be enjoined. Such a motion is shown in Exhibit 8.5.

Exhibit 8.5. Motion for a Preliminary Injunction

[Caption]

<u>MOTION FOR PRELIMINARY INJUNCTION</u>

Plaintiff moves for a preliminary injunction enjoining defendant, his officers, employees, agents, and any persons working with him, until a trial on the merits is held and final order is entered in this action. In support of his motion plaintiff states:

1. Defendant will act in the manner alleged in the complaint unless enjoined.

2. Defendant's threatened action if carried out will result in irreparable injury, loss, and damage, as more fully alleged in the complaint.

3. The injury to plaintiff, if defendant is not enjoined, will substantially exceed any foreseeable injury to the defendant.

WHEREFORE, plaintiff requests that the court enter a preliminary injunction enjoining defendant from [specify and describe conduct sought to be enjoined].

_____
Attorney for Plaintiff

C. WRITS OF ATTACHMENT

Attachment
Pretrial order of the court seizing property of the defendant for later satisfaction of any judgment received by the plaintiff

Attachment is the legal process in which someone's property is seized to satisfy a judgment not yet rendered. While there are no federal attachment statutes, Rule 64 makes available the attachment procedures allowed under the forum state's law. State statutes often provide for attachment of a debtor's property interest under certain defined circumstances and usually specify the procedures, including service of process and bonds, that must be followed. Some jurisdictions also provide for prefiling attachment or garnishment procedures that may be used to freeze assets that may satisfy any future judgment. The purpose of any attachment is to seize sufficient property or money of the defendant to satisfy any future judgment the plaintiff may obtain against the defendant. This is indeed a very powerful remedy for the plaintiff who naturally would like not to have to wait until a judgment to obtain relief against the defendant. In addition, the remedy protects the plaintiff against a defendant who may have sufficient assets now, but may not have sufficient assets two or three years later, once the plaintiff does have a judgment against him. There are remedies for wrongful attachment, however, so caution is obviously in order.

1. The law

Since attachment law may vary from state to state, it is essential that you check the statutory rules in your state and follow them closely before seeking an attachment remedy. In general, however, there are certain requirements that are standard in determining whether the plaintiff may obtain an attachment against the defendant. Use the checklist below to determine if the plaintiff has a right to an attachment. Only after determining that all grounds for an attachment exist should you seek to obtain an attachment against the defendant.

- ☐ An attachment is available only on contract claims. Thus, if the plaintiff is seeking damages for both contract and tort claims, unless the contract claim is based on separate and distinct facts, the attachment remedy may not be available.
- ☐ The contract claim must be for a specific sum of money. If the amount is not known or cannot be easily ascertained, the plaintiff cannot seek an attachment.
- ☐ The amount owed to the plaintiff must be unsecured. This means that there is no security for the obligation that the defendant has to the plaintiff. If the plaintiff otherwise had security for the obligation, plaintiff's remedy would be to obtain the security from the defendant, not seek an attachment.
- ☐ The claim against an individual must arise out of the individual's trade or profession. This means that a party cannot seek an attachment on any money claim personally owed by the defendant, but only for those claims involving an individual's business.

Once you have determined that there are proper grounds for an attachment, talk with the lawyer to determine whether an attachment should be brought against the defendant.

2. Practice approach

Once you and the lawyer have decided that there are sufficient grounds to seek an attachment, the next step is to draft the attachment papers. In general, the papers will require a motion with notice given to the other side. In the papers, you should demonstrate to the court that all of the grounds for an attachment exist and show that it is probably more likely than not that the plaintiff will prevail at trial.

In rare situations, the court may grant an attachment ex parte. However, in these situations you would have to demonstrate to the court that there is great or irreparable injury that might occur to the plaintiff if relief is not granted immediately. Such cases might include those where the attached property is in danger of being destroyed or sold.

If your client has a motion for a writ of attachment served against her, there are several grounds for opposing the attachment. First, if any of the grounds for an attachment are not met, the defendant should point this out to the court in the opposing papers. If all the grounds are not satisfied, then an attachment will be denied.

Another ground for opposing an attachment is demonstration to the court that the plaintiff is not likely to prevail at trial. If there are sufficient defenses to the plaintiff's claim, the court certainly will not allow the plaintiff to have provisional relief before trial. This does not mean that the plaintiff will not ultimately prevail at trial, only that based on the information presented to the court at this time the plaintiff will probably not prevail. The decision of the court on the writ of attachment, however, cannot be introduced at trial and has no bearing on the outcome of the trial.

Finally, most states have exemptions for the type of property that may be attached to satisfy a writ of attachment. These exemptions include homestead exemptions, which apply to the defendant's personal residences, life insurance policies, motor vehicles, tools of the defendant's trade, and property necessary for the support of the defendant and her family.

D. WRITS OF POSSESSION

Writ of possession
Issued in a case where the defendant has given a plaintiff a security interest in some tangible personal property for repayment of a debt

Writs of possession may be issued when the plaintiff has security in personal property of the defendant. Since attachments are only available for **unsecured** property, the proper remedy if the plaintiff's obligation is secured is a writ of possession.

1. The law

As with attachments, writs of possession are governed by the statutory requirements of state law. Thus, you must check the statutory procedure that governs this remedy for your state. The typical situation in which a writ of possession may be issued is when the defendant has given to the plaintiff a security interest in some tangible personal property for repayment of a debt. If the debt is in default, the plaintiff may then sue for repayment of the debt and delivery of the personal property to the plaintiff. To obtain a writ of possession, the plaintiff should show the following:

- Plaintiff has a security interest in tangible personal property being held by the defendant.
- Plaintiff has an immediate right to possession of the property.
- The property is being wrongfully withheld by the defendant.

If these grounds are met, the plaintiff may seek a writ of possession to obtain possession of the property from the defendant prior to trial.

2. Practice approach

If the requirements for a writ of possession are met, you will need to draft a motion requesting that the defendant turn possession of the property over to the plaintiff. In the motion, demonstrate to the court that all grounds have been met. In addition, you should include a declaration from the plaintiff that explains the security interest in the property. If there is a written security agreement, a true and correct copy of the agreement should be attached to the plaintiff's declaration.

E. LIS PENDENS

A **lis pendens** places a lien on property owned by the defendant. Some jurisdictions require the filing of a lis pendens notice and service on all interested parties whenever a suit involves an interest in real property or tangible personal property. The notice is usually filed in the county office that keeps the public records, usually called the county or city recorder's office. This gives notice of the pending litigation to parties having an interest in the property because prior to purchasing real estate or larger personal property items, potential buyers usually have a title search done to ensure that no one else has an interest in the property they are purchasing. Thus, if anyone purchases the property with notice of the pending litigation, that person must take the property subject to any judgment that may be entered in the litigation.

When your client's suit involves real or personal property, you should always check to see if any lis pendens rules apply. If so, follow them so that a judgment will be valid and enforceable against any parties that purchase the property after the lawsuit has commenced. State lis pendens notice requirements are applicable to federal cases involving real estate. A lis pendens notice is shown in Exhibit 8.6.

> **Lis pendens**
> A notice that is recorded against particular real property alerting potential purchasers that there is a pending dispute

Exhibit 8.6.   Lis Pendens Notice

[Caption]

PLEASE TAKE NOTICE THAT the above-captioned action, by plaintiff Sammy Sobel against Casey Anderson, affects title to and/or possession of real property in that plaintiff seeks specific performance of a contract to purchase the real property located in Los Angeles County at 1325 Northridge Drive, Granada Hills, California, and described as: The Northeast Corner of Lot 345 as recorded in Map 234 page 124.

Dated: <u>August 29, 2006</u>

———————————————
Counsel for Plaintiff

CHAPTER SUMMARY

Provisional remedies are important tools for a plaintiff. In this chapter, you have learned the most common provisional remedies available to plaintiffs in civil litigation. One of the most frequently used provisional remedies is the injunction. Injunctions can only be granted under limited circumstances, and you must be familiar with the injunction rules, so that the papers may be drafted correctly. You also may be responsible for arranging for the posting of a bond in the event a temporary restraining order or preliminary injunction is granted.

Other provisional remedies that you need to be familiar with are attachments, writs of possession, and notices of lis pendens. An attachment is available to a plaintiff when the plaintiff is seeking damages based on a breach of contract. The contract claim must be for a specific sum of money and be unsecured. The defendant may oppose a request for attachment. These grounds include demonstrating that the grounds for a writ of attachment are not satisfied, showing that the plaintiff is not likely to prevail at trial, and finally claiming exemptions for the type of property that may be used to satisfy a writ of attachment.

Writs of possession are used when the plaintiff has security in the personal property of the defendant. This remedy allows the plaintiff to obtain the personal property from the defendant prior to trial.

Finally, you may be asked to file a notice of lis pendens. This remedy places a lien on property owned by the defendant. Some states require that a lis pendens notice be filed and served on all interested parties whenever a lawsuit involves a dispute concerning the ownership of real or personal property. Accordingly, if you are asked to assist in a lawsuit where the ownership of property is in dispute, be sure to check your state rules to determine whether a lis pendens must be filed.

KEY TERMS

Attachment

Ex parte

Injunction

Lis pendens

Movant

Permanent injunction

Preliminary injunction

Provisional remedies

Status quo

Temporary restraining order

Unsecured

Writ of possession

REVIEW QUESTIONS

1. Why might a plaintiff want to seek a provisional remedy?

2. Identify the three types of injunctions. What is the purpose of each type of injunction?

3. What are the grounds for seeking an attachment?

4. When is it appropriate to seek a writ of possession as a provisional remedy?

5. What is the purpose of filing a lis pendens?

ADDITIONAL RESOURCES

forms.lp.findlaw.com. Link to federal and state forms.
www.lectlaw.com. Sample forms.
www.lectlaw.com/def/i046.htm. Explanation of injunctions.
www.legal-database.com. Legal information arranged by subject.
www.law.cornell.edu/topics/injunctions.html. Judicial decisions on injunctions.

9

EVIDENCE

This chapter provides you with an overview of the law of evidence. You will learn

- What constitutes evidence

- Why paralegals must be familiar with the rules of evidence

- How to determine what evidence is relevant

- What evidence is excluded based on the hearsay rules

- Whether hearsay evidence may be admissible under a hearsay exception

- When a witness is competent to testify

- What evidence is protected from disclosure based on a claim of privilege

A. INTRODUCTION

The law of evidence determines which "facts" may be presented to the jury during a trial. Our law of evidence has its beginnings in the English common law but has undergone substantial modifications in the United States. The most significant development in recent years has been its codification, culminating in the enactment of the **Federal Rules of Evidence** in 1975, which have been adopted without substantial alteration by over half of the states.

Federal Rules of Evidence
Rules applicable in federal courts that govern what evidence is admissible

Evidentiary issues are **questions of law** — that is, evidentiary issues that raise legal questions and not factual questions. Thus, the trial judge will make rulings on evidentiary issues. By ruling on motions and objections, the trial judge determines what evidence may be presented to and considered by the jury, the finder of facts during a trial. The law of evidence is the tool the judge uses to filter **testimony** (i.e., oral statements given at trial by witnesses under oath) or **exhibits** (tangible evidence offered at trial) and to determine which will be admissible or inadmissible.

The law of evidence permits only that which is deemed sufficiently pertinent and trustworthy to be received by the jury. The jury is still free to accept or reject the evidence, in whole or in part. A convenient way to consider this filtration process is to remember the three "Rs." All evidence, to be admissible must be

1. **Relevant** (must prove or disprove something in issue)
2. **Reliable** (must be firsthand or otherwise trustworthy information)
3. **Real** (the information must be what it purports to be)

B. THE PARALEGAL'S ROLE

Although paralegals are not responsible for making evidentiary objections at trial, a paralegal must still be familiar with the rules of evidence. Paralegals are charged with significant responsibility during the discovery process and may also assist in preparing declarations and affidavits in support of, or in opposition to, pretrial motions. In addition, paralegals often assist with the preparation of evidence for trial. Accordingly, to perform these tasks adequately, a paralegal must know what evidence is properly admissible.

Familiarity with the rules of evidence in discovery is particularly important. During the course of discovery, numerous documents may be exchanged between the parties. Written responses to interrogatories also will be supplied to the opposing parties. If the documents or any response to discovery contains information that would otherwise be subject to an evidentiary objection, such as the attorney-client privilege or the work product doctrine, the objection may be waived by disclosure of the information to the other parties. Thus, evidence may be admissible against the client at trial that would not otherwise have been admissible if a timely objection had been made.

Declarations and affidavits also must comply with all evidentiary requirements and contain only admissible evidence. **Declarations** are written statements made by a witness and signed under penalty of perjury, while **affidavits** are written statements by a witness made under oath and acknowledged by a notary public. Declarations or **affidavits** that contain inadmissible evidence are subject to a motion to strike and will not be considered by the court. Paralegals drafting these documents should be careful to include only admissible evidence to avoid any motion to strike by the other parties.

Finally, when assisting in trial preparation, the paralegal must be able to discern the difference between what the court will likely allow to be admitted and what the court will clearly rule inadmissible under the rules of evidence. A paralegal familiar with the rules of evidence will be able to simplify evidentiary issues and to assist the lawyer in resolving evidentiary problems in advance of trial.

C. RELEVANCE

To be properly admissible, all evidence must first meet the general relevance test. This test can be summarized by asking yourself three questions:

1. Is the offered evidence "of consequence" to the issues in the action? For example, in a negligence action, plaintiff's contributory negligence is relevant to the amount of damages plaintiff can recover.
2. Does the offered evidence have "any tendency" to make a fact "more or less probable"? For example, in a personal injury action, where the plaintiff is trying to prove that the defendant-driver of an automobile was negligent, the fact that the driver previously lived in Florida or is a Vietnam veteran is irrelevant to the negligence claim and has no tendency to make the fact "more or less probable."
3. Even if relevant, is the **probative** value of the evidence — that is, the ability to prove or disprove a fact — "substantially outweighed" by other considerations? For example, in a wrongful death case, the only contested issue may be the cause of death. If the plaintiff offers color photographs of the victim's body, the photographs should not be admitted because they have minimal probative value (showing only the fact of death, a fact undoubtedly established by other evidence) and are inflammatory.

Consider a breach of contract action in which the contract required that the defendant install a sprinkler system at the plaintiff's home. The plaintiff will need to show that the defendant breached the contract. Evidence from the plaintiff showing that two days after its installation the sprinkler system stopped working is relevant evidence to show breach of the contract. First, the evidence is "of consequence" to an issue in the case. That is, the evidence relates to the issue to be proven. Second, the evidence has some tendency to prove that the installation done by the defendant was not adequate, therefore making the breach of the contract "more or less probable." Finally, the probative value is outweighed by any other considerations since there is little risk here that the jury could be confused, misled, or prejudiced by the introduction of this evidence.

However, assume on the other hand that the plaintiff wishes to introduce evidence on the issue of breach that the defendant had installed a sprinkler system for a neighbor and had given the neighbor a refund for the price paid for the installation based on the neighbor's claim that the installation was faulty. If the plaintiff tried to use this evidence during the litigation, it would probably not meet the relevance test. First, an allegation of the faulty work by a third person does not necessarily mean that the defendant breached the contract to the plaintiff in this instance. Thus, the evidence is not "of consequence" to an issue in this case. Moreover, even if the first test is met, the plaintiff would have a hard time meeting the second and third tests. The fact that the defendant gave a refund to another person does not tend to prove or disprove the fact that there was a breach in the contract between the plaintiff and defendant. In addition, this evidence could confuse a jury and lead the jury to believe that the defendant does poor work on all jobs. For this reason, also, the minimum probative value of the evidence is substantially outweighed by the evidence's potential to confuse and mislead a jury.

If evidence is irrelevant under the general relevance test, the evidence is inadmissible. However, even if the evidence is relevant under the general relevance test, there may be special rules that preclude the introduction of the evidence. Evidence of a person's character or habits, for example, is subject to special evidence rules; in addition, some evidence, while relevant, can be excluded for policy reasons. These rules are found in Rules 404 through 412 of the Federal Rules of Evidence. The key exclusions are discussed below.

1. Character traits

Common sense and experience tell us that a person is likely to act consistently with the kind of person he really is, that is, with his **"character traits."** However, evidence of someone's character traits (such as whether he is honest, aggressive, trustworthy, and so on), although perhaps relevant under the general test, will only be admissible if character is an essential element of a claim or defense. For example, in an action for libel, where the defendant stated that the plaintiff is a chronic liar and the defendant's defense is "truth," an essential element of that defense is the plaintiff's truth-telling character.

> **Character traits**
> A person's distinctive qualities; admissible as evidence only if character is an essential element of a claim or defense

2. Habit evidence

The "habit" of a person may be relevant to prove that the conduct of the person on a particular occasion was in conformity with the habit or routine practice of that person. Evidence of conduct that is routine enough to be considered a "habit" will be admissible.[1] Thus, a routine business practice in handling and processing outgoing mail will be habit

---

1. Fed. R. Evid. 406.

evidence admissible to prove circumstantially that a particular letter was actually put in the mail.

3. Policy exclusions

Certain evidence automatically is inadmissible to prove negligence or fault based on policy reasons: Three of the more common exclusions are evidence of subsequent remedial repairs, payment (or offer of payment) of medical expenses, and liability insurance.[2]

Evidence of subsequent remedial repairs is excluded because a party may not make a repair if the fact that he made such a repair can be used against him to prove negligence or fault. Thus, by excluding the evidence, the policy promotes repairs and improvements. Moreover, such repairs and improvements do not necessarily show negligence, but there is a danger that the jury will think that they do.

Payment or the offer of payment of medical expenses also is excluded because such offers or payments may be motivated by reasons other than fault, but again the jury may think the payment or offer shows fault.

Finally, evidence that a person had liability insurance is not admissible to prove negligence or fault. The rationale is that the existence of liability insurance is simply not relevant to the issue of negligence.

D. HEARSAY

Hearsay represents the second of the three "Rs"—"reliable" evidence. The Federal Rules of Evidence, and the rules of most states, define hearsay as "a statement, other than one made by the declarant while testifying at the trial or hearing, offered in evidence to prove the truth of the matter asserted."[3]

The hearsay rules filter offered evidence and permit only that which is sufficiently reliable to be admitted. You must distinguish between hearsay and nonhearsay. If evidence is nonhearsay, it is admissible. If evidence is hearsay, it is inadmissible unless a hearsay exception applies. Hearsay can be a very complex area. The intent of this chapter is to simplify the hearsay rules as much as possible, without going into

2. The Federal Rules of Evidence prohibit the introduction of this evidence to prove negligence or fault; however, such evidence may be introduced for purposes *other* than showing negligence or fault. For example, the Federal Rules of Evidence do not bar the use of the evidence of subsequent repairs in order to prove ownership, control, or feasibility of precautionary measures, if controverted.

3. Fed. R. Evid. 801(C).

too much detail. You probably will not fully understand the hearsay rules and exceptions until you have had an opportunity to work more with the concepts.

The simplest way to determine if a statement is hearsay is to break down the Rule quoted above into three elements:

1. a statement
2. made out of court
3. offered to prove the truth of the matter asserted in the statement

If the statement fulfills all three elements, it is considered hearsay and subject to exclusion in court unless an exception applies.[4]

1. Is it a "statement"?

Under the Federal Rules of Evidence there are three categories of "statements": oral assertions, written assertions, and assertive conduct (nonverbal conduct that is intended as an assertion). The following examples of testimony of a witness in court are illustrative of the rules.

E X A M P L E

1. "I saw the defendant run the red light." Under the hearsay rules this is not a statement; the witness on the stand is merely saying what he previously saw rather than making an assertion.
2. "John told me he saw the defendant run the red light." This is an oral assertion and considered a statement.
3. "John gave me a note that said: 'I saw the defendant run the red light.'" This is a written assertion and considered a statement.
4. "I met John and asked him: 'Did you see the defendant run the red light?' John nodded his head." This is an example of assertive conduct, since John's nodding his head is the functional equivalent of John's saying "yes." This too is considered a statement.

2. Was the statement made "out of court"?

The hearsay rule does not apply to the actual oral testimony of the witness in court. Obviously, if it did, witnesses could not say anything

---

4. Exceptions are discussed subsequently in section E.

on the witness stand. The hearsay rule does apply whenever the witness, while on the witness stand, repeats any "statement" that either he or another person made at any other time or place. The following are examples of out-of-court statements.

1. "Yesterday I saw John, and he said, 'Tom, your car needs a tune-up.'" This is a statement of John, made out of court.

2. "Yesterday I saw John, and I said 'John, my car needs a tune-up.'" This is also an out-of-court statement, even though the out-of-court declarant is the same person as the witness testifying in court.

3. Is the out-of-court statement "offered to prove the truth of the matter asserted in the statement"?

This final element merely requires you to determine what it is you are trying to prove by use of a statement. In the examples above, if you are trying to prove that the defendant ran a red light or that Tom's car needs a tune-up, you would be using the statements to prove the truth of the matter asserted. However, what if you were using the statements to prove something else? For example, what if you were trying to prove that John could speak, or write, or was present at a certain location? Then, the statements would not be used to prove the matter asserted in the statements, but used to prove something else. Under such circumstances, the statements do not fulfill the third element, and the statements would not be considered hearsay.

E. HEARSAY EXCEPTIONS

The hearsay rule traditionally guarantees reliability by the personal presence of the declarant at trial, under oath, and subject to cross-examination by the opposing parties. The basic reasons for testimonial unreliability are lack of perception, poor memory, inability to communicate, and motive to fabricate. Remember, if evidence is deemed to be hearsay, it is inadmissable unless a hearsay exception applies. Since the hearsay rule is designed to admit only reliable evidence, it may seem strange at first to have any hearsay exceptions. Yet the hearsay exceptions are based, in part, on the premise that the particular circumstances eliminate one or more of the reasons for testimonial unreliability. Thus, after you have determined that a statement is hearsay, you must next determine whether there is any exception to the hearsay rules. If such an exception exists, then the statement will be admitted into evidence. Ten of the most common exceptions are discussed below.

1. Admission of a party opponent

The most common exception to the hearsay rules is an admission of a party opponent. In fact, under the Federal Rules of Evidence, such an admission is not even considered hearsay.[5]

An **admission of a party opponent** is any statement made by an adverse party in the lawsuit. The rationale for admitting the statement is that the adverse party is in court and can hardly complain about the inability to cross-examine himself. In addition, the adverse party can certainly testify in court to either deny or explain the statement that was made. The following are examples of admission of a party opponent.

EXAMPLE

1. **In an automobile negligence action, the plaintiff may offer the testimony of a bystander that the defendant-driver said: "I don't know, but perhaps the light was red."**

2. **In a breach of contract action, the plaintiff testifies that the defendant told her, "I am not going to pay for the goods that were delivered."**

2. Prior statements by witnesses

The Federal Rules treat as nonhearsay prior statements by witnesses that were made under oath at a previous hearing or deposition. Most states either treat the prior statement as nonhearsay or admit the statement as an exception to the hearsay rule. The purpose is to allow prior inconsistent statements to be used to impeach a witness.[6]

EXAMPLE

The defendant states at an earlier deposition that he knew that his brakes were bad before the accident. During trial, the defendant now says that he cannot

---

5. Fed. R. Evid. 801(d)(2).
6. Fed. R. Evid. 801(d)(1). See also section F, infra.

remember whether he knew that his brakes were bad, or that the brakes were not bad prior to the accident. The previous out-of-court statement may come into evidence as an exception to the hearsay rule.

---

3. Statements against interest[7]

When the declarant is unavailable to testify at trial, certain statements of the declarant may be admitted under an exception to the hearsay rule.[8] A statement made by a declarant that is against his interest is admissible as an exception to the hearsay rule. The statement may be against the declarant's pecuniary, proprietary, or penal interest. The statement must be within the declarant's personal knowledge and against the declarant's interest when it is made. It is not enough that the statement became against the declarant's interest at a later time.

The rationale for this hearsay exception is that a witness is not likely to make a statement against his interest unless it is true. In addition, because the witness is unavailable to testify at trial, the evidence is necessary.

The following are examples of statements against interest.

EXAMPLE

1. In an automobile negligence action, plaintiff claims that defendant was the driver of the other car involved in the accident. Defendant denies this allegation. Defendant calls a witness who testifies that he heard Al Jones say the following a few days after the accident: "I was actually driving the car that was in the accident the defendant is getting blamed for." If Jones is now unavailable, the statement is admissible, since it is a statement by Jones against his interest.

2. Defendant is on trial for slander. Susan Bailey testifies that she heard Al Jones say: "Poor defendant is being sued for slander when I am the one who slandered the plaintiff." Again, if Jones is now unavailable, the statement is admissible.

---

7. Fed. R. Evid. 804(b)(3).

8. Some exceptions to the hearsay rule require that a witness be unavailable in order for the exception to apply. Under the Federal Rules of Evidence, "unavailable" means that the witness is exempted by the court from testifying on the grounds of privilege, refusal to testify, testifying to a lack of memory, or inability to be present or testify at the hearing because of illness or infirmity, or that the proponent of the statement is unable to compel the declarant's attendance at the hearing by process or other reasonable means.

The statements against interest are not the same as admissions by party opponents. The differences are illustrated in the following chart:

Admissions by a Party Opponent	*Statements Against Interest*
a. only by a party opponent	a. by any witness
b. need not be unavailable	b. witness must be unavailable
c. need not be against interest when made	c. must be against interest of witness when made
d. need not be within personal knowledge of party	d. must be within personal knowledge of declarant

4. Former testimony[9]

If a witness is unavailable, former testimony of the witness may be admissible. To be admissible, the following requirements must be met. First, the witness must be unavailable. Second, the former testimony must have been given under oath in another action or at a former hearing or trial in the same action. Under the Federal Rules, former testimony also includes depositions taken in the same action, although this is not the case under some state rules. Third, the former testimony must have been offered by the adversary in the former proceeding, or if it was offered against the adversary in the former proceeding, the adversary must have had an opportunity to examine the witness with the same opportunity and motive as it does now. If the adversary was not a party to the former proceeding, then the former testimony may be used in civil cases only if the person against whom the testimony was offered in the former proceeding has the same motive and interest as the adversary now.

When faced with a former testimony situation, one should analyze the statement by asking four questions:

1. Is the witness unavailable?
2. Was the testimony under oath in a former action or proceeding?
3. Was the former testimony offered against the same party you wish to offer the evidence against now or the party's predecessor in interest?
4. Did the opposing party or the predecessor in interest have the same motive and opportunity to examine the witness then as now?

The following example shows how to determine whether former testimony is admissible.

---

9. Fed. R. Evid. 804(b)(1).

Plaintiff Smith sues Jones, the defendant-driver, for negligence arising from an automobile accident. During the trial, plaintiff called Williams as a witness, and defendant called Franklin as a witness. Both Williams and Franklin were eyewitnesses to the accident.

In a separate action, Roberts, a passenger in Smith's car, also sues Jones. Neither Williams nor Franklin is now available. Plaintiff Roberts wants to introduce into the trial the former testimony of Williams, and Jones wants to introduce the transcript of Franklin's former testimony. Can they introduce the testimony?

The answer depends on which witness is involved:

1. Williams' former testimony is admissible. He is presently unavailable, the testimony is being offered against Jones, the same party, and Jones would have had a similar motive and opportunity to develop the witness' testimony in the earlier trial.

2. Franklin's former testimony is inadmissible. He is presently unavailable, but his testimony is not being offered against the same party or a predecessor in interest. The current plaintiff, Roberts, is not the same party as Smith, nor is Roberts a predecessor in interest of Smith.

5. Present sense impressions[10]

A statement made during or immediately after an event that describes or explains the event is admissible. The rationale for this exception is that reliability is reasonably assured because the statement is made contemporaneously with the event and is usually made in the presence of witnesses.

After seeing another car pass them on a highway, the driver of the passed car says to his passenger: "The way they're speeding, they'll crash for sure." The statement is admissible as an exception to the hearsay rule.

6. Excited utterances[11]

A statement made under the stress of excitement that relates to a startling event or condition and is made while the declarant is perceiving the

---

10. Fed. R. Evid. 803(1).
11. Fed. R. Evid. 803(2).

event or condition, or immediately thereafter, is admissible. The rationale for this exception is that these statements are considered reliable because the declarant has no time to fabricate.

E X A M P L E

A pedestrian sees a car coming toward the intersection and yells: "Look out! He ran the red light!" Thus, a witness could testify as to the statement made by the pedestrian.

Keep in mind that there are differences between present sense impressions and excited utterances. The following chart illustrates the differences:

Present Sense Impressions	*Excited Utterances*
a. an "event"	a. a "startling event"
b. statement must be made "during or immediately after" the event	b. statement must be made under the stress of excitement" caused by the event
c. statement must "describe or explain event"	c. statement must "relate to a startling event"

7. Statement of present or past conditions for medical diagnosis[12]

Statements about a patient's condition are admissible. The rationale behind this exception is that these statements are reliable because a patient, presumably interested in getting well, will not deliberately falsify his medical history or present symptoms. Thus, both doctors and related parties, such as nurses and clerks, can testify about the statement made by the declarant.

E X A M P L E

A patient, brought to the hospital after an accident, says to the nurse: "I broke my arm, I ache all over, my head hurts, and I think I have a concussion. The other driver went right through the red light and rammed me with his car going about 35 miles per hour."

---

12. Fed. R. Evid. 803(4).

If the nurse is called to testify, she may testify to everything the patient-declarant told her, with the exception of the last sentence. The last sentence does not relate to the declarant's present or past condition and is not necessary for diagnosis. Thus, the last sentence would be hearsay and excluded from the testimony at trial.

---

8. Statement of present state of mind[13]

A statement made by a declarant about her present physical or mental condition is admissible. The rationale for this exception is that the declarant knows best what is going on in her mind.

EXAMPLE

Witness testifies at trial that the declarant told her: "I intend to go to Baker's house tonight." To prove that the declarant actually went to Baker's house, this testimony will be admissible as a statement of the present state of mind of the declarant.

---

9. Dying declarations[14]

A statement by a declarant is admissible if made while the declarant believes that he or she is about to die and the statement is about the circumstances of the declarant's injury. The declarant must now be unavailable to testify at the hearing. The rationale for this exception is that persons who believe they are dying are likely, as their last act, to tell the truth. In addition, the testimony is necessary because the declarant is now unavailable. In a few states, the declarant must actually die. Under the Federal Rules and the rules of some states, the declarant does not actually have to die. If the declarant recovers from the injury, the dying declaration may be admitted so long as the declarant is now unavailable.

EXAMPLE

In a wrongful death action, a witness testifies that Jones stated, just before he died, that the car driven by Smith went through the red light. The statement of Jones is admitted as a dying declaration.

---

13. Fed. R. Evid. 803(3).
14. Fed. R. Evid. 804(b)(2).

10. Records exceptions

There are several exceptions to the hearsay rule that allow records to be admitted into evidence. Remember that statements may be oral, nonverbal, or written. Accordingly, written records may be admitted under a number of exceptions identified in the Federal Rules.[15] The three most common exceptions are discussed in this section.

The first exception is **recorded recollections**.[16] If a witness has forgotten an earlier event, but made an accurate record of the event, the record is considered reliable. It is preferable to admit the record than lose the evidence altogether. This exception requires that some foundation be laid before the document will be read into evidence. Use the following as a checklist to determine whether a proper foundation for the document can be made:

Recorded recollections
A record made of events at about the time the events occurred

- ☐ The witness once had personal knowledge of the facts.
- ☐ The witness now does not have a full and accurate memory of the facts at or near the time the event occurred.
- ☐ The witness made a record of the facts involved.
- ☐ The record was accurate when made.
- ☐ The record in court is the actual record the witness made.

The second record exception is the **business records** exception.[17] The complexity of modern commerce requires that business records be admitted into evidence to prove the occurrence of certain business transactions. Moreover, since businesses need accurate records to conduct their affairs and the records are made by employees who have a duty to create accurate records, the records are considered reliable. Business records include memoranda, reports, or data compilations in any form. Use the following checklist of elements to determine whether a proper foundation can be laid for the admission of the business record:

Business records
Records made by employees in the course of their employment and made on behalf of the business

- ☐ a record of the business
- ☐ made at or near the time of the events recorded on the record
- ☐ by a person who had knowledge of the facts recorded, or made from information transmitted by a person having knowledge of the facts,
- ☐ made as part of the regular practice of that business, and
- ☐ kept in the course of a regularly conducted business activity.

15. See Fed. R. Evid. 803.
16. Fed. R. Evid. 803(5).
17. Fed. R. Evid. 803(6).

To use this exception, an appropriate witness will need to testify to each of the five elements identified. Accordingly, if a business record needs to be admitted into evidence, you may be asked to contact the custodian of records for the business who will probably be able to testify to each requirement.

Public records
Business records generated by governmental entities

Finally, **public records** and reports are admissible.[18] This exception is similar to the business records exception. Under this exception, however, a witness does not need to testify in court in order to lay a foundation for the document. It is sufficient if a certified copy of the public document or report is made available in court.

11. Other exceptions

Under the Federal Rules and the evidence rules of your state, other hearsay exceptions also may be available. The more common exceptions have been identified in this chapter. However, if faced with a hearsay problem, review the evidence carefully to determine whether another exception may apply. In addition, under the Federal Rules, a "catch-all" hearsay exception exists.[19] This exception provides that the judge may admit hearsay evidence if the evidence is relevant; the evidence is more valuable than the witness otherwise could be expected to find; the admission of the evidence serves the interests of justice; and advance notice of the identity of the declarant is given to the adversary. Use this category only as the last resort in the event no other hearsay exception applies.

F. WITNESSES, EXHIBITS, JUDICIAL NOTICE, AND OBJECTIONS

Up to this point we have been examining the nature of relevant and reliable evidence. We are now involved with the third "R"—"real" evidence. Evidence otherwise admissible under relevance and hearsay rules must also be real; that is, the presentation of the evidence must pass certain standards. The three areas of concern for real evidence involve witnesses, exhibits, and judicial notice.

---

18. Fed. R. Evid. 803(8).
19. Fed. R. Evid. 807.

1. Witnesses

A person called to testify at trial is either a "lay" witness or an "expert" witness. A lay witness is any witness who has not been qualified as an expert in a particular area. Almost all witnesses are considered lay witnesses; these are the witnesses who, based on their personal knowledge, will testify to the facts as they have observed or perceived them. Lay witnesses are sometimes referred to as "percipient" witnesses.

Two principal issues arise with respect to every witness who testifies at trial. These issues are whether the witness is "competent" to testify and, if the witness does testify, how that witness may be "impeached."

a. Competency

The threshold issue with any witness is whether the witness is competent to testify. In federal criminal and federal question civil cases, the Federal Rules of Evidence on competency apply.[20] However, in diversity cases and in all state court trials, the state evidence rules on competency apply. Accordingly, you need to be familiar with both the Federal Rules of Evidence and your state rules.

In general, a witness is competent to testify if she has the ability to communicate either orally or by gestures. Even a child may testify, so long as the judge is satisfied that the child can observe, recollect, and communicate. Under the rules of most states, persons of unsound mind are presumed to be incompetent to testify.

To be competent to testify, a witness also must have personal knowledge. It is not sufficient that the witness knows of the facts because they were related by someone else to the witness.[21] The witness must have independent knowledge of the facts.

b. Impeachment[22]

Impeachment refers to the discrediting of a witness' testimony so that the statements made by the witness will not be believed by the trier of fact. Impeachment evidence can be divided into two types: cross-examination of the witness or the introduction of other evidence, called extrinsic evidence, that serves to discredit the witness. A witness may be impeached by a number of methods.

---

20. Fed. R. Evid. 601.
21. The only exception to this rule is in the case of expert witnesses. Fed. R. Evid. 703.
22. Fed. R. Evid. 607.

One method of impeaching a witness is to show that the witness is biased or has an interest in the outcome of the lawsuit. For example, on cross-examination, the attorney may ask the following questions of the witness to show bias or interest:

E X A M P L E

Bias

Q: **Aren't you the plaintiff's brother?**
Q: **Weren't you fired last year by the defendant?**

Interest

Q: **Aren't you an equal partner with the plaintiff in this construction venture?**
Q: **If this will is held invalid, you'll inherit half the estate, won't you?**

A witness also may be impeached by a prior inconsistent statement.[23] For example, if a witness previously has testified at a deposition inconsistently with the testimony at trial, the prior inconsistent statement may be used to impeach the witness. This prior inconsistent statement detracts from the credibility of the witness. In some states, it is necessary for the attorney to cross-examine the witness first about the inconsistent statement before introducing the inconsistent statement into court.

The Federal Rules of Evidence also permit impeachment by introducing evidence of a prior conviction of the witness. Under Rule 609, the prior conviction is admissible if the crime was punishable by death or imprisonment in excess of one year or involved "dishonesty or false statement." In instances where the prior conviction is over ten years old, the prior conviction is admissible only if the probative value of the evidence outweighs its prejudicial effect.

Whenever any witness testifies, her credibility is in issue. Accordingly, the opponent can call at trial a reputation witness who will testify that the earlier witness' reputation for truthfulness is bad.[24] Of course, the proponent can thereafter present contrary testimony of the witness' good reputation for telling the truth. This scenario could be played out as in the example that follows.

---

23. Fed. R. Evid. 613, 801(d)(1)(A).
24. Fed. R. Evid. 608.

Plaintiff in a personal injury case calls Clifford as a witness in plaintiff's case-in-chief. Plaintiff then rests. Defendant in his case-in-chief calls Davis, who testifies that Clifford has a bad reputation for truthfulness. Defendant then rests. Plaintiff in rebuttal calls Adams, who testifies that Clifford has a good reputation for truthfulness.

Similar to evidence of the bad reputation of a witness for truthfulness is evidence of a witness' prior bad acts. Under the Federal Rules, prior bad acts are admissible to attack the credibility of a witness if the acts are "probative of truthfulness." The cross-examiner must always have a good faith basis for asking questions about prior bad acts.[25]

Prior Bad Acts

Q: Didn't you fill out a false employment application last year?

Q: Didn't you file a false state income tax return two years ago?

In some states that do not follow the Federal Rules, evidence of prior bad acts to attack a witness' credibility is not allowed. Accordingly, if your case is in state court, you must be certain to always check your state rules of evidence.

A final method of impeachment is by **contradiction**. Under certain circumstances a cross-examiner may wish to show that the true facts are different from those the witness claims. This is often called impeachment by contradiction.

Contradiction
Method of impeachment that shows that the true facts are different from those stated by the witness

Impeachment by Contradiction

The witness in an automobile negligence action testifies that he was 10 feet from the accident when it happened. On cross-examination, the witness is asked, "Weren't you 100 feet from the accident?" and the witness denies this fact. Here,

---

25. Fed. R. Evid. 608(b).

the cross-examiner can bring in other evidence to prove that the witness was indeed 100 feet from the accident to "contradict" the witness' testimony.

___

2. Expert witnesses[26]

Under the Federal Rules of Evidence and the rules of most states, expert testimony is proper whenever it will "assist the trier of fact to understand the evidence" or "determine a fact in issue." Experts are almost essential in all personal injury cases or in any case involving a large amount of technical information. The expert can explain the medical or technical terms to the jury and render an opinion as to a particular issue. For example, in an automobile negligence action, a doctor may be asked to give an opinion as to the chances of plaintiff completely recovering from the injuries. Such an opinion will assist the judge or jury in determining how much compensation to award the plaintiff if the defendant is found liable.

Any person having specialized knowledge can be qualified as an expert. Unlike a lay witness, an expert witness does not need to have firsthand knowledge of all the facts on which she bases her opinion. Rather, she also can give an opinion if facts are conveyed to her (as when she sits in court and hears all the evidence presented), or if the facts come from a source relied on by persons in her field (such as where a doctor relies on lab tests actually performed by a hospital laboratory).

3. Exhibits

Authenticate
Establish through witness testimony a foundation for the evidence presented before the trier of fact

Exhibits are tangible items of evidence. Common examples are photographs, diagrams, and business records. To be admissible, exhibits must be relevant. In addition, the proponent of the evidence must show that the offered exhibit is what it appears to be.[27] Thus, it is often said that the exhibit must be **authenticated**. To authenticate an exhibit, a witness must testify who can "establish a foundation" for the offered exhibit. Once the judge determines that sufficient credible evidence has been submitted so a foundation for admission has been established, the exhibit may be admitted into evidence and considered by the **trier of fact**—that is, either the judge or the jury who will decide questions of fact. The kind of foundation required to have an exhibit admitted into evidence depends on the type of exhibit involved. There are five basic types of exhibits, each of which is discussed below.

___

26. Fed. R. Evid. 702, 706.
27. Fed. R. Evid. 901.

a. Real evidence

Real evidence refers to physical objects. Here the exhibit is the actual piece of evidence. The foundation necessary for admissibility from a competent witness is:

1. The exhibit is the actual physical object
2. The exhibit is in substantially the same condition now as when it was first obtained

b. Demonstrative evidence

Demonstrative evidence refers to exhibits that represent real things, such as photographs, diagrams, models, and maps. Here the exhibit is only a representation of the actual object. The foundation necessary for admissibility from a competent witness is:

1. The exhibit is a representation of the real thing as it was at the pertinent date
2. The exhibit is reasonably accurate or to scale

c. Writings

Certain types of writings have independent legal significance. Common examples are wills, contracts, promissory notes, and checks. The only foundation requirement for these kinds of writings is whether the writing was in fact signed or written by the undersigned person. In other words, the signatures or handwriting must be authenticated. This can be done through any witness who saw the document being signed or written or is familiar with the signature or handwriting and can identify it. If such a witness is unavailable, handwriting comparisons may be used or any other method that identifies the maker of the document.

d. Business records

As discussed previously, business records are obviously hearsay and must therefore be qualified as an exception to the hearsay rules.[28] The

---

28. See Section D(10).

foundation for the business records may properly be laid by using the following checklist:[29]

- ☐ The witness is the "custodian or other qualified witness"
- ☐ The record must be a "memorandum, report, record, or data compilation, in any form"
- ☐ The record was "made by a person with knowledge" of the facts or was "made from information transmitted by a person with knowledge" of the facts
- ☐ The record was "made at or near the time" of the acts and events recorded on it
- ☐ The record was made as part of "the regular practice of that business activity"
- ☐ The record was "kept in the course of a regularly conducted business activity"

e. Public records[30]

Public records are simply business records generated by governmental entities. Such records are self-authenticating and need no qualifying witness to lay a foundation. A properly certified copy of the public records will be admissible.

4. Best evidence rule[31]

Best evidence rule
Under the common law, a requirement that an original writing had to be produced if the writing was going to be used as evidence

The **best evidence rule** is more accurately called the original document rule, since it applies principally to writings. The common law rule stated that whenever a writing's contents were to be introduced into evidence, the original had to be produced. The rule was a response to the errors and inaccuracies of handmade copies.

Under the Federal Rules of Evidence and the rules of most states, duplicates are generally admissible to the same extent as the original. Faxes are considered under the federal and state rules to be duplicates. In all courts, even though duplicates are permitted, if there is a genuine dispute over authenticity or it would be unfair to admit a duplicate, the original must still be produced.

29. Fed. R. Evid. 803(6).
30. Fed. R. Evid. 902.
31. Fed. R. Evid. 1001-1004.

5. Judicial notice[32]

Judicial notice is an evidentiary procedure in which the trial judge is asked to rule that certain facts are true. The purpose is to promote trial efficiency, sharpen issues, and permit the introduction of indisputable evidence where formal proof would be difficult and lengthy.

There are three types of facts that may be judicially noticed:

1. Facts generally known within the particular geographical area
2. Facts capable of accurate and readily available determination from an unquestionably accurate source
3. Scientific basis for accepted scientific tests

G. PRIVILEGES

Privileges,[33] which are rules providing that certain communications are inadmissible because of confidentiality issues, are based on policy considerations. Under certain situations, a higher social good is obtained (promoting open and candid conversations between specified persons) that outweighs the evidentiary cost of losing relevant evidence. Privileges were developed through the common law and, more recently, by statutes. Unfortunately, the privileges that are recognized vary between jurisdictions, and it is always necessary to research which privileges are recognized in your jurisdiction. The following are the more common privileges that you should be familiar with regardless of the jurisdiction in which you practice.

1. Attorney-client privilege

The **attorney-client privilege** applies to confidential communications between a client and a lawyer and the lawyer's representatives relating to the rendering of legal services. The client is the holder of the privilege, and the privilege can be asserted by the client or the client's personal representative, and by the lawyer on behalf of the client.

Attorney-client privilege
Protection that allows communications between an attorney and client to remain confidential

As with most things in the law, there are exceptions to the privilege. These exceptions vary from jurisdiction to jurisdiction. However, two examples are provided.

First, there is no attorney-client privilege if the services of the lawyer are sought to enable or aid one to commit or plan a crime or fraud.

---

32. Fed. R. Evid. 201.
33. Fed. R. Evid. 501.

Obviously, no social good is advanced by keeping such communications privileged.

Second, when a client claims a breach of duty by the lawyers, the attorney-client privilege may not be invoked. The rationale is that it would be unfair to permit a client to accuse the attorney of a breach of duty and to thereafter invoke the privilege to prevent the attorney from bringing forth evidence in the attorney's defense.

Most important, the privilege may be waived if the "confidential communication" is disclosed to others. This is why, when responding to interrogatories or document requests, a paralegal must be certain not to disclose any such communication (whether the communication is oral or in writing) to the adverse party.

2. Work product privilege

Work product
Work performed by an attorney during the course of representing a client

The **work product** privilege is a qualified privilege for the workpapers, notes, memoranda, and reports gathered or prepared by attorneys in anticipation of litigation. This qualified privilege is intended to encourage an attorney to pursue an exhaustive pretrial investigation and analysis of facts without fear that the fruits of this labor will be discoverable by the other side.

The privilege is qualified because in some instances the attorney's work product may be discoverable. In cases where the work product does not contain the lawyer's opinion, mental impression, or legal theories, a party seeking disclosure may be able to demonstrate that there is a substantial need for such materials, and there is no other way to obtain the materials. In such a case, the court may order that such materials be produced to the other side. However, in cases where the materials contain the lawyer's opinion, mental impressions, or legal theories, the materials are never discoverable.

Although the privilege is referred to as the "attorney work product," the privilege applies equally to materials prepared by a legal assistant or agents of the lawyer working under the direction of the lawyer.

3. Physician-patient privilege

A patient, whether or not a party, has a privilege to not disclose—and to prevent the physician from disclosing—any information acquired by the physician in confidence while attending to the patient. Again, there are exceptions. For example, if the patient puts her health in issue, such as in the case of a personal injury action, the physician-patient privilege will not apply.

Some states also recognize a psychotherapist-patient privilege. Thus, confidential communications between a psychotherapist and the patient for purposes of diagnosing or treating a mental condition of the patient will be privileged. However, if the patient has placed her mental condition in evidence, the privilege may not be asserted.

4. Marital privileges

Confidential communications made by one spouse to the other during a legally valid marriage are protected from disclosure. The policy behind allowing such a privilege is to promote candid conversations between spouses. Either spouse may prohibit the other spouse from disclosing the privileged communication. A majority of states also extend the privilege even after the marriage has ended in divorce, so long as the communication itself was made during the marriage.

In addition, some states also recognize other marital privileges, such as a privilege not to testify against a spouse. The privilege provides that a spouse can refuse to testify as a witness against the other spouse. The policy behind this privilege is to promote marital harmony between spouses.

CHAPTER SUMMARY

This chapter has provided an overview of the law of evidence. A paralegal must be familiar with the rules of evidence in order to adequately assist the lawyer in determining what evidence can or cannot be admitted into evidence at trial. Familiarity with the rules of evidence is also essential for assisting with pretrial motions and preparing responses to discovery requests.

To be admissible, all evidence must be relevant, reliable, and real. Some evidence, even though relevant, will be excluded under special circumstances. In addition, even though some evidence may not be considered reliable because the evidence is hearsay, there may be exceptions to the hearsay rule available. The exceptions still are designed to guarantee reliability by the personal presence of the declarant at trial, under oath, and subject to cross-examination by the opposing parties, or because the exceptions acknowledge other indications of reliability.

Real evidence principally involves issues concerning witnesses, exhibits, and judicial notice. A witness must be competent to testify. A witness' testimony can be impeached by opposing parties. There are several methods of impeachment, including bias, prior inconsistent statements, and contradiction.

Exhibits must be authenticated to show that the exhibit is what it purports to be before the exhibit may be introduced into evidence. An exhibit may be authenticated by a witness who can establish a foundation for the exhibit.

Finally, as a paralegal, you must be aware of privileges that may exist. A privilege protects certain communications from being disclosed to opposing parties. These privileges include communications between an attorney and client, and documents generated by the attorney in the course of representing the client.

KEY TERMS

Admission of a party opponent	Judicial notice
Affidavit	Privileges
Attorney-client privilege	Probative
Authenticated	Public records
Best evidence rule	Question of law
Business records	Real
Character traits	Real evidence
Contradiction	Recorded recollections
Declaration	Relevant
Demonstrative evidence	Reliable
Exhibits	Testimony
Federal Rules of Evidence	Trier of fact
Hearsay	Work product
Impeachment	

REVIEW QUESTIONS

1. What do we mean by the term "relevant evidence"?

2. What types of relevant evidence are excluded for policy reasons? What are the policy reasons behind excluding such evidence?

3. What are the three elements necessary for determining whether a statement is "hearsay"?

4. There are several exceptions to the hearsay rule. Identify at least three exceptions, and give an example of each.

5. Why are communications between a lawyer and the client subject to the attorney-client privilege?

6. What does "judicial notice" mean? Can you give an example of a fact that the court may be able to take judicial notice of?

7. How might a statement of a witness be impeached?

8. What is the best evidence rule?

ADDITIONAL RESOURCES

Best, Arthur, *Evidence: Examples and Explanations*, (Aspen Publishers, 2004).

Epstein, Edna Selan, *The Attorney-Client Privilege and the Work-Product Doctrine*, (ABA 2001).

Imwinkelried, Edward, *Evidentiary Foundation*, (Matthew Bender, 2002).

Mauet, Thomas A., Wolfson, Warren D., *Trial Evidence*, (Aspen Publishers, 2004).

Palmer, Michael G., *The Hearsay Rule*, (Carolina Academic Press, 2002).

Rice, Paul R., *Electronic Evidence*, (ABA, 2005).

Walkowski, Vincent S., *Attorney-Client Privilege in Civil Litigation*, (ABA, 2004).

Chapter 10

DISCOVERY

CHAPTER OBJECTIVES

Discovery is one of the primary tools that a paralegal uses to ascertain facts during the course of a lawsuit. In this chapter, you will learn

♦ What discovery devices you may use to obtain facts

♦ How you may use computers for litigation support

♦ When you can conduct discovery

♦ How to draft the different forms of discovery

♦ How to prepare a witness for deposition

♦ How to prepare a deposition summary in different ways

♦ When a discovery motion may be necessary

A. INTRODUCTION

Discovery is the principal fact-gathering method in the formal litigation process. In today's litigation environment, the discovery stage is where most of the battles are fought and where the war is largely won or lost. Consequently, understanding discovery so that you can effectively use the permissible discovery methods as tactical and strategic tools is critical for every litigation paralegal.

Discovery has three main characteristics. First, for the most part, you may conduct discovery without judicial approval, participation, or regulation. Second, the discovery rules are flexible and permit any sequence—and repeated use—of the various discovery methods subject only to court protection against abuse. Third, orders regulating discovery are usually not appealable orders. Since discovery issues will often be moot by the time a final judgment is entered in the case, appeals are relatively infrequent. This means that issues concerning discovery are principally resolved at the trial court level.

While the federal rules of procedure and evidence regarding discovery are discussed in this chapter, it is still important either when preparing discovery requests or responding to discovery to check your local federal rules of court. Many federal and state courts have special requirements concerning the format for preparing and responding to discovery requests and for filing the discovery. If you understand the federal discovery rules discussed in this chapter, you will easily be able to apply this understanding to the discovery rules in your state.

B. DISCOVERY OVERVIEW

1. Types of discovery

Discovery is designed to prevent trial by surprise. The purpose is to allow each party to find out the other side's facts supporting the various issues in the litigation so that each party may prepare his or her case for trial. However, in civil actions, where the majority of cases are resolved without trial, it is obvious that discovery has its advantages in the settlement context as well. Properly used, discovery highlights the strengths and weaknesses of one's case. Once these strengths and weaknesses are fully exposed, the parties are usually able to discover the true "value" of the case and come to a settlement.

There are five methods of discovery permitted under the Federal Rules of Civil Procedure:

- Interrogatories
- Requests to produce
- Depositions
- Physical and mental examinations
- Requests for admission

Interrogatories are written questions sent by one party to another party. This sending of interrogatories to another party is sometimes referred to as "propounding" interrogatories. The party receiving the interrogatories must give a written response under oath to each question. Under the Federal Rules, the responding party has 30 days to respond. If you are responding to interrogatories in state court, be sure to check your state rules for the time to respond.

Interrogatories
Written questions submitted by one party to another during the discovery stage

Interrogatories are most effective for obtaining basic factual data from other parties, such as the identity of proper parties, agents, employees, witnesses, and experts and the identity and location of documents, records, and tangible evidence. They are also useful in obtaining other parties' positions on disputed facts and experts' opinions and bases for opinions. On the other hand, interrogatories are not usually effective instruments for getting detailed facts, impressions, or versions of events.

A **request to produce** is a written request by one party to another seeking formal permission to obtain copies of records, documents, and other tangible items for inspection, copying, and testing. Such a request also permits entry onto another party's land or property to inspect, photograph, and analyze things on the land or property. By using this discovery device, a party can force the opponent to produce records and other evidence and to permit entry onto property to copy, photograph, or study evidence that is within the opponent's possession, custody, or control.

Depositions
Oral questions asked by one party to another during the discovery stage

Depositions are oral questions by one party to another. Although depositions are often taken in a conference room in an attorney's office, the testimony given by the witness (referred to as the **deponent**) is under oath and taken down by a shorthand reporter who is usually a notary public. The oral questions and answers are then transcribed in a booklet form that the deponent is asked to read and sign. The deponent may be cross-examined, and the deponent's attorney may make objections to the questions that are asked.

Depositions are most effective in tying down parties and witnesses to details and in discovering everything they know pertinent to the case. It is the only discovery vehicle that permits your side to assess how good a witness a person is likely to be at trial. It is an excellent vehicle to secure admissions or other evidence favorable to your side and it is the only one that can be used on nonparty witnesses. Furthermore, a deposition is the only method to preserve testimony if a witness will become unavailable for trial.

A **physical or mental examination** of a party can be obtained if the party's physical or mental condition is in issue. This is often the case in personal injury cases. The examination can only be done if a court order is obtained or if the party agrees to voluntarily submit to an examination. The examination is usually conducted by a doctor chosen by the party requesting the examination. Although other discovery methods can be used to get records of past examinations, this is the only means of forcing a party to be examined and tested for proof of her current condition. For that reason, it is the best method for evaluating a party on such damages elements as permanence, extent of injury, and medical prognosis.

Finally, a **request to admit** is a written statement that forces a party to admit or deny a fact or a document's genuineness. An admitted fact is deemed conclusively admitted for the purpose of the pending trial. This discovery method is effective if limited to simple factual data, such as someone's employment on a specific date or the genuineness of signatures on a contract. It is not a good method for dealing with opinions or evaluative information.

All of these methods will be discussed in greater depth later in this chapter.

2. The paralegal's role

As a litigation paralegal, you can expect to have significant involvement in the discovery process. In addition to preparing discovery requests to the other side, you will often be responsible for obtaining information and responding to the discovery the other side serves upon your client. For example, you may be asked to prepare interrogatories and document requests to ascertain facts from the opposing side. This requires that you not only have a complete understanding of the nature of the case but also know and understand the rules for when and how the discovery should be prepared.

Similarly, you may be asked to obtain information or documents from your client in order to properly respond to the discovery requests served by the other side. Knowing when and how to respond to the discovery are essential paralegal skills.

Lawyers frequently rely on paralegals to prepare witnesses for deposition, to digest documents, and to summarize deposition testimony. Since depositions are frequently scheduled at the convenience of the attorneys and the deponent, you may be responsible for scheduling a date for the deposition and selecting a court reporter to attend.

You also may be asked to select a physician to conduct a medical examination, arrange for the examination, and obtain the medical reports prepared as a result of the examination. In summary, other than appearing on behalf of a deponent at a deposition, there is virtually no part of the discovery process in which you will not be involved.

3. Computerized litigation support

Computers are becoming a significant tool in assisting with the litigation process. There are three areas in which computers can be extremely valuable:

- ◆ Conducting research
- ◆ Locating information about parties and witnesses
- ◆ Organizing discovery

a. Conducting research

Computers have been used for years to assist lawyers and paralegals in conducting research for their litigation cases. Two different computer services, LEXIS and WESTLAW, are available. These services provide computerized access to virtually every primary legal resource available, including court cases, statutes, and codes. By inputting a request for particular information, the computer will locate the materials available in that area.

Of course, there are limitations to this service, since it may not be possible to design a computer search that fits your particular area of inquiry. In addition, the list of materials you receive from your search request may be so lengthy that it may be virtually impossible to review all the material found. Your law firm may also have financial restrictions on how much time can be spent in computer research. Most paralegal schools now have at least one computer service that the school uses to train paralegals. If your school does not have such a service and the law firm you work for does use a computer service, training will be provided to you (usually for free) by a representative of the computer service. The Internet now offers many legal sites that are available free of charge (see Chapter 2, section G).

b. Locating information about parties and witnesses

A second area in which computers are now being used is the location of information about parties or witnesses. Some computer services give you access to records of the secretary of state or other corporate information such as Dun & Bradstreet reports. By accessing this information, you may be able to find out who the officers and directors of a particular business are, who the corporation's agent for service of process is, and the nature of the business. In addition to LEXIS and WESTLAW, other software vendors for this type of service are Information America located in Atlanta, and Prentice Hall Legal & Financial Services located in New York City. The Internet also offers many web sites devoted to locating witnesses and businesses.

c. Organizing discovery

Finally, computers may be used to assist in the discovery process. In large litigation matters, you may need to input discovery information into your firm's computer. For example, if documents are produced by the other side, the documents can be numbered and a description of the document entered into the computer. A computer can be a valuable tool for keeping track of documents and quickly locating specific information. A deposition transcript may also be available on computer disk. This allows you to search for particular testimony without having to read the entire transcript. The court reporter who took the deposition can give you a disk that is formatted for the type of computer software your firm uses.

Computer use in law firms is rapidly increasing, and paralegals should learn to utilize a computer not only for word processing but for litigation support as well. Numerous litigation support programs are available, and your law firm, if it uses computers, will probably have one of these. Some of these programs are available from Aspen Litigation Support, American Legal Systems, and Techlaw Systems, Inc. Again, in most instances, training on the job is available. However, if you are unfamiliar with computers, you should consider enrolling in a basic computer class. Paralegal schools, as well as continuing education programs, often offer these classes.

C. SCOPE OF DISCOVERY

Rule 26(b) of the Federal Rules of Civil Procedure, the basic discovery rule that controls the scope of discovery, provides that a party may discover "any matter, not privileged, that is relevant to the subject matter involved in the pending action." This section discusses what "relevance" means in the discovery context. It also reviews the specialized areas now expressly regulated by Rule 26: insurance, statements, experts, privileges, and work product (or trial preparation materials).

1. Relevance

Relevance for discovery purposes is exceptionally broad. Information sought need not be admissible at trial, nor need the information itself be relevant. Rule 26(b)(1) states that if the information sought to be discovered "appears reasonably calculated to lead to the discovery of admissible evidence" on the subject matter of the lawsuit, it is discoverable. In short, a "fishing expedition" is proper if it might unveil probative evidence.

Rule 26(b)(1) expressly permits discovery of the "identity and location of persons having knowledge of any discoverable matter," including the names and addresses of those persons. The discovery of this information has been made even easier by the Federal Rules relating to discovery that went into effect in December 1993. Under Rule 26(a)(1) a party must, without even waiting for a discovery request, make an initial disclosure to the other party that includes the name and any known address and telephone number for each individual likely to have information relevant to the facts alleged in the pleadings.

Rule 26(b)(1) also expressly permits discovery of "books, documents or other tangible things." However, also under Rule 26(a)(1) parties are required to describe and categorize the nature and location of all potentially relevant documents and records so that opposing parties can make decisions about which documents actually need to be examined. Again, this information must be exchanged between the parties as part of the initial disclosures made prior to any discovery requests.

2. Insurance agreements

To end a long-standing dispute over the discoverability of insurance, Rule 26(a)(1)(D) expressly requires the disclosure, without a discovery request, of a liability insurance policy held by any party that may satisfy a judgment. This information is critical for assessing the "value" of a case and the defendant's ability to pay a judgment. However, under Federal Rule of Evidence 411, the disclosure of insurance information does not necessarily make it admissible as evidence.

3. Statements

For discovery purposes, there are three types of statements: witness statements, party statements made to the party's attorney, and party statements made to anyone else. Different rules apply to each.

A written statement made by a nonparty witness that is in the possession of an adversary is discoverable since it is a relevant, tangible thing. A problem arises when a witness has been interviewed by the opposing side but no statement was made. Under these circumstances, the opposing party has no tangible thing that is discoverable, and any notes of the interview taken by the lawyer or paralegal that contain the lawyer's or paralegal's mental impressions of the witness are probably privileged. Of course, the identity and location of such a witness are discoverable.

Statements made by a party to his own lawyer are not discoverable, principally because the attorney-client privilege will usually apply to such communications. However, Rule 26(b)(3) expressly allows a party to obtain his own statement in the possession of anyone else on demand, without a court order or any showing of need. A party is considered to have a right to his own written or recorded oral statement.

4. Experts

There are three basic kinds of experts: testifying experts, consulting experts, and informally consulted experts. Different rules govern the discoverability of their identity, opinions, and reports.

Rule 26(b)(4)(A) makes discoverable the identity of each party's experts who are expected to be called as witnesses at trial. Through interrogatory answers, a party must also disclose what subject matter the expert will testify about, the substance of the expert's facts and opinions, and a summary of the grounds for each opinion. However, further discovery, such as a deposition of an expert or subpoena of the expert's files, may only be obtained by motion and court order. This rule protects experts from being drawn into the discovery process directly without prior approval of the court.

Nevertheless, Rule 26(b)(4)(A) provides that experts who are expected to be witnesses are subject to deposition prior to trial. However, since Rule 26(a)(2) requires parties to give to the other side a complete and detailed written report of the expected testimony of certain experts, such experts can only be deposed after the report has been served.

Rule 26(b)(4)(B) governs consulting experts, those who have been retained or employed to help assist during the litigation process but are not expected to be witnesses at trial. Such experts ordinarily cannot be subjected to the discovery process unless a requesting party can show "exceptional circumstances under which it is impracticable . . . to obtain facts or opinions on the same subject by other means." The Rule in effect establishes a qualified privilege for the work of a consulting expert, one akin to that for a lawyer's trial preparation materials. The only exception is Rule 35(b), which makes the reports of a physician's mental or physical examination of a party discoverable in certain circumstances.[1]

Informally consulted experts, those experts who have not been retained but have provided information, are not governed by discovery rules. Therefore, neither the existence, identity, nor opinions of such an expert is discoverable. This prevents experts with minimal contacts with a lawyer from being drawn into the discovery process.

5. Privileges

As discussed in Chapter 9, there are various privileges that may protect the disclosure of certain evidence to the other parties. Rule 26(b)(5) now requires that a party notify the opposing parties if it is withholding materials because it is asserting a claim of privilege. The party must also provide enough information to allow the other parties to evaluate the applicability of the claimed privilege. Withholding materials without such notification subjects the party to sanctions under Rule 37(b)(2) and may constitute a waiver of the privilege.

Federal privileges are controlled by Rule 501 of the Federal Rules of Evidence, which continues the development of privileges by case law, statutes, and constitutional provisions.

a. What privilege law applies?

Rule 501 provides that federal privileges, as developed by the courts, will apply. The exception is that in civil cases for which state law has "supplie[d] the rule of decision" as to an element of a claim or defense, state privileges will apply. This essentially means that in federal criminal cases and in federal civil cases based on federal question jurisdiction, federal privilege law will apply. However, in federal civil cases

---

1. See section H.

based on diversity jurisdiction, state privilege rules will apply. Where a privilege is based on the U.S. Constitution, principally the Fifth Amendment's self-incrimination clause, it applies regardless of the type of federal case involved.

b. What is the applicable federal or state privilege law?

When the Federal Rules of Evidence were enacted, Congress chose not to codify federal common law privileges, preferring to let federal privileges continue to develop in the courts. Therefore, care must always be taken to research the law of the appropriate jurisdiction because privilege law can vary.

State privileges, by contrast, are developed by both the courts and the legislatures, although in recent years the trend has been to codify privileges. Keep in mind that state jurisdictions vary widely in their privilege law. While all states recognize frequently used privileges such as marital, attorney-client, and doctor-patient, they vary substantially in their recognition of others such as the privilege for accountants, reporters' informants, and governmental secrets. The scope of any privilege and whether it applies in civil or criminal cases also varies significantly. This area of evidence law always requires substantial research.

6. Trial preparation materials

Ever since the Supreme Court decided Hickman v. Taylor, 329 U.S. 495 (1947), federal courts have recognized a two-tier privilege rule applicable to an attorney's work product; that rule, with some changes and added details, is now incorporated in Rule 26(b)(3) of the Federal Rules of Civil Procedure.

The attorney's work product, now called "trial preparation materials," is protected by a qualified privilege. Trial preparation materials include any "documents and tangible things" that were "prepared in anticipation of litigation" by another party or that party's "representative." A representative includes not only the lawyer but other agents such as an insurance adjuster or claims investigator.

If the privilege applies, it is only a qualified privilege. The Rule permits a party seeking discovery to obtain protected documents and tangible things upon a showing of "substantial need" because the party cannot obtain the "substantial equivalent" by other means without "undue hardship." Under this provision of the Rule, it is clear that undue hardship cannot be shown simply by demonstrating added expense or inconvenience. With witness statements, the area where this issue most frequently arises, there must be some demonstrable reason why the requesting party cannot get the substantial equivalent of the statement himself before production can be ordered.

The second tier of the privilege, the one covering the lawyer's "mental impressions, conclusions, opinions on legal theories," is absolutely protected by the privilege. Hence, disclosure can never be compelled.

D. DISCOVERY STRATEGY: A SEVEN-STEP PROCESS

The discovery rules in the Federal Rules of Civil Procedure are both broad and extensive, and in most cases they permit more discovery than either party will wish to make. Consequently, the overriding concern at the discovery stage is: What will be an effective discovery strategy for this particular case? As outlined previously, discovery planning is essentially a seven-step process.

1. What facts are needed in order to establish a winning case on the client's claims (or to defeat the opponent's claims)?

2. What facts already have been obtained through informal fact investigation?

These questions should already be answered in your developing litigation chart.

3. What "missing" facts must still be obtained through formal discovery?

Discovery is the vehicle your side will use to force other parties, and nonparties, to disclose information they have pertinent to the litigation. Your first question, therefore, should be, What additional information do I need to know to assist in preparing the case for a possible trial? While the answer will vary with each case, use the following checklist to ascertain whether you already have information as a result of informal investigation or whether further discovery is necessary:

CHECKLIST OF INFORMATION OBTAINED

☐ Identity of proper parties
☐ Defendant's ability to pay a judgment

☐ Identity of agents and employees
☐ Opponent's factual basis for legal claims
☐ Opponent's position on factual issues
☐ Identity and location of witnesses
☐ Prospective testimony of adverse parties, agents, and employees
☐ Prospective testimony of important witnesses
☐ Identity, opinions, and reasoning of experts
☐ Prospective testimony of experts
☐ Tangible evidence
☐ Documents
☐ Records
☐ Statements of parties and witnesses
☐ Testimony of favorable witnesses that may become unavailable for trial

Not all of this information is necessarily discoverable. However, you should always compile a similar roster for each case because it will control the information you will try to discover. On your litigation chart, you will have noted information that can only be found through discovery. Your chart will help lead you through the checklist above for each case.

4. What discovery methods are most effective for obtaining the missing facts?

Although there is some overlap in the discovery methods you may use to obtain the missing information, each method is particularly well suited for certain kinds of information.

For example, under Rule 26(b)(4)(A) "a party may depose any person who has been identified as an expert whose opinions may be presented at trial." If the expert is one who is required by Rule 26(a)(2)(B) to prepare a written report of the expected testimony, the deposition of the expert may only be taken after the report has been provided. During the deposition, it is important to get the details underlying expert testing and opinions.

You can obtain discovery of your opponent's consulting expert only on a showing of "exceptional circumstances under which it is impractical . . . to obtain facts or opinions on the same subject by other means." While this is obviously a difficult standard, the Rule contemplates those rare cases, such as when a consulting expert has engaged in destructive testing of a product, when relevant expert information is solely in the possession of one party's expert.

Trial preparation materials, which are protected from disclosure by a qualified privilege, can be obtained from an opponent "only upon a showing of substantial need." The party seeking production must also be "unable without undue hardship to obtain the substantial equivalent of the materials by other means." This exception to the attorney's work product rule arises most often in regard to witness statements, which are not automatically discoverable. When one side has taken a statement from a witness who now refuses to talk to other lawyers, who cannot be subpoenaed, or who has a lapse of memory, and the substantial equivalent of the statement cannot be obtained, the court may order the production of the statement.

5. What facts and witnesses, already identified through informal investigation, must be pinned down by formal discovery?

There is little point in using formal discovery methods with the favorable witnesses, unless those witnesses are old, sick, or are likely to move away. If this is the case, the lawyer will want to take the witness' deposition to preserve the testimony for trial, since the transcript will usually qualify as former testimony.[2]

With unfavorable, hostile, or adverse witnesses and parties, however, there are good reasons for deposing them, even if your side already knows from the informal fact investigation what these witnesses will say at trial. First, there are always benefits in learning in detail what those witnesses will say. Second, witnesses may testify inconsistently in respect to their previous statements or in respect to each other. Third, it may be possible to limit the witnesses' trial testimony by getting the witnesses to admit to topics they have no firsthand knowledge of, are not sure of, or are only approximating or guessing at.

6. What restrictions does the client's litigation budget place on the discovery plan?

Information gathering, especially formal discovery, is expensive, and any discovery strategy must necessarily consider the expenses involved. Accordingly, always consult with the lawyer responsible for the litigation before you prepare any discovery requests.

In addition, responding to discovery, particularly interrogatories and documents requests, can become expensive because of the time involved in researching and preparing responses and reviewing the necessary documents. Before you begin preparing any responses, discuss with the lawyer the time you expect will be necessary to prepare the responses properly.

---

2. Fed. R. Evid. 804(b)(1).

7. In what order should the discovery proceed?

Formal discovery should be used as a progressive device in which each discovery method is utilized as a sequential building block. Rule 26 attempts to accelerate the exchange of basic information about the case and to eliminate the paperwork involved in requesting such information. First, Rule 26 imposes on the parties a duty to disclose basic information without waiting for formal discovery requests. Rule 26(a)(1) requires all parties to exchange information about potential witnesses, documentary evidence, damages, and insurance. Rule 26(a)(2) requires the parties to identify all expert witnesses who will provide substantive evidence and to provide a complete and detailed written report of the expected testimony of experts. Second, Rule 26 requires the court to set the scope, timing, and extent of discovery and disclosure. In order to help the court, Rule 26(f) requires that unless the case is exempted by local rules or special orders, the parties must meet as soon as practicable, plan for discovery, and submit their proposals to the court. Rule 26(f) describes the matters that should be accomplished at the meeting and included in the discovery plan presented to the court. A sample plan is shown in Exhibit 10.1.

Because the discovery process is largely governed by the parties, the relevant questions are: When should discovery start? In what order should discovery be carried out?

a. When should discovery start?

The initial question can be answered simply. Discovery should start as soon as the rules in your state or the Federal Rules permit and as soon as practical. Note that under Rule 26(d) formal discovery is prohibited until after the parties have met as required by Rule 26(f).

In state court, if the prefiling investigation and preparation work are done, discovery may begin during the pleading stage. For instance, defendants frequently serve interrogatories with their answers and sometimes serve notice to take the plaintiff's deposition at the same time. Doing this shows the plaintiff that the defendant intends to litigate vigorously and gives the defendant a head start on any discovery cut-off dates.

b. In what order should discovery be carried out?

The following is a common discovery sequence:

1. Interrogatories
2. Requests to produce and subpoenas

Exhibit 10.1.   Sample Discovery Plan

[Caption]

REPORT OF PARTIES' PLANNING MEETING

The parties submit the following written report, pursuant to Rule 26(f):

1. A meeting was held on June 1, 2006, at the offices of Johnson & Barnes, 100 Main Street, Boise, Idaho. Present were William Johnson, plaintiff's attorney, and Sarah Anton, defendant's attorney. The parties jointly propose to the court the following:

2. <u>Scheduling conference</u>. The parties request a scheduling conference before the entry of a scheduling order.

3. <u>Pleadings</u>. Plaintiff should have until July 1, 2006, to add additional parties and amend pleadings. Defendant should have until August 1, 2006, to add additional parties and amend pleadings.

4. <u>Discovery</u>.
    a. Initial disclosures under Rule 26(a)(1) will be exchanged by June 15, 2006.
    b. Discovery will be needed on the following subjects: plaintiff's and defendant's conduct before, during, and after the collision, plaintiff's medical treatment, plaintiff's future medical needs, plaintiff's present and future lost income, and other claimed damages.
    c. Interrogatories will be limited to 20 by each party to another party, and will be served by July 15, 2006. Responses are due 30 days after service.
    d. Documents requests will be limited to 20 by each party to another party, and will be served by September 15, 2006. Responses are due 30 days after service.
    e. Depositions of nonexperts will be limited to 8 by each party, and will be taken by December 1, 2006. Each deposition will be limited to 3 hours, unless extended by agreement of the parties.
    f. Written reports from plaintiff's retained experts under Rule 26(a)(2) are due December 15, 2006. Written reports from defendant's retained experts are due January 15, 2007.
    g. Depositions of experts will be limited to 2 by each party, and will be taken between December 15, 2006, and February 15, 2007. Each deposition will be limited to 4 hours, unless extended by agreement of the parties.
    h. Requests to admit will be limited to 15 by each party to another party, and will be served by March 1, 2007. Responses are due 30 days after service.

continued on next page

Exhibit 10.1. Continued

i. Supplementation under Rule 26(e) is due by April 1, 2007.
j. Discovery cut-off date is April 1, 2007.

5. <u>Dispositive motions</u>. Dispositive motions will be served and filed by April 15, 2007. Responses are due by May 15, 2007.

6. <u>Settlement</u>. Settlement cannot be evaluated until after the experts' reports have been received. The parties request that the court schedule a conference to discuss settlement after February 15, 2007.

7. <u>Trial</u>.
a. Witness and exhibits lists under Rule 26(b)(3) should be due from plaintiff by May 1, 2007, and from defendant by May 15, 2007.
b. Parties should have 15 days after service of witness and exhibits lists to specify objections under Rule 26(a)(3).
c. The case should be ready for trial by July 1, 2007. The trial is expected to take approximately 4 days.

Respectfully submitted,

_____
William Johnson, attorney for
plaintiff

_____
Sarah Anton, attorney for defendant

3. Depositions of parties, witnesses, and experts
4. Physical and mental examinations
5. Requests for admission

This sequence utilizes the building block approach to discovery. Interrogatory answers should identify the opponent's witnesses, documents, and positions on the facts. Once the answers are received, serving requests to produce on parties and subpoenas on nonparty witnesses is useful to obtain the documents, records, and other evidence identified in the interrogatory answers. After receiving this information, it is time to take depositions of parties, witnesses, and, if permitted, experts. In personal injury cases, the physical and mental examinations of parties are ordinarily conducted later in the litigation process, because these examinations usually focus on such issues as permanence of injury, prognosis, and loss of earning capacity. Once these steps have been completed, requests for admission can further pinpoint areas of dispute and eliminate the need to prove uncontested facts at trial.

This sequence, of course, can be and often is modified. Amended, supplemental, or additional pleadings may be filed that will necessarily alter the course of discovery. In addition, there may be tactical benefits in changing the usual sequence or in serving more than one discovery device at the same time. Keep in mind that the discovery process educates the opponent as well as the party requesting the discovery. Accordingly, lawyers sometimes take the deposition of an adverse party before interrogatories or notices to produce have been sent out, on the theory that the adverse party will have neither the time nor the inclination to prepare thoroughly by collecting and reviewing all the pertinent records beforehand. Also, lawyers frequently schedule depositions of the adverse party and that party's employees and agents back to back so that successive deponents cannot review the testimony of earlier deponents before being deposed themselves. Furthermore, lawyers frequently couple interrogatories requesting the existence of documents with a request to produce the documents identified, and use early requests for admission facts in order to narrow the scope of discovery.

There is no magic formula for deciding on the best sequence for discovery. Discovery may be tailored to the specific needs and circumstances of each case. An important point to remember, however, is that discovery should not be used simply because it is available. Each step must have a specific purpose and be part of an overall discovery strategy.

E. INTERROGATORIES

Submitting interrogatories—that is, a list of written questions—to the opposing parties is usually the first step in the discovery process because interrogatories are the best method for getting basic facts about the other side's case. Once interrogatory answers have been received, further discovery can develop this basic information in greater detail.

See the Litigation File at the end of this book for sample interrogatories and sample answers.

1. Law

Although interrogatories are governed by Rule 33 of the Federal Rules of Civil Procedure, the Rule is often supplemented by local rules because discovery abuse tends to be more extensive with interrogatories than with other discovery methods. These local rules frequently impose additional constraints, most commonly placing limits on the number of interrogatories that can be served and requiring court approval for additional sets of interrogatories. Hence, one should always check the rules for the particular jurisdiction.

Pattern interrogatories
Preprinted questions approved by some districts in common types of cases

Some districts have approved **pattern interrogatories** for common cases such as automobile personal injury suits. Usually taking the form of preprinted questions that relate to a specific area of the law, pattern interrogatories seek information commonly requested in all cases in that particular area. For example, in personal injury cases, recurring interrogatory questions include identification of past injuries, the treating physicians, and the amount of damages sustained. A sample set of pattern interrogatories is included in the workbook.

Interrogatories may be used to identify witnesses and experts; to obtain the subject matter, opinions, and bases for the opinions of experts; and to identify documents and other tangible things. Also, they can be used to inquire about any claim or defense and about any relevant matter that is not privileged, since the scope of discovery is defined by Rule 26(b)(1). However, Rule 33(c) also permits interrogatories that ask for "an opinion or contention that relates to fact or the application of law to fact." The line between what is "opinion" and what is a question of "pure law" is admittedly imprecise and has generated substantial litigation. Because such issues usually become either clearer or moot as discovery progresses, the court may order that such interrogatories remain unanswered until a later time.

Under Rule 33(a), the number of interrogatories each party can serve on another is limited to 25 and requires a court order or stipulation of the parties to serve a larger number. The reason for the limitation is to prevent overly extensive interrogatories, which is a common means of discovery abuse, and because Rule 26(a) already requires disclosure of most information. However, to be consistent with Rule 26(b)(2), service of additional interrogatories should be allowed because the intent is not to prevent discovery but to provide judicial protection against excessive use of this discovery device.

A party cannot avoid the number limit on interrogatories by using distinct subparts. For example, an interrogatory such as the following would count as three separate interrogatories:

EXAMPLE

1. **State all facts upon which you base your contention that the defendant was negligent.**
   (a) For each fact, identify all documents to support your contention.
   (b) For each fact, identify all witnesses.

At least under the Federal Rules, however, it is permissible to divide up an interrogatory into subparts so long as the subparts only divide a single topic. For example, the following would be treated as a single interrogatory:

E X A M P L E

1. **Identify all oral communications you had with the defendant concerning the alleged breach of contract and for each communication state**
   (a) the time
   (b) the place
   (c) the persons present

While these subparts are permissible in federal court, many state courts do not allow subparts. For example, in California no subparts are allowed, and each subpart will be counted as a separate interrogatory. Thus, when in doubt, it is better to draft each interrogatory separately to avoid inadvertently using the number of interrogatories your side is permitted to ask. Many state courts also have rules limiting the number of interrogatories.

Interrogatories can be served by any party on any other party. Without a court order or written stipulation of the parties, Rule 33(a) permits interrogatories to be served only after the parties have met. This limitation results from Rule 26(d), which prohibits formal discovery until after the parties have met as required by Rule 26(f). In state court, interrogatories are often served with the initial pleading or response or shortly afterward.

Answers are due within 30 days of service of the interrogatories, except that defendants are entitled to 45 days from the time of service of the summons and complaint upon them. The answer must respond to each interrogatory separately with either an answer or an objection. An answer must be a "full" answer that fairly meets the substance of the interrogatory. The answering party has an obligation to find the information if it is within the party's possession, even if not within the personal knowledge of the actual person answering.

Under Rule 33(d), the answering party may specify business records from which an answer may be derived or ascertained instead of giving a direct answer, if the "burden of deriving or ascertaining the answer is substantially the same for the party serving the interrogatory as for the party served." When this is the case, the answer need only specify the records in sufficient detail to allow the requesting party to locate and identify the records, and to give the requesting party a reasonable opportunity to inspect and copy them.

An answer must be signed under oath by the person making it. If any interrogatories are objected to, the lawyer making the objection must sign as well.

Finally, an answering party has a continuing obligation to supplement certain answers. Rule 26(e) requires supplementation of responses or disclosures, even though the interrogatory response was complete and accurate when originally made. This obligation applies whenever a party learns that prior disclosures or responses are incomplete or incorrect in some material respect. The obligation to supplement is particularly important with respect to experts, since at the time that the answers to the interrogatories are served, the answering party will frequently not yet know who the testifying experts will be. Failing to supplement answers within a reasonable time can subject the answering party to Rule 37 sanctions.

This duty to supplement may be different in state court. Some state courts do not require any duty to supplement so long as the answer was complete and accurate when made. In California, a party may propound an additional interrogatory before trial that asks the responding party to supplement any previous interrogatory response. In all courts, if a previous answer is later found to be incorrect, the parties have a duty to correct the inaccurate information.

2. Practice approach

When you are asked by the lawyer to send interrogatories to another party, ask yourself two basic questions: What kind of information should I seek? How should I organize and draft interrogatories to get the desired information?

The Litigation File at the end of the book shows an example of a defendant's interrogatories to a plaintiff.

a. Topics: what information should I seek?

Before drafting the interrogatories, ask yourself: What information do I want now so that I can use subsequent discovery methods to develop the information more fully? If you have thought through and discussed with the lawyer the discovery strategy, you should know what information you need that is well suited to obtaining thorough interrogatories. This initial information usually includes the following topics that you can use as a checklist to assist in drafting the interrogatories.

☐ Identity of parties, agents, and employees

Identifying the parties, agents, and employees is not as straightforward as it sounds. Frequently in commercial litigation, you will not know the proper formal names of parties, parent corporations, subsidiaries; where they are incorporated or licensed to do business; or the type of legal entities they are or their relationships to other parties. You need to know this information for a variety of purposes—jurisdictional and joinder issues, for instance. You will also need to learn the identity of all agents and employees, and their relationships to the party. Interrogatories are the best method for getting this information.

☐ Identity of witnesses

Most lawsuits will have witnesses to the events and transactions on which the claims are based. Interrogatories are a good method for obtaining the witnesses' identities, locations, and relationships to the parties.

☐ Identity of documents and tangible things

Similarly, most lawsuits will have certain documents, records, and other tangible things on which the claims are based or that are relevant to the claims. Interrogatories are the best method for identifying and locating these and for determining who has custody or control of them.

☐ Identity of experts, facts, and opinions

At this early stage, of course, the answering party may not yet have selected the experts who ultimately will be witnesses at trial. However, Rule 26(e) requires reasonably prompt supplementation of responses when an interrogatory requests this information. Hence, there is a purpose for requesting it in the initial interrogatories. Sometimes, however, you and the lawyer may decide to ask for this information in a second set of interrogatories after a substantial amount of discovery has been taken, the theory being that a useful response is more likely to be received at that time.

Rule 26(b)(4)(A) provides that experts who are expected to be witnesses are subject to deposition prior to trial. However, since Rule 26(a)(2)(B) requires a complete and detailed written report of the expected testimony of certain experts, such experts can only be deposed after the report has been served.

☐ Details and sequences of events and transactions

Interrogatories are a useful method for obtaining concrete facts under-lying vague or generalized claims. For this reason, they are particularly useful in the commercial litigation area where lawsuits are frequently based on a series of events and transactions spread out over time but not detailed in any way in the pleadings.

☐ Damages information and ability to pay

The plaintiff's complaint will often contain only a general request for damages "in excess of $75,000" or whatever the minimum jurisdictional amount is. Damages interrogatories to the plaintiff are useful for draw-ing out the specific legal theories of recovery the plaintiff is asserting, the dollar amount claimed for each element of damages, and the basis for each claim.

Since it is vital for a plaintiff to determine the defendant's ability to pay a judgment, it is necessary to know whether there are any insurance policies that may cover the event or transaction. In federal court, Rule 26(a)(1)(D) expressly requires this disclosure without a discovery request. In state court, a standard interrogatory question should ask about insurance policies and the details of the coverage. If the pleadings make the defendant's financial condition relevant by alleging a claim such as punitive damages, this information should also be requested.

☐ Identity of persons who prepared answers and of sources used

When interrogatories are served on a corporate party, they should ask for the identity of each person who participated in preparing the answers and the identity of the documents used to prepare each answer. This information will be important in deciding whom to depose and what documents to request.

☐ Positions on issues and opinions of fact

Interrogatories that ask for "opinions," "contentions relating to facts," or the "application of law to facts" are usually proper. On the other hand, interrogatories that ask for matters directly about the law are objectionable. The dividing line is unclear, and a great many discovery motions deal with this problem. Where a pleading is vague, however, a proper interrogatory can prove to be a useful request. For example, it is proper in a negligence action to ask what specific conduct plaintiff claims constituted the negligence, just as in a contract action it is proper to ask what conduct plaintiff claims constituted a breach.

The court has the power under Rule 33(c) to postpone answering such interrogatories. Accordingly, you may wish to avoid such requests in the initial interrogatories because they may trigger objections and delay receiving answers to the more basic interrogatories.

b. Drafting the interrogatories

When you draft interrogatories, your principal task is to prepare a set of interrogatories that will successfully elicit the desired information. The questions must be drafted so as to force the answering party to respond to them squarely and to eliminate the possibility of evasive, though superficially responsive, answers. In addition, the questions should be organized sequentially to make sure that all desired topics are covered. Basic interrogatories for recurrent types of actions are frequently stored in word processors, making them easy to modify for a specific case.

i. Headings

An interrogatory, like any court document, must contain a caption showing the court, parties, and civil case number. Furthermore, the interrogatories should include a heading that identifies which party is raising the interrogatories to which other party. It is also a good practice to label interrogatories "First Set," "Second Set," and so on, and to number them sequentially, with a later set picking up where the previous set left off. This avoids confusion when references are later made to interrogatories and answers. Exhibits 10.2 and 10.3 show sample headings.

Exhibit 10.2.   Interrogatory Headings

[Caption]

PLAINTIFF JOHNSON'S INTERROGATORIES TO DEFENDANT ACME CORPORATION

(First Set)

Plaintiff Johnson requests that defendant Acme Corporation, through an officer or authorized agent of the corporation, answer the following interrogatories under oath and serve them upon plaintiff within 30 days, pursuant to Rule 33 of the Federal Rules of Civil Procedure:

1. . . .
2. . . .
3. . . .

Exhibit 10.3.   Interrogatory Headings

> [Caption]
>
> <u>PLAINTIFF JOHNSON'S INTERROGATORIES TO DEFENDANT</u>
> <u>ACME CORPORATION</u>
>
> (Second Set)
>
> Plaintiff Johnson requests that . . . .
>   23. . . .
>   24. . . .
>   25. . . .

ii. Definitions and instructions

A common practice in more complex interrogatories is to have the actual interrogatories preceded by a definitions and instructions section. Terms used repeatedly in the interrogatories can be defined, making the interrogatories easier to follow while effectively deterring evasive answers. Terms commonly defined in interrogatories include "record," "document," "communication," "witness," "participate," "transaction," "occurrence," "collision," "state," "describe," and "identify." Use broad descriptions of these basic terms so that the answering party cannot give a superficially accurate but effectively unresponsive answer. Sample definitions are shown in Exhibit 10.4.

It is sometimes useful to have an instruction section detail how interrogatories should be answered. Again, it makes the particular interrogatories easier to understand. Sample instructions are shown in Exhibit 10.5.

Finally, in cases where a series of events or transactions is involved, it may be useful to state the time frame the interrogatories are intended to cover. The following example shows how you might state this limit.

EXAMPLE

Unless expressly stated otherwise, each interrogatory relates to the time period beginning June 1, 2006, through and including the date on which answers to these interrogatories are signed.

Keep in mind, however, that this and the other preambles shown in Exhibits 10.4 and 10.5 are useful only in more complex interrogatories.

Exhibit 10.4.   Interrogatories: Sample Definitions

DEFINITIONS

The following terms used in these interrogatories have the following meanings:

1. To "identify" means to (a) state a person's full name, home address, business occupation, business address, and present and past relationship to any party; (b) state the title of any document, who prepared it, when it was prepared, where it is located, and who its custodian is.

2. A "document" means all written or printed matter of any kind, including but not limited to legal documents, letters, memoranda, business records, interoffice communications, and data stored electronically, which are in the possession or control of the answering party.

3. A "communication" means all oral conversations, discussions, letters, telegrams, memoranda, and any other transmission of information in any form, both oral and written.

Exhibit 10.5.   Interrogatories: Sample Instructions

INSTRUCTIONS

In answering each interrogatory:

(a) state whether the answer is within the personal knowledge of the person answering the interrogatory and, if not, the identity of each person known to have personal knowledge of the answer;

(b) identify each document that was used in any way to formulate the answer.

For instance, they are frequently employed in commercial cases. In other cases, such as simple contract or personal injury actions, they are usually unnecessary because they make the interrogatories more complex than they need to be. The intensity of discovery, including interrogatories, must be commensurate with the case's complexity.

In addition, keep in mind that clear, simple interrogatories are more likely to yield clear, simple answers that will provide useful information. The more complex the interrogatories, the more complex and less useful the answers are likely to be. Accordingly, it is usually better to err on the side of simplicity.

iii. Interrogatory style

Interrogatories must be clear and must adequately cover the necessary subjects. They are usually drafted as imperative statements, not as actual questions, since the imperative form affirmatively requires the answering party to supply information.

The first purpose of interrogatories is to identify parties, witnesses, documents, and experts. Exhibits 10.6 through 10.9 show how to draft interrogatories requesting this information.

Note that rather than ask for witnesses in a general way, the interrogatories in Exhibit 10.7 first focus on witnesses to a particular transaction

Exhibit 10.6. Interrogatories: Request to Identify Parties and Agents

1. State the full name of the defendant, where and when incorporated, where and when licensed to do business, where it has its principal place of business, and all names under which it does business.

2. Identify each officer and director of the defendant during the time period of June 2, 2006, through the date answers to these interrogatories are signed.

3. Identify each company, subdivision, and subsidiary in which the defendant has any ownership, control, or interest of any amount for the period referred to in Interrogatory #2 above.

Exhibit 10.7. Interrogatories: Request to Identify Witnesses

1. Identify each person who was present during the execution of the contract that forms the basis of Count I of plaintiff's complaint.

2. Identify each person who participated in or was present during any of the negotiations of the contract executed by plaintiff and defendant on June 2, 2006.

3. State the full name and address of each person who witnessed, or claims to have witnessed, the collision between vehicles driven by the plaintiff and defendant occurring on June 2, 2006.

4. State the full name and address of each person who was present, or claims to have been present, at the scene of the collision during and after the collision, other than the persons identified in Interrogatory #3 above.

5. State the full name and address of each person who has any knowledge of the facts of the collision, other than those persons already identified in Interrogatories #3 and 4 above.

Exhibit 10.8.   Interrogatories: Request to Identify Documents

> 1. Identify each document that relates to the contract executed by plaintiff and defendant on June 2, 2006.
> 2. Identify each document in your possession and control that relates to the accident that is the basis for plaintiff's complaint.

Exhibit 10.9.   Interrogatories Regarding Experts

> 1. As to each expert expected to testify at trial, state:
>   (a) his full name, address, and professional qualifications;
>   (b) the subject matter on which he is expected to testify;
>   (c) the substance of the facts and opinions to which the expert is expected to testify; and
>   (d) a summary of the grounds of each opinion.

or event, then expand the scope in subsequent questions to ensure that all possible known witnesses are identified. This organizes the information into useful categories.

An interrogatory that asks for the identity of documents is commonly combined with a request to produce all documents identified in the interrogatory answer. This has the advantage of getting copies of the identified documents more quickly.[3]

For interrogatories requesting information about experts expected to testify at trial, the use of a basic imperative with subsections is recommended.[4] See Exhibit 10.9.

The categories of interrogatory in Exhibits 10.6 through 10.9 are a part of almost every interrogatory set. These questions obtain the hard data that will provide the springboard for further investigation and discovery.

Interrogatories should also ask for the specific facts on which the pleadings are based. This is particularly important since, due to the minimal requirements of federal "notice pleading," the pleadings frequently contain general conclusory language that gives little information about the facts on which claims, defenses, or damages are based. Interrogatories should develop the basic facts so that the parties can focus on specific

---

3. See section F on drafting document requests.
4. As indicated previously, in courts that limit the number of interrogatories, you may have to count each subpart as a separate interrogatory.

facts underlying the legal claims. Exhibit 10.10 shows a request for this type of information.

If a single interrogatory asks for several categories of information, it is more effective to set out those categories in lettered subsections. This makes it clear what information you want, and makes it more likely that you will elicit complete answers. See Exhibit 10.11.

The kinds of questions shown in Exhibit 10.11 serve to systematically discover the facts on which the plaintiff's case is based, and the answers will point to the areas that need to be explored in greater detail.

Finally, interrogatories should be used to identify the facts on which specific claims are based. Complaints commonly allege that the defendant "breached the contract" or "negligently operated a motor vehicle." An interrogatory is an effective means of developing the facts that the other party claims support the legal contentions. The following are example of how to further develop facts through interrogatories:

EXAMPLE

Developing Facts

1. State the facts upon which you base your claim that defendant acted negligently.
2. State the conduct by the plaintiff and any of its officers, employees, or agents that you claim constituted a breach of the contract.
3. Do you contend that Samuel Jones lacked authority to enter into a contract on behalf of the defendant corporation? If so, state the facts on which you base this contention.

iv. Signing, serving, and filing

The interrogatories must be signed by the attorney and served on each party. In some courts, you must also file the interrogatories with the court. Service is made by any permitted method under Rule 5, most

Exhibit 10.10.   Interrogatories: Facts Underlying Complaint in Personal Injury Action

1. Describe the personal injuries you sustained as a result of this occurrence.

2. Were you hospitalized as a result of this occurrence? If so, state the name and address of each such hospital or clinic, the dates of your hospitalization at each facility, and the amount of each facility's bill.

Exhibit 10.11.   Interrogatories: Categories of Information Regarding Underlying Facts

3. Were you treated by any physicians as a result of this occurrence? If so, state:

(a) the name and address of each such physician;

(b) each physician's areas of specialty;

(c) the dates of each examination, consultation, or appointment; and

(d) the amount of each physician's bill.

4. Were you unable to work as a result of this occurrence? If so, state:

(a) the dates during which you were unable to work;

(b) your employers during those dates;

(c) the type of work you were unable to do; and

(d) the amount of lost wages or income.

5. State any other losses or expenses you claim resulted from this occurrence, other than those already stated above.

6. During the past 10 years, have you suffered any other personal injuries? If so, state:

(a) when, where, and how you were injured;

(b) the nature and extent of the injuries;

(c) the name and address of each medical facility where you were treated; and

(d) physicians by whom you were treated for those injuries.

7. During the past 10 years, have you been hospitalized, treated, examined, or tested at any hospital, clinic, or physician's office for any medical condition other than personal injuries? If so, state:

(a) the name and address of each such medical facility and physician;

(b) the dates such services were provided; and

(c) the medical conditions involved.

commonly by mailing a copy to the lawyers for the other parties. The original interrogatories, with an attached proof of service statement, are then filed with the clerk of the court or, if not permissible in your court, simply retained in your firm's files. A sample set of interrogatories is shown in Exhibit 10.12.

c. Responses to interrogatories

A party must usually answer interrogatories within 30 days of service of the interrogatories. Since they frequently require a substantial amount of work, information necessary to prepare the answers must be

Exhibit 10.12. Sample Set of Interrogatories

[Caption]

Plaintiff Johnson requests that defendant Acme Corporation, through an authorized agent of the corporation, answer the following interrogatories under oath and serve them upon plaintiff within 30 days, pursuant to Rule 33 of the Federal Rules of Civil Procedure.

DEFINITIONS

The following terms used in these interrogatories have the following meanings:

1. To "identify" means to (a) state a person's full name, home address, business occupation, business address, and present and past relationship to any party; (b) state the title of any document, who prepared it, when it was prepared, where it is located, and who its custodian is.

2. A "document" means all written or printed matter of any kind including but not limited to legal documents, letters, memoranda, business records, interoffice communications, and data stored electronically, which are in the possession or control of the answering party.

3. A "communication" means all oral conversations, discussions, letters, telegrams, memoranda, and any other transmission of information in any form, both oral and written.

INSTRUCTIONS

1. In answering each interrogatory:

(a) state whether the answer is within the personal knowledge of the person answering the interrogatory and, if not, the identity of each person known to have personal knowledge of the answer;

(b) identify each document that was used in any way to formulate the answer.

2. Unless expressly stated otherwise, each interrogatory relates to the time period beginning June 2, 2006, through and including the date on which answers to these interrogatories are signed.

INTERROGATORIES

1. State the full name of the defendant.

2. Identify each officer and director of the defendant during the time period of June 2, 2006, through the date answers to these interrogatories are signed.

Exhibit 10.12. Continued

3. Identify each person who was present during the execution of the contract that forms the basis of Count I of the plaintiff's complaint.

4. Identify each person who participated in or was present during any of the negotiations of the contract executed by plaintiff and defendant on June 2, 2006.

5. Identify each document that relates to the contract executed by plaintiff and defendant on June 2, 2006.

6. State all facts which support your denial of the claim stated by plaintiff in Count I of plaintiff's complaint.

Dated: <u>January 18, 2008</u>

J.J. Rayson
Attorney at law

---

obtained reasonably quickly. If the client is out of town or unavailable, or the interrogatories are lengthy, it may be necessary for your side to move for additional time to respond. It is usually a good idea for you or the lawyer to call the opposing lawyer, explain the problem, and ask the opposing lawyer to agree to stipulate to allow additional time. In some courts, a court order approving the stipulation must still be obtained.

i. Researching and preparing answers

A common procedure in answering interrogatories is to send the interrogatories to the client and ask her to respond to the request for information from her own records and from personal recall and to then return the information to you or the lawyer. After you receive the responses back, you can then draft the actual answers by incorporating the client's responses and making any appropriate objections. After you prepare the answers, the client should review the answers for accuracy and completeness, then sign the verification and return the document to you. This procedure works best with individual clients.

Corporate parties and other artificial entities, however, present special considerations. First, you must ascertain who in the corporation should answer the interrogatories. Ordinarily a corporate officer who has personal knowledge of the transactions involved or who has knowledge of the corporate recordkeeping system is an appropriate choice. The selection of the person is more significant than might first appear, however, because although whoever provides the answer will be bound by it, the answer will also be binding on the corporate party.

Second, the corporate party has an obligation to investigate files that are in its possession or control, to collect the requested information, and to put that information in the answer. Records are considered in a party's possession or control if they are records that are kept at the company's offices, or if they are physically in the possession of another, such as an accountant or a storage company, but the party has the power to get the records returned. The corporation's duty to investigate is limited only by the extent of its own records, but there is no duty to conduct an independent outside investigation. A corporate party cannot avoid answering a proper interrogatory through the device of selecting someone to answer the interrogatories who has no personal knowledge of any relevant facts.

Third, under Rule 33(d) a party can answer an interrogatory by specifying the business records from which the requested information can be derived if the burden of obtaining the desired information from those records is substantially the same for either party. This is a most useful device because it avoids "doing the homework" for the requesting party and permits answers to be made more quickly.

ii. Objections

Objection
Statement made by the responding party in an interrogatory that indicates a reason for not answering the question asked

A party on whom interrogatories have been served has two possible responses: an answer or an **objection**. If the response is an objection, simply state the objection as your answer to a particular interrogatory.

Rule 33(b)(4) requires each objection to be specifically justified; unstated or untimely grounds for objection will generally be considered to be waived. However, under Rule 33(b)(1) the responding party still has a duty to provide "answers to the extent the interrogatory is not objectionable."

There are several bases for objecting. First, a party may object on the basis that the information sought is irrelevant. However, since the Rule 26 definition of relevance for discovery purposes is quite broad, such an objection is difficult to make successfully. In addition, the court can grant sanctions for frivolous objections.

Second, a party may object on the ground of privilege, relying on either the privilege for qualified trial preparation materials and absolute mental impressions under Rule 26(b) or on the privileges under Rule 501 of the Federal Rules of Evidence.

Third, an objection can be made to interrogatories that ask for information that cannot be obtained by interrogatories, such as an interrogatory that demands the production of records.

Fourth, an objection can be made on the basis that the interrogatory is annoying, embarrassing, oppressive, or unduly burdensome and expensive. This is probably the most frequently raised objection, one that has generated a substantial body of case law. When such an objection is raised, the answering party should move for a protective order under Rule 26(c).[5] The claim that an interrogatory is unduly burdensome and expensive requires that the court balance the burden of collecting the information requested with the benefit to the requesting party. When the work involved in obtaining the information is enormous and the benefit to the requesting party is small in light of the issues in the case, an objection to the interrogatory should be sustained.

Where an objection exists, it should be made on the interrogatory answer. Exhibit 10.13 shows examples of objections.

iii. Answers

The other possible response is to answer the interrogatory. There are three basic types of responses.

First, the party can answer the interrogatory by supplying the requested information if it is either known or ascertainable from the party's personal knowledge or records. The answer should be as brief as possible, since you ordinarily don't want to volunteer information that has not been requested. On the other hand, you must answer with the essential facts at your disposal, since failing to disclose can subject your side to serious sanctions.

In addition, if your side has a strong case and the attorney is looking toward a favorable settlement, you may want to volunteer information.

Exhibit 10.13.   Objections to Interrogatories

> Interrogatory No. 8: State which officers were involved in the sale of fork-lift trucks to the XYZ Corporation on August 1, 2006.
>
> Answer: Defendant objects to Interrogatory No. 8 on the ground that it asks for information that is not relevant to the subject matter of this action, nor likely to lead to the discovery of admissible evidence because it pertains to a transaction with a nonparty, the XYZ Corporation, that has no relevance to the controversy between the plaintiff and defendant.
>
> Interrogatory No. 9: Identify all conversations between defendant's employees and defendant's corporate counsel between August 1, 2006, and the present date.
>
> Answer: Defendant objects to Interrogatory No. 9 on the ground that it asks for material that is privileged under the attorney-client privilege.

5. See section J1 *supra*.

The goal in answering interrogatories is to strike an appropriate balance between the advantages of brevity and a full, detailed answer. Exhibit 10.14 shows appropriate answers.

When the interrogatory asks for information on which the answering party has some personal knowledge but not to the detail requested, and no records exist that can supply those details, the answer should accurately reflect this situation. In this instance you might reply as follows:

EXAMPLE

Interrogatory No. 6: Identify each communication between John Marlowe and Phillip Johnson that relates to the contract that forms the basis of Count I of plaintiff's complaint.

Answer: There were several telephone conversations between Marlowe and Johnson during a period of approximately four weeks preceding the execution of the contract. The exact dates and substance of each of these conversations are unknown.

This type of answer is satisfactory when the answer cannot state facts that are not within the knowledge or recall of the answering party and no records exist to supply the details. The better practice is to follow up on this type of response through depositions, which allow the extent and details of the party's recall to be explored and developed.

When an interrogatory asks for a party's contentions, a more complete answer is called for, since the answering party does not wish to limit its proof or theories of liability. This more complex response might be framed as follows:

EXAMPLE

Interrogatory No. 4: State all the facts on which you claim that defendant acted negligently.

Answer: Defendant (1) drove in excess of the posted speed limit; (2) drove in excess of a reasonable speed under the existing conditions and circumstances; (3) failed to keep a proper lookout to ensure the safety of others; (4) failed to keep his vehicle in the proper lane; (5) failed to yield the right of way; and (6) failed to obey traffic signals, markers, and "rules of the road." Investigation continues.

In this type of answer, the "investigation continues" response is important because additional investigation and discovery may develop additional facts to support the negligence claim.

A second type of response is simply to state "no knowledge" when this is accurate:

Interrogatory No. 4: **State if any witnesses to the collision prepared written reports of any kind regarding the collision.**

   Answer: **No knowledge.**

Keep in mind that an answering party must search her own records to determine if the information exists and, if it does, use the information to answer the interrogatory.

Rule 26(e) imposes a continuing duty to supplement answers regarding the identity of witnesses, testifying experts, and answers that were

Exhibit 10.14.   Answers Supplying the Requested Information

Interrogatory No. 2: Identify each person who was present during the execution of the contract that forms the basis of Count I of plaintiff's complaint.

Answer: John Marlowe and Phillip Johnson.

Interrogatory No. 3: Identify each physician who treated you as a result of this occurrence.
Answer: Dr. William Jackson, Mercy Hospital, Seattle, Washington; Dr. Erica Olson, 3420 Cascades Highway, Seattle, Washington; possibly other physicians at Mercy Hospital, whose names are unknown; investigation continues.

Interrogatory No. 4: State the name and address of each person who was present or claims to have been present during the collision.

Answer: Mary Carter, 2440 Congress St., Tucson, Arizona; Frank Wilson, 1831 N. Campbell Ave., Tucson, Arizona; Abby Carter, 2440 Congress St., Tucson, Arizona; Jennifer Carter, 2440 Congress St., Tucson, Arizona; in addition, there were several other pedestrians in the vicinity, but the names and addresses of such persons are presently unknown; investigation continues.

incorrect or were correct when made but must be supplemented because failing to do so would constitute knowing concealment. A common response in such instances is to answer based on present knowledge and acknowledge the continuing duty under the Rule. The following are example of this type of response:

EXAMPLE

Interrogatory No. 2: Identify each person who saw or heard something during the collision.

Answer: Other than plaintiff and defendant, none presently known; investigation continues.

Interrogatory No. 3: Identify each expert expected to be called as a witness at trial.

Answer: None at present; plaintiff is aware of her continuing duty to supplement responses under Rule 26(e).

The third type of answer is to identify business records that provide the information. Rule 33(d) requires only that the answer specify the records and give the requesting party a reasonable opportunity to examine and copy them. Actual production with the interrogatory answer is not required; however, such records are always discoverable through a notice to produce under Rule 34. For this reason, there may be times when you will want to simply attach copies of the pertinent documents as exhibits to the interrogatory answers. Below are examples of answers to requests to identify records:

EXAMPLE

Interrogatory No. 5: Identify each communication between Phillip Johnson and Jane East between June 1, 2006, and August 4, 2007, relating to the contract that forms the basis of Count I of plaintiff's complaint.

Answer: Any such communications are kept in the defendant's telephone logbook, the pertinent dates of which may be examined and copied at a reasonable time at the defendant's place of business.

Interrogatory No. 6: Identify each sales transaction entered into between plaintiff and defendant for the period of January 1, 2006, through August 4, 2007.

Answer: These transactions are recorded in the defendant's sales records, which are computerized after sales transactions are completed. A printout of these transactions is attached as Exhibit A.

---

iv. Signing, serving, and filing

The format for interrogatory answers, like any other court document, should include a case caption and document title. The answers must be signed and sworn to by the person making them.[6] If any interrogatories are objected to, the attorney must sign them as well.

The completed interrogatory answers must then be served on each party and, where required, filed with the court. Service is made by any proper method under Rule 5, commonly by mailing a copy to the lawyers for the other parties. If required by the court, the original answer, with an attached proof of service, is filed with the clerk of the court. Some court rules require that the original answer be served on the party requesting the interrogatories, with a copy retained in your law firm's files. Always check the rules for the particular court before serving the interrogatory answers. A sample answer is shown in Exhibit 10.15, as well as in the Litigation File at the end of the book.

F. REQUESTS TO PRODUCE DOCUMENTS AND SUBPOENAS

After answers to interrogatories have been received, you will usually have enough detailed information to ask for copies of identified documents through a request to produce. Hence, requests to produce are usually the second step in the discovery process. Simple requests to produce documents identified in the interrogatory answers are also frequently served with interrogatories. In federal court, you will already have obtained documents as part of the Rule 26(a)(1) disclosures. Accordingly, your request to produce will seek documents not already provided by the other party.

In addition, do not forget the ability to obtain public records from government entities. If a government entity is involved in the litigation, you may be able to obtain any records kept by the entity by simply making a public records request.

1. Law

Requests to produce documents and other physical or tangible evidence and for entry upon land to inspect are governed by Rule 34 of the

---

6. The sworn statement is often referred to as the verification (since the person is verifying the accuracy of the statements). Under the Federal Rules and the rules of most states, the verification may be sworn to under oath and acknowledged by a notary public, or stated under penalty of perjury under the laws of the United States and/or the applicable state.

Exhibit 10.15.   *Format for Sample Answer to Interrogatories*

[Caption]

DEFENDANT ACME CORPORATION'S ANSWERS TO PLAINTIFF'S INTERROGATORIES

Defendant Acme Corporation answers the first set of interrogatories put forth by plaintiff as follows:

Interrogatory No. 1: . . .

Answer: . . .

Acme Corporation

By_____

William Phillips
    Vice President for
    Administration of
    Acme Corporation

State of Arizona | SS.
County of Pima |

William Phillips, after being first duly sworn, states that he is an officer of Acme Corporation and is authorized to make the above interrogatory answers on behalf of Acme Corporation, that the above answers have been prepared with the assistance of counsel, that the answers are based either on his personal knowledge, the personal knowledge of Acme Corporation employees, or on information obtained from Acme Corporation records, and that the answers are true to the best of his knowledge, information, and belief.

_____
William Phillips

Signed and sworn to before me on this _____ day of _____,_____.

_____
Notary Public.

My commission expires on_____

Federal Rules of Civil Procedure. A request to produce can be served upon another party and also nonparties under Rule 34(c). The scope of the request, like other discovery, is controlled by Rule 26(b), which permits discovery of any relevant matter that is not privileged.

Rule 34 permits requests to produce for three things:

1. Documents for inspection and copying
2. Tangible things for inspection, copying, and testing
3. Entry on land or property for inspection and testing

Of these, production of documents is the principal use of Rule 34 requests. Documents include all "writings, drawings, graphs, charts, photographs, phonorecords, and other data compilations from which information can be obtained, translated, if necessary, by the respondent through detection devices into reasonably usable form."

The Rule also requires a party to produce all documents that are in that party's "possession, custody or control." This obligates a party to produce all relevant documents, even those not in the party's actual possession, if the party has a lawful right to get them from another person or entity. In short, a party cannot avoid production through the simple device of transferring the documents to another person or entity such as the party's lawyer, accountant, insurer, or corporate subsidiary. When this avoidance device is used, the party is deemed to have retained "control" of the documents and is required to get them returned in order to comply with the production request.

A request to produce must describe each item or category to be produced with "reasonable particularity." This is usually read to require that, in the context of the case and the overall nature of the documents involved, a responding party must reasonably be able to determine what particular documents are called for. (Sample requests with particularity are shown later in this chapter at page 313.) This is obviously a flexible standard that varies from case to case.

Rule 34 requires that the documents produced for inspection must be produced in either the same order as they are normally kept or in the order, with labels, that corresponds to the categories of the request. The producing party cannot purposefully disorganize documents and records to make them more difficult to comprehend. Furthermore, the request to produce must specify a "reasonable time, place, and manner" for the inspection. The responding party must serve a written response for each category requested, usually within 30 days of service of the request, stating whether he objects, with reasons for the objection, or will comply.

2. Practice approach

a. Timing

Without a court order or written stipulation of the parties, Rule 34(b) only allows requests to produce documents after the parties have met. This limitation results again from Rule 26(d), which prohibits formal discovery until after the parties have met as required by Rule 26(f).

Before serving a request to produce documents or a request for entry upon land to inspect, you need to know what documents you want produced and what things you want to inspect. Rule 34 requires "reasonable particularity." If you have drafted your interrogatories carefully and have asked for descriptions of relevant documents and for the identity of those whose custody those documents are in, answers to the interrogatories should provide sufficient detail to meet the particularity requirement for production requests. Hence, requests to produce should normally be served as soon as possible after the answers to interrogatories have been received. Sometimes, as previously mentioned, production requests are served at the same time as interrogatories.

This timetable presumes that the party has adequately, and in a timely fashion, answered your interrogatories. If the answering party has objected, failed to answer, or served evasive or incomplete answers, these problems must be resolved through appropriate discovery motions.[7] Doing this, however, will necessarily delay serving the requests to produce. In this situation, you should consider serving a request to produce anyway, since you can ordinarily determine in a general way what documents the other party is likely to have and describe them sufficiently by topic or subject matter to meet the particularity requirement. It is easy for discovery to become sidetracked or to stall completely. In these situations, you must weigh the benefits and liabilities of waiting or going ahead in light of the overall discovery strategy for the case.

b. Organization

Before actually drafting the request to produce, you need to organize your thoughts on what you want from the other party. If you have thoroughly discussed the discovery strategy with the supervising attorney and intelligently thought it through, and put forth your interrogatories to and received answers from that party, then the bulk of your work is

---

7. See section J of this chapter.

already done. You will know in sufficient detail what documents you want, what documents the answering party admits having, how those documents are described or labeled, and who their custodian is.

If you have not yet received interrogatory answers but are asked by the lawyer to send out requests to produce anyway, you will have to evaluate what documents the other party is likely to have, how they are likely to be labeled and organized, and who their custodian is. Some of this information may be within the client's knowledge. Accordingly, you should check with the client before serving the document request.

c. Drafting requests to produce

i. Heading

A request to produce should be drafted like any other court document. It must have a caption showing the court, case title, and docket number and be properly labeled. When a case has several parties, it is useful to designate which party is sending the request to which other party; otherwise, the simple title "Requests To Produce Documents" will suffice. A sample heading is shown in Exhibit 10.16.

ii. Definitions

Requests to produce present the same problems concerning definitions as interrogatories. Accordingly, terms and phrases frequently used, such as "document," "record," "relating to," "transaction," and "occurrence," should be defined. It is best to use definitions identical to

Exhibit 10.16.   Request to Produce: Heading

[Caption]

<u>PLAINTIFF JOHNSON'S REQUESTS TO PRODUCE DOCUMENTS TO DEFENDANT ACME CORPORATION</u>

Plaintiff Johnson requests defendant Acme Corporation to produce the documents and things listed below, pursuant to Rule 34 of the Federal Rules of Civil Procedure:

1. . . .
2. . . .
3. . . .

those used in the interrogatories. Exhibit 10.17 shows a sample format for definitions.

iii. Requests format

There are three basic requests permitted under Rule 34: to inspect and copy documents, to inspect and examine tangible things, and to enter upon land to inspect and examine things. The requests should follow a basic format.

The requests to produce must specify a reasonable date, time, and place for the production. Rule 34 requires only that this be "reasonable," which must necessarily take into account the volume and complexity of the records sought. Since the Rule requires a response within 30 days of service, the date set for the production should be a longer time period. Exhibit 10.18 shows the request format.

Exhibit 10.17.   Request to Produce: Definitions

<u>DEFINITIONS</u>

The following terms used in this request to produce have the following meanings:
    1. A "document" means . . . .
    2. A "transaction" means . . . .

Exhibit 10.18.   Request to Produce: Request Format

A. Plaintiff requests that defendant produce the following documents for inspection and copying at the offices of Mary Anton, plaintiff's attorney, 200 Main Street, Suite 400, Tucson, Arizona, on August 1, 2006, at 2:00 P.M.:
    1. . . .
    2. . . .
B. Plaintiff requests that defendant produce the following things for inspection, copying, and testing at the offices of Independent Testing, 2000 Main Street, Tucson, Arizona, on August 1, 2006, at 9:00 A.M.:
    1. . . .
    2. . . .
C. Plaintiff requests that defendant permit plaintiff to enter defendant's lumberyard located at 4000 Monroe Street, Tucson, Arizona, for the purpose of inspecting, photographing, and measuring the premises on August 1, 2006, at 2:00 P.M.

Most requests to produce involve documents. There are several ways to draft requests that will meet Rule 34's particularity requirement.

First, you can use the interrogatory answers. If those answers have listed and described a variety of documents, referring to the descriptions should be adequate. The responding party will be in a poor position to claim that a description it furnished is now suddenly insufficient.

E X A M P L E

Request Based on Interrogatory Answer

1. Each document identified in defendant's answer to Interrogatory No. 6 in plaintiff's first set of interrogatories.

Second, ask for all documents that relate to a specific transaction or event. By making the request specific, it should not be challenged on the grounds of being too vague.

E X A M P L E

Request Based on Specific Transaction

2. All documents relating to the sale of property located at 4931 Sunrise St., Tucson, Arizona, entered into between plaintiff and defendant on July 31, 2004.

Third, you can ask for specific types of documents that relate to a more general time frame or course of conduct.

E X A M P L E

Request for Specific Types of Documents

3. All bills of lading, invoices, and shipping confirmation notices relating to all goods shipped from plaintiff to defendant during the period from January 1, 2006, through April 30, 2006.

In each of the above examples, the party responding to the request to produce should not have difficulty in either understanding the request or identifying the documents requested. In contrast, a request calling for the production of "all documents relating to the allegations in plaintiff's complaint" or similarly vague language is defective and unenforceable because it does not meet Rule 34's specificity requirement.

It is possible that the responding party will not object to a general request, but, regardless, it is usually not an effective approach for discovery. Requests to produce should balance the safety of inclusiveness with the utility of a more focused request. A request that is too broad may result in a huge volume of paperwork being deposited in your office; you may have neither the time nor assistance to review all of it in order to extract the few documents that are relevant to the case.

Fourth, it is always useful to ask for the identity of any documents that existed at one time but have since been destroyed. This prevents the literally true but misleading response that there are "no records" of the description requested.

iv. Signing, serving, and filing

The request to produce should be signed by the lawyer, served on each party, and filed with the court. Service is made by any permitted method under Rule 5, commonly by mailing a copy to the lawyers for the other parties. The original requests to produce, with an attached proof of service statement, are then retained in the firm's files or, if required, filed with the clerk of the court. A sample request to produce is shown in Exhibit 10.19, as well as in the Litigation File at the end of the book.

d. Responses to requests to produce

A party served with a request to produce usually must respond within 30 days of service of the request. Even though the lawyers for the requesting and responding parties frequently reach an informal agreement on how and when to produce documents and conduct inspections,[8] the responding party should serve and file a response since this is required by Rule 34.

i. Researching and preparing responses

If the preliminary investigation has been done and answers to interrogatories have been prepared and served, you already will have done

---

8. See pages 318-319.

Exhibit 10.19.   Sample Request to Produce

[Caption]

PLAINTIFF JOHNSON'S REQUESTS TO PRODUCE DOCUMENTS TO DEFENDANT ACME CORPORATION

Pursuant to Rule 34 of the Federal Rules of Civil Procedure, Plaintiff Johnson requests defendant Acme Corporation to produce for inspection and copying the documents and things listed below, on August 22, 2007, at 2:00 P.M. at the law offices of Mary Anton, located at 200 Main Street, Suite 400, Tucson, Arizona.

DEFINITIONS

The following terms used in this request to produce have the following meanings:

1. A "Document" means all written or printed matter of any kind including, but not limited to legal documents, letters, memoranda, business records, interoffice communications, and data stored electronically, which are in the possession or control of the answering party.

2. The "Transaction" refers to the circumstances surrounding the contract entered into between Plaintiff Johnson and Defendant Acme Corporation on or about June 1, 2007.

3. A "Communication" means all oral conversations, discussions, letters, telegrams, memoranda, and any other transmission of information in any form, both oral and written.

DOCUMENTS REQUESTED

1. All documents reflecting, referring, or otherwise relating to any communications between Defendant and anyone else concerning the Transaction.

2. All bills of lading, invoices, and shipping confirmation notices relating to all goods shipped from plaintiff to defendant during the period from June 1, 2007, through and including December 15, 2007.

3. All documents identified in defendant's answer to Interrogatory No. 5 in plaintiff's first set of interrogatories.

Dated: <u>March 3, 2008</u>

_____

J.J. Rayson

most of the initial work involved in responding to requests to produce. In addition, you should always send the requests to the client and ask the client a couple of questions about the requests. First, does the client know what the requests actually call for? If not, your side may want to object on grounds of vagueness. Second, how much effort will be required to collect the documents requested? If it is substantial and the case is not complex, your side may be able to object on the grounds that the requests are unduly burdensome and move for a protective order or at least for additional time to respond.

After the client has collected the documents, review the material to determine if all of it is relevant. If there are any privileged communications, now is the time to object, since privileges are waived unless timely asserted. Finally, make sure that those documents are in fact all the available documents the client has in his possession, custody, or control. You can be sure that the client and other witnesses will be questioned about the completeness of the tendered documents during their depositions. Now is the time to review the documents with the client for completeness. Also be sure to check your firm's files because documents responsive to the request may be in the files.

ii. Objections

As with interrogatories, a party on whom requests to produce have been served has two possible responses: an answer or an objection. Under Rule 34(b) an objection to a part, item, or category must be specific, and production should still be allowed for the portions that are unobjectionable.

If the response is an objection, there are several possible bases. First, an objection may be made on the ground that the documents sought are irrelevant. However, since Rule 26 has such a broad definition of relevance for discovery purposes, this is a difficult ground on which to prevail. Moreover, this ground will probably have been ruled on if the same objection was made to the interrogatory that asked for the identity of the documents. Second, an objection can be based on a privilege, either the privilege for trial preparation materials and mental impressions under Rule 26(b)(5), or the privileges recognized under Rule 501 of the Federal Rules of Evidence. Third, an objection can be based on the request being annoying, embarrassing, oppressive, or unduly burdensome and expensive. Here, the answering party should seek a protective order under Rule 26(c); still, an objection to a request to produce should be made on the response. A response with an objection is shown in Exhibit 10.20.

As noted above, a request can frequently be objectionable in part. When this is so, the response should make clear what part is being objected to and what the responding party agrees to produce. Such an

Exhibit 10.20.   Response to Request to Produce: Objection

[Caption]

<u>RESPONSE TO PLAINTIFF'S REQUESTS TO PRODUCE</u>

Defendant Acme Corporation responds to plaintiff's Requests to Produce Documents as follows:

    1. Defendant objects to plaintiff's Request No. 1 on the ground that it requests documents the disclosure of which would violate the attorney-client privilege, since the request on its face asks for the production of "all correspondence from corporate officers to corporate counsel regarding the contract dated July 1, 2007."

---

objection is a common response to a broad request asking for a variety of documents, some of which may be privileged. In this case you might phrase the objection as follows.

EXAMPLE

2. Defendant objects to plaintiff's Request No. 2 to the extent it asks for privileged communications protected by the attorney-client privilege. Plaintiff's Request No. 2 asks for the production of "memoranda by defendant's subsidiary, Acme Productions, relating to a bid on U.S. Government Contract No. 89-3287, commonly known as the `Tristar Contract.' " These memoranda include documents prepared by Acme Productions officers and employees, documents prepared at the request of and sent to Acme Corporation's General Counsel, which relate to the pending litigation and are protected from disclosure by the attorney-client privilege.

---

iii. Answers

If a request to produce is not objected to, it must be answered. An answer involves two considerations: the formal response and the practical concerns involved in arranging for the actual production of the documents. There should be a formal answer even if, as is often the case, the production is worked out informally between the attorneys because Rule 34 requires a response. Exhibit 10.21 shows a typical answer.

Exhibit 10.21.   Response to Request to Produce: Answer

[Caption]

<u>RESPONSE TO PLAINTIFF'S REQUESTS FOR PRODUCTION AND INSPECTION</u>

Defendant Acme Corporation responds to plaintiff's requests for production of documents and inspection as follows:

1-8. Defendant has agreed to produce the documents requested in plaintiff's Request Nos. 1 through 8 at the offices of plaintiff's attorney on or before August 15, 2007.

9. Defendant has agreed to permit the inspection of the items described in plaintiff's Request No. 9 at its manufacturing plant located at 9000 Main St., Tucson, Arizona, at a mutually agreed-upon date and time, but not later than August 31, 2007.

_____
Attorney for Defendant
Acme Corporation

If records requested do not exist, the response should clearly establish this fact. In this case your response would be phrased like the following example.

EXAMPLE

---

3. There are no documents in the possession, custody, or control of defendant Acme Corporation requested by plaintiff's Request No. 3.

Most production requests are worked out informally between the lawyers, who usually call each other and agree on the mechanics of delivering and copying the pertinent records. This will usually include when and where the documents will be produced, how the documents will be organized, and who will perform and pay for the actual copying. The usual procedure is for the documents to be produced at, or delivered to, the requesting attorney's offices on an agreed-upon date. The responding party has the option of producing the records either in the order in which they are ordinarily kept or labeled to correspond to the categories of the request. Since most production requests overlap on particulars to ensure completeness, a common approach in responding is to produce the documents in their usual order because this is easier for the responding party.

Regarding an informal agreement on the mechanics of reproducing the records, the Rule requires only production—not copying—by the responding party. However, it is usually desirable for the responding party to make copies so as to retain possession of the original documents. For this reason, it is common for the responding party to make copies of the records that comply with the requests; the cost of reproduction is then paid by the requesting party.

When the documents involved are so voluminous that copying all of them would be prohibitively expensive, a common solution is to have the lawyer for the requesting party review the documents at the offices of either the answering party or the answering party's lawyer. The requesting lawyer can then select the relevant documents for photocopying.

If your client is the answering party, make sure that you keep a copy of everything submitted to the opposing side so that no issue arises later over what was actually delivered. In addition, all documents produced should be stamped in the lower right-hand corner with a number so that an exact count of the documents can be made. The number also makes it easier to identify the documents for depositions and trial preparation.

In addition, the numbers can serve to identify which party produced the document. For example, the parties may agree that the plaintiff will number her documents that are produced as numbers 1-1,000, while the defendant will use numbers 2,000-3,000. Alternatively, you may simply set up a code to identify the documents, such as placing a "p" in front of all documents produced by the plaintiff. Whichever method you use, be consistent in the numbering.

iv. Signing, serving, and filing

The written response to requests to produce must be signed, then served on every other party and filed with the court. Service is made by any permitted method under Rule 5, commonly by mailing a copy to the lawyers for the other parties. The original response, with an attached proof of service, is then filed with the clerk of the court, or, if not permitted under your local court rules, maintained in the firm's files.

3. Document requests and subpoenas to nonparties

Rule 34(c) permits document requests to be used against nonparties to the same extent as parties if the procedures of Rule 45 are followed.

Rule 45 provides that subpoenas can be issued to command any person "to produce and permit inspection and copying of designated books, documents or tangible things in the possession, custody or control of that person, or to permit inspection of premises, at a time and place therein specified." The subpoena must be issued for the court of the district in which the production will be made. If the subpoena is unreasonable or oppressive, the court can, on motion of the party upon whom the subpoena is served, quash the subpoena or require that the party issuing the subpoena to pay in advance the reasonable costs of complying with the subpoena.

Although in federal court it is not necessary to also notice a deposition in connection with obtaining the documents from a nonparty, the practice may be different in state court. In some state courts, when a party wishes to obtain records or tangible things from a nonparty before trial, the only proper discovery procedure is to subpoena the witness for a deposition and include in the subpoena a command to produce and permit inspection and copying of designated records and things. This is sometimes called a **subpoena duces tecum**. An example appears in the Litigation File at the end of the book.

Subpoena duces tecum
An order of the court requiring a witness to appear and produce documents

4. Document productions

Every litigation paralegal will undoubtedly be called on at some point to attend a production of documents. Usually, in document-intensive cases, documents are produced to the other party by making the documents available for photocopying and inspection at either the office of the lawyer of the party producing the documents or, if they are too voluminous to transport, the place where the documents are located. As a litigation paralegal, you may be asked to attend a production of documents produced by the other side or be asked to review documents that are going to be produced by your side to the other side.

If you are asked to attend a production of documents produced by the other party, take the following steps before reviewing the documents:

1. Review the request for production of documents and the response to ascertain what documents need to be produced.
2. Discuss with the lawyer the type of documents you should look for that may be of particular interest.
3. Decide on the method of photocopying and the client's budget for photocopying.

With respect to the latter point, in an ideal situation you will want to photocopy all documents that have even the slightest relevance to the case at issue. However, large volumes of photocopying can become expensive, especially if it is necessary to bring in a mobile copy machine and have someone undo stapled pages and copy each document individually. On the other hand, if the opposing side will release the documents to an outside copy service and the documents can be automatically fed into the copy machine, the cost is much less. Accordingly, it is important to discuss with the lawyer the type of copy service you will use and any limits on costs of production.

Once you are at the location where the documents are being produced, you will need to review the documents carefully and determine which documents should be copied. If you are unsure about certain documents, you may wish to tab the documents and verify with the attorney the significance of the particular document. If cost is not an object, when you are in doubt the document should be copied.

After the documents have been copied, you will need to devise a method for indexing the documents. As with the documents you produce to the other side, all pages of each document should be number stamped. Avoid the temptation of listing every document produced with the corresponding number. Although this method may work in cases where few documents are produced, in larger cases the sheer volume of documents makes it impractical to review such a list for a specific document. Rather, the documents can be set up chronologically, by subject matter, or by type of document (i.e., correspondence, draft contracts, executed contracts, memoranda). Choose the method that works best for you and ensures that you will be able to quickly locate a document when needed.

If your side is producing the documents, you may be asked to review the documents prior to the production. This review is essential since you must be careful to remove any documents that are subject to an attorney-client or work product privilege. Failure to remove the privileged document may result in a waiver of the privilege. In addition, you will want to remove any documents that are not relevant to the request made by the opposing party.

Sometimes, documents will contain both privileged and unprivileged or relevant and irrelevant matter. In this situation, you will need to **redact** the portion of the document that is privileged or nonresponsive. "Redacting" refers to the covering up of the portions of the document that should not be produced. To redact a document, photocopy the document first, then use white-out or white tape to cover up the portions of the photocopied document that should not be produced. After you have redacted all necessary parts of the document, photocopy the document again. This latter photocopy document will be produced. This document should contain a notation that it has been redacted and the reason for the redaction, such as "Document Redacted — Attorney-Client Privilege."

If you are producing a small number of documents, you may wish simply to send photocopies of the documents to your adversary without engaging in a formal document production. If the attorney agrees that the documents may be produced informally, send a transmittal letter along with the documents produced. This will act as a record that the documents were sent and a record of the day the documents were sent and of the documents that were produced. A sample transmittal letter is shown in Exhibit 10.22.

G. DEPOSITIONS

Depositions are usually taken after both interrogatory answers and responses to documents requests have been received, since those answers and documents will usually be used to plan an intelligent deposition. Although depositions are both expensive and time consuming, they are quite useful in assessing witness credibility, learning what witnesses know, and pinning witnesses down. Other than a subpoena for documents, they are the only discovery method that can be used on nonparties, and the only method in which the opposing counsel does not directly control the responses. For these reasons, depositions play a critical role in the discovery plan of virtually every case.

Exhibit 10.22.   *Sample Transmittal Letter*

Dear Mr. Jones:

Pursuant to Defendant's Response to Plaintiff's First Request for Production of Documents, enclosed are copies of documents number stamped 1,000 to 1,200. The number represents a control number placed by our office to identify the documents as coming from our client. The documents being produced are as follows:

Description	Number
Invoices	1,000-1,075
Correspondence	1,076-1,196
Contract dated June 1, 2007	1,197-1,200

If you find any document to be missing, or if any document is illegible and you would like to review the original, please notify me immediately.

Sincerely,

_____
Thomas Flannery
Legal Assistant

Rules 27 through 32 of the Federal Rules of Civil Procedure govern depositions. Rule 30, which regulates oral depositions, is the principal one, however, since oral depositions are the predominant way in which depositions are taken.[9] Although you may attend a deposition, only the lawyer may take the deposition or defend a witness at a deposition.

1. Law

a. Timing

Oral depositions may be taken of any party or nonparty, and can be taken after the parties have met and conferred as required by Rule 26(d) and (e). Leave of court is not necessary to take the deposition before the meeting, so long as the depositing notice indicates with supporting facts that the deponent is expected to leave the country and will thereafter be unavailable for examination.

The timing of the depositions should be considered carefully since under Rule 30 each side has a limit of ten depositions. Thus, in cases with multiple plaintiffs and defendants, each side must get together to decide how to use the depositions. This number can be enlarged only by court order or written stipulation of the parties.

No person can be deposed more than once without court order or written stipulation of the parties. While Rule 26 does not put time limitations on depositions, Rule 26(b)(2) gives the court discretion to impose limits, and some local rules impose them as well.

b. Notice

Whenever a deposition will be taken, the party taking the deposition must give "reasonable" notice to every party to the action. Rule 30(b) does not specify what is reasonable, although some local rules specify minimum requirements, frequently ten days. Also, many courts have addressed the question, most finding that reasonable notice is a flexible standard that depends on the nature of the case and the deponent involved.

The notice must state the name and address of each person to be deposed. If the name is not known, the notice must describe the person to be deposed in sufficient detail to identify that person individually or as part of a class or group. This is frequently the case with corporations and other artificial entities where the actual name of the proper person

---

9. Depositions on written questions are governed by Rule 31. This type of deposition is rarely used.

to be deposed is unknown. In such a case, the corporation, or other entity, must designate an officer, director, managing agent, or other person to testify on its behalf. The notice must also state the time and place for the deposition.

In addition to the notice to other parties, of course the person to be deposed must also be notified. A sample notice of deposition appears in the Litigation File at the end of the book. When the deponent is also a party, the notice of deposition is sufficient. When the deponent is a nonparty, he must be subpoenaed in accordance with Rule 45—this is called a **subpoena ad testificandum**. Witness fees and mileage costs must accompany the subpoena, as set by 28 U.S.C. §1821. A problem that frequently arises concerns the amount of fees and costs that the witness is entitled to receive. A common practice is to tender the witness a check for the probable mileage and one day's witness fees, and to take care of any differences after the deposition.

> **Subpoena ad testificandum**
> An order of the court requiring a witness to appear and give testimony

Finally, the deponent can be commanded to produce records, documents, and tangible things for inspection and copying at the deposition. With parties, this is simply achieved by serving on the deponent a request to produce under Rule 34 for the same date and place on which the deposition will be held. Nonparties can also be commanded to produce records by serving a subpoena under Rule 45(a)—a subpoena duces tecum (see page 328). When such a subpoena is served, a copy of it must be sent to each party by attaching the copy to the notice of deposition.

c. Location

Rule 30 does not specify where a deposition may be conducted. Accordingly, the deposition of a party can be held anywhere. If for some reason the location is unreasonable, the deposed party must seek a protective order under Rule 26(c). The deposition of a nonparty must meet the requirements of Rule 45, discussed in more detail below.

In state court, there are often limits on how far a nonparty deponent may have to travel to attend a deposition. Be sure to check your local state rules before noticing the deposition of a nonparty witness.

d. Persons present

Who may be present at a deposition? The usual persons are the person being deposed, the parties' lawyers, and the court reporter. If the deposition will be videotaped, a videotape operator will also be there.

Often you, as the paralegal, will also be present to assist the lawyer in taking notes or handling exhibits during the deposition. In some cases, if your client is not being deposed and another party is taking the deposition of a witness, you may be asked to attend the deposition in place of the lawyer who represents your client. In these cases, you may be present to take notes for the lawyer and observe the proceedings. However, since you are not authorized to practice law, you will not be allowed to make any objections or statements for the record. In addition, you must be certain to represent to all parties present that you are a paralegal and not a lawyer, so that no one will have the misimpression that you are there in the capacity of a lawyer representing a client.

Parties usually have the right to be present at any deposition, although they appear infrequently. However, if a party's appearance is for an improper purpose, such as intimidation or harassment of a deponent, a protective order can be obtained to prohibit the party from attending. Nonparties and members of the media are usually held to have no right to attend depositions, since a deposition, unlike a trial, is not considered to be a public forum.

e. Recording

Under Rule 28, a deposition must be taken in the presence of someone authorized to administer oaths. Invariably, a certified court reporter, who will stenographically record the testimony, is also a notary public and therefore able to perform both functions. Rule 30(b)(2) allows the deposition to be recorded by sound and video or stenographically. Rule 30(b)(7) also authorizes depositions to be taken by telephone or "other remote electronic means."

While the predominant means of recording remains the court reporter, since this method produces a written transcript, the other available methods are utilized more as ways to reduce costs or to make a more vivid re-creation of the deponent's testimony. These other methods have become a common way of recording experts' depositions when the experts are not expected to testify at trial and their depositions will be introduced in evidence during the trial. Video depositions are also a good idea if the opposing counsel is unduly interfering when the counsel for your side is taking the deposition, such as by repeatedly making objections that serve no proper purpose and are made only to coach the witness on a desirable response.

f. Signing, correcting, and filing

There is no requirement that a deposition be transcribed. However, if any party or the witness requests it, the court reporter must prepare a **deposition transcript**, which is the written record of the questions, answers, and objections made during the deposition. The witness has the right to review the transcript for accuracy and sign it, and any party may also request that the deponent review and sign, so long as the request is made before the deposition is completed. The deponent has 30 days after receiving notice that the transcript is ready to review it and, if there are any changes to make, sign a statement noting the changes and the reasons for them. That statement will then be appended to the deposition transcript.

The reporter must certify that the witness was sworn and that the transcript is accurate. The reporter should then seal the original, which should include any exhibits that were marked and used during the deposition, and file it with the clerk of the court, unless local rules provide otherwise.

g. Objections

Rule 30(c) provides that the reporter shall note on the deposition all objections to the qualifications of the reporter or other officer, to the procedure, evidence, and conduct of parties, as well as any other objections. The Rule states that testimony objected to "shall be taken subject to the objections," the intent being that the witness should answer the questions asked with all objections being noted. This permits a judge to rule on the objections later, in the event that any party wishes to use the transcript at trial.

Under Rule 32(d), objections to a witness' competency, or to the materiality or relevance of the testimony, need not be made during the taking of the deposition, unless the ground for the objection could have been eliminated if made known at that time. However, objections to the form of questions and other errors that might have been corrected if the objection had been made are waived unless timely made.

Neither Rule 30 nor Rule 32 addresses the special problems concerning privilege objections. The usual procedure of requiring answers "subject to the objections" will not work. If the answer is privileged, providing the answer will constitute a waiver of the privilege. Therefore, a timely objection must be made, and if the deponent is a party, the deponent's lawyer should instruct the deponent not to answer. The party taking the deposition then has the option of moving for an order to compel discovery under Rule 37.

If the examination is being conducted in bad faith to annoy, embarrass, or harass the deponent, then a party or the deponent can demand that the deposition be suspended so that the party or deponent can move for a protective order under Rule 26 to terminate or limit the examination.

2. Practice approach

Although as a paralegal you are not permitted to take the deposition of any witnesses, you will nevertheless have several responsibilities with respect to the deposition process. You may be asked to

- Schedule the deposition
- Prepare an outline of questions and issues for the lawyer to use at the deposition
- Prepare your witnesses for the taking of their depositions
- Attend the deposition to assist the lawyer in taking notes
- Summarize the deposition transcripts for future reference

Each of these areas is discussed in detail below.

a. Scheduling the deposition

Scheduling a deposition involves two decisions: when and where. When is determined primarily by tactical considerations that the lawyer will make. Where depends on the lawyer's personal preference and what the Rules allow. Since paralegals are often responsible for scheduling depositions, you must be familiar with the rules on choosing a location. Rule 30 does not deal with location, so it leaves the choice up to the party taking the deposition of another party. However, Rule 45(c) has specific location rules for deposing nonparty witnesses. In general, such a witness can only be deposed in the county where he resides, is employed, or personally transacts business. When planning depositions, in short, you can make a party come to you, but you must go to a nonparty witness.

The usual location for deposing a party is in your own offices. The lawyer will have files there — which can be useful should the lawyer need to refer to them during the deposition — and the deponent will be away from familiar surroundings.

To depose a nonparty witness, you will usually have to schedule the deposition in the witness' county, unless you can get the witness to come to you. While the Rule is designed to accommodate nonparty witnesses, it can have the effect of inconveniencing everyone else. Therefore, it is usually a good idea to try to have the witness come to you. The party deposing the witness, and perhaps even the other parties, will offer to compensate the witness for actual travel expenses and lost wages in addition to the usual mileage and witness fees. This offer may make the witness more likely to come to your offices to be deposed. This is often preferable, since it saves time and, in the long run, saves the client money.

To depose an expert, it is frequently better to schedule the deposition at the expert's offices. It will be convenient for the expert, and the lawyer will have access to the expert's reports, records, and reference material. This will avoid what otherwise is a common problem: the expert who, for one reason or another, fails to bring all necessary paperwork, thereby making a thorough deposition impossible.

After you and the lawyer have selected a time and place for the depositions, take the following steps:

1. Send notices to parties
2. Serve subpoenas on witnesses
3. Send notices to produce or serve subpoenas duces tecum
4. Reserve a suitable room for the deposition
5. Arrange for a court reporter
6. Reconfirm deposition date and attendance

The notices to parties and subpoenas to witnesses, along with any notices to produce or subpoenas duces tecum, should be served with a reasonable lead time. Given the busy schedules of most people, 20 or 30 days' notice is certainly appropriate. When your side is deposing a party, the lawyer may ask you to call that party's lawyer and select a mutually convenient time before preparing the notices. This avoids delays, avoids motions to reset deposition dates, and generally helps create good working relationships between opposing sides, which benefits everyone. With nonparty witnesses, it is frequently a good idea to serve a subpoena first, and subsequently try to arrange for the witness to travel to your office.

The notices must be sent to every party to the action. If the deposition is for a party, nothing else need be done, unless you also need to send a notice to produce records. If the deposition is for a nonparty, you must serve a subpoena on that witness or, if necessary, a subpoena duces tecum for records. Keep in mind that the subpoena under Rule 45(a)(2) must be issued by the clerk of the district in which the deposition will be taken. The clerk will only issue a subpoena to a nonparty if you demonstrate that your side has given notice of the deposition to all parties. Bring a duplicate or, if the clerk's office requires it, a certified copy of the notice and proof of service to the issuing clerk. A sample notice is shown in Exhibit 10.23, as well as in the Litigation File at the end of the book.

If your side wishes to have the party deponent produce records, simply add, "The deponent shall produce the following documents and records," and attach a list describing the relevant documents. If the deposition is of a nonparty, the notice should have a copy of the subpoena attached if possible. It is also a good practice to send a copy of the notice to the court reporter who is scheduled to take the deposition. The subpoena for a nonparty will be on a standard form that is presigned and sealed and issued by the appropriate clerk's office. A sample form is shown in Exhibit 10.24. Make sure you attach a check for the necessary witness and mileage fees, as governed under 28 U.S.C. §§1821 et seq.

After the notice and subpoena have been served, arrange for a suitable place in which the deposition can be taken. Make sure a court

Exhibit 10.23.   Notice of Deposition

[Caption]

<u>NOTICE OF DEPOSITION</u>

To: _[defendant's attorney]_

Please take notice that I will take the deposition of Rudolf Watson, defendant, before a notary public, or any other authorized officer, on August 30, 2007, at 2:00 P.M., at Room 201, 400 Elm St., Chicago, Illinois, pursuant to Rule 30 of the Federal Rules of Civil Procedure. You are required to have the deponent present at that date, time, and place for oral examination.

_____
Attorney for Plaintiff

reporter is scheduled and told where and when the deposition will be held. Those who should be present include the deponent, the court reporter, the lawyers for the parties, and perhaps the parties themselves. A conference room or private office in your law office suite is usually the best place for the lawyer to take the deposition. The lawyer will be comfortable there and have all necessary files available. However, if your side wants to be particularly accommodating to a witness for tactical reasons, use a location convenient for the witness. If the deponent is required to produce documents and you are afraid she will not fully comply, depose her where the records are kept.

Finally, it is always a good idea to reconfirm the deposition with the parties, lawyers, witnesses, and court reporter involved. Rule 30(g) provides for costs against the deposing party when a notice to depose a witness is given, the witness is not served, and other parties and lawyers are not notified of this fact. When a witness cannot be served and the deposition must be canceled, promptly notify all other persons involved.

b. Preparing for the deposition

A good deposition obviously requires preparation. The attorney may ask you to collect all the documentation in the firm's files that has any bearing on the witness' anticipated testimony, to review it, and to have

Exhibit 10.24.   Subpoena for a Nonparty

AO 90 (Rev 5.85) Deposition Subpoena

United States District Court

CENTRAL ____ DISTRICT OF ____ CALIFORNIA

Perry Johnson,

v.

Acme Corporation

DEPOSITION SUBPOENA

CASE NUMBER: 34854

SUBPOENA FOR
☐ PERSON   ☒ DOCUMENT(S) or OBJECT(S)

TO: The Custodian of Records for Discover Trucking

YOU ARE HEREBY COMMANDED to appear at the place, date, and time specified below to testify at the taking of a deposition in the above case.

PLACE	DATE AND TIME
233 Berg Street Suite 314 Woodland Hills, CA 91357	August 15, 2007

YOU ARE ALSO COMMANDED to bring with you the following document(s) or object(s):*

1. All documents concerning any business transacted by Acme Corporation with Discover Trucking that involved goods shipped to Perry Johnson.

2. All invoices for goods shipped by Acme Corporation to Perry Johnson.

☐ Please see additional information on reverse

Any subpoenaed organization not a party to this suit is hereby admonished pursuant to Rule 30(b)(6), Federal Rules of Civil Procedure, to file a designation with the court specifying one or more officers, directors, or managing agents, or other persons who consent to testify on its behalf, and setting forth, for each person designated, the matters on which he will testify or product documents or things. The persons so designated shall testify as to matters known or reasonably available to the organization.

U.S. MAGISTRATE OR CLERK OF COURT	DATE
(signature) , CLERK, U.S. DISTRICT COURT (BY) DEPUTY CLERK	July 20, 2007

This subpoena is issued upon application of the:	QUESTIONS MAY BE ADDRESSED TO:
☒ Plaintiff ☐ Defendant ☐ U.S. Attorney	J.J. Rayson, Esq. Law Offices of Mary Anton 200 Main Street, Tucson, Arizona ATTORNEY'S NAME, ADDRESS AND PHONE NUMBER 334-9954

*If not applicable enter none

CV - 33 (11/86)

Exhibit 10.24.   Continued

AO 9* Rev 5/85) Deposition Subpoena

RETURN OF SERVICE [1]			
RECEIVED BY SERVER	DATE	PLACE	
SERVED	DATE	PLACE	
SERVED ON (NAME)		FEES TENDERED ☐ YES ☐ NO AMOUNT $_____	
SERVED BY		TITLE	

STATEMENT OF SERVICE FEES		
TRAVEL	SERVICES	TOTAL

DECLARATION OF SERVER [2]

I declare under penalty of perjury under the laws of the United States of America that the foregoing information contained in the Return of Service and Statement of Service Fees is true and correct.

Executed on _____   _____
　　　　　　　　　Date　　　　　　　　　*Signature of Server*

　　　　　　　　　　　　　　　　　　　　　_____
　　　　　　　　　　　　　　　　　　　　　Address of Server

ADDITIONAL INFORMATION

(1) As to who may serve a subpoena and the manner of its service see Rule 17(d), Federal Rules of Criminal Procedure, or Rule 45(c), Federal Rules of Civil Procedure.

(2) "Fees and mileage need not be tendered to the deponent upon service of a subpoena issued on behalf of the United States or an officer or agency thereof (Rule 45(c), Federal Rules of Civil Procedure; Rule 17(d), Federal Rules of Criminal Procedure) or on behalf of certain indigent parties and criminal defendants who are unable to pay such costs (28 USC 1*~5, Rule 17(b) Federal Rules of Criminal Procedures)"

copies available for use during the deposition. A copy can be marked by the witness during the deposition, and the lawyer can give the copy to the court reporter to attach as an exhibit to the deposition transcript.

When you have reviewed the available material, you and the lawyer should begin to discuss and outline how the lawyer will take the particular deposition. This depends on several considerations:

- Is the deponent an adverse party, unfavorable witness, or friendly witness?
- What information does your side need to obtain?
- What foundations for exhibits does the lawyer want to establish?
- What admissions or impeachment should the lawyer try to obtain?
- Is the lawyer taking the deposition only to discover information, or taking the deposition with an eye toward preserving the witness' testimony for possible later use?
- What are the risks in deposing this person?

These considerations must be evaluated so that you and the lawyer have good answers to the fundamental question that must be resolved: Why is this deposition important?

These considerations affect how the lawyer will take a particular deposition. Regardless of the approach, the questioning should be thorough because a basic purpose for depositions is to find out what the deponent knows. It is usually a good practice to make an outline of the anticipated topics with suitable references to the exhibits that the attorney will want to use. Paralegals are often asked to draw up this formal outline. Although such an outline must obviously be tailored to the facts of each case, certain general topics should usually be explored. A sample outline is shown in Exhibit 10.25.

The background topics shown in Exhibit 10.25 should be pursued regardless of the deponent. When the deponent is a party, most of this information should already have been received in the interrogatory answers, but the lawyer should have the deponent reconfirm the information and explain it in greater detail where necessary.

There are also numerous books available that contain checklists for various types of cases and witnesses. These are useful for considering the types of topics that can be explored and the sensible order for them, but such checklists should never be a substitute for the lawyer's tailoring questions to the particular deponent.

Once you organize the preliminary matters, outline the substantive areas, which depend on the type of case, legal and factual issues, and the witness' relationship to them. The key to the deposition here is detail. You need to make sure that the outline covers all the topics and is logically organized, usually chronologically. Sample outlines for different substantive areas are shown in Exhibits 10.26 through 10.28.

Exhibit 10.25.   Deposition Outline: Preliminary Matters

1. Background
   Name and address
   Personal and family history
   Education
   Job history
2. Documents and records
   Notice to produce and subpoenas
   Record-keeping
   Record search
   Identifying produced records
   Names and addresses of other persons and entities that may have
     records related to case
3. Identity of party
   Officers, directors, employees, agents
   Parent corporation and subsidiaries, licensees
   Incorporation and places of business
   Residence
   Place where licensed to do business
   Names used in business
4. Witnesses
   Names and addresses of persons witnessing events and transactions
   Names and addresses of persons deponent has communicated with
   Names and addresses of persons who may know something about
     case

Exhibit 10.26.   Deposition Outline: Substantive Issues (Personal Injury Case)

Deponent: Plaintiff in Personal Injury Case

1. Background questions
   (Preliminary matters as outlined above)
   Health history before accident
2. Vehicles involved
   Make, year, registration
   Insurance
   Condition, inspection, repair records
3. Scene of collision
   Neighborhood
   Roads
   Traffic markings and controls

continued on next page

Exhibit 10.26.   Continued

4. Weather and road conditions
5. Events before accident
    Activities earlier in day
    Food, alcohol, drugs
    Physical condition at time
    Earlier activities
6. Events immediately before collision
    Location and direction of vehicles
    Passengers
    Traffic conditions
    Visibility and weather conditions
    Other distractions
    Where first saw defendant's car
    Marking diagrams and photographs
7. Collision
    Speed of cars before impact
    Traffic signals
    Braking and other conduct of plaintiff
    Braking and other conduct of defendant
    Point of impact
    Where cars ended up
    Marking diagrams and photographs
8. Events after collision
    Bystander activities
    Police activities
    What plaintiff and defendant did
    What plaintiff and defendant said
    Plaintiff's and defendant's condition after collision
    Ambulance
9. Medical treatment
    At hospital -diagnosis and treatment
    Doctors' visits after discharge -treatments
    Medication, therapy
10. Present physical condition
    Any physical limitations
    Medication
11. Damages
    Vehicle
    Hospital expenses
    Doctors' bills
    Lost wages
    Insurance payments
    Other claimed losses

Exhibit 10.27.   Deposition Outline: Substantive Issues (Contract Breach Case)

Deponent: Corporate Plaintiff in Contract Breach Case

1. Background questions
   (Preliminary matters as outlined above)
2. First contact with defendant
   Reasons -how came about
   Persons involved
3. Course of dealing up to contract
   Types of business conducted
   Business practices
   Specific contracts entered into
   Performance history
4. Negotiations leading up to contract
   Dates, times, places, participants
   All communications
5. Contract execution
   Date, time, place, participants
6. Conduct following execution
   Performance by each party
7. Breach claimed
   When, what
   Witnesses
8. Conduct following breach
   Attempts to mitigate
9. Damages claimed
   Breach damages
   Consequential damages

The deposition should extract from the witness everything the deponent knows that is pertinent to the case. Remember that there is usually only one opportunity to depose a person so the lawyer must be prepared, with the help of your outline, to get the most out of that opportunity.

A sample deposition appears in the Litigation File at the end of the book.

c. Preparing the client for deposition

When your office receives a notice for deposition of your client, you may be asked to prepare the client for the deposition. Preparing the

Exhibit 10.28. Deposition Outline: Substantive Issues (Personal Injury Case)

Deponent: Physician in Personal Injury Case

1. Professional background
   Education
   Internship and residency
   Licenses and specialty boards
   Description of practice
   Experience in type of injury involved here
2. Physician's medical records and reports
   Identify them
   Treatises he relies on
   Consultations
3. First contact with plaintiff at hospital
   Where and when
   History
   Symptoms
   Examination and findings
   Tests
   Diagnosis
   Treatment
4. Subsequent contacts with plaintiff
   Where and when
   Symptoms
   Examinations and findings
   Tests
   Prognosis
5. Opinions and conclusions
   Extent of injuries
   Permanence of injuries
   Effect on plaintiff
   Causation
   Why physician disagrees with other experts
6. Fees
   How much
   Future fees

client for the upcoming deposition may well be the most important single event in the litigation process. The opposing lawyers will use the deposition to determine what the client knows, develop admissions and impeachment, pin the client down to details about what he does or does not know, and generally size up the client as a trial witness. If the deposition goes well, the settlement value of the case will rise as well. Hence, preparation for the deposition is critical.

Shortly before the deposition date, have the client come to your office with enough time allocated to prepare him thoroughly. Scheduling this for the afternoon, as the last appointment for the day, is a good idea so you will not be rushed by other appointments. On the other hand, you may prefer to schedule such interviews in the morning, when you and the client are fresh. Take all of the following steps when preparing a client for deposition.

First, have the pleadings, discovery, documents, records, reports, photographs, diagrams, and sketches available for the client to review. However, show the client only his statements, not those of others. Showing the client other persons' statements will always create the impression, particularly at trial, that the client has tailored his testimony to be consistent with other witnesses or has used the other statements to acquire information he himself does not personally have. This may also make such statements disclosable at trial because under Rule 612 of the Federal Rules of Evidence an adverse party may be able to obtain any documents used to refresh the witness' recollection, even if used before trial; the adverse party may be able to use them during the witness' cross-examination and to introduce in evidence relevant portions of the documents. It is usually better to avoid this problem by not showing the client other witnesses' statements.

Second, review with the client what a deposition is, what its purpose is, why it is so critical, and what the procedure will be. Explain to the client that once the deposition begins, the lawyer representing the client will be relatively inactive, except to make objections in order to preserve error when necessary, or to instruct him not to answer if critical to do so. Make sure that the client knows to dress appropriately. There are commercial videotapes on deposition preparation available, and some are very useful to show what actually goes on during a deposition.

Third, review how your client should answer questions accurately. Impress upon him that even though the atmosphere will probably be informal, he must answer carefully. Standard suggestions given to the client include the following:

1. Make sure that you understand the question. If you don't, say so and ask that the question be rephrased.
2. If you know the answer, give it. If you don't know, say so. If you know but can't remember just then, say so. If you can only estimate or approximate, say so. However, give positive, assertive answers whenever possible.

3. Don't volunteer information. Answer only what the question specifically calls for. Don't exaggerate or speculate. Give the best short, accurate, truthful answer possible.
4. Answer questions only with what you personally know, saw, heard, or did, unless the question asks otherwise.
5. Read every document the questioner shows to you before answering any questions about the document.
6. Be calm at all times. Avoid arguing with the lawyers or getting upset over the questions. Your lawyer will be there to protect you from unfair questions and procedures by making objections and instructing you on what to do and say.

Fourth, discuss how objections will be handled. Explain that many objections are made "for the record," and that usually the witness must answer despite the objection, which is made for possible later use at trial. However, be sure that the client knows not to answer when an objection is made and the client's attorney tells him not to answer. This will be the case if the objection is based on privilege or harassment grounds, when answering the question may waive any error.

Fifth, review with the client what questions the lawyers are likely to ask. This involves creating a short outline as discussed previously. Make sure that the client can accurately respond to those expected questions in a positive, convincing manner whenever possible. Let the client know that other lawyers present may ask additional questions, but that the client's lawyer will probably not ask questions unless necessary to correct a mistake or clarify something ambiguous.

Finally, explain that the client has a right to review the deposition if it is transcribed, noting any corrections and the reasons for them, and to sign it. However, you should also explain that, in the event any corrections are made, the attorneys will be able to comment on that fact at the time of trial. Accordingly, it is best to give the best testimony possible now, and not rely on the ability to correct errors in the transcript later.

d. Taking notes at the deposition

Although the deposition transcript will provide a written record of the statements made by the witness during the deposition, you may still be asked to be present during the deposition to take notes. Notes taken during a deposition are important in cases where several witnesses will be deposed within a short period of time, or a motion is pending or planned in which the deposition testimony is needed. In these cases, the transcript, if not specially ordered on an expedited basis, may not be ready in sufficient time to use it for preparing for depositions of the other witnesses or for preparing or opposing a motion. The transcript usually will not be prepared for two to three weeks, thus requiring reference to the notes taken during the deposition. In addition, if the client does not attend the deposition, you may be asked to send a letter or memorandum to advise the client of the substance of the deposition testimony.

When taking notes, try not to take down everything. The transcript will contain all the questions and answers. Your task is to simply write down the important information that the witness gives. If you are not familiar with the issues in the case, discuss the issues with the lawyer in advance of the deposition and decide which questions and answers require particular attention.

After the deposition, promptly prepare a memorandum summarizing your notes. The memorandum should be in a narrative form and provide only the facts, not the questions that are given. The first two paragraphs of a sample memorandum are provided in Exhibit 10.29.

e. Summarizing the deposition

Summarizing depositions based on the deposition transcript is one of the more important roles you will undertake as a paralegal. A good

Exhibit 10.29.   Sample Memorandum Summarizing Deposition Notes

To: Litigation Attorney
From: Litigation Paralegal

Re: Smith v. Alliance Realty Company

On June 2, 2006, I attended the deposition of the plaintiff David Smith ("Smith"). The following is a summary of my notes taken during the deposition.

Smith was born on April 3, 1955, in Pasadena, California. He graduated from Pepper High School in 1973, and graduated from the University of Southern California in 1977 with a degree in business administration. He immediately went to work for the Alliance Realty Company as a bookkeeper. He remained in that position until 1985, at which time he was promoted to senior bookkeeper. In 1988 Smith was given the job title of Vice President of Accounting. However, his duties did not change. During the entire time of his employment, Smith was never informed of any problems with his work product, was never disciplined for any reason, and always received year-end bonuses. Smith was terminated on October 10, 2005, without any advance warning.

summary will assist the lawyer in easily locating key deposition testimony for depositions of other witnesses or for trial. There are several types of deposition summaries. You should choose the type based on the importance of the particular witness to the issues in the case and the purpose for which the deposition summary will be used. For example, a deposition summary for a primary witness in the case will need to be more detailed than a summary for a witness whose testimony may be relevant to only one or two minor issues. A summary prepared for use at trial will need to be organized to quickly locate specific topics and page numbers where the topics are found. Discuss with the lawyer in advance the type of deposition summary that she wants you to prepare.

The different types of deposition summaries are identified below, along with a sample of each type.

i. Chronological summary

Chronological summary
A deposition summary organized sequentially

The most common type of summary is the **chronological summary**. This type of summary starts at the beginning of the deposition and continues through to the end of the deposition. On the left-hand side of the page, general topic headings and line and page numbers are given. On the right-hand side of the page, a summary of the testimony is given. This type of summary will be the most detailed and should contain enough information that anyone who did not attend the deposition will still know what was stated at the deposition without having to read the entire transcript. However, remember that all deposition summaries are "summaries," and you should avoid including the witness' testimony word for word. The format of a chronological summary is shown in Exhibit 10.30.

Exhibit 10.30. Format: Chronological Deposition Summary

<u>Personal Background</u> pgs 1-6	Born April 3, 1955, in Pasadena, California. Graduated U.S.C. in 1977 with B.S. in Business Administration. Married. Two children.
<u>Employment</u> pg 6, lines 10-25	Alliance Realty Company. 1977 to October 10, 1996.
<u>Promotions</u> pgs 7-10	Started as bookkeeper. Promoted to senior bookkeeper in 1985. Vice President of Accounting 1988.

ii. Subject matter summary

The **subject matter summary** does not digest the deposition in the order in which the topics appear chronologically. Rather, each subject matter is dealt with separately, regardless of where the subject appears in the deposition. The advantage of this type of summary is that if questioning has skipped around to various topics, the summary helps to organize the topics. This summary is probably the most useful in preparing for depositions of other witnesses and for trial, since the lawyer will not need to read through the entire summary in order to locate all the testimony on a particular issue. The format for this type of summary is shown in Exhibit 10.31.

Subject matter summary
A deposition summary that categorizes each topic by subject matter

iii. Topic index

The **topic index** provides a quick reference for the lawyer on particular areas covered within the deposition. No attempt is made to completely summarize the deposition. Rather, it is merely an outline of the general topic areas. This type of summary may be used in addition to one of the other summaries to provide easy access at trial to specific testimony. The topic index may be arranged chronologically or by subject matter. A sample is shown in Exhibit 10.32.

Topic index
A type of deposition summary that is an outline of the general topic areas

Exhibit 10.31.   Format: Subject Matter Deposition Summary

Discussions with Other Employees	
pg 14, lines 10-15	Jay Becker
pg 18, lines 12-14	Kevin McDonald
pg 50, lines 22-24	Marcia Sawyer
Employment After Termination	
pg 22, lines 3-23	Office clerk BBB Cable Company 12/1-3/14
pg 28, lines 14-18	Accountant Aerial Business Systems 3/20 to present

Exhibit 10.32.   Format: Deposition Topic Index

Page	Topic
pg 10, lines 23-24	Educational background
pg 15, lines 12-15	Employment background
pg 18, lines 8-14	Present employment

iv. Narrative summary

Narrative
A type of deposition summary that is in memorandum form with no reference to particular page and line numbers

The final type of summary is the **narrative** format. This summary is similar to the memorandum you may do immediately following the deposition. The only difference is that you will now have the benefit of the deposition transcript to prepare your summary. This type of summary is generally not useful for trial preparation. However, it is a useful summary to send to the client since the client will be more interested in the substance of the testimony than the page and line numbers where the testimony can be located. A sample narrative summary is shown in Exhibit 10.33.

H. PHYSICAL AND MENTAL EXAMINATIONS

In some cases, primarily personal injury cases, the physical and mental condition of a party is a critical fact affecting both liability and damages. Under those circumstances, that party should be examined to evaluate the genuineness of the condition, its extent and causes, and to develop a prognosis. Rule 35 of the Federal Rules of Civil Procedure governs this process.

1. Law

Rule 35 applies to physical and mental examinations of a party and of a "person in the custody or under the legal control of a party." The Rule

Exhibit 10.33.   Format: Narrative Deposition Summary

David Smith ("Smith") is 47 years old, married with two children. He was terminated from his employment at Alliance Realty Company on October 10, 2005. Since his termination, he has worked for two different companies: BBB Cable Company and Aerial Business Systems. He is presently earning $53,000 a year, which is $30,000 less than what he was earning at Alliance when he was terminated.

Smith does not know why he was terminated. He claims not to have been advised of any problems with his work during his 24 years of employment. In addition, he was never disciplined for any reason, and always received year-end bonuses based on his work performance. Smith testified that his immediate supervisor, Marcia Sawyer, always spoke very highly of him.

clearly applies to minors and other legally incapacitated persons who are not the actual named parties but are the real parties in interest.

A court order is required for such examinations, unless the person to be examined voluntarily agrees to the examination, which is permitted under Rule 29 so long as there is a written stipulation. In other situations, your side must move for a court order and give notice to the person and all parties. For the court to order an examination, the physical or mental condition of a party or related person must be "in controversy," and your side must show "good cause" for requesting it.

The good cause requirement has sometimes caused difficulty. In most cases, however, typically personal injury cases or paternity cases where the physical condition of a party is important, there are few problems and the parties often informally arrange for the necessary examinations. In these types of cases, the need for the examinations is apparent from the pleadings. However, issues such as testimonial competency will not be apparent from the pleadings; therefore, the moving party must make a sufficient showing of need in the motion to satisfy the good cause requirement.

The court's order must specify the date, time, place, manner, conditions, and scope of the examination, as well as the person or persons who will perform it. The scope of the examination is determined by the nature of the claims, defenses, and facts and issues in controversy. However, Rule 35 is silent on who should perform the examination. In practice, the moving party usually suggests a physician, and the court ordinarily approves the selection unless another party or the person to be examined has a serious objection. The court has discretion to approve or disapprove, and some districts have local rules that provide for the selection of "impartial experts" from approved lists.

The party moving for the examination must, upon request by the examined party, deliver a detailed written report of the examining physician setting out findings, results of tests, diagnoses, and conclusions, as well as reports of all earlier examinations for the same conditions. The party moving for the examination can then, upon request, get any previous or future reports about the same person for the same condition, unless, when a nonparty is examined, the party shows he cannot obtain the report. This procedure essentially provides for reciprocal discovery when one side requests a report from the examining physician. When the party examined requests a copy of the report of the physician who examined him, this operates as a waiver of the doctor-patient privilege not only as to that physician, but also as to any other physician who has or may later examine him as to the same conditions.

These disclosure requirements and waiver effects apply regardless of whether the examinations are made pursuant to a court order or through agreement of the parties, unless that agreement expressly provides otherwise. In addition, the discovery permitted under Rule 35 does not restrict other permissible discovery. However, Rule 35 is the only rule that can compel discovery where otherwise the doctor-patient privilege would prevent disclosure.

2. Practice approach

Since the situations in which physical and mental examinations can be compelled are usually obvious, these examinations are frequently arranged informally between the parties. Even when there is an informal agreement, however, it is always a good idea to put it in a letter or, even better, in a stipulation under Rule 29 that is then filed with the court.

Where an arrangement cannot be worked out, the party must move for a court order compelling the desired examination. To comply with Rule 35, the motion must

1. Ask for the examination of a party or a person in the custody or control of the party
2. Allege a genuine controversy about that person's physical or mental condition
3. Demonstrate good cause for the examination
4. Request the date, time, place, manner, conditions, and scope of the examination
5. Designate the physician who should conduct it

A sample motion for an order to compel physical examination is shown in Exhibit 10.34, as well as in the Litigation File at the end of the book.

If the court grants the motion, an order must be entered. In federal courts the practice is for the court clerk to prepare orders, which the judge then signs. Where permitted, however, it is always a useful approach to draft an appropriate order in situations when a nonparty, here the physician, is involved because the physician will want a copy of the order before conducting the examination. A sample order granting request for physical examination is shown in Exhibit 10.35.

Finally, keep in mind the reciprocal discovery provisions of Rule 35(b)(1). If the examined party requests a copy of the doctor's report, the party moving for the examination has the right to receive from the examined party other reports dealing with the same conditions, regardless of when made; however, your side must request those reports. Perhaps the safer approach is to send that party a document entitled "Request For Medical Reports," show that it is made under the provisions of Rule 35(b)(1), and file the request with the court. If the other party fails to deliver, or later attempts to use such reports, your side has made a record of your request and can object to the introduction of those reports at trial because the party did not comply with Rule 35.

Exhibit 10.34.   Motion for Order to Compel Physical Examination

[Caption]

<u>MOTION FOR ORDER COMPELLING PLAINTIFF'S PHYSICAL
EXAMINATION</u>

Defendant moves under Rule 35 of the Federal Rules of Civil Procedure for an order compelling plaintiff to submit to a physical examination. In support of her motion defendant states:

1. Plaintiff's physical condition is genuinely in controversy, since plaintiff's complaint on its face alleges that "as a result of this collision, plaintiff has suffered severe and permanent injuries to his back and legs."

2. Since plaintiff alleges that his physical limitations are compensable, there exists good cause for a physical examination to evaluate the plaintiff's current physical condition, physical limitations, and prognosis.

3. William B. Rudolf, M.D., a board certified orthopedic surgeon, has agreed to examine the plaintiff at his offices at 200 Main Street, Suite 301, Washington, D.C., on August 15, 2006, at 4:00 P.M., or at another time if directed by this court.

WHEREFORE, defendant requests that this court enter an order directing the plaintiff to be examined on the terms set forth above.

_____
Attorney for Defendant

I. REQUESTS FOR ADMISSION

A request to admit facts and the genuineness of documents is the fifth method of discovery permitted under the Federal Rules of Civil Procedure and is usually the last employed during the litigation process. Its purposes are to sharpen trial issues, streamline trials, and eliminate the need to formally prove controverted facts.

1. Law

Requests for admission and the genuineness of documents, governed by Rule 36, apply only to parties. Admissions made in response to the requests are admissions for the purposes of the pending action only and

Exhibit 10.35.   Sample Order Granting Request for Physical Examination

---

[Caption]

<u>ORDER</u>

This matter being heard on defendant's motion to compel the physical examination of plaintiff, all parties having been given notice, and the court having heard arguments, it is hereby ordered that:

1. Plaintiff John Williams be examined by William B. Rudolf, M.D., at 200 Main Street, Suite 301, Washington, D.C., on August 15, 2006, at 4:00 P.M., unless the plaintiff and Dr. Rudolf mutually agree to an earlier date and time.

2. Plaintiff shall submit to such orthopedic examinations and tests as are necessary to diagnose and evaluate the plaintiff's back and legs, so that Dr. Rudolf may reach opinions and conclusions about the extent of any injuries, their origin, and prognosis.

3. Dr. Rudolf shall prepare a written report detailing his findings, test results, diagnosis, and opinions, along with any earlier similar reports on the same conditions, and deliver it to defendant's attorneys on or before September 15, 2006.

Entered:

Dated: _____

_____
United States District Judge

---

cannot be used for any other purposes. This encourages a party to admit facts without worrying about collateral consequences.

In federal court, requests may be served on other parties at any time after the parties meet to develop a discovery plan under Rule 26(f). In state courts, requests may be sent after service of the summons or complaint on that party or, as to the plaintiff, after commencement of the action. In both courts, like other discovery provisions, requests can be employed essentially at any time during the litigation process.

A request can be directed to three categories:

◆ Genuineness of documents
◆ Truth of facts
◆ "Application of law to fact"

The general scope of these requests is the same as for discovery in general; they apply to anything that is relevant but not privileged. Each request must be separately stated.

After a request has been served on a party, that party must serve a response within 30 days or the matters requested will be deemed admitted. This automatic provision of Rule 36 makes it a formidable weapon because inertia or inattentiveness can have an automatic, and usually devastating, consequence. Hence, there is one cardinal rule for practice under this provision: Your side must respond and serve the response within the 30-day period.

There are four basic responses permitted. First, the party can object to a matter in the request, in which case the party must state the reasons for the objection. Second, the party can admit the matter; if admitted, the matter is deemed conclusively established, unless the court allows withdrawal or amendment in accordance with Rule 16. Third, the party can deny the matter. Fourth, the party can neither admit nor deny because the matter is genuinely in dispute or because, after reasonable inquiry, the party does not have sufficient information to determine if the matter is true or not, setting forth the reasons.

How your side responds, and whether the response is justified under the circumstances, will determine whether Rule 37 sanctions can be imposed. Rule 37(c) usually provides that the expenses—including attorney's fees—incurred in proving a denied matter can be taxed as costs against the losing party. However, if your side neither admits nor denies on the basis of there being a genuine issue for trial or because of genuine insufficient knowledge, Rule 37 sanctions cannot be imposed.

Once a response has been received, your side can move the court to review the adequacy of the objections and responses. The Rule requires that a response must specifically deny the matter or set forth in detail why the answering party cannot admit or deny after making a reasonable inquiry. A denial must fairly meet the substance of the requested admission. The better practice is to make a motion under Rule 36(a) to determine the sufficiency of an answer and see if the court will deem the matter admitted. This will avoid surprises at trial. The court can enter an order compelling an answer or amended answer if appropriate, order that the matter be deemed admitted, or continue the motion to the pretrial conference or to another date.

2. Practice approach

Since the scope of Rule 36 is so broad, using and responding to requests for admission are principally tactical concerns that must be discussed thoroughly with the lawyer in coordinating the overall discovery strategy. Requests for admissions are best seen not as a method for getting additional facts but as a technique for eliminating the need for formal proof and for determining what facts opposing parties intend to contest at trial.

a. Timing

Rule 36 permits requests for admission at any time after the parties meet to plan discovery, so the decision on when to use it is controlled by practical considerations. Frequently, however, the requests are used at the end of the discovery stage. Discovery is essentially complete when the initial disclosures have been made, interrogatory answers and records pursuant to document requests have been received, the parties and necessary witnesses have been deposed, and, when appropriate, physical and mental examinations have been conducted. Requests for admissions are most commonly served at this point because the existing discovery will identify what still remains in issue. The requests should focus on the remaining facts still in issue and be served after other discovery has been completed, but before the pretrial conference is scheduled or summary judgment motions are made. Requests for admission served at that time will help determine what facts the other side will concede or contest if the case goes to trial.

Another approach is to serve requests for admission early in the discovery process to bring the potential Rule 37 sanctions into play. This forces the opponent to decide what facts and issues she intends to dispute and allows later discovery to become more focused. If a party denies a fact in a request to admit without a substantial basis for the denial, and that fact is later proved at trial, the party proving the fact can receive as court costs the reasonable expense of proving the denied fact at trial, including attorney's fees. If requests for admission are made early, the period starts for which your client may be entitled to get Rule 37 costs.

In addition, if there is a belief that the opposing party will use dilatory tactics or avoid serious settlement discussions on a case that should be settled quickly, making a request to admit early raises the risks for the party using those tactics. This can be effective in forcing the opponent to admit facts.

b. What to request

To determine what to request, look first at the elements of your side's claims. Second, analyze each "fact" that the client will need to prove to meet the burden of proof at trial on each element. Once this is accomplished, you can organize those "facts" into the three categories permitted under Rule 36: (1) genuineness of documents, (2) truth of facts, and (3) application of law to facts. Third, review the pleadings to see what has been admitted, and review your side's discovery results to see what facts are conceded. Reviewing the discovery is critical because a fact, when admitted in interrogatory answers or by a party deposition, is only an admission by a party opponent. This means that the party admitting a fact can still present contrary evidence at trial. However, if a party admits facts in a request to admit, this is a conclusive admission. This means that a party cannot present contrary evidence at trial unless the court permits amendment or withdrawal of the admission under Rule 36. Thus, look for admissions to your previous discovery requests, and ask for the same admission of facts in the requests for admission.

c. Drafting the requests

The cardinal rule for the drafting of requests for admissions is to keep them simple. A lengthy, complicated request practically begs to be denied, objected to, or responded to with a lengthy, equivocal response. This will merely generate further motions and probably achieve nothing.

Simplicity requires that a request be short and contain a single statement of fact. Such requests are difficult to quibble with, and they stand the best chance of being admitted outright. They should also comply with admissibility rules, such as those concerning relevance and hearsay.

Organize your requests into the three permitted categories:

1. Genuineness of documents
2. Truth of facts
3. Opinions of fact and application of law to facts

Examples of requests for each of these categories are shown in Exhibits 10.36, 10.37, and 10.38. See also the Litigation File at the end of this book.

Requests for admission regarding "opinions of fact" and the "application of law to fact" are a problematic area because questions of "pure law" cannot be asked. For instance, a request that asks a party to admit negligence or culpability is objectionable. Where the line is between "opinions of fact" and "application of law to fact," as against "pure law," remains unclear. Regardless of where that line is, treading close to it will probably draw objections. Accordingly, it is usually better to be on the safe side and leave the legal disputes for resolution at trial. Common situations in which the application of law to fact is raised are issues of title, ownership, agency, and employment.

The requests for admission should be signed by the lawyer, served on each party, and filed with the court if required by your local rules.

Exhibit 10.36.   Request to Admit Facts: Genuineness of Documents

---

[Caption]

REQUESTS TO ADMIT FACTS AND GENUINENESS OF DOCUMENTS

Plaintiff Ralph Johnson requests defendant Marian Smith to make the following admissions, within 30 days after service of this request, for the purposes of this action only:

That each of the following documents is genuine:

    1. A contract, attached as Exhibit A, is a true and accurate copy of the contract signed by plaintiff and defendant on August 1, 2007.

Exhibit 10.37.   Request to Admit Facts: Truth of Facts

That each of the following facts is true:

    1. The signature on the contract, attached as Exhibit A, purporting to be that of the defendant, is in fact that of the defendant.

    2. The defendant signed the original of Exhibit A.

    3. Defendant signed the original of Exhibit A on August 1, 2007.

Exhibit 10.38.   Request to Admit Facts: Opinions of Fact and
                          Application of Law to Fact

That each of the following statements is true:

    1. Defendant was the legal titleholder of a lot commonly known as 3401 Fifth Street, Tucson, Arizona, on August 1, 2007.

    2. On August 1, 2007, William Oats was an employee of XYZ Corporation.

    3. On August 1, 2007, William Oats was authorized to enter into sales contracts on behalf of XYZ Corporation.

Service is made by any permitted method under Rule 5, commonly by mailing a copy to the lawyers of the other parties. In some courts the original requests for admission, with an attached proof of service statement, are then filed with the clerk of the court. If the particular court does not accept discovery requests for filing, the original should be kept in the client's file.

d. Choosing a response

A party on whom requests for admission have been served must respond, usually within 30 days of receiving the requests, or else the matters in the requests will automatically be deemed admitted. There are four basic responses to a request.

First, your side can object to the request. As with discovery generally, you can object that the matter requested is irrelevant or privileged. In addition, you can object and seek a protective order if the request is unduly burdensome or harassing.

Second, your side can admit the request. When you do so, you conclusively admit the matter for the purpose of the pending action only. Such an admission prevents you from presenting contrary evidence at trial.

Third, your side can deny the request. The denial must be based on good faith. If the requesting party later proves the denied matter at trial, under Rule 37 that party may get expenses, including attorney's fees, involved in proving the matter. The response can, of course, admit to some parts of a request and deny others.

Fourth, under certain circumstances your side can neither admit nor deny. This is allowed if the answering party has made a "reasonable inquiry" in an effort to acquire necessary information for responding to the request but is still unable to respond. In addition, if the answering party considers the requested matter to be a genuine trial issue, it can either deny or set forth reasons for neither admitting nor denying.

When you and the lawyer have decided what the appropriate response should be, drafting the response is similar to drafting answers to complaints. However, the better format is that used for interrogatory answers, where the answers and interrogatories both appear together. A sample response to requests for admission is shown in Exhibit 10.39.

The response to requests for admission should be signed by the party's lawyer, served on each party, and filed with the court. Service is made by any permitted method under Rule 5, commonly by mailing a copy to the lawyers for the other parties. The original response, with an attached proof of service statement, is then filed with the clerk of the court, unless a local rule directs that discovery is not filed until a need arises.

e. Requesting party's responses

When a party has made and served responses to requests for admissions on the requesting party, the requesting party can do two things:

Exhibit 10.39.   Response to Requests for Admission

[Caption]

RESPONSE TO REQUESTS FOR ADMISSIONS

Defendant Marian Smith responds to plaintiff Ralph Johnson's requests for admissions as follows:

Request No. 1: A contract, attached as Exhibit A, is a true and accurate copy of the contract signed by plaintiff on August 1, 2007.

Answer: Admit.

Request No. 2: Plaintiff performed all his obligations under the contract.

Answer: Deny.

Request No. 3: On August 1, 2007, William Oats was authorized to enter into sales contracts on behalf of XYZ Corporation.

Answer: Objection. Responding to this request would disclose the substance of conversations between William Oats, an attorney, and the XYZ Corporation, which are protected from disclosure by the attorney-client privilege.

Request No. 4: Mary Doyle was the sole titleholder of a lot commonly known as 3401 Fifth Street, Seattle, Washington.

Answer: Defendant can neither admit nor deny this request. Public records neither confirm nor deny, and defendant has no access to any documents that could confirm or deny it.

---

first, move to review the sufficiency of an answer; second, move to review the validity of an objection. Both of these are directed to the court's discretion. The court can enter any appropriate order, such as deeming a matter admitted, requiring an amended answer, or continuing the issue to the pretrial conference or other time.

When the answering party denies a request to admit facts, a good approach is to send the answering party interrogatories that ask for the basis of the denial. Another approach is to send **"contention interrogatories"** along with the requests for admission, again asking for the basis of each denial of a request. This sometimes causes the answering party to admit the request rather than attempt to justify the denial in the accompanying interrogatory answer. You should discuss this strategy with the attorney responsible for the matter.

Contention interrogatories
Questions that ask the opposing side for the basis of any denial of a request

J. DISCOVERY MOTIONS

Discovery under both federal and state rules is largely undertaken without judicial intervention, except for the specific areas discussed here. Generally, only when there is a dispute over discovery need the courts become involved.

Three points should be remembered when making any discovery motion. First, under Rule 37(a) of the Federal Rules and in many state courts the moving party's lawyer must certify what good faith efforts have been made to resolve a dispute before the court will intervene.

Second, discovery abuse has probably been the subject of more controversy and proposals than any other aspect of the litigation process. Courts have responded to the problem by becoming more involved in discovery, particularly by having discovery plan conferences and by dealing more actively with abuses and imposing stiffer sanctions.

Third, amendments to Rule 26 and Rule 16 give courts additional powers to regulate discovery. Rule 26(b)(2) gives courts the power to limit discovery where it is unnecessarily cumulative or duplicative, or is obtainable from other sources with less effort and expense. Rule 16 gives courts power to hold discovery conferences and impose a discovery plan. Under Rule 26(g), the lawyer's signature is a certification that she has read the discovery document; has made a reasonable inquiry; and that the document is consistent with the Rules and law, is not made for any improper purpose, and is not unreasonably burdensome or expensive. In today's climate, abusing discovery by filing frivolous, needless, or unduly burdensome discovery requests, responses, or motions often results in severe sanctions.

There are two principal types of discovery motions, those for protective orders and those for orders compelling discovery.

1. Protective orders

Rule 26(c) and, in the case of oral depositions, Rule 30(d)(3) govern **protective orders**. Whenever an entity or person from whom discovery is sought feels that they are being subjected to annoying, embarrassing, oppressive, unduly burdensome, or unduly expensive discovery demands, the appropriate procedure is to move for a protective order. Before filing a motion for a protective order, Rule 26(c) requires that the moving party meet and confer with the other party and make a good faith effort to resolve the discovery dispute without the need for court intervention. Both parties and nonparty deponents can seek protective orders.

Protective orders
An order from the court restricting or limiting discovery by one party to another

The motion must usually be brought in the district where the action is pending. However, when a deposition has been terminated so that a protective order can be obtained, the proper jurisdiction under Rule 30(d)(3) is either the district where the action is pending or the district when the deposition is being taken. The latter may well be proper when a nonparty deponent is seeking the protective order, since the deposition is often taken where the deponent resides or does business.

The moving party must show **good cause**. While grounds for protection are numerous, the most common grounds are that the discovery requested is so lengthy and detailed that it is unduly oppressive and expensive—for example, discovery involving lengthy or repetitive interrogatories and depositions, and overly detailed documents requests and requests for admission. Another common ground is the serving of notice for depositions on high corporate officers who have no firsthand knowledge of any relevant facts. If the dominant purpose of the discovery is not to develop information reasonably necessary to prepare for trial or settlement, but to bend the opposition into submission, Rule 26(b)(2) is violated and the protective order is appropriate. Other motions frequently seek to limit disclosure, such as restricting persons present at depositions and preventing the disclosure of business secrets to persons outside the litigation.

Keep in mind that many discovery matters come up by motions to compel after a party has objected to discovery requests. Objections are permitted in answers to interrogatories, document requests, and requests for admission. In these circumstances, the objection protects the responding party. The requesting party must move for an order compelling discovery, and there is no need for the responding party to move for a protective order.

If a protective order is appropriate, Rule 26(c) provides a variety of remedies that can protect a party or person from embarrassment, oppression, and undue burden or expense. These include barring the requested discovery; regulating the terms, conditions, methods, and scope of discovery; limiting persons present at the discovery; requiring the sealing of depositions and documents; and regulating or barring disclosure of trade secrets and confidential information.

The motion for a protective order must be prepared like any other motion and must include statements of the facts as well as a request for the relief sought. Under some local rules, the motion must be accompanied by a notice of motion indicating the date, time, and place of the hearing on the motion, and include a supporting memorandum of law and a declaration or affidavit from someone with personal knowledge of the facts stated in the motion.[10] Sample motions are shown in Exhibits 10.40 and 10.41.

---

10. The format and content of motions in general are discussed in Chapter 6, section B.

Exhibit 10.40.   Motion for a Protective Order

[Caption]

<u>MOTION FOR PROTECTIVE ORDER</u>

Plaintiff Willard Johnson requests that this court enter a protective order pursuant to Rule 26(c) against defendant Clark Lawrence, and in support of his motion states:

1. On August 8, 2006, defendant took plaintiff's first deposition. This deposition took approximately four hours and generated a transcript of 238 pages. The transcript has been filed with the clerk of this court.

2. On April 15, 2007, defendant again took plaintiff's deposition. This deposition took approximately three hours and generated a transcript of 181 pages. This transcript has also been filed with the clerk of this court.

3. On July 2, 2007, plaintiff was served with another notice of deposition. On that date the undersigned counsel called defendant's counsel and asked why a third deposition was necessary. The only offered explanation was that counsel "wanted to make sure he'd covered all the bases."

4. This pending action involves a simple intersection collision. The two previous depositions have exhaustively covered what plaintiff knows about the collision, what happened afterwards, his medical treatment, and all claimed damages.

5. The notice for a third deposition, under these circumstances, constitutes an attempt to annoy, oppress, and place undue burdens on the plaintiff, and has no proper purpose. Since plaintiff lives out of state, another deposition will again impose significant financial and time expenses.

WHEREFORE, plaintiff Willard Johnson requests that this court enter a protective order barring defendant Clark Lawrence from taking further depositions of the plaintiff or, in the alternative, restricting this deposition to such matters as counsel can demonstrate are relevant and were not inquired into at the previous depositions.

_____
Attorney for Plaintiff

Exhibit 10.41.   Motion for a Protective Order

[Caption]

<u>MOTION FOR PROTECTIVE ORDER</u>

Plaintiff Nancy Jones moves, pursuant to Rule 26(c), for a protective order against defendant XYZ Corporation, and in support of the motion states:

1. The pending case is a product liability case involving a rubber hose manufactured by defendant XYZ.

2. Plaintiff has previously served a motion to produce the rubber hose involved for the purposes of inspection and testing. Defendant's response stated that the rubber hose has already been shipped to ABC Laboratories for testing.

3. There is a substantial danger that any testing by ABC Laboratories will alter or destroy the rubber hose and forever prevent plaintiff from inspecting and testing it.

WHEREFORE, plaintiff requests this court to enter a protective order against defendant as follows:

(a) prevent anything from being done with or to the rubber hose until plaintiff has had a reasonable opportunity to inspect and photograph it;

(b) prevent any tests that would destroy or affect the appearance and integrity of the rubber hose;

(c) if destructive testing is necessary, order that such testing be conducted at a time and place so that plaintiff's experts can be present and observe the testing procedures, and obtain a copy of all test results;

(d) award payment of reasonable expenses, including attorney's fees, to plaintiff incurred as a result of making this motion.

_____
Attorney for Plaintiff

Each discovery motion must be accompanied by a certificate of compliance, which should look like Exhibit 10.42.

A common practice is to prepare a proposed order and attach it to the motion. The proposed order should parallel the motion by setting out what information needs to be protected and how it will be protected.

After the motion is prepared and signed, a copy, along with a notice of motion, must be served on every other party under Rule 5. The original of the motion and notice of motion, with a proof of service, must be filed with the clerk of the court. Keep in mind that many federal judges

Exhibit 10.42. Certificate of Compliance

<u>CERTIFICATE OF COMPLIANCE WITH RULE 26(c)</u>

I, Allen Smith, attorney of record for defendant Plaintiff Willard Johnson, certify that I have complied with the requirements of Rule 26(c) by doing the following:

1. On July 3, 2007, I sent a letter to defendant's counsel asking why a third deposition of the plaintiff was necessary. I received no written or oral reply to my letter.

2. On July 10, I called defendant's counsel and personally spoke with him. He stated that he noticed the plaintiff's deposition a third time to "make sure he'd covered all the bases," and gave no other reason for wanting a third deposition.

3. I requested that defendant's counsel withdraw the notice for the plaintiff's deposition, but he refused. Consequently the bringing of this motion for a protective order is necessary.

Dated: _____   _____
                                          Attorney for Plaintiff

---

delegate discovery matters to magistrates, so make sure your notice of motion correctly specifies who will hear the motion.

2. Orders compelling discovery

Rule 37(a) governs motions for an order compelling disclosure or discovery. A motion for an appropriate order for disclosure or discovery directed to a party to the lawsuit must be made in the court in which the action is pending. If the disclosure or discovery order is to be made to a nonparty to the lawsuit, the application must be made in the district court where the discovery is to be taken.

Rule 37(a)(2)(B) requires that litigants make a good faith effort to resolve discovery disputes informally before filing motions to compel discovery or disclosure with the court. The attorney must attach a certification to the motion showing what steps were taken to attempt to resolve the dispute. (A sample certificate is shown in Exhibit 10.44.)

A party can move for an order compelling discovery whenever a party fails to answer or gives evasive or incomplete answers to proper discovery. Frequently the issue arises when a party responds by objecting to an interrogatory, request to produce, or request to admit. A motion to compel must then be made to determine whether the objection is proper. The issue also frequently arises when a party fails to answer interrogatories, fails to produce documents after being served with a request to produce, refuses to designate a deponent on behalf of a corporate party, or, in the case of deponents, refuses to appear, be sworn, or answer questions. It also arises when a Rule 26(a) disclosure is claimed to be inadequate or not in compliance with the Rule.

Under Rule 37(a)(4), the court has authority to award reasonable expenses, including attorney's fees, to the prevailing party when a motion to compel is granted and also when the discovery sought is provided after the motion has been filed. However, even if the motion is granted, the court may deny a request for fees and costs if it determines that no good faith effort to resolve the dispute was made prior to making the motion.

The most common motions to compel usually involve either a party's failure to respond to discovery at all, or responding with evasive or incomplete answers that do not fairly meet the substance of the request. A typical motion is shown in Exhibit 10.43, and the required certificate

Exhibit 10.43.   Motion to Compel Discovery

[Caption]

MOTION TO COMPEL DISCOVERY

Defendant Alfred Jenkens moves that this court enter an order compelling plaintiff Thomas Smith to answer interrogatories, and in support of his motion states:

1. On June 5, 2007, defendant served his first set of interrogatories on plaintiff.

2. On July 15, 2007, defendant by letter reminded plaintiff's lawyer that answers to interrogatories were overdue and had not yet been received. A copy of this letter is attached as Exhibit A. No response to this letter has been received.

3. Over 100 days have passed since defendant served interrogatories on plaintiff and to date no answers have been received.

WHEREFORE, defendant requests the court to order plaintiff to serve interrogatory answers within five days and award reasonable expenses, including attorney's fees, to defendant incurred as a result of making this motion.

_____
Attorney for Defendant

of compliance showing good faith efforts to resolve discovery disputes in Exhibit 10.44. A sample motion and notice of motion appear in the Litigation File.

The steps to follow with the motion to compel are the same as those for a motion for a protective order: After the motion is prepared and signed, a copy along with a notice of motion must be served on every other party under Rule 5. The originals of the motion and notice of motion, with a proof of service, must be filed with the clerk of the court. Keep in mind that many judges delegate discovery matters to magistrates, so make sure that your notice of motion correctly specifies who will hear the motion.

3. Sanctions for abuse

Rule 37(c) includes a sanction for the failure to make a disclosure that is required by Rule 26(a). The sanction prevents a party from using as evidence, either at a hearing, in a motion, or at trial, any witness or information that was not disclosed in the initial disclosures unless the failure to disclose did not harm the other party. This sanction is automatic and does not require a motion under Rule 37(a)(2)(A).

For other discovery abuses, a motion is required. The sanctions that may be granted depend on the seriousness of the abuse. There are two basic sanctions that may be imposed.

Exhibit 10.44. Certificate of Compliance

I, Allen Smith, attorney of record for defendant Alfred Jenkens, certify that I have complied with the requirements of Rule 37(a)(2)(B) by doing the following:

1. On July 15, 2007, I sent a letter to plaintiff's attorney reminding her that her interrogatory answers were overdue. I received no response to this letter. A true and correct copy of my letter is attached hereto.

2. Approximately three times during the past month I have called plaintiff's attorney and left messages requesting the overdue answers.

3. Three days ago I left a message with plaintiff's attorney advising her that I would make a motion to compel unless I received answers within 48 hours. I received no response of any kind from plaintiff's attorney or her office.

[Add, if appropriate, "I declare under penalty of perjury under the laws of the United States that the foregoing is true and correct."]

Dated: _____

_____
Attorney for Defendant

First, under Rule 37(a)(4) sanctions "shall" be imposed, after a hearing, against the losing party or that party's lawyer, unless the moving party failed to make a good faith effort to resolve the dispute informally before bringing the motion, or other circumstances exist that would make the awarding of sanctions unjust. These sanctions can include the reasonable expenses incurred by the winning party in making or opposing the motion, including reasonable attorney's fees. If the discovery motion is denied, the court can also enter any appropriate protective order.

Second, under Rule 37(b) sanctions for discovery abuse can be imposed when a deponent or party fails to obey a previous court order regarding discovery. In this situation, the court can enter essentially any sanction appropriate, given the misconduct involved. Such sanctions can include ordering that certain facts be admitted, barring a party from presenting evidence on an issue, striking the abusing party's pleading, dismissing all or part of the action, entering a judgment against the abusing party, and treating a refusal to obey as a contempt of court. Sanctions can also include awarding reasonable expenses, including attorney's fees, if appropriate under the circumstances.

CHAPTER SUMMARY

This chapter has discussed the formal tools for obtaining facts in a lawsuit. Basically, there are five discovery devices that you may use: interrogatories, requests to produce, depositions, medical examinations, and requests for admission. Each of these devices serves a different purpose. Interrogatories are beneficial for obtaining basic factual information. Requests to produce allow you to obtain documents and other tangible items that are in the control of other parties. Depositions are an effective method for tying down parties and witnesses to details. A physical and/or mental examination helps a party assess medical damages. And a request to admit provides a way to have a fact conclusively established without having to prove the fact at trial.

Each discovery device has its own format requirements and timing requirements that must be followed. If the party responding to the discovery believes that the discovery is annoying, embarrassing, oppressive, unduly burdensome, or unduly expensive, the responding party may move for a protective order to limit or restrict the discovery. If a protective order is not sought, the responding party must answer and/or assert a valid objection to the discovery.

The paralegal must perform many tasks with respect to depositions. These tasks include preparing a witness for deposition, taking notes during the deposition, and summarizing the transcript of the deposition.

Different methods are available for summarizing the deposition transcript; you must choose a method that fits your particular needs and purposes.

Although for the most part discovery is conducted without court intervention, it sometimes becomes necessary to make a discovery motion before the court. Thus, the paralegal must be familiar with how to obtain a protective order from the court and how to compel a party to respond to discovery requests.

Finally, this chapter has detailed the various ways a computer can be utilized for litigation support. This includes using a computer to organize documents and to locate key testimony in a deposition transcript.

KEY TERMS

Chronological summary
Contention interrogatories
Deponent
Deposition
Deposition transcript
Good cause
Interrogatories
Narrative
Objection
Physical and mental
   examinations

Protective order
Redact
Request to admit
Request to produce
Subject matter summary
Subpoena ad testificandum
Subpoena duces tecum
Topic index

REVIEW QUESTIONS

1. Identify the five different discovery devices. What is the purpose of each device?
2. How can computers be used to assist in the litigation process?
3. In federal court, what information must be disclosed as part of the initial disclosure?
4. What are the different ways a deposition summary may be prepared?
5. Identify at least three grounds a party may have for objecting to interrogatories.
6. What is a protective order? Why is it important to move for a protective order as quickly as possible?
7. Why is it sometimes necessary to serve a subpoena duces tecum?
8. Why is it necessary to sometimes "redact" portions of a document that is produced to the opposing side?

9. What items of information must be included in a notice of deposition?
10. If you are preparing a client for a deposition, what rules for responding to deposition questions should you review with the client?

ADDITIONAL RESOURCES

Grim, Pauyl W., Fax, Charles S., *Discovery Problems and Their Solution*, (ABA, 2005).

Martiniak, Chris L.J., *How to Take and Defend Depositions*, (Aspen Law, 2002).

Part

III

SETTLEMENT, TRIAL, AND POST-TRIAL

Chapter

11

Settlements

Since most cases are settled before trial, it is important for a paralegal to be thoroughly familiar with the settlement process. This chapter provides details on

◆ When to use a settlement brochure

◆ How to draft a settlement agreement

◆ What the different types of settlement agreements are

◆ How to enforce a settlement agreement

A. INTRODUCTION

Pretrial conference
A meeting between the parties before the court after litigation has commenced, but before trial begins

More than 90 percent of civil cases filed in court settle before trial. The law prefers settlement and has created several methods to accomplish it. Judges prefer settlement, and the trend has been toward greater judicial involvement, principally by using **pretrial conferences** to get the adversaries together to discuss settlement possibilities. Finally, most clients ultimately prefer settlement over the increased expenses and uncertainties of a trial. Small wonder, then, that lawyers settle most cases before trial.

Settling a case involves three basic steps:

1. Determining the case's settlement value
2. Selling such assessment to the opposing side
3. Getting the client to agree

While a case can be settled at any time, settlement possibilities are almost always explored when a case nears the pretrial conference stage and a trial is just around the corner. Discovery will be complete at this point, and there is sufficient information to accurately assess the case.[1]

As a paralegal, you are not authorized to engage in the practice of law and, accordingly, do not have authority to negotiate a settlement. However, you may be requested by the lawyer to prepare a settlement brochure to send to the opposing party or to draft the settlement agreement.

---

1. Obviously, settlement is sometimes explored earlier as well, for instance, just before or just after filing suit or after the plaintiff's deposition has been taken, when the costs both in terms of time delay and litigation expenses can be held down.

B. PREPARING A SETTLEMENT BROCHURE

In recent years it has become fashionable among plaintiffs' personal injury lawyers to prepare **settlement brochures** in major cases. These brochures essentially set out the background of the plaintiff and the plaintiff's family along with the evidence showing liability and damages. The fact summaries are usually supplemented by photographs and documents such as employment records, hospital and other medical records, bills, and medical and economic expert reports detailing the extent of injuries, the degree of permanent physical losses, and the plaintiff's economic future. Some lawyers believe that developing such a brochure is the most effective way of presenting the plaintiff's case before trial and obtaining a favorable settlement. The settlement brochure should graphically show the nature and extent of the injuries, summarize the quality of the plaintiff's case, and demonstrate the jury appeal of a plaintiff.

Settlement brochure
A brochure that sets out the background of the plaintiff along with the evidence showing liability and damages

C. SETTLEMENT CONTRACTS

Since settlements are simply agreements between parties, general contract law principles apply. Good practice generally requires that the agreement be in writing and signed by each party, and some local rules require it.

Settlements are generally made using either a release, a covenant not to sue, or a loan receipt. The agreement is then presented to the court, and the case is dismissed with prejudice. It is critical to understand the legal differences between the various settlement methods. The choice of method is influenced by the types of legal claims and the number of parties involved, whether the settlement is intended to be complete or partial, the type of court action or approval that may be necessary, and the applicable law of contribution. You must know the law of the jurisdiction that governs the settlement contract because statutes and case law concerning releases, covenants not to sue, and loan receipts vary among the jurisdictions.

Also, the drafting of the agreement is important, since you need to ensure that it is treated under the applicable law in the way you and the lawyer want it treated, and that it has the effect you intend. This is particularly important in cases with **joint tortfeasors**, when two or more persons are liable to plaintiff for the same injury. In cases with joint tortfeasors the issue of contribution among the tortfeasors may arise. **Contribution** is a theory for apportioning liability among joint tortfeasors, so that the paying party may receive a proportionate sum from the other nonpaying joint tortfeasors.

1. Releases, covenants not to sue, and loan receipts

Release
A discharge of all claims against the parties as well as against any persons against whom the same claims are or could have been asserted

A basic common law **release** is a complete discharge, or satisfaction, of an action. It operates as a discharge of all claims against the parties to the release as well as against any persons against whom the same claims are or could have been asserted. A release is used only when there is a settlement of the entire lawsuit involving every claim and every party.

A **covenant not to sue** does not discharge any parties. It is simply a contract between two or more parties in which the plaintiff agrees not to sue or to pursue an existing claim against one or more defendants. For this reason a covenant not to sue is used when there is a partial settlement not involving every party.

The need for covenants not to sue has an historic basis. Since under common law a release was a discharge of all joint tortfeasors, a plaintiff could not use a release when he wished to settle a tort claim with fewer than all defendants. The covenant not to sue solved this problem. Today, the effect of the common law release rule has been eliminated in those jurisdictions that have adopted the Uniform Contribution Among Joint Tortfeasors Act. However, the laws of the states are not uniform, and the relevant laws must be understood to determine the effect on contribution whenever the settlement involves a tort claim having multiple joint tortfeasors. A simple covenant not to sue does not prevent a nonsettling defendant from later bringing a contribution claim against the settling defendant after a final judgment, unless a statute (like the Uniform Contribution Among Joint Tortfeasors Act) in the applicable jurisdiction prevents this result. Therefore, it is critical to know how a given jurisdiction deals with the question of contribution.

Loan receipt/Mary Carter agreement
Refers to a loan by one defendant of a certain amount to the plaintiff

In recent years the **loan receipt**, sometimes called a **Mary Carter agreement**, named for the case of Booth v. Mary Carter Paint Co., 262 So. 2d 8 (Fla. Dist. Ct. App. 1967), has been used to generate some contribution among joint tortfeasors. Under this settlement approach, one defendant agrees to "loan" a certain amount to the plaintiff. The plaintiff in turn agrees to dismiss the case as to that defendant only, pursue the case against the other defendants, and repay the loan to the settling defendant from any recovery against the remaining defendants. Through the loan receipt approach, a defendant can settle for a given amount, which might be recouped after trial. Plaintiff for her part gets an early partial recovery and a cooperative defendant. The legality of this basic settlement technique has been upheld in most jurisdictions over public policy objections, but courts have also generally required that the existence and terms of a loan receipt be disclosed to the remaining defendants and have allowed it to be used to show the bias and interest of a witness who testifies at trial if the witness is associated with the settled defendant.

Any number of variations of the basic loan receipt formula are possible. In some situations, the loaning defendant is not dismissed as a defendant but is kept as a nominal party who "agrees" to defend the suit. Sometimes the loaning defendant is dismissed with prejudice, sometimes without. The choices are numerous and are affected by the extent to which the details of such arrangements are admissible at trial and by whether the jurisdiction's law of contribution among joint tort-feasors is affected by any particular agreement's structure. The jurisdictions vary widely on the validity and enforceability of the numerous variations of Mary Carter agreements. It should be apparent that a loan receipt agreement should never be entered into without a complete familiarity with the particular jurisdiction's applicable law.

2. Drafting the agreement

Regardless of which type of settlement is used, care obviously must be taken in drafting the agreement to ensure that it is tailored to the case involved.

- ◆ The agreement should clearly state whether it is a release, covenant not to sue, or loan receipt, and state what matters it does and does not resolve
- ◆ The agreement should describe the events involved in the case, since the discharge will only be for those events
- ◆ The agreement should state the claims of liability and damages and the defendant's denial of them, since it is the compromise of these disputed claims that constitutes the mutual consideration in the agreement
- ◆ The agreement should specify how the pending court case is to be terminated
- ◆ The agreement can contain a choice-of-law clause and specify the details of any contribution in a covenant not to sue, if appropriate and permitted under the applicable jurisdiction's law

Exhibits 11.1, 11.2, and 11.3 are simple examples of a release, covenant not to sue, and loan receipt. They should be modified to fit the facts of any particular situation. The Litigation File at the end of the book contains another sample release.

If you are requested by the lawyer to draft the settlement contract, you must research the law of the applicable jurisdiction to determine the validity and effect of these settlement devices and you must keep the following basic concepts clear.

First, a common law release terminates all of plaintiff's claims against all existing and potential defendants, not just the settling defendant. A plaintiff must never agree to a release unless the plaintiff intends to terminate all present and future litigation.

Exhibit 11.1. Sample Release

RELEASE

In consideration of the sum of $ _____, which Plaintiff acknowledges receiving, Plaintiff _____ agrees to release Defendants _____ and _____ _____ and their heirs, survivors, agents, and personal representatives from all claims, suits, or actions in any form or on any basis, because of anything that was done or not done at any time, on account of the following:

All claims for personal injuries, property damage, physical disabilities, medical expenses, lost income, loss of consortium, and all other claims that have been or could be brought, including all claims now known or which in the future might be known, which arise out of an occurrence on or about _____[date]_____, at _____[location]_____, when Plaintiff claims to have sustained injuries as a result of a collision between an automobile driven by Plaintiff and automobiles driven by the Defendants.

As a result of this collision, Plaintiff has brought suit against the Defendants for damages. The Defendants have denied both liability and the claimed extent of damages. This release is a compromise settlement between Plaintiff _____ and the Defendant _____ _____ and Defendant _____.

This agreement is a release and shall operate as a total discharge of any claims Plaintiff has or may have arising out of the above occurrence against these Defendants and any other persons.

Plaintiff _____ and Defendant _____ _____ and Defendant _____ also expressly agree to terminate any actions that have been filed, particularly a claim by this Plaintiff against these Defendants currently filed as civil action no. _____ in the United States District Court for the District of _____, in _____. Plaintiff and these Defendants agree to execute a Stipulation of Dismissal, with prejudice, and file it with the Clerk of the above Court, thereby terminating that action in its entirety, within seven days of the execution of this agreement.

Date: _____

_____
Plaintiff

_____
Defendant

_____
Defendant

Exhibit 11.2.   Sample Covenant Not to Sue

COVENANT NOT TO SUE

In consideration of the sum of $ _____, which Plaintiff acknowledges receiving, Plaintiff _____ agrees not to institute, pursue, or continue any claim, suit, or action in any form or on any basis, because of anything that was done or not done at any time, against Defendant _____ and his heirs, survivors, agents, or personal representatives on account of the following:

Any claims against Defendant _____ for personal injuries, property damage, physical disabilities, medical expenses, lost income, loss of consortium, and any other claims that have been or could be brought, including all claims now known or which in the future might become known, which arise out of an occurrence on or about _____[date]_____, at _____[location]_____, when Plaintiff claims to have sustained injuries as a result of a collision between an automobile driven by Plaintiff and an automobile driven by Defendant.

As a result of this collision, Plaintiff has brought suit against Defendant for damages. Defendant has denied both liability and the claimed extent of damages. This covenant not to sue is a compromise settlement between Plaintiff _____ and Defendant _____ _____.

This agreement is a covenant not to sue, and not a release or an accord and satisfaction. Nothing in this agreement shall operate as a discharge against any other persons, and Plaintiff _____ expressly reserves the right to pursue any claims against any other persons other than Defendant _____ and his heirs, survivors, agents, and personal representatives.

Plaintiff _____ and Defendant _____ _____ also expressly agree to terminate any actions between them, particularly a claim by Plaintiff against this Defendant currently filed as civil action no. _____ in the United States District Court for the District of _____, in _____. Plaintiff and Defendant agree to execute a Stipulation of Dismissal, with prejudice, and file it with the Clerk of the above Court, to terminate that action against this Defendant only, within seven days of the execution of this agreement.

Date: _____

_____
Plaintiff

_____
Defendant

Exhibit 11.3.   Sample Loan Agreement

<u>LOAN AGREEMENT</u>

Plaintiff _____ and Defendant _____ _____ enter into the following agreement:

Plaintiff _____ has filed suit against Defendant _____ and other Defendants. This suit, civil action no. _____, is pending in the United States District Court for the District of _____ in _____. Defendant _____ and the other Defendants have denied the claims.

Plaintiff's pending suit is based on a collision that occurred on or about _____*[date]*_____, at _____*[location]*_____ in which Plaintiff claims to have suffered injuries as a result of a collision between an automobile in which Plaintiff was a passenger and other automobiles. Defendant _____ was the driver of the automobile in which Plaintiff was a passenger. Defendant _____ has denied liability for Plaintiff's claimed injuries.

Plaintiff wishes to dispose of her claim against Defendant _____ _____ and continue her claims against the other Defendants in the pending suit. Defendant _____ wishes to dispose of Plaintiff's claim against him. Plaintiff _____ _____ and Defendant _____ agree to the following:

Plaintiff _____ agrees to dismiss the complaint only against Defendant _____ in the above action, with prejudice, and continue her action against the remaining defendants until her action is terminated by settlement or judgment.

Defendant _____ agrees to loan Plaintiff the sum of $ _____. This loan is without interest. Plaintiff promises to repay the loan from any judgment or settlement Plaintiff actually receives and collects from any of the remaining Defendants in the above action. Plaintiff will be obligated to repay the loan only to the extent of any recovery actually collected from any of the remaining Defendants, and in any event Plaintiff shall have no obligation to pay Defendant _____ any sum exceeding $ _____*[loan amount]*_____.

Date: _____   _____
                            Plaintiff

                            _____
                            Defendant

Second, a covenant not to sue, first created to avoid the effect of the common law release rule, technically keeps the claims alive against the settling defendant since the plaintiff only agrees not to enforce the claims against that defendant. As a result, a settling defendant is still exposed to contribution claims by the other defendants who are still in the lawsuit. A defendant should never agree to a covenant not to sue unless the defendant has adequate protection against later contribution claims, either by statute or by the settlement agreement.

Third, contribution among joint tortfeasors is not the same thing as **indemnification,** which allows one party who has paid for a liability to recover completely from another party.[2] Contribution does not affect valid indemnification claims against any parties.

Indemnification
A claim allowing one party who has paid for a liability to recover completely from another party

Fourth, many states by statute protect a settling joint tortfeasor defendant by providing that any judgment against the nonsettling defendants be reduced by the amount the settling defendant paid the plaintiff, and by discharging the settling defendant from any later contribution claims by nonsettling defendants and other joint tortfeasors (a provision of the Uniform Contribution Among Joint Tortfeasors Act). However, not all states have such statutes, so the settling defendant must know the applicable jurisdiction's law to assess his exposure to later contribution claims.

It should be apparent that the drafting of a settlement can be complex, particularly in situations involving multiple joint tortfeasors. In general, every plaintiff wants a guaranteed dollar amount from the settling defendant, wants to keep claims alive against the nonsettling defendants, and wants no relief from contribution for the settling defendant. Every settling defendant, by contrast, wants to get out of the case with a guaranteed dollar amount to cap his exposure, and wants adequate protection from later contribution claims if a statute does not already provide it. Accordingly, you should confer with the lawyer in charge about the legal effect of these settlement devices and the contribution law that applies to the tort claims. This way, you will be able to prepare a carefully drafted instrument that fits the particulars of the case so that the final agreement achieves what the lawyer needs in order to adequately protect the client.

3. Structured and installment settlements

In recent years, so-called structured settlements have become common, particularly in the personal injury area when plaintiffs have been

---

2. Contribution may exist when one party to a joint and several obligation pays more than his share of the obligation. In this situation, the paying party may be entitled to receive a proportionate contribution from the other jointly liable parties. Indemnification exists to completely save another from any legal consequences.

seriously and permanently injured. **A structured settlement** is simply a settlement under which the plaintiff receives periodic payments rather than one lump sum. The benefit to the plaintiff is that she is assured of support over a period of years. Defendant's insurance companies are also benefited, since paying a settlement over a number of years reduces the true cost of the settlement. Socially, structured settlements help ensure that the plaintiff will not become indigent and depend on the state for support. Under the Internal Revenue Code, periodic payments receive the same tax treatment as lump sum payments.[3]

The most frequently used approach in structured settlements is to provide for an initial lump sum and a series of periodic payments. The lump sum is large enough to cover the plaintiff's attorney's fee, other legal expenses, and the plaintiff's unpaid bills. The periodic payments cover either a fixed period of years or the lifetime of the plaintiff; the periods are either annual or a shorter time. If the payments may extend over a number of years, they may be tied to the inflation rate by providing for increases based on the Consumer Price Index or other measure of inflation rates. The defendant's insurer usually funds the periodic payments by purchasing an annuity from an established life insurance company that will automatically make the payments required under the agreement.

Even if the action does not involve personal injury claims, it is possible that the parties may agree to have the settlement funds paid in installments. This is particularly the case when the settling defendant may not be able to afford to pay a lump sum settlement, but can afford to make monthly payments and pay the settlement amount in installments.

Although uncommon, a party may sometimes breach a settlement. Since a settlement agreement is a contract, the settlement can always be enforced in a separate contract action. However, this is not the preferred method as it would require a party having to wait until the termination of the separate lawsuit before enforcing a judgment.

The best way to enforce a settlement is to include a separate provision in the settlement for immediate entry of a judgment in the event of a default in the settlement. Some courts may require the injured party to make a motion to enforce the settlement, even if there is a provision for entry of judgment in the settlement agreement. If a motion is required, the motion should be brought in the same court and preferably before the same judge to whom the case had been assigned. At the hearing on the motion, the settling party must be prepared to prove up the breach of the settlement agreement. Once the motion is granted, a judgment can be entered against the defendant, and the judgment

---

3. In general, § 104 of Internal Revenue Code excluded from gross income damages for personal injuries, whether paid as lump sums or periodic payments.

enforced using the methods discussed in Chapter 13. A sample of an installment settlement agreement is found in Exhibit 11.4.

4. Terminating the suit

After a settlement agreement has been reached, the lawsuit must be terminated. The standard method is to file a stipulation to dismiss with the clerk of the court. Under Rule 41 a court order is no longer necessary.

Make sure the stipulation to dismiss is with prejudice as to the settling defendant, since this bars the plaintiff from refiling the claim later. If the settlement is only partial, as is the case with a covenant not to sue or a loan receipt, the stipulation must clearly show which party is being dismissed and which parties remain in the case. The stipulation is signed by the lawyers for the parties who have agreed to settle. Sample stipulations are shown in Exhibit 11.5 and Exhibit 11.6.

In certain types of cases, court approval is needed for any settlement. Settlements in class actions must have court approval under Rule 23(e). Also, settlements involving decedents' estates or incapacitated parties such as minors and incompetents usually require court approval. In these situations, the action will be brought in the name of the representative party, such as a guardian, guardian ad litem, conservator, administrator, or executor. Local statutes and rules must always be checked to ensure compliance with technical requirements. The usual procedure is to present a petition to the court having jurisdiction over the party, usually a probate or family court, and to serve notice to all parties and other interested persons. A hearing is then conducted on the proposed settlement, and, if approved, an appropriate court order authorizing the settlement will be entered.

5. Offers of judgment

Rule 68 of the Federal Rules of Civil Procedure provides that either party can serve an **offer of judgment** upon the opposing party more than ten days before the trial. The purpose of Rule 68 is to encourage settlements when reasonable offers to settle have been made. If the offer is refused and a judgment following trial is the same or less favorable to the refusing party than the pretrial offer of judgment, the refusing party becomes responsible for the offering party's "costs" incurred from the time of the offer.

Offer of judgment
An offer by a party defending a claim to have judgment entered in a specific amount

In the past few years, Rule 68 has become a prominent weapon in the settlement stage of the litigation process and has generated substantial case law. For example, Rule 68 applies whenever a final judgment is in a plaintiff's favor but is less favorable than the offer to settle made by a

Exhibit 11.4.   Sample Structured Settlement

WHEREAS, plaintiff _____, and defendant _____, are parties to a civil action Case Number 224435, presently pending in the [identify court] (hereinafter referred to as the "Civil Action"); and

WHEREAS, the parties to the Civil Action are desirous of avoiding the time and expense associated with the further prosecution and defense of the Civil Action; and

WHEREAS, said parties are desirous of being released of any and all claims with respect to the Civil Action;

NOW THEREFORE, in consideration of the releases and covenants contained herein, Plaintiff and Defendant agree as follows:

1. Except with respect to the obligations under this Agreement Plaintiff, hereby forever and fully releases and discharges the Defendant from all liabilities, losses, cost, expenses (including, without limitation, attorneys' fees), and damages related to all or any part of the subject matter of the Civil Action, or the prosecution or defense thereof.

2. Except with respect to the obligations under this Agreement Defendant, hereby forever and fully releases and discharges the Plaintiff from all liabilities, losses, cost, expenses (including, without limitation, attorneys' fees), and damages related to all or any part of the subject matter of the Civil Action, or the prosecution or defense thereof.

3. With respect to the covenants contained in paragraphs 1 and 2 of this Agreement, each of the parties hereby expressly waives all benefits under any code, statute or rule of law which provides, in essence, that a general release does not extend to unknown or unsuspected claims which, if known by the creditor would have materially affected the settlement with the debtor. The parties understand and acknowledge the significance and consequence of such a waiver and assume full responsibility for any damages or losses sustained by them of any sort or nature which might otherwise have been or be assertable as claims.

4. In consideration of Plaintiff dismissing its complaint in the Civil Action and the releases, representations, and agreements as set forth in this Agreement, the Defendant will pay to Plaintiff the sum of Sixty Thousand Dollars ($60,000.00), said sum to be payable by cashier's check to Plaintiff as follows:

   a. $10,000 to be paid at the time of execution of this Agreement;

   b. $10,000 to be paid on or before March 1, 2006;

   c. $10,000 to be paid on or before December 1, 2006;

   d. The balance of $30,000 to be paid on or before March 1, 2007.

5. The parties agree that no interest is to accrue on the above amounts.

Exhibit 11.4. Continued

6. The parties agree that in the event that the defendant defaults in the payment of any of the above amounts, that the plaintiff has the right to obtain by ex parte application, and without any further notice to the defendant, a judgment for the entire amount that remains due and owing, plus interest on said amount at the rate of 10% from the date of the breach of this settlement agreement.

7. If an action is commenced between the parties to this Agreement in connection with the enforcement of any provision of this Agreement, the prevailing party shall be entitled to reasonable costs and expenses, including attorneys' fees.

8. This Agreement shall be interpreted in accordance with the laws of the State of [name].

IN WITNESS WHEREOF, the parties hereto have each approved and executed this Agreement on the dates set forth opposite their signatures.

Exhibit 11.5. Sample Stipulation of Dismissal (Full Settlement)

[Caption]

<u>STIPULATION OF DISMISSAL</u>

Plaintiff _____, Defendant _____
_____, and Defendant _____ agree to dismiss this action with prejudice, and each party will bear its costs.

Date: _____   _____
                           Attorney for Plaintiff

                           _____
                           Attorney for Defendant

                           _____
                           Attorney for Defendant

defendant. The defendant's offer to settle must be reasonably certain in amount and must be unconditional, but there is no requirement that the settlement and cost amounts be itemized.

The principal difficulty in applying Rule 68 has concerned the meaning of the term "costs." It is clear that costs include clerk and marshal fees, witness fees, and court reporter fees, but less so concerning attorney's fees. In Marek v. Chesney, 473 U.S. 1 (1985), the Supreme Court held that

Exhibit 11.6.   Sample Stipulation of Dismissal (Partial Settlement)

[Caption]

<u>STIPULATION OF DISMISSAL</u>

Plaintiff _____ and Defendant _____
_____ agree to dismiss this action with prejudice as to
Defendant _____ only, and the action shall continue as
to the remaining Defendants.

Date: _____

_____
Attorney for Plaintiff

_____
Attorney for Defendant

"costs" refers to all costs that can be awarded under applicable substantive law. In that case, a 42 U.S.C. § 1983 civil rights action, § 1988 allowed attorney's fees to the prevailing party. However, the plaintiff's judgment was not as favorable as the defendant's pretrial offer of judgment. Therefore, plaintiff could not recover as part of costs any attorney's fees incurred from the date of the defendant's offer. Since this included the attorney's fees for the entire trial, plaintiff could not collect attorney's fees amounting to over $100,000.

Case law to date has generally rejected a similar argument in attorney's fees cases that the plaintiff who gets a judgment less favorable than a previous offer should also be required to pay defendant's post-offer attorney's fees.

The present usefulness of Rule 68 depends largely on whether "costs" include attorney's fees. When they include only court costs and the like, these are likely to be sufficiently small in most cases that they will not exert much pressure on a party to settle. For example, when costs include attorney's fees because a statute expressly so provides, Rule 68 affords substantial leverage against a plaintiff since, if the later judgment is less favorable than defendant's offer of settlement, the plaintiff will forgo recovering attorney's fees from the date of the offer. As Marek v. Chesney illustrates, this can be a substantial amount. Because of this disparity between cases where costs include attorney's fees and those that do not, various proposals to amend Rule 68 have been raised. Most call for Rule 68 costs to include attorney's fees in all cases, but no such proposal has been adopted to date.

If a party wishes to make an offer of judgment to the opposing party, this must be done more than ten days before trial begins. Make sure that the offer is actually delivered to the opposing party's attorney within the permissible time. A sample offer of judgment is shown in Exhibit 11.7, as well as in the Litigation File at the end of the book.

Parties usually make settlement offers under Rule 68 when settlement negotiations have broken down and a trial is to begin soon. However, the offer can be made at any time, and should be made earlier if the value of the case can realistically be assessed, particularly when attorney's fees are included as costs. The offer can be made in a letter, sent by registered mail or hand delivered, or in a formal offer with an attached copy of service.

If the plaintiff elects to accept the offer of judgment, he simply sends a notice to the defendant that he accepts the offer. Judgment can then be entered on the accepted offer.

6. Evidence rules

Under Rule 408 of the Federal Rules of Evidence, compromises and offers of compromise are not admissible to prove liability or damages. Rule 408 is broadly drafted to bar settlement discussions from being introduced at trial on those issues. The Rule, however, does not prevent

Exhibit 11.7.   Offer of Judgment

[Caption]

<u>OFFER OF JUDGMENT</u>

To: _____*[attorney for plaintiff]*_____

Defendant Johnson Corporation, pursuant to Rule 68, offers to allow judgment to be entered against it, in favor of plaintiff Frank Jones, in the amount of fourteen thousand ($14,000) dollars, and costs of suit incurred to the date of this offer.

This offer is made under Rule 68 of the Federal Rules of Civil Procedure and Rule 408 of the Federal Rules of Evidence, is made as a settlement offer, and is not to be taken as an admission of, or any indication of, liability on the part of this defendant.

Date: _____   _____

Attorney for Defendant
Johnson Corporation

admission of such evidence for other purposes, principally to expose bias and interest of a testifying witness. The law is clear that a party that has settled and later becomes a witness at the trial of the same case can be cross-examined on the existence and content of the settlement. The same rule has generally been applied to Mary Carter agreements because they usually show bias and interest.

7. Insurer good faith requirements

In civil litigation, a defendant will often have some insurance coverage. The insurance contract normally has language under which the insurer reserves the right to manage the defense and negotiate a settlement. However, courts have usually imposed a duty on the insurer to deal fairly and in good faith to protect the interests of the insured. This duty comes about because the interests of the insurer sometimes conflict with those of the insured. The insured naturally wants the company to stand behind her and defend vigorously or, if a settlement is reached, to settle within the policy limits. The insurer also has an interest in defending vigorously, but in a settlement situation only has a financial interest in settling the case under the policy limit. Hence, the insurer and insured's interests come most sharply in conflict when there is a risk of exposure over the policy limits since, once the policy limit is reached, only the insured has additional exposure. Because of this conflict, courts have imposed a good faith obligation on the insurer to manage the case fairly and to adequately protect the insured's interests. In other words, the insurer has a fiduciary duty and must conduct the defense in the best interests of the insured as though there were no policy limits.

Any settlement offer from the plaintiff should be communicated to the insured's lawyer, since the insured is the actual party. Case law is not uniform on whether failure to notify the party of a settlement offer is a breach of good faith, but some courts have so held. It is obviously a good practice to notify the client of every settlement offer, regardless of how unrealistic it is. When a duty to defend in good faith has been breached, the insurer is generally liable for the entire judgment, regardless of policy limits.

For the defense counsel, the message from case law should be clear. The defense counsel's client is the insured, and counsel's professional and ethical obligation is to serve the best interests of the client. That counsel was selected and will have fees paid by the insurance company does not alter the professional obligations. When settlement negotiations are in progress, both the insured and insurer must be kept informed of their progress. Whenever possible, the insured and insurer should both agree in writing to any settlement. Since the lawyer serves the client, not the insurer, the lawyer must accept a reasonable settlement, even when it involves the policy limits, if it is in the best interests of the client. When exposure above the policy limits is involved and the lawyer cannot get both the insured and the insurer to agree to a settlement, attention must be given to the status of the law in that particular jurisdiction to determine what the rights, duties, and liabilities of the insured and the insurer are in such circumstances.

CHAPTER SUMMARY

There are several methods available to settle a lawsuit. One method that is popular in encouraging settlement in personal injury actions is the preparation of a settlement brochure. The settlement brochure sets out the plaintiff's background, along with evidence showing liability and damages. The purpose is to graphically show the nature and extent of the injuries and to demonstrate the appeal the plaintiff's case will have to a jury.

If a settlement is reached, the settlement must be reduced to writing. The settlement may use a release, covenant not to sue, or loan receipt. Under the Federal Rules, the defendant may also make an offer of judgment that will be entered against the defendant if accepted by the plaintiff. If you are drafting a settlement agreement, care must be taken to ensure that the settlement is tailored to the case involved. You also must research the law applicable in your jurisdiction to determine the validity and effect of the various settlement devices.

After the settlement agreement is reached, the lawsuit must be terminated. The standard method is to file a stipulation for dismissal with the court. If one party breaches the settlement, the settlement can be enforced in a separate contract action, or the wronged party may be able to make a motion to enforce the settlement.

KEY TERMS

Contribution

Covenant not to sue

Indemnification

Joint tortfeasors

Loan receipt

Mary Carter agreement

Offer of judgment

Pretrial conference

Release

Settlement brochure

Structured settlement

REVIEW QUESTIONS

1. What are the three basic steps involved in settling a case? How can the paralegal assist the lawyer with each of these steps?

2. What is included in a settlement brochure? Why is such a brochure popular in personal injury actions?

3. What are the differences between a "release" and a "covenant not to sue"?

4. How does a "Mary Carter agreement" work? What is the advantage of such a settlement approach to the plaintiff? To the defendant?

5. How can a plaintiff enforce a settlement agreement made by the defendant?

ADDITIONAL RESOURCES

www.findlegalforms.com. Sample settlement agreements.
contracts.onecle.com. Settlement agreements.
www.lawdepot.com. Create release agreements.
www.forms.guru.com. Sample forms.

Chapter 12

TRIAL PREPARATION, TRIAL, AND APPEAL

Paralegals are involved in all aspects of trial preparation and may also assist at trial and with any appeal. In this chapter, you will learn

◆ How to draft a pretrial memorandum

◆ How to organize litigation files for trial

◆ What items must be included in a trial notebook

◆ Why developing a theory of the case is important

◆ How to prepare witnesses for trial

◆ How to prepare exhibits for trial

◆ What the paralegal's role is during trial

◆ What tasks must be performed if a party files an appeal

A. INTRODUCTION

Even though only a small percentage of civil cases filed will actually go to trial, preparation for trial is an integral part of the litigation. Trial preparation usually starts once discovery is complete, and well in advance of the actual trial. It is during this phase of the litigation that the emphasis shifts from gathering the facts to applying the facts to the issues for presentation to a judge or jury. Since the parties' attention is drawn to the issues in dispute and to the evidence available to support or refute the issues, it is no wonder that many cases settle during this stage of the litigation. Accordingly, proper preparation of the case serves two purposes: evaluation of the case for settlement purposes and presentation of the case at trial if there is no settlement.

This chapter discusses the important steps in properly preparing a case for trial and the significant role you will play in this preparation as a paralegal. The conduct of the trial is noted to give you some advance familiarity with the trial process before you must actually attend a trial.

B. THE PARALEGAL'S ROLE

As a paralegal you are an essential member of the litigation team as the case progresses from the fact-gathering and discovery stage to trial.

Paralegals are often responsible for organizing all of the data that have been collected throughout the course of the litigation and for ensuring that the data are readily available during the trial. In addition, paralegals assist with preparing and marking exhibits for trial, preparing witnesses, developing a theory of the case, preparing direct and cross-examination questions, and preparing any final pretrial motions.

During the trial, the paralegal must ensure that all exhibits are properly in place and anticipate any documents that the attorney may need during the examination of witnesses. All trials are different and, regardless of the amount of planning and preparing that is done in advance, surprises often occur at trial. Part of your responsibility is to assist in responding to any unexpected developments during the trial and to help ensure that the presentation of your client's case goes smoothly.

C. PRETRIAL CONFERENCES

Pretrial conferences are governed by Rule 16 of the Federal Rules of Civil Procedure, which gives the trial court broad authority to hold pretrial conferences on a wide spectrum of matters and to enter comprehensive pretrial orders. Rule 16 is not mandatory, however, and trial judges vary widely in how they use the Rule. Many districts and individual judges have also adopted local rules and instructions further regulating pretrial conferences. Hence, in assisting the lawyer in preparing for a pretrial conference, you must comply not only with Rule 16 but also with applicable local rules and be aware of your judge's special instructions on, and attitude toward, pretrial conferences.

The pretrial conference is a meeting held before trial between the attorneys and the judge. The pretrial conference is usually informal and held in the judge's chambers. The purpose is to identify the issues in dispute and the evidence that will be presented. Local rules vary on whether any memoranda must be filed in advance of the pretrial conference. Some courts require a short general memorandum on the case; some require that the parties meet in advance to prepare a joint pretrial memorandum; and still others require no memorandum at all. Even if no memorandum is required, it is still a good idea to prepare a pretrial memorandum because it provides an opportunity to brief the judge in writing about the nature of the case in advance of the trial. The pretrial memorandum generally contains the following sections: uncontested facts, contested issues of fact and law, exhibit list, witness list, and jury instructions. A sample is shown in Exhibit 12.1, as well as in the Litigation File at the end of the book.

Pretrial order
Order that acts as a guide
for the trial

After the pretrial conference, a pretrial order will be prepared, either by the judge or the parties, and signed by the judge. The **pretrial order** is a guide for the trial; it identifies the issues, witnesses, exhibits, and order of proof. The pretrial order must be complete, since no deviations are allowed from the pretrial order at trial. If any omissions or inaccuracies are made in the pretrial order, they must be promptly corrected. A sample pretrial order is shown in Exhibit 12.2 (see page 389).

Exhibit 12.1.   Pretrial Memorandum

[Caption]

JOINT PRETRIAL MEMORANDUM

Counsel for plaintiff Frances Johnson and defendants Robert Jones and Lisa Roberts submit the following Joint Pretrial Memorandum:

I

Uncontested Facts

The accident occurred on June 1, 2007, at approximately 2:00 P.M. Plaintiff Frances Johnson was a passenger in a 2002 Honda Accord owned and driven by defendant Robert Jones. Jones was driving north on Kolb Road intending to turn left (west) on 22d Street. As he was executing this turn, the defendant Lisa Roberts, who was driving her 2005 Buick Skylark south-bound on Kolb Road, struck Jones' vehicle. The intersection is controlled by a traffic light. Both defendant Roberts and defendant Jones claim to have had a green light favoring their direction of travel. At the time of the accident, the plaintiff Johnson was employed as a bank teller by the First National Bank.

II

Contested Issues of Fact and Law

1. Which of the defendants, if either, were negligent?
2. Were both defendants negligent?
3. If the plaintiff was injured as a result of the negligence of one or both defendants, what amount of money is she entitled to recover for her damages?

Exhibit 12.1.   Continued

III

Exhibits

A. Plaintiff Johnson's Exhibits   Objections to Admissibility, if any;
   1. Medical expenses totaling
      $1571.04 as evidenced by
      vouchers in support of each
      expenditure contained in a blue
      brochure with a cover sheet
      listing the medical expenses.
   2. The Police Department official   Objected to by defendant Jones.
      report of the accident.
   3. St. Mary's Hospital emergency
      room records of the plaintiff.
   4. Photographs of the plaintiff
      showing her shoulder deficit.
   5. X-rays taken of the plaintiff.
   6. Photographs and diagrams of
      the intersection involved.

B. Defendant Jones' Exhibits: Objections to Admissibility, if any:
   1. Plaintiff's hospital and medical
      records.
   2. X-rays.
   3. Plaintiff's employment records.
   4. Bills concerning property
      damage.
   5. Time sequence of signal lights.
   6. Photographs of the vehicles.
   7. The police report as far as it is
      admissible.

C. Defendant Roberts' Exhibits: Objections to Admissibility, if any:
   1. Police report of accident.
   2. Photographs of vehicles   Objected to by plaintiff and by
      involved.   defendant Jones, for the reasons
                                        stated in the attached
                                        Memorandum of Law.

   3. Plaintiff's medical records.

continued on next page

Exhibit 12.1.   Continued

IV

Witnesses

A. Plaintiff Johnson's Witnesses:
    1. Plaintiff.
    2. Richard Martin, M.D.
    3. Ernest Jackson, M.D.
    4. Philip Wigmore, a bystander.
    5. Bernie Sullivan, plaintiff's supervisor at First National Bank.
    6. Investigating police officer Frank Johnson.
    7. Defendants.

B. Defendant Jones' Witnesses:
    1. The parties to this action.
    2. Investigating police officer Frank Johnson.

C. Defendant Roberts' Witnesses:
    1. The parties to this action.
    2. Doctors who have seen or treated plaintiff.
    3. Richard Hollister, a bystander.
    4. Officer Horn, Police Department.
    5. Glenda Sylvester, accident reconstruction expert.

V

Jury Instructions

Plaintiff and defendants' proposed jury instructions are attached.

    1. Plaintiff Johnson objects to Jones' instructions numbers 4, 7, and 9, and objects to Roberts' instruction number 6 for the reasons stated in the attached Memorandum of Law.

    2. Both defendants object to plaintiff Johnson's instructions numbers 6, 7, 8, and 13 for the reasons stated in the attached Memorandum of Law.

RESPECTFULLY SUBMITTED this 1st day of May, 2008.

By _____
Attorney for Plaintiff
Johnson

By _____
Attorney for Defendant
Jones

By _____
Attorney for Defendant
Roberts

Exhibit 12.2.   Pretrial Order

[Caption]

FINAL PRETRIAL ORDER

The following are the results of pretrial proceedings in this cause held pursuant to Rule 16 and IT IS ORDERED:

I

This is an action for damages arising out of a collision involving vehicles driven by defendant Jones and defendant Roberts, which occurred on June 1, 2007, at the intersection of Kolb Road and 22d Street.

II

Jurisdiction is based on diversity of citizenship under 18 U.S.C. § 1332. Plaintiff is a citizen of California, defendant Jones is a citizen of Arizona, and defendant Roberts is a citizen of Nevada.

III

The following facts are admitted by the parties and require no proof:

1. The collision occurred on June 1, 2007, at the intersection of Kolb Road and 22d Street.

2. Defendant Jones was the owner and operator of a 2002 Honda Accord that was involved in the collision.

3. Defendant Roberts was the owner and operator of a 2005 Buick Skylark that was involved in the collision.

4. Plaintiff Johnson was a passenger in defendant Jones' vehicle at the time of the collision.

IV

The following facts, though not admitted, will not be contested at trial by evidence to the contrary:

1. Plaintiff was absent from work on June 1, 2007, through June 14, 2007.

continued on next page

Exhibit 12.2. Continued

2. Plaintiff was admitted to St. Mary's Hospital Emergency Room on June 1, 2004, and was discharged from the hospital on June 3, 2007.

3. Plaintiff's hospital bill was $592.83.

4. Plaintiff's doctor bills to date total $978.21.

V

The following are the issues of fact to be tried and determined upon trial:

Issue: Whether the defendants used due care in operating their vehicles?

Plaintiff contends that both defendants were speeding, not driving safely, and were not keeping a proper lookout.

Defendant Jones contends that he was driving within the speed limit and operating his vehicle safely.

Defendant Roberts contends that she was driving within the speed limit and operating her vehicle safely, and that defendant Jones failed to yield the right of way.

VI

The following are the issues of law to be tried and determined upon trial:

Issue: Whether the defendants, or either one of them, were negligent?

Plaintiff contends that both defendants were negligent and that their negligence jointly and directly caused plaintiff's injuries.

Defendant Jones contends that he was not negligent, and that his conduct caused no injuries to plaintiff.

Defendant Roberts contends that she was not negligent, that she did not violate any statutes, and that her conduct caused no injuries to plaintiff.

VII

a. The following exhibits are admissible in evidence in this case and may be marked in evidence by the Clerk:

(1) Plaintiff's exhibits: (see attached List number 1)

(2) Defendants' exhibits: (see attached Lists numbers 2 and 3)

Exhibit 12.2. Continued

b. As to the following exhibits, the party against whom the same will be offered objects to their admission upon the grounds stated:
  (1) Plaintiff's exhibits: (see attached List number 4)
  (2) Defendants' exhibits (see attached Lists numbers 5 and 6)

VIII

The following witnesses will be called by the parties upon trial:
  (a) On behalf of plaintiff: (see attached List number 7)
  (b) On behalf of defendants: (see attached Lists numbers 8 and 9)

IX

A jury trial has been requested, and was timely requested. It is anticipated that the case will require three trial days.

APPROVED AS TO FORM:

_____
Attorney for Plaintiff Johnson

_____
Attorney for Defendant Jones

_____
Attorney for Defendant Roberts

The foregoing constitutes the Final Pretrial Order in the above case. All prior pleadings in the case are superseded by this Order, which shall not be amended except by consent of the parties and by order of this court.

_____
United States District Judge

Dated: _____

D. ORGANIZATION OF FILES

Ours is an age of records, and the field of law is no exception. Everything is routinely recorded and duplicated. By the time it approaches trial, even a simple case can, and invariably will, generate an extensive collection of paperwork. Consequently, one of the first steps to take in preparing for trial is to ensure that the files are in order. All files must be organized, divided, and indexed to provide immediate and accurate access to the contents at any time during trial. The ligitation team that is organized will appear prepared, confident, and professional to both the court and jury.

Files should usually include the following indexed folder categories:

COMMON FILE CATEGORIES

◆ *Court papers.* These should normally be bound in the order filed or entered:

☐ Pleadings
☐ Discovery
☐ Motions and responses
☐ Orders
☐ Subpoenas

◆ *Evidence.* Records should be placed in clear plastic document protectors and have evidence labels attached. While records will depend on the specific case, the following are commonly involved:

☐ Bills, statements, and receipts
☐ Correspondence between parties
☐ Photographs, maps, diagrams
☐ Business records

◆ *Attorney's records*

☐ Running case history (log of attorney's activities in the case)
☐ Retainer contract, bills, costs
☐ Correspondence
☐ Legal research
☐ Miscellaneous

There is no magic in organizing files. Everyone develops their own systems for the types of cases they routinely handle. The important point to remember is that your system must be logical, clearly indexed, and bound whenever possible, so that records can be retrieved quickly and accurately.

In both small and large cases, it is often easier to store the records on the computer. CD-ROM technology has been developed that can store all trial records and exhibits (including transcripts, pleadings, and so on) in a computer. Simply by moving an electronic wand over a bar code, which instantly projects the appropriate exhibit on the computer screen, you can retrieve these records. For trial purposes, the computer can be hooked up to a large screen monitor. The exhibits can be retrieved at trial by the computer and projected on the screen. The exhibit then can be marked, highlighted, and enlarged by either the lawyer or witness at trial. Many courtrooms are now equiped with computer screens and monitors, so that paper copies of exhibits and evidence are quickly becoming obsolete.

E. TRIAL MATERIALS

As the trial date approaches, it will be necessary to organize the material that will be used during trial. Trial material should be organized in the way that is most efficiently useful at trial. This is different from organizing case files, discussed above in section D. Each part of a trial—jury selection, opening statements, direct and cross-examinations, and closing arguments—requires separate organization and preparation. Accordingly, paperwork necessarily generated during the preparation of each phase of the trial should be organized in a logical, easily retrievable, way.

Two methods, the **divider method** and the **trial notebook method**, are most commonly used. While ordinarily either of the two methods is used, they can also effectively be used in conjunction, especially in large cases. In such instances, the notebook can be used as a working trial notebook that keys into a larger divider system. This is frequently done, particularly in large commercial litigation cases.

1. Divider method

Under this method, each part of the trial receives a separate, labeled file divider, which has in it all papers pertinent to that phase of the trial. By merely pulling out the appropriate section, both you and the lawyer will have at your disposal during trial all necessary materials.

The advantage of the divider method is that it is usually better suited to a long, complex case when the paperwork is so voluminous it cannot physically be organized and contained in a trial notebook.

The disadvantages are primarily logistical. A divider method is only as reliable as the person maintaining it. If a file is misfiled or its contents misplaced, it cannot be readily located, and its utility is eliminated. If more than one person is using the files, the possibilities of disruption are much greater.

2. Trial notebook method

Under this method, all necessary materials for each part of the trial are placed in a three-ring notebook in appropriately tabbed sections. The advantages are that once placed in the notebook, the materials cannot be lost or misplaced and are immediately located simply by turning to the appropriate section.

Notes taken during the trial, such as during the cross-examinations of your side's witnesses or the direct examinations of your opponent's witnesses, should be on letter-sized paper, prepunched for three-ring notebooks. (Legal pads of this sort are readily available.) The notes can then be placed in the appropriate section of the trial notebook.

While it should be organized to meet individual needs, the notebook system works best when it contains enough tabbed sections to make the contents easily accessible. The following sections are commonly incorporated in trial notebooks.

a. Facts

This section should contain all reports, witness statements, diagrams, charts, and other factual materials. It should also contain a summary sheet that recites the parties, attorneys (address and telephone), the counts of the complaint or indictment, and the essential facts and chronology of events involved.

b. Pleadings

This section should contain the complaint or indictment, answer, and other pleadings of each party to the suit. The pleadings should be in chronological order. If amended pleadings have been filed, only the currently operative pleadings should be here. When pleadings are sufficiently complex, a pleading abstract, or summary of the pleading, should be included in this section. When the indictment or complaint is based on a specific statute, a copy of the statute should also be included. Keeping the elements instructions for the claims and defenses in this section is also useful.

c. Discovery

Included in this section should be the following discovery documents:

1. Interrogatories and answers to interrogatories
2. Deposition abstracts, cross-indexed to tabbed and marked depositions
3. Requests to admit and responses
4. Requests to produce and responses
5. Other discovery

d. Motions

This section should contain all pretrial motions, responses, and orders that already have been made, as well as any that will be presented prior to or during the trial. It should also contain the pretrial memoranda and final pretrial order.

e. Jury selection

This section should contain:

1. A **jury chart** to record the basic background information about each juror obtained during the voir dire examination. In voir dire examination the judge and, in some courts, the lawyers ask specific questions of the prospective jurors to ascertain any bias, prejudice, or other information that would affect the decision of the prospective juror in the case. The type of chart or diagram you use depends on how jury selection will be conducted. In some courts a **strike system** is used. This means that each prospective juror will be questioned before any challenges are made. Under this system, you can simply use a legal pad to record the basic information about each juror and then strike a juror's name if a challenge is made.

If a more traditional system is used, jurors will usually be called into the jury box and only those in the box will be questioned. As challenges are made and prospective jurors are excused, others will replace them. Under this system it is obviously necessary to develop a system that keeps track of the jurors in the box. Most lawyers and paralegals use a jury box diagram to record the jurors' names and backgrounds. When a challenge (see section J) is exercised, you simply put a large "P" (plaintiff), "D" (defendant), or "C" (cause) through the appropriate box to record which party exercised the challenge. When blank, a jury chart will appear as follows:

Jury chart
A diagram to be used during voir dire examination of the jury

JURY CHART

The diagram will cover most of a page. Then simply write down the basic background information of each juror in the appropriate box during the voir dire examination, as demonstrated below.

> **John Doe** — 40 — carpenter — self-emp. 10 yrs. — 3C in grade school — W part-time bookkeeper 15 yrs. — owns home Chicago, N. side — 2 yrs. army

2. A checklist for questions, if counsel are permitted to conduct the voir dire examination in whole or in part. In some courts the judge conducts the voir dire.

3. A list of questions the lawyer wants the court to ask, if the court does part or all of the voir dire examination.

4. A list that keeps track of the challenges exercised by each party.

f. Charts

This section should contain the following lists and charts, which can easily be made on standardized forms:

1. **Witness list**, showing each witness' name, home address and telephone number, work address, and telephone number, a short synopsis of the witness' testimony, and other information necessary to locating and scheduling the witness during trial. If the list is long, it is useful to put it in alphabetical order. A sample witness list is shown in Exhibit 12.3.

2. An **exhibit chart** for your party as well as all other parties showing the exhibit number, exhibit description, and boxes to check if exhibit was offered, admitted, refused, reserved, or withdrawn. A sample chart is shown in Exhibit 12.4.

Exhibit 12.3. Witness List

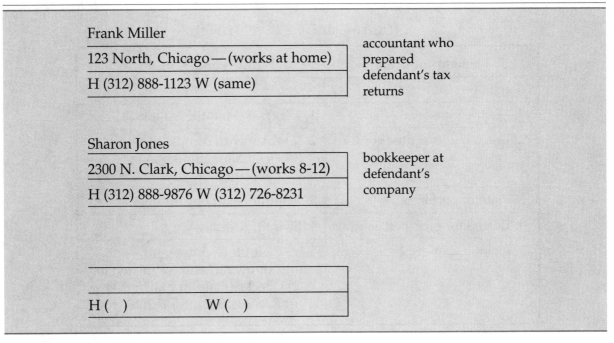

Frank Miller

123 North, Chicago — (works at home)

H (312) 888-1123 W (same)

accountant who prepared defendant's tax returns

Sharon Jones

2300 N. Clark, Chicago — (works 8-12)

H (312) 888-9876 W (312) 726-8231

bookkeeper at defendant's company

H ( )   W ( )

3. A **trial chart** showing each element of each claim or defense and the witnesses and exhibits that will prove each required element. A sample trial chart is shown in Exhibit 12.5.

Exhibit 12.4. Exhibit Chart

		EXHIBIT CHART — PLAINTIFF					
#	**Exhibits marked for identification**		Offered	Admitted	Refused	Reserved	Withdrawn
1	Construction contract		x	x			
2	Final payment check		x		x		
3a-g	Monthly progress reports (7)		x	x			

Exhibit 12.5. Trial Chart

TRIAL CHART—PLAINTIFF

Elements of Claim	Witness and Exhibits
(Count I — Contract)	
1. Contract made	1. Contract (Plaintiff Exhibit #1)

2. Defendant executed contract	2. (a) Answer to complaint
	    (b) Defendant admission in
	        deposition

3. Plaintiff performed	3. Plaintiff testimony
4. Defendant breached contract	4. Plaintiff testimony

5. Plaintiff damages	5. (a) Plaintiff testimony
	    (b) Contractor who completed job
	    (c) Checks (Plaintiff Exhibit #4)
	    (d) Records (Plaintiff Exhibit #6)

g. Direct examinations (your case-in-chief)

For each witness that your side intends to call as part of the case, a separate sheet should be maintained that outlines the direct examination questions. The witness sheets should reflect what exhibits the witness will qualify and the location of all prior statements.

When completed, the witness sheets can then be arranged in the same order as the order of proof. In this way putting on the case-in-chief becomes a matter of simply calling the witnesses according to their witness sheets. Cross-examination notes should be made on paper prepunched for three-ring binders so that they can then easily be put in the notebook behind the witness sheet for each witness.

h. Cross-examinations (opponent's case)

Each witness that you and the lawyer anticipate the opponent will call should have a witness sheet outlining the cross-examination the lawyer plans to conduct. The outline should be placed on one side of the page so brief notes can be made during the direct examination on the other side. The outline should show the location of all prior statements that might be used during the cross-examination.

i. Closing arguments

The closing arguments section should initially contain several blank sheets. Throughout the trial, as certain testimony or other ideas arise that the lawyer may want to use in closing arguments, the lawyer will note them in this section.

j. Jury instructions

This section should contain a copy of all the jury instructions your side intends to offer at the instruction conference, which is usually held shortly before the closing arguments. The instructions should be drafted before trial. In civil cases, the court will usually require each side to submit proposed jury instructions as part of the pretrial memoranda. This section will also eventually contain the other side's instructions, which the court will rule on. During the conference, you can mark each instruction as being given, refused, or withdrawn.

k. Research

This section should contain a copy of trial memoranda, trial briefs, or other legal research on issues that are likely to arise during the course of the trial. It should also contain photocopies of the principal cases and other authority supporting your party's case, so the lawyer can quote the authorities or give them to the judge if necessary. This is also a convenient place to keep a copy of the rules of evidence for the appropriate jurisdiction.

The trial notebook system enables you and the lawyer to locate any necessary information immediately and present the case in a well-organized, professional manner. All paperwork necessary for the trial will be in the notebook, except transcripts and exhibits.

In addition, you may wish to set up a file divider for each witness containing a copy of every prior statement this witness has made, such as in a police report or deposition. This folder will then contain all statements usable to refresh recollection on direct and to impeach during cross-examination.

F. THEORY OF THE CASE

Up to this point, the trial preparation has included organizing the case files, preparing the trial notebook, drafting jury instructions, reviewing the elements of each count, preparing exhibits, and reviewing the probable testimony of all anticipated witnesses. In conjunction with these preparations, you may be asked to assist the lawyer in developing a theory of the case.

As discussed in section D of Chapter 3, it is essential for the lawyer to develop a theory of the case before trial and act in accordance with it throughout the trial itself. A **theory of the case** is simply the lawyer's position on, and approach to, all the undisputed and disputed evidence that will be presented at trial. The lawyer must integrate the undisputed facts with her version of the disputed facts to create a cohesive, logical position at trial. That position must remain consistent during each phase of the trial. At the conclusion of the trial, this position must be the more plausible explanation of "what really happened" to the jury.

The theory of the case must be developed before the trial begins, because the approach to each phase of the trial is dependent on the theory. Consider the following:

EXAMPLE

Theory of the Case

In an automobile negligence case Marcy Walters is struck by Robert Chen's car at an intersection. Some evidence will place Marcy, the plaintiff, within the crosswalk with the walk-light green. Other testimony will show she was outside the crosswalk, jaywalking across the intersection.

Is the theory, as plaintiff, that:

1. Marcy was on the crosswalk and had the right of way? (ordinary negligence)
2. Marcy was not on the crosswalk but was injured because Robert (the defendant) could have stopped his car but didn't? (last clear chance)

G. PREPARATION OF WITNESSES

Witness preparation for trial purposes is not discovery. This is not the time to learn "what the case is all about" or to obtain interesting information. Witnesses favorable to your side must be prepared for testifying in court to those facts that will support your side's theory of the case. Preparation involves reviewing those facts that each witness and exhibit can provide, and preparing the witnesses to testify to those facts in a convincing fashion. Although the lawyer conducting the trial will usually prepare the witnesses, you may be asked to sit in on the meetings with each witness or to conduct the initial preparation. The following checklist should be used in conducting the preparation:

STEPS IN WITNESS PREPARATION

☐ Prepare each witness for trial individually.

Only in this way can you realistically expect each witness to be adequately prepared for his or her particular role in the trial.

☐ Review with the witness all previous testimony, depositions, answers to interrogatories, written and oral statements, and any other material that could be used for impeachment.

Have the witness read these materials or read them to the witness. Determine if his present recollection differs in any way from his previous statements. If so, and the witness insists that his present recollection, not the prior statement, is accurate, explain that the opposing lawyer is allowed to impeach him with the prior statement and how this will be done in court.

☐ Review with the witness all exhibits he will identify or authenticate.
☐ Review the probable testimony of other witnesses to see if any inconsistencies exist.

If there are inconsistencies, look for explanations that can be used to explain them if opposing counsel raises the inconsistencies at trial.

☐ Review the direct examination with the witness—repeatedly.

Make sure the witness can actually testify to what the lawyer anticipates he can. Make sure he can establish the foundation for all necessary exhibits. Once the general outline of the direct examination has been established, go over the actual questions in light of evidentiary requirements. Explain why the lawyer cannot use leading questions. If possible, review the testimony in an empty courtroom as a dress rehearsal, using the actual questions and answers the lawyer intends to present before the jury. Preparation should continue until the witness is thoroughly familiar with the questions, and answers them in the clearest, most accurate way. However, preparation should not continue to the point where the testimony sounds memorized or rehearsed.

☐ After the direct examination has been prepared, review with the witness the areas that the lawyer anticipates the cross-examination will cover.

Explain the different rules that apply to cross-examination and the purposes of the examination. Do a practice cross-examination of the witness, raising the same points and using the demeanor the actual cross-examiner is likely to raise and use at trial. Emphasize that the witness should maintain the same demeanor and attitude on cross as he had on direct and answer only the questions asked.

☐ Prepare the witness for his courtroom appearance.

Explain that he should dress neatly and conservatively. Explain how the courtroom is arranged; where the judge, lawyers, court reporter, clerk, bailiff, and spectators sit; how the witness will enter and leave the courtroom; where and how he will take the oath; where he will sit while giving his testimony; and how he should act while in court. If the witness is a party who will sit with the lawyer at counsel table, remind him that the jury will be watching and assessing him even when he is not testifying. Instruct him not to whisper to the lawyer or to you or interrupt the lawyer when court is in session. Instead, have him write on a notepad anything he wants to tell the lawyer or you when other witnesses are testifying.

☐ Prepare the witness for his courtroom testimony.

Explain that following these rules will favorably affect the way the jury will evaluate and weigh his testimony:

- ◆ Listen carefully to every question. Answer only that question. Do not ramble on or volunteer information. Look at the jury when answering questions. Speak clearly and loudly so that the last juror can easily hear you. Don't look at the judge or lawyer for help on difficult questions.
- ◆ If you do not understand a question, say so and the lawyer will rephrase it. If you cannot remember an answer to a question, say, "I can't recall" or "I can't remember." You will be allowed to review any of your statements to jog your memory. If you don't know an answer, say, "I don't know." If you can only approximate dates, times, and distances, give only your best approximation. If you cannot answer a question "yes" or "no," say so and explain your answer. However, give positive, clear, and direct answers to every question whenever possible. Answer the questions with the words you normally use and feel comfortable with. Don't use someone else's vocabulary, "police talk," or other stilted speech.

◆ Be serious and polite at all times. Do not exaggerate or understate the facts. Don't give cute or clever answers. Never argue with the lawyers or the judge. Never lose your temper. The lawyer on cross-examination may attempt to confuse you, have you argue with him, or have you lose your temper. Resist these temptations.

◆ You will be allowed to testify only to what you personally saw, heard, and did. You generally cannot testify to what others know, or to conclusions, opinions, and speculations.

◆ If an objection is made by either side to any question or answer, stop. Wait for the judge to rule. If he overrules the objections, answer the question. If he sustains the objection, simply wait for the next question. Never try to squeeze an answer in when an objection has been made.

◆ Explain the purposes of direct, cross, redirect, and recross and the forms of questions employed in each type of examination.

◆ Explain trick questions that the other side may ask, such as: "Have you talked to anyone about this case?" "What did your lawyer tell you to say in court?" and "Are you getting paid to testify?" Explain how such questions can be accurately and fairly answered.

◆ Above all, always tell the complete truth according to your best recollection of the facts and events involved.

If a witness is not a party to the lawsuit, the witness will need to be served with a subpoena to appear at trial. Part of your preparation of witnesses should be to ensure that a subpoena is served on all nonparty witnesses. Friendly witnesses can be served with the subpoena at the time of the meeting to prepare them for trial. Explain to witnesses that you are serving them with a subpoena because they are nonparties and a subpoena is necessary to secure their attendance. Even friendly witnesses can sometimes have second thoughts about testifying. If they are not served with a subpoena, there is nothing compelling witnesses to attend. Accordingly, it is best to protect your client's interests by serving the subpoena rather than running the risk that a witness does not appear at trial.

In some jurisdictions, it is also necessary to serve parties to a lawsuit with a subpoena if their testimony is necessary for the trial. Although most parties attend their own trials, serve a subpoena to guarantee the party's attendance if the party is going to be called as a witness as part of your client's case. In some jurisdictions, a notice to appear at trial served upon the party's attorney is sufficient to compel attendance of the party.

H. PREPARATION OF EXHIBITS

In some jurisdictions, trial exhibits are exchanged between the parties in advance of trial. However, even if the exhibits do not need to be exchanged between the parties, you should still ensure that all exhibits are in order before the commencement of trial.

Discuss with the lawyer the documents she wants to use as trial exhibits and the order in which you should mark the exhibits. Once you collect the necessary documents, organize them in the order they will be used at trial. Place each exhibit in a separate folder, and mark the exhibit for identification. Although you will need to check your local court rules, generally numbers are used for the plaintiff and letters are used for the defendant when identifying exhibits.

Remember that the best evidence rule requires you to have the original document. Accordingly, attempt to locate the originals of all documents. Place the original document, along with a copy of the document, in the exhibit folder. If you do not have the original, put a note in the exhibit file as to where you can locate the original if necessary.

Often, certain exhibits are enlarged so they will be easier for the jury to see. This is especially true in the case of photographs. Identify the exhibits that need to be enlarged as soon as practical, so you will have sufficient time to have the enlargements made and mounted.

Demonstrative evidence
Exhibits that represent real things

Demonstrative evidence, sometimes referred to as graphic evidence, is particularly useful in jury trials. Demonstrative evidence, such as charts, models, and diagrams, assists the jury in understanding the issues and facts. All demonstrative evidence should be prepared in advance of trial. Discuss with the lawyer the types of demonstrative evidence that she needs, and then arrange for the preparation of the evidence. If videotapes or slides will be used, arrange to have the necessary equipment available for the trial.

I. ORDER OF TRIAL

To fully prepare for trial, you need to understand the various stages of the trial and when evidence will be presented. The first stage is the selection of the jury. After selection of the jury, the lawyer for each party will present **opening arguments**. Opening arguments are an opportunity for the lawyers to tell the jury (or in nonjury trials, the judge) their respective clients' versions of the facts and what they expect the evidence to prove.

Opening arguments
Statements made by lawyers at the beginning of the trial to explain their clients' version of the facts and evidence they expect to prove

Next, the plaintiff's lawyer will present her case-in-chief. The **case-in-chief** refers to the evidence that a party will present to support the party's position. There is no magic to the order the lawyer will use to call her witnesses. Rather, the witnesses should be called in an order that will logically and forcefully present the evidence. Above all, the jury must be able to easily follow and understand the story as it unfolds. The lawyer, along with your assistance, will determine the order of the witnesses in advance of trial. In this way, you can make arrangements to have the witnesses available for trial on the day they will likely be called on to testify.

After the plaintiff's lawyer presents her case-in-chief, the defendant's lawyer will present his case-in-chief. Again, the witnesses should be called in an order that permits logical and forceful presentation of the defendant's version of the facts.

The plaintiff has the opportunity to present **rebuttal evidence** after the defendant's case-in-chief. Rebuttal evidence is evidence the plaintiff produces to explain or contradict the defendant's evidence. The defendant also has an opportunity to present evidence that explains or denies the rebuttal evidence. This is called **surrebuttal**.

> **Rebuttal evidence**
> Evidence refuting the evidence presented by the defendant as part of the defendant's case-in-chief

After both sides have presented their cases and any rebuttal or surrebuttal evidence, **closing arguments** will be heard. In closing arguments the lawyers summarize the evidence that has been presented and explain why the judge or jury should rule in a particular way.

> **Surrebuttal**
> Evidence presented by the defendant that explains or denies the rebuttal evidence

J. ASSISTANCE DURING TRIAL

1. Planning for the courtroom

As part of your assistance at trial, you will be responsible for ensuring that all necessary files, documents, and equipment are in the courtroom at the start of trial. Planning the logistics of this responsibility takes time. Accordingly, do not wait until the day of trial to determine the proper setup of your materials.

If possible, visit the courtroom a few days before the trial. You will need to determine if adequate space exists for the storage of files, the location of chalkboards and easels for exhibits, and the location of electrical outlets for tape recorders, video equipment, or projectors. If extension cords are necessary, determine the number and length of the cords needed and whether the cords can be placed to avoid anyone's tripping over them. Also observe the location of counsel tables to determine where your files should be placed. You will need to arrange your files so they will not be in the way, but at the same time be close enough so you have easy access. If necessary, diagram the courtroom so that when you return to the office you can draw a map for location of all your materials.

In addition to your trial exhibits and files, pack a **trial box** with necessary items for the trial. This trial box should contain the following:

- ◆ Pens and pencils
- ◆ Notepads
- ◆ Paper clips

- ◆ Post-it tabs
- ◆ A copy of the evidence code and rules of civil procedure for your jurisdiction
- ◆ Manila folders
- ◆ Business cards for you and the lawyer to give to the court reporter
- ◆ Scotch tape
- ◆ Stapler and staples
- ◆ Pleading paper
- ◆ Change for telephoning witnesses who are on call

Ascertain what time the courtroom opens, so that on the morning of trial you can arrive early to set up the materials. Everything should be ready to go before trial starts. If you are using computer software for record retrieval for trial presentation purposes, check with the court clerk several days in advance to ensure that you are familiar with the courtroom equipment.

2. Voir dire

The procedure for jury selection varies from court to court. However, in general, the prospective jurors come into the courtroom and take their place in the jury box. At that time, either the judge or lawyers, depending on each court's particular practice, will conduct a voir dire of the jury.

Voir dire refers to the method used to learn about the prospective jurors. The judge or lawyers will ask questions of each prospective juror in an attempt to ascertain information about the juror. This information can help the lawyer decide whether the prospective juror will be biased in favor or against one side.

If the lawyer wishes to strike a juror from the jury panel, a challenge to that juror can be made. A challenge may be peremptory or for cause. A **peremptory challenge** allows a lawyer to strike a juror from the panel without having any stated reason—for example, perhaps the lawyer believes the juror does not have the right personality or experience to render a decision favorable to the lawyer's client. However, recent case law prohibits the use of race and gender as the basis for exercising peremptory challenges.

To avoid too many challenges, the lawyers are each given only a limited number of peremptory challenges (usually no more than four or five). In most jurisdictions, the number of challenges is contained in statutes and rules. The numbers vary widely, and you must read the applicable statutes and rules prior to trial to find out the exact number. If a juror is biased, or has some interest in the litigation, or personally

---

Voir dire
Process of the judge and lawyers asking specific questions to learn information about prospective jurors

Peremptory challenge
Allows a lawyer to strike a juror from the panel without having any stated reason

knows any of the parties to the litigation, the juror may be stricken from the panel **for cause**.

Your role as a paralegal during the voir dire is to keep a chart of the names and information given by the prospective jurors. This information will then be reviewed with the lawyer to assist the lawyer in exercising the challenges. A sample chart is included in section E of this chapter. You should also keep track of the number of peremptory challenges that the lawyer uses so that you can advise the lawyer how many challenges remain. The lawyer will want to save at least one challenge until the complete jury is picked to avoid running out of challenges and having to accept a juror that may be detrimental to the client's case.

For cause
When a juror is stricken from the jury panel because of a particular reason

3. The trial

During trial, you must watch and listen to everything. Be alert for documents the lawyer needs for direct and cross-examination and for impeachment. Take notes during each witness' testimony, so that you can review the testimony with the lawyer during breaks and recesses. You also will be responsible for keeping the exhibit chart. You must note the identity of each document, and whether the exhibit was offered into evidence, admitted, refused, reserved, or withdrawn.

Nonparty witnesses generally will not sit through the entire trial. Rather, they will usually be **on call**, requiring that you call them when it is time for them to appear and testify. It is essential that you telephone the on-call witnesses well in advance of the time their testimony is expected. You do not want there to be any unnecessary breaks in the trial because a witness is late. Moreover, if a witness chooses not to appear on time, the court may require the lawyer to call another witness to keep the trial moving. This could significantly alter the planned order of proof and presentation of the evidence.

At the conclusion of each day's evidence, determine with the lawyer whether a daily transcript or any portion of the transcript is needed. Many times, the lawyer will want at least a portion of the transcript to use for examination of future witnesses or for the closing arguments. If a transcript is necessary, arrange with the court reporter for the portion you desire before you leave for the day. This will maximize the possibility that the reporter will have the transcript ready when you need it. However, remember that daily transcript copies are expensive and should be obtained only if genuinely needed.

At the end of each day of trial, you should meet with the lawyer, even if for only a few minutes, to discuss the day's events and what materials will be necessary for the next day.

K. THE PARALEGAL'S CONDUCT DURING TRIAL

No chapter on trial can be complete without mentioning some basic rules that govern paralegals' conduct during a trial, rules that are best reflected on each time you attend a trial.

Remember that the litigation team, as well as the parties, is on trial; that trial begins when you first enter the courtroom and ends when the court rules on the last post-trial motion. Remember that the lawyer's conduct and your conduct are constantly being evaluated and compared by everyone in the courtroom.

During the testimony of witnesses you should never appear worried or anxious. If the evidence is unfavorable, incorrect, or a surprise, never let your expression show any sign of your reaction. In short, you should maintain a "poker face" at all times. Also, avoid nodding or shaking your head or making any other gestures that can be distracting to the jury.

Talking with the lawyer at the counsel table should be limited. Rather, make a note of anything you need to communicate. You should instruct the client also to make notes if he or she wants to communicate something to either you or the lawyer during the testimony of witnesses.

Finally, a couple of ethical reminders for trial. First, be careful not to speak with any of the jurors. Your inadvertent communication with a juror could lead to claims of impropriety by the adverse party and a mistrial. Second, avoid discussion of the case in the elevators, corridors, and restrooms. You never know who may overhear your conversation.

L. APPEAL

Simply because the trial is over does not mean that the litigation is put to rest. Rather, if there is a possibility of obtaining a reversal, the losing party will undoubtedly appeal the judgment. The paralegal can provide organizational, analytical, and substantive assistance during the appellate process.

1. The appellate process

The rules governing the appellate process in federal courts are found in the Federal Rules of Appellate Procedure. These rules are similar to rules that have been adopted in state courts and must be carefully followed to avoid forfeiture of your client's rights.

Every party has an appeal as a matter of right from a district court to a court of appeals. This means that the losing party is permitted to appeal the trial court's judgment, and the court of appeals must hear the appeal. If a party loses in the court of appeals, however, that party must petition the Supreme Court to hear the appeal; the appeal will be heard by the Supreme Court only if the petition is granted. This petition is called a **petition for a writ of certiorari**. Since petitions to the Supreme Court are rare, this chapter will focus on the appeals from a trial court to the court of appeals.

The losing party in the trial court may file an appeal by filing a document called a **notice of appeal**. This notice must contain the name of the party or parties making the appeal. The notice must also state the judgment, or part of the judgment, that the party is appealing from. For example, the plaintiff may have obtained a judgment in the trial court against the defendant for breach of contract and received damages in the amount of $10,000. However, even though the plaintiff won, the plaintiff may not have been satisfied with the amount of the judgment. Therefore, the plaintiff would specify in the notice of appeal that the plaintiff is appealing from the amount of damages that has been awarded.

If the defendant were filing the appeal in this case, the defendant would probably want to appeal the entire judgment since the defendant lost on both the issues of liability and damages. The appeal must also contain the name of the court to which the appeal is taken. A sample notice of appeal is shown in Exhibit 12.6.

In federal court, it is permissible to identify the parties in the notice of appeal by their status in the trial court. For example, in the trial court the parties are identified as plaintiffs and defendants. However, subsequent to the filing of the notice of appeal, the parties will be identified based on who is making the appeal. The party bringing the appeal is called the **appellant**. The party defending against the appeal is called the **appellee**. In state court, the names of the parties on appeal may be different. For example, in California state court, the party bringing the appeal is called the appellant, but the party defending against the appeal is called the **respondent**.

The notice of appeal is filed with the trial court. The clerk of the court will then mail out notice of the appeal to each party or their counsel of record. The fee for filing a notice of appeal varies from state to state and between districts. Be sure to check with the court to determine the amount of the filing fee before filing the notice of appeal.

The notice of appeal must be filed within 30 days after entering of the judgment. In cases where the United States or one of its officers or agencies is a party, the appeal may be filed within 60 days after entry of the judgment. Accordingly, you must keep careful track of the dates, so that an appeal may be timely filed.

Petition for a writ of certiorari
Request that the United States Supreme Court grant an appeal of a decision made by a federal court of appeals

Exhibit 12.6.   Notice of Appeal

UNITED STATES DISTRICT COURT FOR THE CENTRAL
DISTRICT OF CALIFORNIA

Amy Baldwin Plaintiff	File No. 99351944
v.	
LJJ Motor Company Defendant	<u>NOTICE OF APPEAL</u>

   Notice is hereby given that Amy Baldwin, plaintiff in the above action, hereby appeals to the United States Court of Appeals for the Ninth Circuit from that portion of the final judgment entered on September 12, 2007, awarding the plaintiff only $10,000 in damages.

Dated: <u>October 7, 2007</u>

_____
Mark Jacobs
Attorney for Plaintiff
Amy Baldwin

---

2. The record on appeal

As discussed in Chapter 1, an appellate court is limited to reviewing the record of the court below. Thus, there are no witnesses called to give testimony. Instead, the parties must submit to the appellate court the transcript of the trial court proceedings and any documents and exhibits that were filed in the trial court. The transcript, original documents, exhibits, and a copy of the docket sheet that lists all the documents that were filed in the trial court are collectively referred to as the **record on appeal**.

Record on appeal
The transcript and any documents and exhibits filed in trial court, which are submitted to the appellate court for review

   Under Rule 10 of the Federal Rules of Appellate Procedure, the appellant has ten days from the filing of the notice of appeal to order the written transcript of the trial court proceedings from the court reporter. If there has been a trial, the appellant will generally order a transcript of the entire trial. The order must be in writing. A sample order requesting a transcript is shown in Exhibit 12.7.

   Rule 10 also governs situations when there is no transcript. If there is no transcript of the proceedings available, the appellant may prepare a statement of the evidence and proceedings from the best available means. This includes the attorney's notes and the attorney's own recollection. The appellee will have ten days in which to serve objections to or amendments to the statement filed by the appellant.

Exhibit 12.7.   Order Requesting Transcript

UNITED STATES DISTRICT COURT FOR THE CENTRAL
DISTRICT OF CALIFORNIA

Amy Baldwin
                 Plaintiff   File No. 99351944
        v.
LJJ Motor Company   <u>NOTICE OF APPEAL</u>
                 Defendant   <u>REPORTER'S TRANSCRIPT</u>

Notice is hereby given that appellant Amy Baldwin requests that the
court reporter prepare a transcript of the trial in the above matter which
commenced on September 1, 2007, and continued until September 8, 2007.

Dated: <u>October 7, 2007</u>

                                        Mark Jacobs
                                        Attorney for Plaintiff
                                        Amy Baldwin

3. Written briefs

Rule 28 of the Federal Rules of Appellate Procedure governs the content
and format of the written briefs. The appellant's brief must contain the
following items:

- ◆ A table of contents, with page numbers
- ◆ A table of cases (arranged alphabetically) and a list of all statutes
  used and other authorities cited, with a reference to the page of the
  brief where the case, statute, or authority appears
- ◆ A statement that indicates the basis for subject matter jurisdiction in
  the district court and the basis for jurisdiction in the court of appeal
- ◆ A statement of the issues presented in the appeal
- ◆ A statement of the case, which is the procedural history of the case
  and how it was decided in the trial court
- ◆ A statement of facts relevant to the issues in the appeal
- ◆ An argument that contains the contentions of the appellant, the rea-
  sons for the contentions, and citations to appropriate authority
- ◆ A short conclusion that states the relief that you want on the appeal

One item in this list, the argument, requires explanation. The argument is very similar to a memorandum of points and authorities that

Standard of review
Determines how an appellate court should look at the issues in deciding an appeal

accompanies a motion. However, in an appellate brief, the argument needs to include a section on the appropriate **standard of review**. A standard of review is how the appellate court should look at the issues in making a decision. For example, depending on the issues, the court may look to see whether there is substantial evidence to support the judgment of the court. If there is substantial evidence to support the judgment, the judgment will be affirmed. Another standard of review is to look to see if there was any procedural error that prejudiced your side. You will need to do legal research to determine what the standard of review is for your case. In many cases, treatises and handbooks on appeals will be helpful in determining the standard of review.

After the appellant files and serves a written brief, the appellee has 30 days to serve and file a response to the appellant's brief. The appellee's brief should contain the following:

♦ A jurisdictional statement indicating the basis for subject matter jurisdiction in the district court and the jurisdictional basis in the court of appeal
♦ A statement of the issues
♦ A statement of the case
♦ A statement of the standard of review

Rule 32 provides specific rules on the type size that may be used in briefs, and the covers that must appear on each brief submitted. In federal court, the cover of the appellant's brief must be blue, and the cover of the appellee's brief must be red. In state court, the color of the briefs may be different. Accordingly, always check your state rules before filing an appellate brief in state court.

4. The paralegal's role

As indicated in this chapter, the appellate process is governed by detailed court rules. To ensure that all deadlines and rules are met, keep a chart such as the one in Exhibit 12.8 for every case that identifies the deadline for any appeal, whether an appeal is filed, the deadline for filing cross-appeals, whether a cross-appeal is filed, and dates for filing written briefs. This chart should be kept, regardless of whether you represent the party appealing the judgment or the responding party.

The chart should be expanded to include any special rules for your particular court, such as filing notices to the reporter to prepare the trial transcript, requests for extensions of time to file written briefs, and the time for filing any appellate motions.

Exhibit 12.8.   Appellate Process Chart

Date judgment was entered	
Deadline for filing appeal	
Was appeal filed?	
Deadline for filing cross-appeal	
Was cross-appeal filed?	
Deadline for opening brief	
Deadline for responding brief	
Deadline for reply brief	

If your side is appealing the judgment, you can assist in analyzing the trial transcript to locate any **prejudicial errors**. The prejudicial errors that may justify grounds for appeal include objections that were improperly ruled on by the judge, evidence that was improperly denied or admitted, or jury instructions improperly given or denied.

Prejudicial errors
Errors that occur in the trial that, if such errors had not occurred, might have changed the outcome of the trial

If your side is defending against the appeal, your analysis of the trial transcript will focus on locating trial excerpts that show there were no errors or, at a minimum, the error claimed by the opposing side did not affect the trial outcome. For example, if the trial judge refused to allow a witness to testify to certain evidence, perhaps similar evidence was admitted through another witness. Thus, any error was harmless and should not justify a reversal.

In addition to analyzing the trial records, the paralegal can provide writing and research support to the lawyer. Written briefs by all parties will need to be submitted to the court. Thus, excerpts from the records will need to be woven into a statement of the facts. In addition, the paralegal can assist with conducting research for legal authority to support the client's position. In fact, the experienced paralegal can take full responsibility for the appellate process, leaving only minimal supervision and oral argument to the lawyer.

CHAPTER SUMMARY

This chapter has outlined all the essential steps for successful trial preparation. Adequate trial preparation is necessary not only for presentation of the case at trial but also to help evaluate the case for settlement purposes.

As part of the trial preparation, you may be asked to draft a pretrial memorandum. Many courts require a pretrial conference between the parties and the trial judge. If a pretrial conference is held, prepare a memorandum in advance of the conference. Even if such a memorandum is not required by the local rules, prepare a memorandum nevertheless, for it will help familiarize the judge with the various issues in the lawsuit. The memorandum generally contains sections on uncontested facts, contested issues of fact and law, exhibits, witnesses, and jury instructions.

As the case proceeds to trial, organize the litigation files for easy access during trial. The files should include file folders for court papers, evidence, and attorney's records. The material to be used at trial should be organized using either the divider method or the trial notebook method.

During trial preparation, the lawyer will develop a theory of the case. A theory of the case is the lawyer's position on, and approach to, all the evidence that will be presented at trial. The theory of the case will influence the approaches taken to each phase of the trial. To adequately assist with trial preparation, the paralegal should be familiar with the theory of the case.

Even though witnesses have been prepared for deposition during the discovery phase, trial preparation requires that witnesses be specifically prepared for testifying at trials. Use the checklist in this chapter to conduct the preparation of trial witnesses. Similarly, documents gathered in discovery must be marked as trial exhibits. Some exhibits may need to be enlarged and mounted for use at trial.

During trial, the paralegal will be an integral part of the litigation team. Some of the paralegal responsibilities during trial include recording information during jury voir dire, taking notes of each witness' testimony, keeping the exhibit chart, arranging for on-call witnesses to be present at the appropriate time, setting up any equipment for demonstrative evidence, and utilizing computer software for trial presentation.

Once the trial is over, one or more parties may appeal the judgment. If an appeal is brought, trial transcripts must be carefully analyzed and written briefs prepared for submission to the appellate court.

KEY TERMS

Appellant	Divider method
Appellee	Exhibit chart
Case-in-chief	For cause
Closing argument	Jury chart
Demonstrative evidence	Notice of appeal

On-call witnesses

Opening argument

Peremptory challenge

Petition for writ of certiorari

Prejudicial errors

Pretrial conference

Pretrial order

Rebuttal evidence

Record on appeal

Respondent

Standard of review

Strike system

Surrebuttal

Theory of the case

Trial box

Trial chart

Trial notebook method

Voir dire

Witness list

REVIEW QUESTIONS

1. What is the purpose of a pretrial conference?

2. Identify the two ways that trial material may be organized. What are the advantages and disadvantages of each method?

3. What does the phrase "theory of the case" mean? Why is it important to develop a theory of the case in advance of trial?

4. Why is it necessary to serve nonparty witnesses with a subpoena to appear at trial?

5. How can a paralegal assist a lawyer with the voir dire of the jury?

6. What is the role of the paralegal during trial? What ethical considerations should govern your conduct during the trial?

7. What is the process for starting an appeal?

8. Why is it important to keep a chart of all deadlines during the appellate process?

ADDITIONAL RESOURCES

www.chesslaw.com/freebriefs.htm. Access to sample appellate briefs.
Mauet, Thomas A., *Trial Techniques*, (Aspen Publishers, 2002).
McElhaney, James W., *McElhaney's Trial Notebook*, (ABA, 2005).

Chapter

13

ENFORCEMENT OF JUDGMENTS

CHAPTER OBJECTIVES

This chapter provides a checklist of the various methods available for enforcing a judgment. You will become familiar with

◆ How to draft a demand letter

◆ Why you should record an abstract of judgment

◆ When a writ of execution is required

◆ What the differences are between a till tap, a keeper, and a bank levy

◆ How to locate assets of the debtor

A. INTRODUCTION

Now that the trial is over and you have a judgment, what do you do next? The client obviously will be pleased if a favorable monetary judgment has been rendered in her favor, but complete satisfaction only will be had once the money is in the client's hand. Not surprisingly, many defendants against whom a judgment has been entered do not automatically turn over payment to the plaintiff without sufficient prodding. Once judgment is obtained, there are several steps you can take to see that your client's rights are protected and to maximize a quick payment on the judgment.

Use the steps in this chapter as a checklist to help identify what action you should take. Always research your local state rules to ensure that each action is proper in your state.

B. DEMAND LETTER

Judgment debtor
The party that owes money

The easiest and quickest step to take is to send a **demand letter** for payment on the judgment. Although the **judgment debtor**, the party that owes money, may not send a check for the entire amount, you may be able to elicit an offer to pay a reduced sum or to pay in installments. Both options should be considered by your client if you and the lawyer believe it may be difficult to ever collect the full amount of the judgment from the debtor. The letter may be sent to the judgment debtor directly or, if represented by counsel, the judgment debtor's counsel.

Although you may draft the demand letter, the lawyer should sign the letter. A typical demand letter is shown in Exhibit 13.1.

Exhibit 13.1.   Demand Letter

Mr. J.J. Jones
123 Main Street
Los Angeles, California 93048

Re: Smith v. Jones

Dear Mr. Jones:

As you are aware, on June 1, 2007, a judgment was entered against you and in favor of our client Susan Smith. The amount of the judgment, plus interest to date, is $37,141.96. Interest continues to accrue at the daily rate of $10.14. Accordingly, demand is hereby made upon you to pay the entire sum due on or before July 1, 2007. Your personal check, cashier's check, or money order should be made payable to Susan Smith and sent to my attention at the above address. Once your check has cleared, we will file an acknowledgment of satisfaction of judgment and cease all further enforcement activities.

If we do not receive your payment, we will have no choice but to continue our enforcement activities, the cost of which will be charged against you.

We look forward to your prompt payment.

Sincerely,

_____

A.T. Terny

C. ABSTRACTS OF JUDGMENT

An **abstract of judgment**[1] places a lien on all real property owned by the debtor. In some states, the lien also will attach to any property the debtor acquires for a period of time after the recording of the lien. When a lien is recorded, it places all buyers of the property on notice of your client's claim against the judgment debtor. The property cannot be sold until your client's judgment is satisfied. If it is sold, the buyer must take the property subject to the lien. Naturally, few buyers are willing to take on such obligations.

Lien
A claim by the creditor against property of the debtor as security for the debt

---

1. Pursuant to Rule 69 of the Federal Rules of Civil Procedure, the procedures for enforcement of a judgment are to be in accordance with the law of the state in which the district court sits, unless an applicable statute of the United States governs. The methods discussed in this chapter are ones used in virtually every state.

Although this remedy can be very effective in obtaining payment of your client's judgment, it also has its drawbacks. If the debtor is not paying your client, it is likely he has other creditors who are not being paid. Thus, if a senior lienholder forecloses on the property, your client's lien will be extinguished unless there is sufficient equity in the property to pay the junior liens. However, this drawback should never discourage you from recording an abstract of judgment, since an abstract of judgment is simple and inexpensive.

The form for the abstract of judgment can be obtained from your county recorder. Although the form will differ from state to state, all forms generally require identification of the case title and number, the amount of the judgment, the name of the judgment debtor, and the date judgment was entered. Depending on the requirements of your state, the abstract of judgment will need to be recorded in all geographical areas in which the debtor owns property. A sample form is shown in Exhibit 13.2.

D. WRITS OF EXECUTION

Levy
The procedure by which assets of the debtor are seized for satisfaction of a judgment

Rule 69 of the Federal Rules of Civil Procedure provides, in part, that the "[p]rocess to enforce a judgment for the payment of money shall be a writ of execution, unless the court directs otherwise."[2] A **writ of execution** is an order from the court empowering the sheriff, marshal, or other appropriate law enforcement agency to **levy** upon the assets of the debtor in order to satisfy the judgment. The writ of execution is generally a form that is filled out by the judgment creditor and issued by the clerk of the court. Upon issuance of the writ of execution, the judgment creditor can transfer the writ to the sheriff, marshal, or other agency, with instructions to levy upon certain assets of the judgment debtor. There are primarily three types of levy: the till tap, the keeper, and the bank levy.

1. The till tap

Till tap
Collection of cash and checks on hand at a business in order to satisfy a judgment

If the judgment debtor is the owner of a business, or if the debtor is a business entity, a **till tap** is an effective method to collect the cash and checks on hand at the business. The law enforcement agent will go into the business and stay for a short period of time, usually no more than

---

2. As noted earlier, the procedures for enforcing a judgment are governed by state law. Accordingly, while the Federal Rules identify the requirement of a writ of execution, the procedure for use of such writ is determined by state law.

Exhibit 13.2. Abstract of Judgment

WHEN RECORDED, RETURN TO:

Mary Stowe, Esq.
4242 Gilmore Street
West Hills, California 91307

UNITED STATES DISTRICT COURT CENTRAL DISTRICT OF CALIFORNIA	
PLAINTIFF(S) Kaspter Industries	CASE NUMBER 995293
DEFENDANT(S) Baker & Livingston Corporation	ABSTRACT OF JUDGMENT

  I certify that in the above-entitled action and Court, Judgment was entered
on   September 23, 2007   , in favor of

     Plaintiff Kaspter Industries

for $ 75,000.00   Principal, $ 3,400.00   Interest, $ 565.00 Costs,
and $ 1,500.00   Attorney Fees.

ATTESTED this   27th day of   October   , 2007.

Driver's License No._____
Social Security No._____
☐ Driver's License No. or Social Security No. is unknown
☒ No stay of enforcement ordered by Court
☐ Stay of enforcement ordered by Court, stay date ends_____
Judgment debtor or debtor's attorney's name and address which summons was
served:

  Kevin Roberts_____

  354 Mason Avenue_____
  Chatsworth, California 91544

                              Clerk, U.S. District Court

                         By_____
                              Deputy Clerk
              ABSTRACT OF JUDGMENT

three or four hours. During this time, the agent will collect any cash or checks that are in the register or that come into the business while the law enforcement agent is present.

The length of time you want to instruct the agent to remain on the premises depends on the type of business of the debtor. If the business is, say, a furniture store and does not have very much walk-in trade, you may want to instruct the law enforcement agent to collect the funds on hand when the agent arrives, but not stay on the premises. However, if the business is a fast-food restaurant, keeping agent on the premises through the lunch hour may be enough to satisfy the debt owed to your client. Keep in mind that it is expensive to have a law enforcement agent stay on the premises. Accordingly, instruct the agent to stay only as long as you believe it is worthwhile. The judgment creditor usually can charge the expense by adding the expense to the judgment. However, this is little comfort if the judgment creditor is unlikely to recover the entire amount of the judgment from the debtor.

2. The keeper

Keeper
A law enforcement agent who stays on the premises of a business and collects cash or checks sufficient to satisfy a judgment

Similar to a till tap is the installation of a **keeper**. A keeper will stay at the business premises for a longer period of time, usually 24 to 48 hours. During this time, the keeper collects any money that comes into the business. At the end of the time, if sufficient funds have not been collected, the keeper will take possession of personal property. This property will be sold at an execution of sale, and proceeds sufficient to satisfy the judgment will be given to the judgment creditor. Any excess funds would, of course, go back to the judgment debtor.

The real value of this method is that once a keeper is installed, debtors are usually very anxious to negotiate a payment with the judgment creditor. Thus, it is likely that you will receive a telephone call from the debtor shortly after the keeper arrives on the premises.

As with a till tap, the keeper also is a member of a law enforcement agency. Since not all law enforcement agencies will install a keeper, check with the agency before sending instructions and the writ of execution.

3. The bank levy

Bank levy
A seizure of funds held in a debtor's bank account

If the judgment debtor is an individual who does not own his own business, the choices for enforcing the judgment are more limited. The most common enforcement technique is the **bank levy**. If you know the name and location of the debtor's bank, you can instruct the law enforcement agency to levy upon all funds in the debtor's bank account. It is not necessary that you know the account number. However, you will need to know the particular branch office if the bank has more than one office.

Upon notice of the levy, the bank will turn over to the law enforcement agency serving the notice all funds in the debtor's account on the date the notice is received, up to the amount necessary to satisfy the judgment. This procedure usually works only once. After the debtor learns of the levy, it is likely he will close his account or, at a minimum, not deposit any additional sums at that particular branch.

E. WAGE GARNISHMENTS

A **wage garnishment** is a direction to the employer of the judgment debtor to withhold a certain amount of money from each paycheck of the debtor for a limited period of time. The amount is generally set by statute, and there are certain statutory exemptions that vary from state to state. For example, in California, there are exemptions for child support and taxes. Federal law also provides for certain exemptions. Accordingly, unless the amount of the judgment is small, it is unlikely that a wage garnishment will ever satisfy the full amount of the judgment.

F. LOCATING ASSETS

All the methods discussed for enforcement of judgments are fine, so long as you know what property and assets the debtor owns. If you do not know, you will need to attempt to locate the assets before you can give instructions to the law enforcement agency.

There are several steps you can take to locate assets of the debtor. The first step is to check with the client to see what information the client has about the debtor. For example, the client may have a returned check from the debtor, a financial application, or a report from a credit reporting agency.

If the client does not have sufficient information, your next step is to use the information available on the Internet. You may be able to discover a good deal about the debtor and the debtor's assets by doing your own search. Run a name search of the debtor. This may turn up information on businesses owned by the debor. In addition, use the Internet to search for public records in county and states that record property information, tax information, liens and other asset-related information.

If your Internet search does not produce sufficient information, you may take discovery from the debtor. This discovery can be in the form of post-judgment written interrogatories or an oral examination of a debtor. The advantage of requiring the debtor to submit to a debtor's examination rather than responding to interrogatories is time. Obviously, you will be able to obtain quicker results if the debtor is required to respond orally to the location and identification of his assets. The disadvantage is that the debtor may state during the examination that he does not recall certain information. For this reason, you should always request that the debtor bring with him documents such as check ledgers, savings account numbers, and grant deeds so the debtor can refer to the documents to answer questions.

If you are still unable to locate assets of the debtor, either because you do not have sufficient information or you suspect the debtor is hiding assets, you may wish to hire a private investigator. A private investigator will locate real property and bank accounts of the debtor. Many investigators charge their fees based on the number of bank accounts or property they are able to locate. Since retaining an investigator can be expensive, this should be your last resort and should only be used once you have tried to located this same information on the Internet.

CHAPTER SUMMARY

There are several methods to enforce a judgment. The easiest and quickest method is to send a letter demanding payment. However, this method is rarely successful, and the paralegal's job is to be familiar with the other ways a judgment can be enforced. This chapter has described some of the more common methods of enforcement.

Abstracts of judgments place a lien on all real property owned by the debtor. This method can be very effective if the debtor owns real property and there are not many senior lienholders.

A writ of execution must be obtained before a sheriff, marshal, or other law enforcement agent can levy against any assets of the debtor. If a writ of execution is obtained, the judgment creditor may request a till tap, installation of a keeper, or a bank levy. The method chosen will depend on the nature of the assets held by the debtor. If the debtor is employed, the writ of execution can be used to obtain a garnishment of the debtor's wages.

Each of the enforcement of judgment methods requires that you know where the assets of the debtor are located. In attempting to locate assets, you can check with the client for information, propound post-judgment interrogatories, or conduct a debtor examination.

KEY TERMS

Abstract of judgment

Bank levy

Demand letter

Judgment debtor

Keeper

Levy

Lien

Till tap

Wage garnishment

Writ of execution

REVIEW QUESTIONS

1. What is the purpose of an abstract of judgment? Why is an abstract of judgment an effective way to enforce a judgment?

2. What is a "writ of execution"?

3. Identify the differences between a till tap and the installation of a keeper. What are the advantages and disadvantages of each?

4. How can a judgment creditor obtain funds in a judgment debtor's bank account?

5. Identify at least three ways you can obtain information about the location of the debtor's assets.

ADDITIONAL RESOURCES

www.abika.com/Reports/Samples/howtofindassets.htm. Summary of information on how to enforce judgments and questions to ask in a debtor's examination.

www.inc.com/articles/1999/10/14809.html. Enforcement of small claim court judgments.

www.ifes.org/searchable/ifessite. Checklist for enforcing judgments. File Format: PDF.

www.askjeeves.com. Search engine to locate companies that will collect on judgments.

Chapter

14

ALTERNATIVE DISPUTE RESOLUTION

This chapter introduces you to the alternatives to resolving disputes through the litigation process. You will learn

- What the differences are between arbitration and mediation
- What the benefits of mediation are
- How to submit a claim to private arbitration
- Why parties may wish to arbitrate a claim
- When parties must arbitrate their disputes

A. INTRODUCTION

With the increasing costs of litigation in courts, alternatives to resolve disputes between parties are becoming increasingly popular. The two most widely used alternatives to the court system are mediation and arbitration. **Mediation** is where the parties sit down with a neutral third party, called the **mediator**, and the mediator assists the parties in coming to a resolution of their dispute. **Arbitration** is the parties' submission of their dispute to an impartial tribunal for resolution by one or more arbitrators.

Arbitration
The submission by the parties of their dispute to an impartial tribunal for resolution

Many of court and admininstrative hearing rules now provide an opportunity for mediation prior to proceeding with the litigation. In addition, in many courts, depending on the amount in controversy, arbitration may be required prior to obtaining a trial. For example, in California any matter filed in the superior court in which the amount in controversy is less than $50,000 is subject to mandatory arbitration. Arbitration of smaller matters helps to ease the court backlog and can provide a quicker and less expensive forum for the parties. Arbitration through the court system is referred to as **judicial arbitration**. Unless otherwise agreed to by the parties, judicial arbitration is nonbinding. This means that the parties have a right to either appeal the arbitrator's decision to a court of law or in some cases obtain a new trial in the court.

In addition to arbitration through the court, nonjudicial arbitration, sometimes referred to as private arbitration, is available through private agencies and is usually paid for by the parties. The most frequently used private agency is the **American Arbitration Association** (AAA), which has offices all over the country. Arbitration administered through private agencies such as the AAA is generally binding. Thus, the parties would have no right to appeal a decision by the arbitrator.

This chapter covers the general rules governing mediation and arbitration. Since judicial arbitration rules vary from state to state, if you are litigating a case in state court that has either been ordered to judicial arbitration or the parties have agreed to judicial arbitration, carefully review your state's arbitration procedures to determine any special rules that may apply.

B. MEDIATION

Arbitration and mediation are not the same. **Mediation** is a much more informal resolution of a dispute between the parties since there will not be a judge or arbitrator hearing the case.

In mediation, which is also available through the AAA and other private organizations, the mediator will listen to both sides of the dispute. The mediator will not give any legal advice, nor will the mediator express a decision in favor of one party. Rather than rendering a decision for one side against the other, the mediator will help the parties attempt to reach an acceptable settlement. Thus, mediation can be especially useful if the parties have had difficulty communicating with one another or have not been able to work out an agreeable settlement on their own.

In some cases, the parties may choose to mediate their dispute prior to an arbitration hearing or trial. If the mediation is successful, the parties will simply confirm this through a written settlement agreement. If the mediation is not successful, the parties will then set a hearing for the arbitration or trial and proceed as if no attempt at mediation had taken place. Any evidence of settlement negotiations during the course of the mediation cannot be used as evidence in a subsequent arbitration or trial.

The advantages to a mediation are many. First, there is no winner or loser in mediation. Rather, the mediator facilitates the parties arriving at their own solution. Thus, the parties, with the assistance of the mediator, can be creative in coming up with a solution for the dispute. In arbitrations and civil litigation, there is generally no opportunity for coming up with an acceptable middle position. For example, assume that a dispute exists over damage to a fence that divides the property line of two neighbors. If neighbor A brings a lawsuit against neighbor B claiming that B is responsible to pay for the damage, absent a settlement the court, and any court required arbitration, is bound to determine whether B is required to pay the amount requested by A. However, in a mediation, the parties may decide, during the mediation process, that they would like to share the cost of a new brick wall. Not only is the ability to fashion a creative solution a benefit, but the parties are now more likely to preserve their relationship rather than have it destroyed by the outcome of a lawsuit.

Mediation
A formal conference between the parties and a neutral person with the intent to arrive at a settlement

Since mediation does not involve a hearing to determine who is liable and the amount of liability, the mediator will not hear from witnesses other than the parties, or consider numerous evidentiary exhibits to determine an outcome. Rather, the parties will appear, give their side of the dispute, and the mediator will attempt to facilitate a resolution from the information given. Thus, the cost involved in preparing witnesses and preparing exhibits are eliminated. In addition, if the mediation occurs early in the process, the costs of discovery and trial preparation can also be greatly reduced.

Finally, having the benefit of a neutral party to listen to, and comment upon, the information provided is often a useful way for parties to see both the strengths and weaknesses of their individual cases.

C. THE ARBITRATION PROCESS

In an arbitration proceeding, an arbitrator will hear both sides of the dispute. The parties will present evidence, call witnesses, and conduct a proceeding that is very similar to a trial. At the conclusion of the arbitration, the arbitrator will make a ruling in favor of one party and against another. This ruling is similar to a judgment and is called the **arbitration award**.

Arbitration award
The ruling arising from arbitration

Arbitration is available through the AAA, or through other private entities, whenever the parties either have a contract that has a provision in it for arbitration of disputes or if the parties agree to submit an existing dispute to arbitration. The AAA recommends that in drafting a contract to include an arbitration provision, you use the following language:

> Any controversy or claim arising out of or relating to this contract, or the breach thereof, shall be settled by arbitration administered by the American Arbitration Association in accordance with its Commercial Arbitration Rules, and judgment on the award rendered by the arbitrator(s) may be entered in any court having jurisdiction thereof.

This is the standard arbitration clause you will see in many business contracts. Of course, arbitration clauses will also appear in many other types of contracts. The AAA has specific rules and guidelines for arbitration of disputes concerning hospital and medical claims, construction claims, labor claims, and security claims. You should obtain from the AAA the specific rules for the type of claim that you are arbitrating.[1]

Demand for arbitration
The form that a party files to commence arbitration through the AAA

Under the rules of the AAA, all types of arbitration are commenced by filing a **demand for arbitration**, along with the appropriate administrative

---

1. While this chapter discusses the arbitration process through the AAA, a similar process is used in other private arbitrations and most court ordered arbitrations.

fee, with the AAA. The demand also must be served upon all opposing parties. The party filing the demand is called the **claimant**. The party responding to the demand is the **respondent**. Once the demand is filed, the AAA takes care of all other details, including scheduling an arbitration date and arranging for the arbitration. An AAA arbitration demand form is shown in Exhibit 14.1. In judicial arbitrations, there is no need to file a demand for arbitration, since the matter will be submitted to arbitration either automatically by the court or by agreement of the parties.

D. PREPARING FOR ARBITRATION

Once the demand for arbitration has been received by the AAA, the AAA will assign the case to a staff member referred to as the **case administrator**. The **case administrator** will send out a list of potential arbitrators to the parties, as well as a request for dates when the parties will be available for the arbitration hearing. The parties have the right to strike any names of arbitrators that they object to and to rank in order of preference the remaining arbitrators. The case administrator will then review both lists submitted by the parties and choose an arbitrator who has not been objected to by either party. In judicial arbitrations, usually only one arbitrator is assigned. However, the parties still have the right to object to the assigned arbitrator for good cause.

The hearing will generally be held within a few months of filing the demand for arbitration. The case administrator will set a date for the arbitration hearing based on the request for dates received from the parties and the availability of the arbitrator.

Since the arbitration will proceed similarly to a trial and the arbitrator in a private arbitration will render a binding decision at the conclusion of the hearing, it is important to carefully prepare for the arbitration hearing. Accordingly, you may be asked as a paralegal to assist the lawyer with the following preparations:

PREPARATION FOR ARBITRATION?

☐ Gather all documentation and papers that support your side's position.

You will need to make sufficient copies of the documents and papers so that the attorney may give one copy to the arbitrator and one copy to each opposing party, and retain one copy for the attorney's own use during the arbitration.

Exhibit 14.1.   AAA Arbitration Demand Form

American Arbitration Association

COMMERCIAL ARBITRATION RULES

To institute proceedings, please send three copies of this demand and the arbitration agreement, with the administrative fee as provided in the rules, to the AAA. Send the original demand to the respondent.

DEMAND FOR ARBITRATION

DATE: April 17, 2007

TO: Name Victoria Peller
(of the Party on Whom the Demand Is Made)

Address 17083 Empire Road

City and State Longwood, Florida   ZIP Code 32750

Telephone (407) 826-7635   Fax

Name of Representative Kevin Patterson

Name of Firm (if Applicable) Patterson & Arnold   (if Known)

Representative's Address 3377 Main Street

City and State Orlando, Florida   ZIP Code 32801

Telephone (407) 345-6437   Fax 407-345-7676

The named claimant, a party to an arbitration agreement contained in a written contract, dated _____
August 12, 2002 _____ and providing for arbitration under the
Commercial Arbitration Rules of the American Arbitration Association, hereby demands arbitration thereunder.

THE NATURE OF THE DISPUTE:

Failure of party to perform under a written employment contract.

THE CLAIM OR RELIEF SOUGHT (the Amount, if Any):

Back pay and future salary due under the contract in the amount of not less than $50,000.

TYPES OF BUSINESS: Claimant Salesperson   Respondent Supplier of medical goods

HEARING LOCALE REQUESTED: Orlando, Florida
(City and State)

You are hereby notified that copies of our arbitration agreement and this demand are being filed with the American Arbitration Association at its Orlando office, with a request that it commence administration of the arbitration. Under the rules, you may file an answering statement within ten days after notice from the administrator.

Signed *Beverly Garner*   Title Attorney
(May Be Signed by a Representative)

Name of Claimant Laura Fidler

Address (to Be Used in Connection with This Case) 3464 Main Street, Suite 407

City and State Orlando, Florida   ZIP Code 32801

Telephone (407) 345-2455   Fax 407-345-2897

Name of Representative Beverly Garner

Name of Firm (if Applicable) Resnick, Howe & Park

Representative's Address Same as above

City and State   ZIP Code

Telephone (   )   Fax

XXX   **MEDIATION is a nonbinding process. The mediator assists the parties in working out a solution that is acceptable to them. If you wish for the AAA to contact the other parties to ascertain whether they wish to mediate this matter, please check this box (there is no additional administrative fee for this service).**

Form C2–6/93

☐ Subpoena documents from other parties if your client does not have access to all the documentation needed for the arbitration.

Many states have rules permitting the arbitrator to issue a subpoena to compel other parties or even nonparties to bring the documents to the arbitration hearing.

☐ Determine who will be called as witnesses at the arbitration.

If possible, interview all the witnesses in advance and make a written summary of what each witness' testimony will be.

☐ Assist the attorney in preparing questions for direct and cross-examination of each of the witnesses.
☐ Assist the attorney in preparing a written arbitration brief.

The arbitration brief is similar to a trial brief. It will outline your client's version of the facts and cite appropriate legal authorities that will help the arbitrator decide the law to be applied to the facts in the case.

Although arbitrations are simple to initiate, the preparation for the arbitration hearing demands work similar to the preparation for a trial. Keep in mind that nonjudicial arbitrations are binding and, except under very limited circumstances (such as fraud or bias by the arbitrator), the award of the arbitrator cannot be appealed if your side is the losing party. Accordingly, it is necessary for both sides to do their best in presenting the case.

E. THE ARBITRATION HEARING

In general, the arbitration will proceed very much like a trial, with both sides presenting their witnesses and evidence. The arbitrator, however, is not bound by the rules of evidence. Accordingly, arbitrators usually listen to all the evidence, and then make their own determination about the relevancy or admissibility of the evidence.

Unlike a trial, a court reporter will not be present at the arbitration to make a written transcript of the proceedings unless requested by the parties. In addition, the hearing will be much less formal than a trial; it will take place in an office at the AAA, probably in a small conference room. This usually makes for a much more relaxed atmosphere for both the parties and their attorneys.

After both sides have presented their cases, the arbitrator will declare the hearings to be closed. The arbitrator then has 30 days in which to render the arbitration award. The prevailing party may then petition the appropriate court to confirm the award. The arbitration award will be confirmed unless there are special circumstances, such as proof of bias on the part of the arbitrator or some fraud in the proceedings on the part of the prevailing party or arbitrator. Once the award is confirmed, it becomes an enforceable judgment.

CHAPTER SUMMARY

With rising legal costs, arbitration and mediation are popular alternatives to litigation. Mediation may help the parties resolve their dispute by reaching an acceptable settlement. If mediation is not possible, arbitration can provide a faster and less expensive alternative to proceeding in court.

Arbitration is available whenever the parties have a contract that specifically provides for arbitration. In addition, even if no such contract provision exists, the parties can voluntarily agree to submit their dispute to arbitration. The agency most frequently used to arbitrate disputes is the American Arbitration Association.

Once a demand for arbitration is filed with the AAA, the case administrator will take care of the procedural details, such as setting a hearing and arranging for the appointment of an arbitrator. However, thorough preparation is still needed for the arbitration hearing since there are limited circumstances in which a party can have a court trial after resolution of a dispute through arbitration.

KEY TERMS

American Arbitration   Demand for arbitration
    Association   Judicial arbitration
Arbitration   Mediation
Arbitration award   Mediator
Case administrator   Respondent
Claimant

REVIEW QUESTIONS

1. What are the differences between judicial and nonjudicial arbitration?

2. What are the advantages and disadvantages between arbitration and litigation?

3. How is an arbitration commenced?

4. Describe the mediation process.

ADDITIONAL RESOURCES

www.adr.org. Official site for the American Arbitration Association.
www.findlaw.com. Link to arbitration and mediation information.

This appendix is part of the litigation file in Jones v. Smith, an automobile collision case. It illustrates each basic step in the pleadings, discovery, motions, and settlement stages of the litigation process.

FACTS

John Jones, a 23-year-old delivery truck driver, was involved in a collision with Susan Smith. The collision occurred on September 2, 2005, at the intersection of 40th Street and Thomas Road in Phoenix, Arizona. Jones injured his stomach, neck, back, a shoulder, and an ankle and was out of work for a month. His car was also damaged.

Jones brings suit in federal court in Phoenix, Arizona. He claims that Smith negligently ran a red light at the intersection and crashed into his car (he was not operating a delivery truck at the time). Jones is a citizen of Arizona; Smith is a citizen of Nevada. The lawsuit was filed on January 3, 2006.

UNITED STATES DISTRICT COURT
FOR THE DISTRICT OF ARIZONA

John Jones, Plaintiff	No. _____ Civil Action
v.	
Susan Smith, Defendant	<u>JURY TRIAL</u> <u>DEMANDED</u>

The 'Caption' includes the court, the parties, and the case number.

The jury demand is usually put in the caption as well as at the end of the complaint.

<u>COMPLAINT</u>

Plaintiff John Jones complains of defendant Susan Smith as follows:

1. Jurisdiction in this case is based on diversity of citizenship and the amount in controversy. Plaintiff is a citizen of the State of Arizona. Defendant is a citizen of the State of Nevada. The amount in controversy exceeds, exclusive of interest and costs, the sum of seventy-five thousand ($75,000) dollars.

This is the standard jurisdictional allegation in diversity cases. It should be the first paragraph of the complaint.

2. On September 2, 2005, at approximately 2:00 P.M., plaintiff John Jones ("Jones") was driving a vehicle northbound on 40th Street toward the intersection of 40th Street and Thomas Road in Phoenix, Arizona. Defendant Susan Smith ("Smith") was driving a vehicle eastbound on Thomas Road toward the same intersection.

The factual allegations should be clear and simple. This makes it more likely that they will be either admitted or denied outright, making the pleadings easier to understand.

3. Smith failed to stop for a red light at the intersection of 40th Street and Thomas Road, and negligently drove her vehicle into Jones' vehicle.

The negligence and causation claims are kept single. This is adequate under "notice pleading" requirements.

4. As a direct and proximate result of Smith's negligence, Jones injured his stomach, neck, back, a shoulder, an ankle, and other bodily parts, received other physical injuries, suffered physical and mental pain and suffering, incurred medical expenses, lost income, and will incur further medical expenses and lost income in the future.

The injury allegations are usually spelled out in some detail.

Many complaints simply ask for "a sum in excess of $75,000," the jurisdictional limit. This avoids requesting unrealistic damages. The danger of exaggerated damages is that, unless amended, the pleadings can be read to the jury at trial, making the plaintiff look greedy.

WHEREFORE, plaintiff John Jones demands judgment against defendant Susan Smith for the sum of $100,000, with interest and costs.

Dated: <u>January 3, 2006</u>

anne Johnson
_____
anne Johnson
Attorney for Plaintiff
100 Congress Street
Phoenix, AZ 85001
882-1000

Most jurisdictions also require submitting a jury demand form and paying a jury demand fee to preserve the right to a jury trial.

<u>**PLAINTIFF DEMANDS TRIAL BY JURY**</u>

UNITED STATES DISTRICT COURT
FOR THE DISTRICT OF ARIZONA

John Jones,
            Plaintiff

        v.   No. _____

Susan Smith,
            Defendant

SUMMONS

TO THE ABOVE-NAMED DEFENDANT:
Susan Smith
200 Palmer Way
Las Vegas, Nevada

A good practice is to give the person who serves the complaint and summons any additional information about the defendant that may help make an effective service.

You are hereby summoned and required to serve upon Anne Johnson, plaintiff's attorney, whose address is 100 Congress Street, Phoenix, AZ 85001, an answer to the complaint which is herewith served upon you, within 20 days after service of this summons upon you, exclusive of the day of service.

In this case service must be made under the Arizona long-arm statute. Make sure that the service complies with the statute, since this is required by Rule 4(e).

If you fail to do so, judgment by default will be taken against you for the relief demanded in the complaint.

John Clark
Clerk of the Court

The person making the service must prepare an Affidavit of Service showing how service on the defendant was actually made.

[Seal of U.S. District Court]

Dated: January 3, 2006

The Affidavit of Service form is frequently attached to the summons form.

UNITED STATES DISTRICT COURT
FOR THE DISTRICT OF ARIZONA

John Jones,
Plaintiff

v.   No. 03 C 1000

Susan Smith,
Defendant

ANSWER

Defendant Susan Smith answers the complaint as follows:

Simple responses are more likely to be made since the complaint's allegations are correspondingly simple.

1. Admit
2. Admit
3. Deny
4. Defendant denies plaintiff was injured as a result of any negligence by the defendant, and is without knowledge or information sufficient to form a belief as to the truth of all other allegations in Par. 4, and therefore denies them.

Each defense should be set out separately.

First Defense

Plaintiff's claimed injuries and damages were caused by plaintiff's own negligence, which was the sole proximate cause of any injuries and damages plaintiff may have received.

WHEREFORE, defendant requests that plaintiff receive nothing, and that judgment be entered for the defendant, including costs of this action.

Dated: January 15, 2006

William Sharp
William Sharp
Attorney for Defendant
100 Broadway
Phoenix, AZ 85001
881-1000

AFFIDAVIT OF SERVICE

I, Helen Thompson, having been first duly sworn, state that I served a copy of defendant's Answer on plaintiff by personally delivering it to Anne Johnson, attorney for plaintiff, at 100 Congress Street, Phoenix, Arizona, on January 15, 2006.

Helen Thompson
_____
Helen Thompson

Signed and sworn to before me on January 15, 2006.

Ned Lark
_____
Notary Public

My commission expires on December 31, 2007.

[Seal]

After the complaint has been served, every other court paper must be served on every other party in accordance with Rule 5. The usual service is personal delivery or mailing to the party's attorney of record.

An affidavit or certification of service should always be attached to every court paper showing how proper service was made.

All court papers must be filed with the court either before service or within a reasonable time after service.

In practice, court papers are usually filed with the court clerk the same day service is made.

UNITED STATES DISTRICT COURT
FOR THE DISTRICT OF ARIZONA

John Jones,
        Plaintiff

v.

Susan Smith,
        Defendant

No. 03 C 1000

Interrogatories will usually be the first discovery device the parties serve on each other.

In this example, the defendant served interrogatories on plaintiff two weeks after answering the complaint. (Many defendants serve interrogatories with the answer.)

Note how each interrogatory deals with a separate, defined category and asks for all relevant data for the category. This will usually generate more complete answers. It also gives the answering party the opportunity of answering the interrogatory by producing the relevant records that contain the answers.

DEFENDANT'S INTERROGATORIES TO PLAINTIFF

Pursuant to Rule 33 of the Federal Rules of Civil Procedure, defendant Smith requests that plaintiff Jones answer the following interrogatories under oath, and serve them on the defendant within 30 days:

1. Describe the personal injuries you received as a result of the occurrence described in the complaint (hereafter "this occurrence").

2. State the full names and present addresses of any physicians, osteopaths, chiropractors, and other medical personnel who treated you as a result of this occurrence, each such person's areas of specialty, the dates of each examination, consultation, or appointment, the amount of each such person's bill, and whether each bill has been paid.

3. Were you confined to a hospital or clinic as a result of this occurrence? If so, state the name and address of each such hospital or clinic, the dates of your confinement at each facility, the amount of each such facility's bills, and whether each bill has been paid.

4. Have you incurred other medical expenses, other than these requested in Interrogatory Nos. 2 and 3, as a result of this occurrence? If so, state each expense incurred, the nature of each expense, when the expense was incurred, to whom it was incurred, and whether each expense has been paid.

5. Have you incurred any expenses as a result of this occurrence other than medical expenses? If so, state the nature of each expense, the date incurred, the amount of each

expense, the reason for incurring each expense, and whether each expense has been paid.

6. Were you unable to work as a result of this occurrence? If so, state the dates during which you were unable to work, each employer during these dates, the type of work you were unable to do, and the amount of lost wages or income from each employer.

7. Have you recovered from the claimed injuries that resulted from this occurrence? If not, state the claimed injuries from which you have not recovered and any present disability.

The plaintiff's current condition and medical history are important areas that should be explored thoroughly. This can then be verified during the plaintiff's deposition.

8. During the ten years preceding September 2, 2002, have you suffered any other personal injuries? If so, state when, where, and how you were injured and the name and address of each medical facility where, and physicians by whom, you were treated for these injuries.

9. During the ten years preceding September 2, 2002, have you been hospitalized, treated, examined, or tested at any hospital, clinic, physician's office, or other medical facility for any conditions other than those requested in Interrogatory No. 8? If so, state the name and address of each such medical facility and physician, the dates of such services, and the medical conditions involved.

10. State the full name and address of each person who witnessed, or claims to have witnessed, the collision between the vehicles involved in this occurrence.

Occurrence witnesses are obviously important in this kind of case. It's a good practice to break them up by category in appropriate cases.

11. State the full name and address of each person who has any knowledge of the facts of the collision other than those persons already identified in Interrogatory No. 10.

12. Describe your vehicle that was involved in this occurrence, any damage to your vehicle as a result of this occurrence, the name and address of any firm repairing your vehicle, the amount billed for repairs, when such repairs took place, and whether the repair bills have been paid. If your vehicle has not been repaired, state where it is presently located and its condition.

13. Identify by date, description, and source any medical records and any other records or documents of any kind in your or your attorney's possession or control that relate in any way to this occurrence and the injuries and damages you claim resulted from this occurrence.

Medical records are obviously critical in this kind of case. The descriptions you get will be used to send production requests to the plaintiff and subpoenas to third-party sources.

This interrogatory tracks the language of Rule 33.

14. For each expert expected to testify at trial, state:

(a) expert's full name, address, and professional qualifications;
(b) the subject matter on which the expert is expected to testify;
(c) the substance of the facts and opinions to which the expert is expected to testify; and
(d) a summary of the grounds of each opinion.

Dated: <u>February 3, 2006</u>

William Sharp
_____

William Sharp
Attorney for Defendant
100 Broadway
Phoenix, AZ 85001
881-1000

A proof of service must be attached.

UNITED STATES DISTRICT COURT
FOR THE DISTRICT OF ARIZONA

John Jones,
            Plaintiff

        v.   No. 03 C 1000

Susan Smith,
            Defendant

PLAINTIFF'S ANSWERS TO INTERROGATORIES

Plaintiff John Jones answers Defendant's interrogatories as follows:

Interrogatory No. 1: Describe the personal injuries you received as a result of the occurrence described in the complaint (hereafter "this occurrence").

The usual way of answering interrogatories is to set out the questions and the answers, making it easy to correlate the two.

Answer: Cervical, dorsal, and lumbar sprain and strain; cerebral concussion; multiple contraction headaches and concussion headaches; left hemiparesis with ataxia; ankle sprain; numbness; multiple contusions and abrasions.

Interrogatory No. 2: State in full the names and present addresses of any physicians, osteopaths, chiropractors, and other medical personnel who treated you as a result of this occurrence.

ANSWER:

Doctors Hospital
1947 East Thomas Road
Phoenix, Arizona 85016

Leo L. Lang, M.D.
333 East Campbell Avenue
Phoenix, Arizona 85016

Frank Hoffman, M.D.
222 West Thomas
Suite 100
Phoenix, Arizona 85013

J. Franks, D.C.
55 North 27th Avenue
Phoenix, Arizona 85007

Here the plaintiff has prepared partial answers, and acknowledges that further information will generate supplemental answers later. However, these partial answers were prepared within the 30-day requirement of Rule 33.

(Answer may be supplemented as discovery and investigation continues.)

Interrogatory No. 3: Were you confined to a hospital or clinic as a result of this occurrence? If so, state the name and address of each such hospital or clinic, the dates of your confinement at each facility, the amount of each facility's bills, and whether each bill has been paid.

Answer: No; treated, but not confined, at Doctors Hospital.

Interrogatory No. 4: State each medical expense incurred, and whether each expense has been paid.

Answer:

Doctors Hospital	$957.50
Leo Lang, M.D.	339.70
Frank Hoffman, M.D.	440.00
J. Franks, D.C.	2,700.00
Walgreen Pharmacy	58.13

Those bills have been paid.

(Answer may be supplemented as discovery and investigation continues.)

Interrogatory No. 5: Have you incurred any expenses as a result of this occurrence other than medical expenses? If so, state the nature of each expense, and whether each expense has been paid.

<u>Answer:</u>

Broken wristwatch	$125.00
College tuition and books	
(tuition $750/books $52)	802.00

Wristwatch repair bill has been paid.

<u>Interrogatory No. 6:</u> Were you unable to work as a result of this occurrence? If so, state the dates during which you were unable to work, each employer during these dates, the type of work you were unable to do, and the amount of lost wages or income from each employer.

<u>Answer:</u> Yes. September 2, 2005, to October 1, 2005. Devo Wholesale Florist. Delivery truck driver. $2,600—one month's salary.

This is a typical interrogatory answer. It provides all the facts requested, does so efficiently, and does not volunteer anything not asked for.

<u>Interrogatory No. 7:</u> Have you recovered from the claimed injuries that resulted from this occurrence? If not, state the claimed injuries from which you have not recovered and any present disability.

<u>Answer:</u> Plaintiff still experiences headaches, neck pain, and lower back pain.

<u>Interrogatory No. 8:</u> During the ten years preceding September 2, 2005, have you suffered any other personal injuries? If so, state when, where, and how you were injured and the name and address of each medical facility where, and physicians by whom, you were treated for these injuries.

<u>Answer:</u> No.

<u>Interrogatory No. 9:</u> During the ten years preceding September 2, 2005, have you been hospitalized, treated, examined, or tested at any hospital, clinic, physician's office, or other medical facility for any conditions other than those requested in Interrogatory No. 8? If so, state the name and address of each such medical facility and physician, the dates of such services, and the medical conditions involved.

<u>Answer:</u> No.

<u>Interrogatory No. 10:</u> State the full name and address of each person who witnessed, or claims to have witnessed, the collision between the vehicles involved in this occurrence.

<u>Answer:</u>

John Jones, plaintiff
Susan Smith, defendant
Carol Brown, 42 E. Cambridge, Phoenix, AZ
Mary Porter, 42 E. Cambridge, Phoenix, AZ
Officer Steven Pitcher, Phoenix Police Department

Witness lists must frequently be supplemented over time, since the ongoing investigation will often uncover additional witnesses.

(Answer may be supplemented as discovery and investigation continues.)

<u>Interrogatory No. 11:</u> State the full name and address of each person who has any knowledge of the facts of the collision other than those persons already identified in Interrogatory No. 10.

<u>Answer:</u> See persons listed in answer to Interrogatory No. 4: John Jones, Sr., and Mary Jones, plaintiff's parents; James Devo, plaintiff's employer.

(Answer may be supplemented as discovery and investigation continues.)

<u>Interrogatory No. 12:</u> Describe your vehicle that was involved in this occurrence, any damage to your vehicle as a result of this occurrence, the name and address of any firm repairing your vehicle, the amount billed for repairs, when such repairs took place, and whether the repair bills have been paid. If your vehicle has not been repaired, state where it is presently located and its condition.

This is another typical answer. It provides the facts called for, yet does not volunteer anything.

<u>Answer:</u> 2001 Toyota Corolla four-door sedan. Extensive damage to left and front side of car. Jack's Auto Repair, 2000 E. Valley Road, Phoenix. $4,213. Repairs completed about September 30, 2005. Repair bill has been paid.

<u>Interrogatory No. 13:</u> Identify by date, description, and source any medical records and any other records or documents of any kind in your or your attorney's possession or control that relate in any way to this occurrence and the injuries and damages you claim resulted from this occurrence.

Answer:

Employment records of Devo Wholesale Florist
Doctors Hospital records
Dr. Lang's office records
Dr. Hoffman's office records
Dr. Franks' office records
Medical bills
X rays taken by the above health care providers
Phoenix Police Department accident report
Photographs of the scene of the accident

(Answer may be supplemented as discovery and investigation proceeds.)

Interrogatory No. 14: For each expert expected to testify at trial, state the expert's full name and address.

Answer:

Frank Hoffman, M.D.
222 West Thomas
Suite 100
Phoenix, AZ 85013

The initial answer to this standard interrogatory is frequently "None known at present—investigation continues," on the basis that the answering party has not yet decided who its testifying experts will be.

J. Franks, D.C.
55 North 27th Avenue
Phoenix, AZ 85007

Here the treating physicians will obviously be witnesses at trial, so their names are disclosed with supplemental answers to follow.

Leo L. Lang, M.D.
333 East Campbell Avenue
Phoenix, AZ 85016

(Answer may be supplemented as discovery and investigation continues.)

Dated: <u>February 25, 2007</u>

John Jones
_____
John Jones, Plaintiff

State of Arizona   SS.
County of Maricopa

Interrogatory answers must be signed under oath by the party making them.

I, John Jones, being first duly sworn, state that:
    I am the plaintiff in this case. I have made the foregoing Answers to Interrogatories and know the answers to be true to the best of my knowledge, information, and belief.

John Jones
_____
John Jones, Plaintiff

Subscribed and sworn to before me this 25th day of February 2007, by John Jones, Plaintiff.

Like any court papers, the answers must be served on every party. A proof of service, showing how service was made, must be attached to the answer.

Mary Ryan
_____
Mary Ryan, Notary Public

My commission expires on December 31, 2007.

[Seal]

UNITED STATES DISTRICT COURT
FOR THE DISTRICT OF ARIZONA

John Jones,
      Plaintiff

   v.   No. 03 C 1000

Susan Smith,
      Defendant

REQUEST FOR PRODUCTION OF DOCUMENTS

Pursuant to Rule 34 of the Federal Rules of Civil Procedure, defendant requests that plaintiff produce within 30 days, in the law offices of William Sharp, 100 Broadway, Phoenix, AZ 85001, the following documents for inspection and copying:

1. All medical reports, records, charts, X-ray reports, and all other records regarding any medical examinations and treatment received by plaintiff for the injuries claimed in the complaint.

2. All United States Income Tax returns filed by plaintiff for the years 2000, 2001, 2002, 2003, 2004.

3. All exhibits plaintiff will offer at the trial of this case.

Dated: <u>February 3, 2007</u>

William Sharp
_____
William Sharp
Attorney for Defendant
100 Broadway
Phoenix, AZ 85001
881-1000

Note that this documents request was served at the same time as the interrogatories.

Documents requests usually depend on interrogatory answers to identify the relevant documents. Here, however, what the defendant wants is both simple and obvious, so the defendant decides to serve the requests with interrogatories.

These kinds of records should already be in the plaintiff's possession.

A proof of service must be attached.

UNITED STATES DISTRICT COURT
FOR THE DISTRICT OF ARIZONA

John Jones,
        Plaintiff

v.   No. 03 C 1000

Susan Smith,
        Defendant

PLAINTIFF'S RESPONSE TO REQUEST FOR PRODUCTION OF DOCUMENTS

A response to a production request should be filed so there is a court record that shows how and when the request was complied with. If photocopying will be expensive, the requesting party will usually have to pay for the photocopying charges.

Since plaintiff may have additional trial exhibits, the notation "investigation continues" may be appropriate. A supplemental response may then need to be filed as plaintiff decides on additional exhibits.

Plaintiff responds to defendant's Request for Production of Documents as follows:

1. Plaintiff will produce copies of all reports in plaintiff's possession regarding medical examinations and treatment of plaintiff for his injuries. These copies will be delivered to defendant's attorney on or before March 3, 2003.

2. Plaintiff herewith produces his U.S. Income Tax Returns for the years 2000 through 2004.

3. Plaintiff to the extent known at present will produce copies of all exhibits he will offer at the trial of this case. These copies will be delivered to defendant's attorney on or before March 1, 2004.

Dated: February 25, 2007

Anne Johnson
Anne Johnson
Attorney for Plaintiff
100 Congress Street
Phoenix, AZ 85001
882-1000

A proof of service must be attached.

UNITED STATES DISTRICT COURT
FOR THE DISTRICT OF ARIZONA

John Jones,
      Plaintiff

    v.   No. 03 C 1000

Susan Smith,
      Defendant

SUBPOENA DUCES TECUM

To: James Devo, President
      Devo Wholesale Florist
      3731 40th Street
      Phoenix, AZ 85010

    YOU ARE HEREBY COMMANDED to appear and give testimony under oath at the law office of William Sharp, 100 Broadway, Phoenix, AZ 85001 on March 17, 2007, at 1:30 P.M. You are also commanded to bring the following:

    All records relating to the employment of John Jones at Devo Wholesale Florist from the first day of employment through the present date, including but not limited to records showing wages received, hours worked, and the condition of John Jones' health.

A deposition subpoena that also requires the party to bring specified records is the only discovery method that can be used to obtain records from nonparty witnesses.

Make sure that you serve a Notice of Deposition on every other party, because other parties always have a right to attend any deposition and question the deponent.

Dated: <u>March 3, 2007</u>

[Seal]

John Clark
Clerk of the Court

UNITED STATES DISTRICT COURT
FOR THE DISTRICT OF ARIZONA

John Jones,
         Plaintiff

                  v.   No. 03 C 1000
Susan Smith,
         Defendant

NOTICE OF DEPOSITION

TO: PLAINTIFF JOHN JONES

Two weeks' notice is appropriate in this type of case.

    Please take notice that the undersigned will take the deposition of John Jones, Plaintiff, on March 18, 2007, at 2:00 P.M. at 100 Broadway, Phoenix, AZ 85001. You are hereby notified that the plaintiff is to appear at that time and place and submit to a deposition under oath.

A subpoena is not necessary since the deponent is a party.

Dated: March 3, 2007

                                        William Sharp
                                        _____
                                        William Sharp
                                        Attorney for Defendant
                                        100 Broadway
                                        Phoenix, AZ 85001
A proof of service must be attached.   881-1000

UNITED STATES DISTRICT COURT
FOR THE DISTRICT OF ARIZONA

John Jones,
        Plaintiff

        v.   No. 03 C 1000

Susan Smith,
        Defendant

DEPOSITION OF JOHN JONES

DEPOSITION of John Jones, taken at 2:13 P.M. on March 18, 2007, at the law offices of William Sharp, at 100 Broadway, Phoenix, AZ 85001, before Nancy Post, a Notary Public in Maricopa County, Arizona.

Appearance for the plaintiff:

Anne Johnson
100 Congress St.
Phoenix, AZ 85001

Appearance for the defendant:

William Sharp
100 Broadway
Phoenix, AZ 85001

JOHN JONES

Called as a witness, having been first duly sworn, was examined and testified as follows:

EXAMINATION BY MR. SHARP:

Q.   This is the deposition of the plaintiff, John Jones, being taken in the case of John Jones v. Susan Smith, Case No. 03 C 1000 in the United States District Court for the District of Arizona. It is being held at the law office of William Sharp, 100 Broadway, Phoenix, Arizona 85001. Today's date is March 18, 2006. Present in addition to Mr. Jones are myself, William Sharp, attorney for

This is a standard introductory statement.

a.   Personal background.

Note the form of the questions and the tone of the examination. If the questioner has decided that the principal purposes of the deposition are to acquire information and assess the plaintiff as a trial witness, then, accordingly, the questions are usually open-ended, designed to elicit information and have the plaintiff do the talking. The questions are asked in a pleasant and friendly way.

b.   Work experience.

defendant Smith, Anne Johnson, attorney for plaintiff Jones, and Nancy Post, a certified court reporter and notary public. Mr. Jones, you were just sworn to tell the truth by the court reporter, correct?

A.   That's right.

Q.   It's important that you understand the questions and give accurate answers. If there's anything you don't understand, or anything you don't know or aren't sure of, you let us know, all right?

A.   Yes.

Q.   Please tell us your name.

A.   John J. Jones.

Q.   How old are you?

A.   I'm 23.

Q.   Are you married or single?

A.   Single.

Q.   Where do you live?

A.   1020 North 50th Street, Phoenix, Arizona.

Q.   How far did you go in school?

A.   I graduated from high school—Central High, 2001.

Q.   What did you do after high school?

A.   I joined the army.

Q.   Tell us about your army experience.

A.   After basic training, I was sent to an infantry division, and did most of my three years in Germany. I was a corporal when I received my honorable discharge. That was in August 2004.

Q.   What did you do after that?

A.   I came back to Phoenix, moved into my parents' house, and started working for Devo Wholesale Florist.

Q.   Where is that located?

A.   It's at 3731 40th Street, Phoenix.

Q.   What kind of work do you do there?

A.   I started as a sales clerk, then I became a driver on one of their trucks.

Q.   What do you do as a driver?

A.   I deliver flowers from the store to customers in the Phoenix area.

Q.   What were your hours in August and September 2005?

A.   It varied, but it was usually 6:00 A.M. to 2:00 P.M.

Q.   Were those your hours the day of the accident?

A.   Yes.

Q.   Other than your job for Devo Florist, did you have any other jobs or activities in September 2005?

A.   I didn't have any other job. I was a part-time student at Glendale College.

Q. Mr. Jones, were you ever involved in an automobile accident before September 2, 2005?

A. No.

Q. Did you ever receive personal injuries of any kind before September 2, 2005?

A. No.

Q. During the past ten years, other than for this accident, did you ever see a physician for any reason?

A. Well, our family doctor is Dr. Hoffman. I would see him from time to time for checkups, shots, and things like that. But I never had any serious injury or illness that I went to Dr. Hoffman for.

Q. Mr. Jones, tell me each injury you feel you've received as a result of the accident on September 2.

A. Okay. I hurt the left side of my neck, my lower back, my left ankle, my left shoulder, and my stomach.

Q. Let's start out with the left side of your neck. What injuries did you receive there?

A. I think I whipped my head to the side when the car crashed into me and I strained my neck. I had these shooting pains in my neck whenever I tried to move it.

Q. How long did that pain continue?

A. Well it was pretty severe for about a week, and then it started getting better. I still get pains there from time to time.

Q. Tell me about the injuries to your lower back.

A. Well, that was sort of the same thing. I must have wrenched my back from the force of the collision. Just like my neck, it was stiff and hurt for a while. After about a week it started getting better, and today I only get the pain from time to time, especially toward the end of the work day.

Q. Tell me about your left ankle.

A. I sprained my ankle during the accident. That was probably the worst injury. I had to stay off my feet for about two weeks, and I really couldn't start walking on it for three or four weeks. That's the injury that kept me out of work for a month.

Q. When did your ankle start getting better?

A. About a month after this happened it was well enough so I could start working, although I was still limping for quite a while. It probably took about four months before the ankle healed up completely.

Q. Tell me about the injury to your left shoulder.

A. I got some cuts and scratches and bruises on my left shoulder when I crashed into the dashboard of the car. That hurt for maybe two weeks, and then went away.

Q. Finally, tell me about the injuries to your stomach.

A. I guess I injured my stomach when I smashed against the steering wheel. It was just painful inside of my stomach. That went away after a few days.

c. Accident and health history must be explored, since preexisting injuries would affect the damages picture.

d. Each claimed injury should be explored in detail.

The "tell me" form of questions is used to get the witness to disclose everything.

If the plaintiff at trial tries to claim additional injuries, he can hardly say he didn't mention all his injuries during the deposition because the lawyer didn't give him a chance to do so. Since pain and suffering will probably be the largest single element of damages, these questions are important to "pin down" the witness and prevent later exaggeration at trial.

The "any other injuries" question is always useful. Again, it prevents later exaggeration.

e.   Medical treatment.

Note how this deposition is organized chronologically (with the exception of the accident itself). If you are drafting a deposition outline, this is usually the best way to organize the questions, unless you have a specific reason for doing it another way.

Q.   Other than these injuries to your neck, lower back, ankle, shoulder, and stomach, did you receive any other injuries?

A.   Oh yeah. I received a concussion on the left side of my head. That's what the doctor told me.

Q.   Mr. Jones, let's talk about the medical treatment you received for these injuries following the accident. First, how did you get to Doctors Hospital?

A.   An ambulance came to the intersection and they put me on a stretcher and drove me to the hospital.

Q.   What happened when you arrived at Doctors Hospital?

A.   The ambulance attendants took me into the emergency room, and some nurses checked me over, took my pulse and blood pressure, and stuff like that. After a while one of their doctors examined me. I think his name was Dr. Lang. I told Dr. Lang where I hurt and about the accident.

Q.   What kind of treatment did you receive at the hospital?

A.   Well, they examined me, x-rayed, cleaned up some of the cuts on my shoulder and chest, and put my ankle in a cast. It wasn't one of those big plaster casts; it was a cast that went around the back of my ankle and foot and was surrounded with an elastic bandage. I must have been there a couple of hours, and by that time my parents had come to the hospital, and they took me home.

Q.   Did you receive any medication prescription?

A.   The doctor gave a prescription for Tylenol with codeine, which my mother picked up at the drug store. The doctor told me to follow instructions on the bottle and take the medication if I needed it for the pain.

f.   Recovery period.

Q.   Mr. Jones, tell us about the month you spent before you went back to work.

A.   Well, the first week I pretty much spent in bed. Sometimes I got up and lay on the couch and watched TV. At that time everything was aching—my neck hurt, my head hurt, my stomach hurt, my ankle was swollen up. I spent all my time with my foot up to keep the swelling down, and I was taking the medicine to keep the pain down.

Q.   How long was it before you were able to move around the house?

A.   I'd say the first week or ten days I pretty much spent on my back. After that period of time the pain in my head, shoulder, and stomach started going away, and the swelling in my ankle was starting to go down. I got a pair of crutches and started moving around the house a little bit. I couldn't stay on my feet very long before the foot would swell up if I stood up for any length of time.

Since the defendant's purpose is to minimize the extent and length of the pain, these questions are important. Again, they prevent later exaggeration.

Q.   At the end of September 2005, what was your physical condition like?

A.   The scratches and bruises had gone away. The pains in my neck, shoulder, stomach, leg, and back had started to get better. The only places that really kept on hurting was my lower back and my ankle.

Q. Tell me about those.

A. Well my back would have these stabbing pains from time to time. It felt real stiff. My ankle was stiff. My ankle was still swollen, and I couldn't walk on it yet. Dr. Hoffman, my family doctor, had removed the cast about three weeks after the accident and I could start walking without crutches, but I was still limping and the ankle would get sore if I walked on it for any length of time.

Q. When did you see Dr. Hoffman?

A. My mom took me to Dr. Hoffman about three weeks after the accident. He checked me out, removed the soft cast from my ankle, and told me it was okay to start walking around without the crutches if I could stand it.

Q. When did you stop using the crutches?

A. I stopped using them when I went back to work at the beginning of October.

Q. What did you see Dr. Franks, the chiropractor, for?

A. Well, my mom thought that going to a chiropractor might help my back and ankle. My back still hurt, and my ankle was still sore. She thought that it might be a good idea to get some physical therapy to see if that might help. That's why I went to Dr. Franks.

Q. How many times did you see Dr. Franks?

A. I went to him for the first time around October 1st. I went to see him maybe twice a week for the next couple of months.

Q. What kind of treatment did Dr. Franks perform?

A. He would give me physical therapy. That involved bending my back, stretching it, applying heat treatments, things like that. The same thing was true for the ankle.

Q. Did it help?

A. Yes. About two months later, maybe by Christmas, most of the stiffness and pain had gone away.

Q. From December 2005 to the present day, describe your physical condition.

A. It's better. I still have pain from time to time in my back and ankle.

Q. When do you get the pain there?

A. Well, it depends on how much or how hard I work. The more I work the more likely I am to get those pains.

Q. How often do you get those pains?

A. It's maybe once a week for an hour or two, usually at the end of the work day.

Q. When was the last time you took Tylenol with codeine?

A. I took that stuff for maybe six weeks.

Q. Did you ever take any painkillers other than Tylenol with codeine?

A. I sometimes take aspirin when I get these pains.

Q. Other than what you've told me about, do you have any other injuries or problems that you feel were caused by this accident?

A. No, you pretty much covered it.

The history of the plaintiff's treatments is, of course, available from the medical records, which the defendant will have before the deposition. Nonetheless, these questions test the witness' recall and propensity to exaggerate.

These questions effectively limit the damages.

g.   Expenses and lost income.

While the fact that most of the bills have been paid by insurance is not admissible at trial, it will have some effect on the settlement picture.

Q. Mr. Jones, let's talk about some of the bills involved here. First, the medical bills. Your interrogatory answers show that the bills from Doctors Hospital, Dr. Lang, Dr. Hoffman, and Dr. Franks have all been paid. Who paid those bills?

A. I'm not sure. I know they were paid by my health insurance. I think my mother paid the Walgreen Pharmacy bill.

Q. Who paid for the wristwatch repair?

A. My mom paid that. I'm supposed to pay her back.

Q. You claim college tuition and book expenses in the amount of $802. Tell us about that.

A. Well, I was a part-time student at Glendale College. I had already paid the tuition and bought the books for the two courses I was taking. When I got injured, I couldn't take the courses I signed up for.

Q. How much income did you lose as a result of this accident?

A. I get paid $2,600 a month salary from Devo Florists. I went back to work October 1, 2005. The way I figure it, I lost one month's salary, or $2,600.

Q. The $2,600 is your gross income, isn't it?

A. Yes.

Q. What's your take-home pay?

A. We get paid on the first and fifteenth of the month. My take-home for half a month is about $900.

h. The accident.

Note that here the questioner has saved the accident as the last topic. Some lawyers save the most important part of a deposition for the end, on the theory that the lawyer then has a better "feel" for the witness and the witness' guard will be down by that time.

These scene description questions are useful to see how effectively the plaintiff can describe the scene, and are good questions to see how effective a trial witness he will make.

Q. Mr. Jones, let's talk about how this accident happened. Describe the vehicle you were driving.

A. It's a 2004 Toyota Corolla four-door. I bought it when I got out of the service. It was in really good shape, because I took good care of it.

Q. Is the title to that car in your name?

A. Yes.

Q. The accident happened around 2:00 P.M.?

A. Yes.

Q. At the time of the accident, where were you coming from?

A. I was coming from work at the flower shop.

Q. Where is that flower shop located?

A. On 40th Street and Thomas Road.

Q. 40th Street is the north-south street, correct?

A. Yes.

Q. Where is the flower shop in relation to the intersection?

A. It's not right at the corner. It's on 40th Street, maybe 300 feet south of Thomas.

Q. Which side of 40th Street is the flower shop on?

A. It's on the east side.

Q. Tell me how you went from the flower shop north on 40th Street.

A. My car was parked in the lot next to the flower shop. When I got out of work, I pulled out of the lot and started going north on 40th Street.

Q. Describe what 40th Street looks like.
A. It's a pretty wide street. It has three lanes of traffic in each direction. In addition, it has left-turn lanes at the major intersections.
Q. There are traffic lights at the corner of 40th Street and Thomas, right?
A. Yes.
Q. Where are they located?
A. I think there's one at each corner and on the median strips.
Q. How many lights face the northbound traffic on 40th Street?
A. Probably around three.
Q. When you pulled onto 40th Street, which lane did you pull into?
A. I got into the inside lane, right next to the median strip.
Q. Mr. Jones, when was the first time you looked at the traffic lights at the corner of 40th Street and Thomas?
A. When I first pulled onto 40th Street and got in the inside lane.
Q. How far were you from the intersection at that time?
A. I guess around 100 feet.
Q. How fast were you going at that time?
A. Maybe 20 or 25 miles per hour.
Q. What was the color of the traffic lights at that point?
A. Green.
Q. What happened as you went northbound on 40th Street?
A. Well, it all happened really quickly. As I went north, the light turned yellow just before I got into the intersection. I was going through the intersection on the yellow light when suddenly I got smashed by another car from the driver's side.
Q. How long had the light been yellow at the time the other car collided with you?
A. It couldn't have been more than two or three seconds.
Q. How fast were you going when you were hit?
A. Maybe 25 or 30 miles per hour.
Q. Did you ever see the car that hit you before the impact?
A. Not really. I first saw it just before it was about to smash into me. It couldn't have been more than 10 or 15 feet from me. Before I could even put on my brakes, the car hit me.
Q. Tell us what happened from the moment the two cars hit.
A. Well, I remember putting on my brakes, I kind of skidded in the intersection, and the other car seemed to be stuck against the side of my car. I can remember getting bounced around inside the car and smashing my head and chest against the inside of the car and the steering wheel.
Q. Were you wearing a seat belt at that time?
A. No.
Q. Did your car have seat belts?
A. Yes.

This is a useful answer since he was only about three seconds from the intersection before he looked at the lights.

This answer is also useful since it suggests that the plaintiff was not paying much attention as he entered the intersection.

Note how the questions become more specific. The questioner's purpose now is to "pin down" the witness to specific facts.

This is important, since in some jurisdictions this fact is admissible to show plaintiff's own negligence or failure to prevent damages.

Q. What happened when your car came to a stop?

A. I was pretty much numb. I can remember people coming up to me when I was in the car telling me not to move. I wasn't going to move anyway. I just hurt all over. I don't know how long it was, but after a while an ambulance came and they got me out of the car and put me on a stretcher.

Q. Mr. Jones, just before the impact, describe exactly what you were doing.

A. Well, I remember starting into the intersection. Since the light was yellow, I remember looking to the right to make sure that there weren't any cars taking a turn that might get in my way. I just looked to my right and then looked back up the road, then I saw the other car coming from my left just before it crashed into me.

Q. Did you ever put on your brakes before the impact?

A. No, I don't think so, there wasn't time to react.

Q. Mr. Jones, is there anything you remember about how this accident happened that you haven't told me about this afternoon?

A. No, nothing that comes to mind. I think I've pretty much told you everything.

Q. That's all the questions I have at this time. Do you have any questions, Ms. Johnson?

Ms. Johnson: No.

Mr. Sharp: Will you waive signature?

Ms. Johnson: No, we'd like to see the transcript.

(The deposition was concluded at 3:06 P.M.)

John Jones

_____

John Jones

State of Arizona | SS.
County of Maricopa |

The foregoing deposition was taken before me, Nancy Post, a Notary Public in the County of Maricopa, State of Arizona. The witness was duly sworn by me to testify to the truth. The questions asked of the witness were taken down by me in shorthand and reduced to typewriting under my direction. The deposition was submitted to the witness and read and signed. The foregoing

---

Some lawyers always ask this kind of question, since it's potential impeachment if the plaintiff "remembers" more at trial.

The party deponent should not waive signature, since he should review the transcript for accuracy.

Note that the plaintiff's lawyer asked no questions. This is the usual practice, unless the party gave incorrect or confusing answers that need to be corrected or clarified.

Note also that the plaintiff's lawyer made no objections during the deposition. The questions were proper so objections were unnecessary.

The court reporter must arrange a meeting with the deponent so he can review the transcript, note any claimed inaccuracies, and sign the transcript. Any claimed inaccuracies are usually put on a separate sheet and attached to the transcript.

pages are a true and accurate transcript of the entire proceedings taken during this deposition.

Dated: <u>April 1, 2006</u>

Nancy Post
_____
Notary Public

My commission expires on December 31, 2007.

UNITED STATES DISTRICT COURT
FOR THE DISTRICT OF ARIZONA

John Jones,
                Plaintiff

                v.   No. 03 C 1000

Susan Smith,
                Defendant

NOTICE OF MOTION

TO: Anne Johnson
      Attorney at Law
      100 Congress Street
      Phoenix, AZ 85001

Even with service by mail, this is adequate notice. As a professional courtesy, however, many lawyers call the opposing lawyers and let them know they are serving the motion.

   PLEASE TAKE NOTICE that on June 10, 2006, at 9:00 A.M., or as soon as counsel can be heard, defendant in the above-captioned matter will present the attached Motion to Compel Discovery before the Hon. Joan Howe, Courtroom No. 4, United States Court House, Phoenix, Arizona.

Dated: <u>May 30, 2006</u>

                    William Sharp
                    _____
                    William Sharp
                    Attorney for Defendant
                    100 Broadway
                    Phoenix, AZ 85001
                    881-1000

UNITED STATES DISTRICT COURT
FOR THE DISTRICT OF ARIZONA

John Jones,
      Plaintiff

    v.   No. 03 C 1000

Susan Smith,
      Defendant

MOTION TO COMPEL DISCOVERY

Defendant moves for an order compelling plaintiff to answer in the full interrogatories previously served on plaintiff, pursuant to Rule 37 of the Federal Rules of Civil Procedure. In support of her motion defendant states:

    1. Defendant served interrogatories on plaintiff on February 3, 2006.

    2. Plaintiff partially answered these interrogatories on February 25, 2006. Many of the answers are incomplete and do not provide the facts called for.

    3. Plaintiff's answers to Interrogatory Nos. 2, 4, 10, 11, 13, and 14 stated that "answers may be supplemented as discovery and investigation continues."

    4. To date plaintiff has neither supplemented his interrogatory answers nor advised defendant that no additional answers will be forthcoming, although defendant has requested, by telephone and letter, that plaintiff submit supplemental answers.

    WHEREFORE, defendant requests the court to order plaintiff to serve supplemental interrogatory answers within ten days and award reasonable expenses, including attorney's fees, incurred by defendant as a result of this motion.

Since over three months have passed since plaintiff served incomplete answers to interrogatories, this motion should be brought.

In many jurisdictions local rules require that a motion must be supplemented by a memorandum of points and authorities. In other jurisdictions this is done only for complicated or contested motions, such as for summary judgment. Always show what efforts were made to get compliance before the motion was filed.

Keep in mind that many jurisdictions require a lawyer to certify compliance with local rules that require that the parties first try to resolve discovery disputes informally.

Note that Rule 37 allows the court to award the reasonable costs incurred in being forced to bring this motion. This includes attorney's fees. Asking for perhaps $300 would be reasonable.

Dated: <u>June 2, 2006</u>

William Sharp
_____
William Sharp
Attorney for Defendant
100 Broadway
Phoenix, AZ 85001
881-1000

AFFIDAVIT OF SERVICE

I, Helen Thompson, having been first duly sworn, state that I have served a copy of the attached Notice of Motion and Motion to Compel Discovery on plaintiff's attorney by mail at 100 Congress Street, Phoenix, Arizona 85001, on June 2, 2006.

Helen Thompson
_____
Helen Thompson

Signed and sworn to before me on June 2, 2006.

Ned Lark
_____
Notary Public

My Commission expires on December 31, 2007.

[Seal]

UNITED STATES DISTRICT COURT
FOR THE DISTRICT OF ARIZONA

John Jones,
   Plaintiff

   v.   No. 03 C 1000

Susan Smith,
    Defendant

REQUEST FOR ADMISSION OF FACTS
AND GENUINENESS OF DOCUMENTS

Plaintiff requests defendant, pursuant to Rule 36 of the Federal Rules of Civil Procedure, to admit within 30 days the following facts and genuineness of documents:

  1. Defendant was the owner of a 1998 Buick Skylark sedan on September 2, 2005.

  2. Defendant was driving the 1998 Buick Skylark sedan when the collision occurred on September 2, 2005.

  3. Defendant was a driver licensed by the State of Nevada at the time of the collision.

  4. Each of the following documents, attached as exhibits to this request, is authentic:

Exhibit No.	Description
1.	Phoenix Police Dept. accident report.
2.	Title and registration documents from the Nevada Dept. of Transportation showing defendant to be the owner of a 2001 Buick Skylark sedan.
3.	Driver's licence issued to defendant by the Nevada Dept. of Transportation.

Dated: June 2, 2006

Anne Johnson
_____
Anne Johnson
Attorney for Plaintiff
100 Congress Street
Phoenix, AZ 85001
882-1000

If this case will go to trial, the plaintiff will need to establish basic facts. These requests cover facts that the defendant will probably not contest, and that will streamline the plaintiff's case during trial.

A proof of service must be attached.

UNITED STATES DISTRICT COURT
FOR THE DISTRICT OF ARIZONA

John Jones,
       Plaintiff

v.   No. 03 C 1000

Susan Smith,
       Defendant

DEFENDANT'S ANSWER TO PLAINTIFF'S REQUEST FOR ADMISSION OF FACTS AND GENUINENESS OF DOCUMENTS

Defendant answers plaintiff's Requests for Admission of Facts and Genuineness of Documents as follows:

Like interrogatories, the usual practice in answering is to set out both the request and the answer. This avoids confusion.

<u>Request No. 1:</u> Defendant was the owner of a 2001 Buick Skylark sedan on September 2, 2005.

<u>Answer:</u> Admits.

<u>Request No. 2:</u> Defendant was driving the 1998 Buick Skylark sedan when the collision occurred on September 2, 2005.

<u>Answer:</u> Admits.

<u>Request No. 3:</u> Defendant was a driver licensed by the State of Nevada at the time of the collision.

<u>Answer:</u> Admits.

<u>Request No. 4:</u> Each of the following documents, attached as exhibits to this request, is authentic:

<u>Exhibit No.</u>	<u>Description</u>
1.	Phoenix Police Dept. accident report.
2.	Title and registration documents from the Nevada Dept. of Transportation showing defendant to be the owner of a 2001 Buick Skylark sedan.

3.   Driver's licence issued to defendant by the Nevada
        Dept. of Transportation.

<u>Answer:</u> Admits.

Dated: <u>June 20, 2006</u>

William Sharp
_____

William Sharp
Attorney for Defendant
100 Broadway
Phoenix, AZ 85001
881-1000   A proof of service must be attached.

UNITED STATES DISTRICT COURT
FOR THE DISTRICT OF ARIZONA

John Jones,
    Plaintiff

v.   No. 03 C 1000

Susan Smith,
    Defendant

OFFER OF JUDGMENT

By this time defendant has sufficient facts to assess the case's settlement value. The offer of judgment will put additional pressure on the plaintiff to consider a realistic settlement.

    Pursuant to Rule 68 of the Federal Rules of Civil Procedure, defendant offers to allow judgment to be taken against her in the amount of SEVENTEEN THOUSAND FIVE HUNDRED and 00/100 DOLLARS ($17,500.00), and costs of suit incurred to the date of this offer.

    This offer is being made under Rule 68 of the Federal Rules of Evidence and Rule 408 of the Federal Rules of Evidence.

Dated: <u>August 1, 2006</u>

William Sharp
William Sharp
Attorney for Defendant
100 Broadway
Phoenix, AZ 85001
881-1000

A proof of service must be attached.

UNITED STATES DISTRICT COURT
FOR THE DISTRICT OF ARIZONA

John Jones,
        Plaintiff

        v.   No. 03 C 1000

Susan Smith,
        Defendant

MOTION FOR ORDER TO COMPEL
PLAINTIFF'S PHYSICAL EXAMINATION

Defendant moves under Rule 35 of the Federal Rules of Civil Procedure for an order compelling plaintiff to submit to a physical examination. In support of her motion defendant states:

1. Plaintiff's physical condition is genuinely in controversy since the complaint alleges a variety of physical injuries.

2. Plaintiff during his deposition stated that he still suffers from the consequences of the accident that is the basis for his complaint. These include periodic pain in his back and ankle.

3. There exists good cause, in light of the above, for a physical examination of the plaintiff to evaluate the plaintiff's current physical condition and prognosis.

4. Rudolf B. Anton, M.D., a board certified neurologist, has agreed to examine and evaluate the plaintiff at his medical office located at 4401 N. Scottsdale Road, Scottsdale, Arizona, on September 15, 2006, at 5:00 P.M., or at another time, as directed by this court.

WHEREFORE, defendant requests that the court enter an order directing the plaintiff to be examined on the terms set forth above.

Dated: September 1, 2006

William Sharp

William Sharp
Attorney for Defendant
100 Broadway
Phoenix, AZ 85001
881-1000

Since plaintiff has not accepted the offer of judgment, defendant must continue her trial preparations. Getting a current evaluation of the plaintiff's medical condition and prognosis from a physician who has not previously seen the plaintiff is vital.

Keep in mind that many jurisdictions require a lawyer to certify compliance with local rules that require that the parties first try to resolve discovery disputes informally.

A proof of service must be attached.

UNITED STATES DISTRICT COURT
FOR THE DISTRICT OF ARIZONA

John Jones,
       Plaintiff

      v.   No. 03 C 1000

Susan Smith,
       Defendant

JOINT PRETRIAL MEMORANDUM

Judges frequently have instructions on what the memorandum should contain and how it should be organized.

Pursuant to Local Rule, plaintiff and defendant submit the following joint pretrial memorandum:

I

Uncontested Facts

These facts have all been admitted in the pleadings or during discovery.

Plaintiff Jones and Defendant Smith were involved in a vehicle collision on September 2, 2005. The collision occurred at the intersection of 40th Street and Thomas Road in Phoenix, Arizona, at approximately 2:00 P.M. At the time of the collision Jones was driving his car, a 2001 Toyota Corolla four-door sedan, northbound on 40th Street; Smith was driving her car, a 2001 Buick Skylark sedan, eastbound on Thomas Road. The intersection is controlled by traffic lights.

On September 2, 2006, Jones was employed as a delivery driver by Devo Wholesale Florist and was being paid gross wages of $2,600 per month.

II

Contested Issues of Fact and Law

1. Did Smith run a red light?
2. Did Jones run a red light?
3. Was Smith negligent?
4. Was Jones negligent?

III

Exhibits

A. Plaintiff Jones' Exhibits	Objections, if any

    1. Doctors Hospital
       records

    2. Dr. Lang's office
       records

    3. Dr. Hoffman's office
       records

    4. Dr. Franks' office records

    5. All bills for above

    6. X rays taken by above

    7. Devo Wholesale Florist
       employment records

    8. Phoenix Police Dept.
       reports — **Objection, for reasons stated in attached memorandum.**

> If any evidence is objected to, the judge may rule on the objections, if possible to do so, during the pretrial conference.
>
> If objections are made, the objecting party should state the basis for the objection, with supporting citations.

    9. Accident scene
       photographs

   10. Jack's Auto Repair
       records and bill

   11. Watch repair bill

   12. Glendale Community
       College bills

   13. Walgreen Pharmacy
       bill

   14. Accident scene
       diagrams

B. Defendant Smith's Exhibits	Objections, if any

    1. Plaintiff's hospital
       and medical records

    2. Rudolf Anton, M.D.,
       medical records

    3. Accident scene
       photographs

    4. Accident scene
       diagrams

    5. Phoenix Police Dept.
       reports to extent
       admissible

IV

Witnesses

A. Plaintiff Jones' Witnesses
 1. Plaintiff
 2. Carol Brown, 42 E. Cambridge, Phoenix
 3. Mary Porter, 42 E. Cambridge, Phoenix
 4. Dr. Lang
 5. Dr. Hoffman
 6. Dr. Franks
 7. James Devo, Devo Wholesale Florist
 8. John Jones, Sr., and Mary Jones, plaintiff's
   parents
 9. Officer Steven Pitcher, Phoenix Police Dept.
10. Defendant
11. Personnel from Jack's Auto Repair, to
   qualify exhibits
12. Personnel from above hospitals and physicians,
   to qualify exhibits

B. Defendant Smith's Witnesses
 1. All of plaintiff's witnesses
 2. Dr. Rudolf Anton

V

Jury Instructions

Plaintiff's and defendant's proposed jury instructions are attached.

   1. Plaintiff objects to defendant instruction nos. 6, 7, and 9, for the reasons stated in plaintiff's attached memorandum.

2. Defendant objects to plaintiff instruction nos. 2, 3, 4, and 6, for the reasons stated in defendant's attached memorandum.

RESPECTFULLY SUBMITTED,

Date: <u>November 3, 2006</u>

Anne Johnson

Anne Johnson
Attorney for Plaintiff

William Sharp

William Sharp
Attorney for Defendant

Pretrial memoranda frequently also contain a memorandum of law from each party that discusses any legal issues that the judge will need to resolve before or during trial.

The judge's final pretrial order will usually track the language and organization of the memorandum and contain all rulings on admissibility issues that were made at the conference.

RELEASE

In consideration of the sum of twenty thousand dollars ($20,000), which plaintiff acknowledges receiving, Plaintiff John Jones agrees to release Defendant Susan Smith and her heirs, survivors, agents, and personal representatives from all claims, suits, or actions in any form or on any basis, because of anything that was done or not done at any time, on account of the following:

All claims for personal injuries, property damage, physical disabilities, medical expenses, lost income, loss of consortium, and all other claims that have been or could be brought, including all claims now known or that in the future might be known, which arise out of an occurrence on or about September 2, 2005, at 40th Street and Thomas Road, in Phoenix, Arizona, when plaintiff claims to have sustained injuries as a result of a collision between an automobile driven by plaintiff and an automobile driven by defendant.

A release would be the standard way of settling this case, since it is a complete settlement by all the parties.

The parties would usually execute a separate settlement agreement detailing the terms of the settlement.

As a result of this collision plaintiff has brought suit against defendant for damages. Defendant has denied both liability and the claimed extent of damages. This release is a compromise settlement between Plaintiff John Jones and Defendant Susan Smith.

This agreement is a release and shall operate as a total discharge of any claims plaintiff has or may have, arising out of the above occurrence, against this defendant and any other persons.

Plaintiff John Jones and Defendant Susan Smith also agree to terminate any actions that have been filed, particularly a claim by this plaintiff against this defendant currently filed as civil action No. 03 C 1000 in the United States District Court for the District of Arizona in Phoenix, Arizona. Plaintiff and defendant agree to execute a Stipulation of Dismissal, with prejudice, and file it with the Clerk of the above Court, thereby terminating that action in its entirety, within five days of the execution of this agreement.

Date: <u>December 3, 2006</u>

The parties, not their lawyers, must sign the release.

John Jones
_____
John Jones, Plaintiff

Susan Smith
_____
Susan Smith, Defendant

UNITED STATES DISTRICT COURT
FOR THE DISTRICT OF ARIZONA

John Jones,
        Plaintiff
 	
    v.
Susan Smith,
        Defendant
	No. 03 C 1000

STIPULATION OF DISMISSAL

Plaintiff John Jones and Defendant Susan Smith agree to dismiss this action with prejudice, and each party will bear its costs.

The stipulation of dismissal terminates the lawsuit. No court order is necessary.

Dated: December 3, 2006

Anne Johnson
_____
Anne Johnson
Attorney for Plaintiff

William Sharp
_____
William Sharp
Attorney for Defendant

GLOSSARY

Abstract of judgment. A lien on all real property owned by the debtor.

Administrative litigation. The process by which administrative agencies resolve disputes that concern their administrative rules and regulations.

Admission of a party opponent. Any statement made by an adverse party in the lawsuit.

Affidavit. A written statement by a witness made under oath and acknowledged by a notary public.

Affidavit of service. A notice at the end of a pleading stating that service of the pleading has been made upon a particular party and including the notarized signature of the individual signing the notice.

Affirm. The appellate court rules that the decision of the court below should remain the same.

Affirm with modification. The appellate court rules that the decision of the court below should remain the same with the exception that a particular element of the decision be modified.

Affirmative defense. Defense pled by the defendant in the answer that, if proven, denies recovery to the plaintiff.

Amended pleadings. The changing or correcting of a pleading after the pleading already has been filed and served.

American Arbitration Association. A private tribunal that administers arbitration that does not go through the court system.

Ancillary jurisdiction. The authority of a federal court to hear certain types of pleadings involving claims that do not have an independent basis for federal jurisdiction. Ancillary jurisdiction arises whenever a plaintiff has a proper claim and another party wishes to file a counterclaim, cross-claim, or third-party complaint but the latter claim does not have an independent jurisdictional basis.

Answer. A response by the defendant to the plaintiff's complaint, which response admits or denies the various allegations and usually asserts a number of affirmative defenses.

Appellant. The party bringing an appeal in federal court.

Appellee. The party defending against an appeal in federal court.

Arbitration. The submission by the parties of their dispute to an impartial tribunal for resolution.

Arbitration award. The ruling arising from arbitration.

Assignee. The person or entity that has received a claim through an assignment.

Assignment. A claim that has been transferred to another person or entity. In such a case, the assignee has a right to sue in the assignee's own name.

Assignor. The person or entity that transfers the claim in an assignment.

Attachment. Pretrial order of the court seizing property of the defendant for later satisfaction of any judgment received by the plaintiff.

Attorney-client privilege. Protection that allows communications between an attorney and client to remain confidential; also extends to communications between a client and a paralegal.

Attorney's lien. A claim by the lawyer on any judgment or recovery obtained by the client to ensure payment of the lawyer's fee.

Authenticated. Establishing through witness testimony a foundation for the evidence presented before the trier of fact.

Authorization forms. Forms signed by the client that permit the lawyer to obtain personal records of the client such as medical records, employment records, and police reports.

Bank levy. A seizure of funds held in a debtor's bank account.

Bench. Where the judge sits during a hearing or trial.

Best evidence rule. Under the common law, a requirement that an original writing had to be produced if the writing was going to be used as evidence. Duplicates are generally admissible in evidence under the Federal Rules of Evidence and the rules of most states.

Breach of contract. A cause of action that requires the plaintiff to allege a contract that was breached by the defendant, causing damages to the plaintiff. Plaintiff must also allege that plaintiff has either performed under the contract or is excused from performing on the contract.

Business records. Records made by employees in the course of their employment and made on behalf of the business in which they are employed; admissible as evidence.

Caption. Identification in a pleading of the parties, court, and case number. This information must be included in every pleading.

Case administrator. The staff member at the American Arbitration Association assigned to handle the administrative aspects of the arbitration.

Case-in-chief. The evidence supporting the particular party's position.

Case or controversy. A case that is ripe for adjudication. An actual case that is not moot or merely advisory.

Cases. Court decisions interpreting the law.

Cause of action. Theory of recovery that entitles the plaintiff to recover against the defendant.

Certificate of compliance. A written statement by the lawyer, sometimes required by local rules of court, certifying that the lawyer has attempted to meet in good faith with the opposing party to resolve their discovery dispute before bringing a motion to compel discovery.

Certificate of service. A notice at the end of a pleading indicating that service of the pleading has been made upon a particular party.

Chain of custody. Establishing location of a piece of physical evidence at all times prior to its possible use at trial.

Character traits. A person's distinctive qualities; admissible as evidence only if character is an essential element of a claim or defense.

Choice-of-law decisions. Determining in which court a complaint should be filed.

Chronological summary. A deposition summary organized sequentially; it starts at the beginning of the deposition and continues through to the end of the deposition.

Citizenship. The place where a natural person or legal entity resides. For a natural person, the citizenship is the person's domicile. For a corporation, the citizenship is the place of incorporation and the corporation's principal place of business.

Civil litigation. Resolution of disputes between private parties through the court system.

Claim for relief. Another name for a cause of action.

Claimant. The party filing a demand for arbitration.

Class action. A lawsuit brought by individuals representing a large group of identifiable members.

Closing arguments. The statements made by the lawyers at the close of all the evidence. The statements generally include a summary of the important evidence that was presented during the trial.

Codes. Laws enacted by state or federal legislatures, such as the United States Code.

Commercial litigation. Civil litigation involving businesses.

Common law. Body of law brought to America by colonists; developed in England from custom and usage and affirmed by the English judges and courts. Term sometimes used to refer to case law.

Compensatory damages. Money damages that compensate the injured party, including damages that flow directly from the injury or breach. Compensatory damages may be general, such as compensation for pain and suffering, or specific, such as payment for medical expenses and lost time from work.

Competent witness. A witness who is qualified to testify because such witness has the ability to communicate either orally or by gestures and is capable of relating facts truthfully.

Complaint. The document filed by the aggrieved party to commence litigation.

Complete diversity. A requirement that each plaintiff have a different state of citizenship from each defendant.

Compulsory counterclaim. A counterclaim that must be brought by the defendant against the plaintiff or else the defendant will lose the right to assert the claim.

Concurrent. When used in reference to jurisdiction, term means that a lawsuit may be brought in either federal or state court because each court has jurisdiction over the dispute.

Conflict of interest. Occurs when two or more parties with adverse interests are represented by the same counsel.

Consent order. An order drafted and agreed to by both parties that disposes of a pending motion.

Consolidation. The combining of two trials or hearings into one.

Constitution. The highest law of federal and state governments. In addition to the United States Constitution, each of the fifty states has its own constitution. No state constitution or state or federal law may violate the federal Constitution.

Consulting expert. Expert who has been retained or employed to assist during the litigation process, but who is not expected to be a witness at trial.

Contention interrogatories. which can accompany a request to admit facts, ask the opposing side for the basis of any denial of a request. The answering party may thus decide to admit the request rather than attempt to justify the denial in the interrogatory answer.

Contingency fee. An agreement between the lawyer and client whereby the lawyer will receive as compensation for the lawyer's fee a certain percentage in the recovery ultimately obtained by the client. If the client receives no recovery, the lawyer will not receive any fee. This type of fee arrangement is common in personal injury actions.

Contingent claim. A claim that may arise, but has not yet arisen.

Contradiction. Method of impeachment that shows that the true facts are different from those stated by the witness.

Contribution. A theory of apportioning payment for a liability. When one party to a joint and several obligation pays more than that party's share of the obligation, the paying party may be entitled to receive a proportionate sum from the other jointly liable parties.

Corporation. A legal entity composed of shareholders who own the entity but whose existence is separate and distinct from the entity. Shareholders generally cannot be held liable for the obligations of the corporation.

Costs. The out-of-pocket expenses incurred by the lawyer during the course of representation of the client and that are reimbursed by the client. These costs are distinguished from the fee charged by the lawyer. Costs include such items as filing fees, court reporter fees, travel expenses, postage, and long-distance telephone charges.

Count. Each separate cause of action alleged in a complaint. Each count should be numbered.

Counterclaim. Claim in the form of a pleading brought by the defendant against the plaintiff as part of the same lawsuit.

Court cases. Litigation decisions that are decided in a court of law.

Court of Appeals. The intermediate appellate court under the federal court system.

Covenant not to sue. A contract between two or more parties in which the plaintiff agrees not to sue or to pursue an existing claim against one or more defendants.

Criminal litigation. Litigation commenced by a governmental body against individuals who have committed crimes against society.

Cross-claim. A complaint brought by one codefendant against another codefendant.

Damages. Monetary compensation requested by the plaintiff from the defendant.

Declarant. The person making either a written or oral statement.

Declaration. A written statement by a witness that is signed by the witness under penalty of perjury.

Declaratory relief. Equitable remedy used by the plaintiff when a controversy arises over the rights and obligations of the parties and neither party is yet in breach of these obligations.

Default. A failure of a party to respond to the pleading of the opposing party. Usually occurs in the case of a defendant who does not respond to the plaintiff's complaint.

Default judgment. Judgment entered against a defendant who fails to appear and defend against the lawsuit after having been given proper notice of the lawsuit.

Defendant. The party who defends an action brought by the plaintiff.

Definitions and instructions. A section at the beginning of a discovery request that establishes the meaning of certain terms used in the request and advises the responding party how the request should be answered.

Demand for arbitration. The form that a party files to commence arbitration through the American Arbitration Association.

Demand letter. A letter sent to the opposing side requesting immediate payment of the sum owed.

Demonstrative evidence. Exhibits such as photographs, diagrams, models, and maps that represent real things.

Demurrer. A type of motion that asks the court to dismiss the other side's pleading because the pleading is not legally sufficient.

Deponent. Witness who gives testimony at a desposition. The deponent's testimony is given under oath, and the deponent can be cross-examined by the attorney for the opposing side.

Deposition transcript. A written record of everything communicated orally during the course of a deposition.

Depositions. Oral questions asked by one party to another during the discovery stage. The answers are stated under oath before a court reporter who usually is also a notary public.

Directed verdict. Verdict returned by the jury in favor of a party as directed by the trial judge.

Discovery. The formal method by which a party receives information from the other parties in the lawsuit.

Discovery and motion stage. The stage in the litigation process whereby the parties conduct formal fact investigation through written responses and oral testimony recieved from the other side.

Dispositive motions. Motions heard by the court any time before trial that have the effect of deciding and terminating the lawsuit without the necessity of a trial.

Diversity jurisdiction. The power of the federal court to hear controversies between citizens of different states. In order for the federal district courts to have jurisdiction, "complete diversity" must exist: Each plaintiff must have a different state citizenship from each defendant.

Divider method. A way to organize trial materials. Trial materials are organized by putting all papers pertinent to each phase of the trial in a separate folder.

Domicile. The permanent residence of a natural person. No person can have more than one domicile at one time.

Due process. A constitutional doctrine requiring fairness in judicial proceedings.

Elements. Items that must be proven for each claim, relief, and defense.

Equitable remedy. Relief requested by the plaintiff from the defendant that is usually designed to prevent some future harm. An equitable remedy is distinguished from money damages, which is a legal remedy.

Evidence. Facts presented to the judge or jury.

Ex parte. Without notice to the other side, or very limited notice to the other side.

Exemption. An amount of money that may not be used to satisfy a judgment.

Exhibit chart. A chart used during trial to show the exhibit number, exhibit description, and boxes to check if exhibit was offered, admitted, reserved or withdrawn.

Exhibits. Tangible items of evidence presented at trial.

Expert witness. A witness who has been qualified in a particular area and is used to assist the trier of fact with understanding or determining a fact in issue.

Extrinsic evidence. Evidence outside of the evidence that is being presented at a particular time. Thus, if a witness gives evidence, other evidence (i.e., the extrinsic evidence) may be used to impeach the evidence given by the witness.

Factfinder. The judge or jury that reviews the disputed events and determines the facts.

Federal question jurisdiction. An issue brought before the federal court arising under the Constitution, laws, or treaties of the United States.

Federal Rules of Civil Procedure. The procedural rules governing litigation filed in federal court.

Federal Rules of Evidence. Rules applicable in federal courts that govern what evidence is admissible.

Fixed flat fee. An agreement between the lawyer and client whereby the lawyer receives a predetermined sum as the amount of the fee regardless of how much work is expended on the client's behalf.

For cause. When a juror is stricken from the jury panel for a particular reason. For example, the juror may be biased or prejudiced toward one party, may have an interest in the litigation, or may know any of the parties or attorneys to the litigation.

Former testimony. Testimony given under oath in another action or at a former hearing or trial in the same action.

Forum state. The state where a lawsuit is being brought.

Foundation. Establishment of a basis for admission of evidence.

Good cause. What a party must have before a party can obtain a protective order. Good cause for a protective order includes such reasons as the discovery is unduly oppressive and expensive. Good cause also refers to what a party must have to compel discovery responses by another party. Good cause for compelling discovery includes such reasons as the information is not available from any other source, the information sought is necessary, and the information is relevant to a particular issue in the litigation.

Guardian ad litem. A person appointed by the court to represent another, usually a minor or incompetent, in a lawsuit. The guardian ad litem can sue or be sued on behalf of the person represented.

Habit. The routine conduct of a person; may be admissible as evidence at trial.

Hague Service Convention. An international treaty that governs service of process in countries that are parties to the treaty.

Hearsay. An out-of-court statement used to prove the truth of the matter asserted in the statement.

Hourly rate. When the lawyer charges the client at a specific rate per hour multiplied by the number of hours spent on the client's behalf.

Impeachment. The discrediting of a witness' testimony so that statements made by the witness will not be believed by the trier of fact.

Impleader. The method for bringing into an action new parties who may be liable to a defendant for some or all of the judgment that the plaintiff may obtain against the defendant. Also called third-party complaint.

Improper venue. When the plaintiff files a complaint in the wrong geographic district.

Inconvenient venue. When the plaintiff files a complaint in a proper district but a district that is not convenient for the defendant or witnesses.

In personam jurisdiction. A court's power to personally bind the parties to the court's judgment.

In rem jurisdiction. The court's power to adjudicate rights in property located within the state in which the court sits.

Indemnification. A claim allowing one party who has paid for a liability to recover completely from another party.

Informally consulted expert. Expert who has not been retained to assist with the litigation, but has provided information during the litigation process.

Injunction. Equitable remedy used by the plaintiff to stop certain conduct or actions of the defendant.

Internet. A worldwide computer network of information databases.

Interpleader. Procedure under which a party may deposit into court a fund or property when the party is or may be subjected to double liability because two or more claimants are making a claim on a fund or property. The claimants then are forced to litigate their claim in order to determine who is entitled to the fund or property.

Interrogatories. Written questions submitted by one party to another during the discovery stage.

Intervention. The ability of a person, not a party to the lawsuit, to become a party to the lawsuit when such person has an interest in the outcome of the lawsuit.

Intervention of right. The ability of a person to become a part of the lawsuit when such a person has an interest in the outcome of the lawsuit.

Involuntary dismissal. Method of terminating a claim when the plaintiff or other claimant has been guilty of misconduct or inaction.

Irreparable injury. Injury to the party that cannot be repaired and that can be avoided by the granting of injunctive relief.

Joinder of claims. The bringing together in one lawsuit the different claims that a party may have against another party.

Joinder of parties. The bringing together of different parties in one lawsuit. Under Rules 19 and 20 of the Federal Rules of Civil Procedure, the plaintiff must determine which parties must, should, or can be brought into the lawsuit so that the plaintiff's claim can be properly decided.

Joint tortfeasors. Two or more persons who are liable to plaintiff for the same injury.

Judgment. The decision in the lawsuit.

Judgment debtor. The party who has lost a judgment and owes money to the other party. The other party is called the judgment creditor.

Judgment on the pleadings. A judgment entered after the pleadings have been filed, but before trial, when the undisputed facts as pled show that the movant is entitled to judgment. Similar to a motion to dismiss.

Judicial arbitration refers to arbitration handled through the court system. Unless otherwise agreed to by the parties, such arbitration is nonbinding.

Judicial notice. Evidentiary procedure in which the trial judge is asked to rule that certain facts are true.

Juror. A person who sits as part of the jury panel during trial and decides questions of fact.

Jury. A panel of individuals who decide questions of fact during a trial.

Jury chart. A diagram to be used during voir dire examination of the jury. Information obtained from each prospective juror is recorded on the chart.

Jury demand. A notice by a party that the party requests a trial by jury as opposed to a trial heard only by the judge.

Jury instructions. Instructions that itemize the elements for various claims, reliefs, and defenses.

Keeper. A law enforcement agent who stays on the premises of a business and collects cash or checks sufficient to satisfy a judgment. If insufficient funds exist, the keeper may also take possession of personal property and sell the property in order to satisfy the judgment.

Lawyer's fee. The amount charged by the lawyer for professional services rendered to the client. Also referred to as attorney's fee. A fee for professional services is distinguished from out-of-pocket costs incurred, which are generally not considered part of the fee.

Lay witness. Witness who has not been qualified as an expert in a particular area. Often referred to as a percipient witness, a lay witness is one who will testify to the facts as he or she has observed them.

Leave of court. Permission from the court to file a pleading.

Legal remedy. Generally a request by the plaintiff for money damages from the defendant.

LEXIS. A computer service that provides access to legal research materials.

Levy. The procedure by which assets of the debtor are seized for satisfaction of a judgment.

Lien. A claim by the creditor against property of the debtor as security for the debt.

Limited jurisdiction. A reference to federal district courts since federal district courts cannot hear all controversies, but rather only those controversies that fall under their power as defined in Article **III** of the United States Constitution and those where Congress has extended jurisdiction over a particular type of case.

Lis pendens. A notice that is recorded against particular real property alerting potential purchasers of the property that there is a pending dispute that affects title to or possession of the property.

Litigation. Resolution of disputes through the court system.

Loan receipt. Refers to a loan by one defendant of a certain amount to the plaintiff, and the plaintiff's agreement to dismiss the case as to that defendant and to pursue the case against the other defendants. When the plaintiff recovers from the other defendants, plaintiff agrees to repay the loan.

Local rules of court. Rules of procedure that are adopted by each individual court and apply to all litigation commenced in that particular court.

Long-arm statute. The ability of a court to exercise jurisdiction over a defendant who is outside the geographical boundaries of the court.

Magistrate. An officer of the court authorized to hear routine civil pretrial matters.

Mary Carter agreement. Another name for loan receipt. Used to generate some contribution among joint tortfeasors.

Mediation. A formal conference between the parties and a neutral person with the intent to arrive at a settlement of the parties' dispute.

Mediator. A neutral party who listens to both sides of the dispute and helps the parties to arrive at a mutually acceptable settlement.

Memorandum of law. Legal document submitted with a motion setting forth background facts and legal authorities to support a position.

Minimum contacts. Sufficient contact by a defendant with the state attempting to exercise jurisdiction over the defendant.

Minute order. Form on which the clerk makes an entry reflecting the ruling by the judge.

Moot issue. When an issue no longer exists between the parties in a pending lawsuit. Courts will not decide moot issues.

Motion. Either a written or oral request made by a party to the court for some order or ruling by the court.

Motion calendar. The cases scheduled for hearing in court on any particular day.

Motion for a more definite statement. A motion by the defendant that the plaintiff give more details before the defendant is required to answer the complaint.

Motion for judgment n.o.v. A motion to have judgment entered in a party's favor notwithstanding the jury's verdict against the party.

Motion for new trial after a judgment n.o.v. A motion by a party for a new trial after that party's verdict has been set aside because the judge has granted a motion for judgment n.o.v.

Motion to amend findings and judgment. A motion made after trial and entry of judgment to have the court amend the findings and to amend the judgment in conformity with the amended findings.

Motion to dismiss. A motion by the defendant that the complaint filed by the plaintiff be dismissed because of some specified defect.

Motion to set aside judgment. Motion by a party to set aside the judgment entered by the court. The motion may be based on a number of grounds such as mistake, fraud, or newly discovered evidence.

Motion to strike. A motion to eliminate certain allegations from a complaint.

Movant. The party making a motion. Sometimes referred to as the moving party.

Narrative summary. A type of deposition summary that is in memorandum form with no reference to particular page and line numbers.

Negligence. Type of cause of action. To state a claim for negligence, the plaintiff must allege a duty of care by one party to another that was breached and that was the cause of plaintiff's damages.

Notice and claims provisions. Contract provisions usually requiring notice of intent to sue or presentation of claims before filing suit, and requiring that notice be given within a short period of time, usually much shorter than the applicable statute of limitations period.

Notice of appeal. Documents filed by the losing party in a trial court decision, which must contain the name of the party or parties taking the appeal and the name of the court to which the appeal is taken; it must also state the judgment, or part of the judgment, that the party is appealing from.

Notice pleading. A short and plain statement in the complaint of the claim that the plaintiff seeks to enforce and the relief that the plaintiff is requesting.

Objection. Statement made by the responding party in an interrogatory that indicates a reason for not answering the question asked.

Offer of judgment. An offer by a party defending a claim to have judgment entered in a specific amount. If the plaintiff refuses the offer and a judgment after trial is entered in favor of the plaintiff that is less favorable than the offer, the plaintiff becomes liable to the defendant for the defendant's costs that were incurred since the time of the offer.

On-call witnesses. Witnesses who are going to be called to testify at trial but who do not attend the trial until they are advised of the particular date and time they are needed.

Opening arguments. Statements made by the lawyers at the beginning of trial that explain their respective clients' versions of the facts and what they expect the evidence to prove.

Opponent. The party opposing a motion. Sometimes referred to as the responding party.

Oral argument. Opportunity for lawyers to answer any questions an appellate court may have and to more fully explain their respective clients' positions. Oral argument takes place after the submission by the parties of written briefs.

Original jurisdiction. The first court that has authority to decide the legal dispute.

Partial summary judgment. Judgment granted as to fewer than all counts or on one of several issues within a count.

Parties to an action. A person, group of persons, or legal entity that has the right to bring or defend a litigation case.

Partnership. Legal entity created by two or more individuals who carry on a business and divide any profit or loss of the business.

Party statement. A written statement made by a party to the litigation.

Pattern interrogatories have been approved by some districts for common cases such as automobile personal injury suits. Usually taking the form of preprinted questions, pattern interrogatories seek information commonly requested in all cases relating to a specific area of the law. For example, recurring interrogatory questions in a personal injury suit include identification of past injuries, the treating physicians, and the amount of damages sustained.

Pecuniary. Refers to monetary or economic affairs.

Penal. Refers to legal punishment.

Pendent jurisdiction. Jurisdiction by the federal court over nonfederal claims when both the federal and nonfederal claims derive from a common set of facts.

Percipient witness. A witness who testifies to facts as he or she has observed or perceived them. Same as lay witness.

Peremptory challenge. A method used to strike a juror from the jury panel; the term refers to an absolute right of the lawyer to strike a juror even if no cause for challenging that juror exists. However, the lawyer will be allowed only a limited number of peremptory challenges.

Permanent injunction. An injunction granted only after trial and that will exist for all time until the injunction is dissolved by court order.

Permissive counterclaim. A counterclaim that may be brought by the defendant against the plaintiff but that does not have to be brought in the same action.

Permissive intervention. The ability of a person to join a lawsuit if the claims or defenses are similar to the main action.

Permissive joinder. A joinder of parties that is allowed -but not required -by the court.

Personal jurisdiction. The power of a court to bring a party before it and to make a decision binding on such a person.

Petition for writ of certiorari is directed to the United States Supreme Court and requests that it grant an appeal of a decision made by a federal court of appeals.

Physical and mental examinations. Medical examination of a party usually done by a doctor selected by the opposing party. May be done only if a court order is obtained or if the party agrees to submit voluntarily to the examination. The party's physical or mental condition must be in issue.

Physical evidence. Tangible personal property such as vehicles, machinery, and consumer products that may be used as trial exhibits.

Plaintiff. The party who brings an action.

Pleadings. Formal written documents by the parties to the litigation to either start or respond to the litigation. For example, the initial pleading is usually the complaint.

Prayer for relief. A section at the end of a complaint specifying the relief requested by the plaintiff.

Prejudicial errors. Errors that occur in the trial that, if such errors had not occurred, might have changed the outcome of the trial.

Preliminary injunction. An injunction granted after a hearing. The preliminary injunction maintains the status quo until trial.

Pretrial conference. A meeting between the parties before the court after litigation has commenced, but before trial begins. At the meeting the parties will attempt to agree on all undisputed facts and narrow the issues for trial.

Pretrial memorandum. A written statement provided to the court in advance of trial generally setting forth the uncontested facts, contested issues of fact and law, exhibits, witnesses, and jury instructions.

Pretrial motions. Motions made after litigation has commenced but before the trial begins.

Pretrial order. Order that identifies the issues, witnesses, exhibits, and order of proof for trial, and acts as a guide for the trial. The order is prepared after the pretrial conference.

Prima facie case. Case in which each element in the plaintiff's claim can be proven.

Principal place of business. The state where a corporation conducts a majority of its business, or, if this is not certain, the state where corporate headquarters is located.

Prior statements. Statements made under oath by a witness at a previous hearing or deposition.

Privileges. Rules providing that certain communications are inadmissible because the communications are deemed to be confidential.

Probative. Having a tendency to prove or disprove a fact in issue.

Proof of service. A notice that usually appears at the end of a pleading or motion stating that the pleading or motion was served on the other parties to the lawsuit, the date service was made, and the manner of service.

Propounding. The act of sending discovery requests to another party.

Proprietary. Refers to ownership of property.

Prosecute. To vigorously pursue a claim.

Protective order. An order from the court restricting or limiting discovery by one party to another.

Prove up. Demonstration by a plaintiff at a motion for default hearing that service on the defaulting party was proper and that the allegations of the complaint are true. Plaintiff also must be prepared to show what the proper damages are.

Provisional remedies include temporary restraining orders, preliminary injunctions, writs of attachment and possession, and lis pendens. Under proper circumstances these remedies allow a plaintiff to essentially obtain the relief requested from the defendant before going to trial.

Public bodies. Governmental agencies operated for the benefit of the general public.

Public records. Business records generated by governmental entities; admissible as evidence at trial.

Punitive damages. Damages given to the plaintiff when the defendant's conduct is willful or malicious. Such damages are meant to punish the wrongdoers for their conduct and may be awarded in addition to compensatory damages. Punitive damages are sometimes called exemplary damages.

Qualified privilege. Privilege that is not absolute. The privilege will not exist if the other party can show a substantial need for the information.

Quash. To vacate by court order.

Quasi in rem jurisdiction. Reference to actions in which the court does not have in personam jurisdiction over the defendant, but the court does have jurisdiction over particular property of the defendant that allows the court to subject that property to claims asserted by the plaintiff.

Questions of law. Issues that raise a legal question and not a fact question.

Real. The information is what it purports to be.

Real evidence. Information that is what it purports to be; can also refer to physical objects.

Real party in interest. The party who, under applicable substantive law, has the right that the lawsuit seeks to enforce.

Reasonable inquiry. The requirement that the lawyer has looked into the law and facts and concluded that there is a sound basis for the pleading.

Rebuttal evidence. Evidence refuting the evidence presented by the defendant as part of the defendant's case-in-chief.

Record on appeal includes the transcript, original documents, exhibits, and a copy of the docket sheet listing all documents filed in the trial court.

Recorded recollections. A record made of events at about the time the events occurred.

Recording. An action that places notice of some action, lien, or judgment on the title of real property. Thus, any potential buyers of real property are put on constructive notice that an action, lien, or judgment exists.

Recoupment. A right by the defendant to have any damages awarded to the plaintiff reduced because of some entitlement by the defendant to damages from the plaintiff.

Redact. Covering up a portion of a document that should not be produced to the opposing side.

Relation back. A doctrine that permits a pleading to be deemed to have been filed at an earlier time. For example, an amended complaint will be deemed to have been filed at the time of the initial complaint for purposes of determining if the statute of limitations has run.

Release. A discharge of all claims against the parties as well as against any persons against whom the same claims are or could have been asserted.

Relevant. The evidence either proves or disproves something in issue.

Relevant evidence. Evidence that proves or disproves something in issue in a lawsuit.

Reliable. The evidence must be firsthand or otherwise trustworthy information.

Reliable evidence. Evidence that is based on firsthand knowledge or otherwise trustworthy information.

Remedies. The relief sought by the plaintiff from the defendant.

Removal. The procedure in which a defendant may transfer a case already filed in a state court to the federal district court for the same district in which the state action is pending.

Reply. The plaintiff's answer to the defendant's counterclaim.

Representative. Any individual representing a party such as a lawyer or other agents.

Requests for admission. Written statements by one party to another requesting admission of certain facts or the genuineness of particular documents.

Requests to produce. Written requests by one party to another seeking formal permission to obtain copies of records, documents, and other tangible things for inspection, copying, and testing.

Res. A Latin word referring to either real or personal property, usually in the context of in rem actions.

Res judicata. A doctrine that provides that any judgment is binding on the parties forever. Literally means "a thing decided."

Respondent. The party that "responds" to a charge filed by a plaintiff. In many situations, the respondent is referred to as the defendant.

Retainer fee. The amount the client pays to the lawyer at the commencement of the representation. This fee is credited against the fees and costs incurred by the client.

Reverse. The appellate court rules that the decision of the court below should be changed.

Reverse and remand. The appellate court rules that the decision of the court below should be changed and that the case should be sent back to the court below for further proceedings.

Rule 11. Rule under the Federal Rules of Civil Procedure that requires, before any lawsuit is filed, that a reasonable inquiry into the facts be made in order to ensure that a pleading is well grounded.

Sanctions. A penalty a court may impose for certain violations of court rules and orders. The penalty often includes reasonable expenses such as attorney's fees.

Senior lienholder. Someone who has a claim that is before another's claim. The senior lienholder has priority, and the senior lienholder's claim must be satisfied before any other claims are paid.

Separate trials. Where parts of the same case are tried separately. For example, the court may order separate trials on the complaint and counterclaim.

Service of process. The delivery of a legal document to the opposing party. Usually refers to the actual delivery of the initial pleading to the defendant.

Settlement. A resolution by the parties of their dispute without the necessity of a trial.

Settlement brochure. A brochure that sets out the background of the plaintiff and plaintiff's family along with the evidence showing liability and damages.

Shareholders. The owners of a corporation. The percentage of ownership is determined by the number of shares the owner holds in the corporation.

Sole proprietorship. Business owned by one person and usually operated under a fictitious business name.

Sovereign immunity. The insulation of the government from being sued when functioning in an official government capacity, unless the government consents to being sued.

Special appearance. An appearance by the defendant for the sole purpose of contesting personal jurisdiction.

Stakeholder. The party who holds funds or property for another and has no interest in the funds or property.

Standard of review determines how an appellate court should look at the issues in deciding an appeal. For example, was there substantial evidence to support the judgment of the trial court? The appropriate standard of review should be addressed within the argument in an appellate brief.

Standing. The right of a person to challenge in court the conduct of another.

Status quo. The conditions that presently exist.

Statute of limitations. Statute that limits the time period in which an action may be brought.

Statutes. Laws enacted by state or federal legislatures; sometimes referred to as "codes."

Strike system. A method for jury selection. Each prospective juror will be questioned and then the lawyers will exercise their challenges to the jurors by striking certain jurors from the panel.

Structured settlement. A settlement under which the plaintiff receives periodic payments rather than one lump sum.

Subject matter jurisdiction. The power of the court to hear particular matters.

Subject matter summary. A deposition summary that categorizes each topic by subject matter regardless of where the subject appears in the deposition transcript.

Subpoena. Court order compelling a nonparty to appear or produce documents or other tangible items.

Subpoena ad testificandum. An order of the court requiring a witness to appear and give testimony. Same as subpoena.

Subpoena duces tecum. An order of the court requiring a witness to appear and produce documents.

Subrogation. When one party becomes obligated to pay for the loss sustained by another, that party may be substituted as a proper party to collect against the wrongdoer for such loss.

Substitution of parties. When a different party replaces one of the original parties, such as in the case of the death of a party.

Summary judgment. A judgment rendered by the court before a trial. A summary judgment is a motion brought by one party to the litigation against another in order to obtain a judgment without the necessity of a trial. Summary judgment may be granted only if there are no triable issues of fact. The court's judgment must be based solely on issues of law.

Summons. Notice accompanying the complaint that commands that the defendant appear and defend against the action within a certain period of time or else judgment may be entered against the defendant.

Supplemental pleading. A change or correction in a pleading that already has been filed when transactions, occurrences, and events have occurred since the time of the filing of the original pleading.

Surrebuttal. Evidence presented by the defendant that explains or denies the rebuttal evidence.

Temporary restraining order. An order from the court temporarily prohibiting a party from doing some act until such time as a hearing for an injunction can be heard. A temporary restraining order usually stays in effect for no longer than 10 to 15 days.

Tentative ruling. A ruling by the judge based on the written briefs submitted by the parties and before oral argument is heard. The ruling is subject to change after oral argument.

Testifying expert. An expert who will be called as a witness at trial.

Testimony. Evidence given by a witness under oath.

Theory of the case. The lawyer's position on, and approach to, all the undisputed and disputed evidence that will be presented at trial. Another name for your side's version of the facts.

Third party. Someone who is not a party to the lawsuit but who is in possession of evidence necessary for the lawsuit.

Third-party complaint. A complaint by a defendant in the action against a new party, which has the effect of bringing this new party into the action. Same as impleader.

Third-party practice. The method for bringing into an action new parties who may be liable for some or all of the judgment.

Till tap. Collection of cash and checks on hand at a business in order to satisfy a judgment.

Tolls. Refers to the stopping of the time limitations.

Topic index. A type of deposition summary that is an outline of the general topic areas.

Tort. A civil wrong or injury not based upon contract.

Trial and post-trial proceedings. Motions made by any party either during trial or after trial.

Trial box. A box that contains necessary items for trial such as pens, pencils, and notepads.

Trial chart. A chart used during trial to show each element of each claim or defense and the witnesses and exhibits that will prove each required element.

Trial court. The court where the complaint is filed and litigation commences.

Trial notebook. Method for organizing trial materials. All necessary materials for each part of the trial are placed in a three-ring notebook in appropriately tabbed sections.

Trial preparation materials. Documents and other tangible things prepared by a party or the party's representative in anticipation of litigation.

Trier of fact. Either the judge or jury who decides questions of fact during a trial.

UCC. An abbreviation for the Uniform Commercial Code, which is a code that regulates commercial transactions. It has been adopted in at least some form by most states.

Uncontested. Refers to when a party fails to oppose a motion filed by another party.

Under submission. Refers to the judge delaying decision on a motion until the judge has an opportunity to further research or consider the issues presented by the parties during the course of oral argument.

Unincorporated associations. Social organizations, churches, homeowner groups, etc., that operate under a common name for the common benefit of all members.

United States Code. Laws enacted by Congress.

United States District Court. The name of the trial court under the federal court system.

United States Supreme Court. The highest appellate court in the federal court system.

Unsecured. An obligation from the defendant to the plaintiff that has no security.

Value. In a litigation case the term refers to the monetary worth of the case should the plaintiff prevail.

Venue. The geographic district where a lawsuit may properly be heard.

Verdict. A decision of the judge or jury on a question of fact.

Verified. Refers to a pleading signed by a party and notarized. In some states a notary's signature is not required, but the party must still sign that the pleadings are true and correct to the best of the party's information and belief.

Voir dire. Occurs when the judge and, in some courts, the lawyers ask specific questions of the prospective jurors to ascertain any bias, prejudice, or other information that would affect the decision of the prospective juror in the case.

Voluntary dismissal. A withdrawal of a claim by the party originally asserting the claim.

Wage garnishment. A direction to an employer of the debtor to withhold a certain amount of money from each paycheck of the debtor for a limited period of time.

WESTLAW. A computer service that provides access to legal research materials.

With prejudice. Once dismissed, the claim may not be refiled.

Without prejudice. Once dismissed, the claim may be filed again.

Witness list. A list used during trial showing each witness' name, home address and telephone number, work address and telephone number, a short synopsis of the witness' testimony, and any other information necessary to locating and scheduling the witness during trial.

Witness statements. A written statement made by a nonparty witness.

Work product. Work performed by an attorney during the course of representing a client in anticipation or preparation of litigation, such as notes, internal memoranda, and reports of consulting experts. Also includes work performed by a paralegal. Generally not subject to discovery.

Writ of execution. An order from the court empowering the sheriff, marshal, or other appropriate law enforcement agent to levy upon the assets of the judgment debtor.

Writ of possession is issued in a case where the defendant has given a plaintiff a security interest in some tangible personal property for repayment of a debt. If a debt is in default, the plaintiff may then sue for repayment of the debt and delivery of the personal property to the plaintiff.

INDEX

BURLINGTON COUNTY COLLEGE

3 3072 00207 7618

HDRAWN

KF 8841 M37 2006
Maerowitz, Marlene A.
Fundamentals of litigation
for paralegals
(+ CD-ROM in pocket)

MOUNT LAUREL CAMPUS

BURLINGTON COUNTY COLLEGE
601 PEMBERTON BROWNS MILLS ROAD
PEMBERTON NJ 08068